FISCAL POLICY AND ECONOMIC GROWTH

FISCAL POLICY AND ECONOMIC GROWTH

Lessons for Eastern Europe and Central Asia

Edited by
Cheryl Gray
Tracey Lane
Aristomene Varoudakis

THE WORLD BANK
Washington, DC

1818 H Street, NW
Washington, DC 20433
Telephone: 202-473-1000
Internet: www.worldbank.org
E-mail: feedback@worldbank.org

1 2 3 4 10 9 8 7

ISBN: 0-8213-7181-9
ISBN-13: 978-0-8213-7181-7
e-ISBN: 0-8213-7182-7
e-ISBN-13: 978-0-8213-7182-4
DOI: 10.1596/978-0-8213-7181-7

Library of Congress Cataloging-in-Publication date has been applied for.

Cover design: David Runyon
Cover photos: World Bank Photo Library.

Contents

Boxes

Figures

Tables

Acknowledgments

This study was prepared by a cross-sectoral team of staff and consultants in the Europe and Central Asia (ECA) Region of the World Bank. The editors would like to thank Asad Alam, Leszek Balcerowicz, Arup Banerji, Gordon Betcherman, Armin Fidler, Bernard Funck, Sanjeev Gupta, Felipe Jaramillo, Thomas Laursen, Willi Leibfritz, Pradeep Mitra, Leszek Kasek, Guillermo Perry, Emilia Skrok, Vinaya Swaroop, and Dana Weist for helpful comments on previous drafts. The underlying public finance database for ECA and comparator countries was compiled by Tracey Lane, Olga Vybornaia, and Yulia Makarova with contributions from ECA's country economists. The Public Sector group in the Poverty Reduction and Economic Management (PREM) Vice Presidency provided invaluable assistance with fiscal data for the rest of the world, and the team is particularly indebted to Anand Rajaram, Zhicheng Swift, and Nataliya Biletzka for their assistance. Finally, the editors would like to thank Marinette Guevara and Gabriela Huffman for their excellent administrative support.

Authors and Contributors

Human Development Department, Europe and Central Asia (ECA) Region, World Bank

Dina Abu-Ghaida, *Senior Economist*
Daniel Dulitzky, *Senior Economist*
Ufuk Guven, *Social Protection Specialist*
Xiaohui Hou, *Young Professional*
Jan Rutkowski, *Lead Economist*
Anita Schwarz, *Lead Economist*
Mateusz Walewski, *Consultant (Center for Social and Economic Research, Poland)*

Poverty Reduction and Economic Management Department, ECA Region

Cheryl Gray, *Sector Director*
Leszek Kasek, *Economist*
Tracey Lane, *Senior Economist*
Anton Marcincin, *Economist*
Taras Pushak, *Consultant*
Andrzej Rzonca, *Consultant (National Bank of Poland)*
Pablo Saavedra, *Economist*
Emilia Skrok, *Economist*

Erwin Tiongson, *Economist*
Juraj Valachy, *Consultant*
Aristomene Varoudakis, *Lead Economist*
Olga Vybornaia, *Research Analyst*

Sustainable Development Department, ECA Region

Christine Kessides, *Lead Economist*
Shaheena Khan, *Consultant*

Abbreviations

BEEPS	Business Environment and Enterprise Performance Survey
CEE	Central and Eastern Europe
CENABAS	Chilean Central Supply Facility
CIS	Commonwealth of Independent States
CIT	corporate income tax
CMEA	Council for Mutual Economic Assistance
COMECON	Council for Mutual Economic Assistance
CPI	Country Profile Indicators; Consumer Price Index
CPIA	Country Policy and Institutional Assessment
CSMBS	Civil Servant Medical Benefit Scheme
DRG	Diagnosis Related Group
EAP7	Seven East Asia "Miracle" Countries
EBA	Extreme Bound Analysis
ECA	Europe and Central Asia region
ESA	European Systems of Accounts
EU	European Union
Eurostat	Statistical Office of the European Union
FE	Fixed Effects
FSU	Former Soviet Union
GDP	gross domestic product
GFS	Government Finance Statistics
GFSM	Government Finance Statistics Manual

GMM	Generalized Method of Moments
GNI	gross national income
GNP	gross national product
GRD	General Directorate of Roads
HALE	Healthy Life Expectancy
HIF	Health Insurance Fund
HAS	Health Service Area
ICA	Investment Climate Assessment
ILO	International Labour Organization
IMF	International Monetary Fund
KFD	National Road Fund
kWh	kilowatt hour
LAC	Latin America and the Caribbean region
LSDV	Least Squares Dummy Variable
MAP	Medical Aid Program
MoF	Ministry of Finance
MRI	Magnetic Resonance Imaging
NAEC	National Assessment and Examination Center
OECD	Organisation for Economic Co-operation and Development
OLS	ordinary least squares
PIT	personal income tax
PPP	purchasing power parity
RE	Random Effects
REBIS	Regional Balkans Infrastructure Study
SDS	Department of Statistics
SEE	Southeastern Europe
SHI	social health insurance
SOE	state-owned enterprise
SOP	Sector Operating Plan
SSS	Social Security Scheme
STA	State Tax Authority
STS	State Tax Service
TIMSS	Trends in International Mathematics and Science Study
TIRS	Transport Infrastructure Regional Study
UAW	unaccounted water
UCS	Universal Coverage Scheme
VAT	value added tax
WEO	World Economic Outlook
WDI	World Development Indicators
WHO	World Health Organization

Foreword

Governments around the world must formulate and implement policies for taxation and public spending. These policies can have major impacts on economic growth, income distribution, and poverty, and thus they tend to be at the center of economic and political debates.

This study explores public finance policies in the transition countries of Europe and Central Asia (ECA) and their likely effects on economic growth. It tackles broad questions such as the impact of fiscal deficits, government size, quality of public spending, and structure of taxation on growth, and it explores several key areas of public spending and taxation in detail. While focusing primarily on ECA—in particular a subset of 10 ECA "focus" countries—the study also brings in experiences from rapidly growing economies in other regions of the world and tries to draw policy lessons from these experiences for ECA. Given its primary focus on economic growth, the study does not look as systematically at other important public policy goals, such as poverty reduction, income distribution, and employment, although it does try to touch on these issues or refer the reader to more in-depth work where relevant.

The countries in the ECA region have made major strides over the past 17 years in transforming their economics and political systems. Since the transition recessions of the early 1990s, countries in the region have resumed economic growth. International trade and integration have expanded markedly, and poverty has declined significantly. Yet ECA countries still face daunting challenges in public finance, as demands for public spending to restore crumbling infrastructure, strengthen public services, and protect aging societies come into conflict with the need to reduce the burden of taxation, improve the business environment, and expand employment opportunities. We hope that this study will provide useful and practical insights to our client countries as they tackle these important policy challenges.

Shigeo Katsu
Vice President
Europe and Central Asia Region

Danny Leipziger
Vice President
Poverty Reduction and Economic Management

CHAPTER 1

Fiscal Policy and Economic Growth in Europe and Central Asia: An Overview

Cheryl Gray

Since 1990, the countries of Central and Eastern Europe and Central Asia (ECA) have gone through two historic transitions: a political transition from totalitarianism toward democracy and an economic transition from socialism toward free market systems. These transitions have required a fundamental change in the role of the state, from controlling virtually all major economic assets to providing public goods and facilitating a largely privately owned competitive economy. This change in the role of the state has required a major downsizing and reorientation of public spending and a complete overhaul of tax policy and administration.

This book looks in depth at public finance policies in ECA countries 15 years after the start of transition. The study has five overarching goals:

- to understand public finance policies and trends—including trends in the overall size of the public sector (general government) as well as specific patterns of taxation and public spending—across ECA countries
- to explore how these policies and trends affect economic growth
- to benchmark public finance policies and trends in ECA with those of rapidly growing emerging market countries in other regions

- to help ECA countries identify structural reforms in areas where expenditure pressures are acute (such as pensions and health care) and create fiscal space in other areas critical for growth (such as education and infrastructure)
- to explore ways to improve the efficiency and enhance the impact on employment and growth of tax systems in ECA countries

The analysis is organized in three parts. Part 1 reviews public finance systems across the ECA region with regard to overall size, structure of expenditures and revenues, and patterns of fiscal adjustment over time. It compares these patterns and trends in ECA countries against those in fast-growing economies in other regions, and it explores possible relationships between these public finance variables and rates of economic growth. Part 2 undertakes detailed analysis of public expenditures policies in four major areas: infrastructure, education, health, and pensions. Part 3 turns to the revenue side of the budget and looks in detail at two issues of particular importance in current policy debates: the impact of "flat" income tax reforms and the level and structure of taxes on labor. Box 1.1 establishes the framework for the analysis.

While much of the analysis in the study covers the entire range of ECA countries, a subset of 10 ECA countries receives special focus: Albania, Armenia, Croatia, Georgia, the Kyrgyz Republic, Poland, Romania, the Slovak Republic, Turkey, and Ukraine. These countries vary markedly in size, per capita income, and location and are dealing with a broad range of issues facing the region as a whole. The study also compares subregions within ECA recognizing the diversity of the entire region. These are central Europe's new European Union (EU) member states (EU-5), comprising the Czech Republic, Hungary, Poland, the Slovak Republic, and Slovenia; the Baltics, comprising Estonia, Latvia, and Lithuania; and all initial new member states "EU-8," comprising EU-5 and the Baltics; Southeast Europe (SEE), comprising Albania, Bosnia and Herzegovina, Bulgaria, Croatia, the former Yugoslav Republic of Macedonia, Romania, and Serbia and Montenegro;[1] low-income members of the Commonwealth of Independent States (CIS), comprising Armenia, Azerbaijan, Georgia, the Kyrgyz Republic, Moldova, Tajikistan, and Uzbekistan; and middle-income CIS, comprising Belarus, Kazakhstan, the Russian Federation, and Ukraine. Seven non-ECA countries—Chile, Ireland, the Republic of Korea, Spain, Thailand, Uganda, and Vietnam—are also highlighted in much of the analysis. These seven countries have had higher than average growth rates for the past decade, and their public finance policies hold useful lessons for ECA.

BOX 1.1

A Framework for Analysis

The topics of Parts 1, 2, and 3 of this study—the overall role and size of the state, public expenditure policy, and tax policy—are intimately intertwined. In principle the design of a public finance system entails two major sets of choices. The first set of choices is concerned with the role of the public sector, whether in service provision, or in financing, or both. Is there a clear role for government in a particular area of spending, because of the presence of either public goods (for example, defense, law and order, environmental protection, and public infrastructure) or externalities (certain areas of public health, education, and social protection, for instance)? If there is a role for government, does the public sector need to supply the good in question or can it be supplied as well or better by the private sector with some degree of public financing? The second set of choices, once the rationale and type of government involvement have been determined, is how best to raise the revenues to finance such spending. Should general revenues or earmarked sources of financing be used? Earmarking of revenues may safeguard public spending in certain key areas, such as road maintenance, but it also reduces competition in the use of public funds with possible detrimental effects on expenditure efficiency. Earmarking may also harm growth through distortions in tax structure, such as when payroll taxes designed to fund social protection lead to excessive tax burdens on labor. When general revenues are used in lieu of earmarking, what types and mixes of taxes are preferable, given concerns about economic growth, income and wealth distribution, and administrative capacity?

Ideally, overall public spending should be at a level where the marginal economic benefit of an additional unit of spending equals the marginal economic cost of an additional unit of taxation (or other mode of financing). It is important, therefore, to consider both revenues and expenditures, because policy makers need to balance the economic costs of various forms of taxation against the economic benefits of the spending that such taxation can finance. Many other factors— including difficulties of measurement, distributional concerns, and political factors—clearly complicate such a calculation in any real world setting. History also matters, and ECA's current public finance policies are heavily influenced by its socialist past with its centralized state, its welfare orientation, and its heavy spending on infrastructure, as discussed throughout the study.

Do Government Size and Fiscal Deficits Matter for Economic Growth?

After the turmoil and transition recessions of the early 1990s, most ECA countries returned to economic growth in the late 1990s and have grown steadily for the past decade or so. This growth has led to significant declines in poverty, as some 58 million people have been brought out of poverty since 1998. These economic successes have been accompanied by significant reforms in public finances. Government spending has fallen in line with the changing role of the state, and tax revenues have picked up from low levels as tax policies have been restructured and tax administrations strengthened. Fiscal deficits have narrowed as a result of increasing revenues and controls on spending (figure 1.1), and public debt ratios have fallen. Fiscal deficits in many ECA countries are now lower than in some Western European countries, although the pace of fiscal adjustment has lost some momentum in some countries in Central and Eastern Europe. Furthermore, many ECA countries will need to strengthen their efforts at fiscal consolidation going forward if they are to avoid increasing levels of public debt.

Even with this progress in fiscal adjustment, however, ECA governments are still relatively large on average (figure 1.2) compared with those in non-ECA countries at similar levels of per capita income. Governments are particularly large in Central and Southeast Europe, where primary public expenditure (net of interest payments) accounts on average for about 40 percent of GDP and total public spending averages close to 45 percent of GDP. Generous social protection schemes (figure 1.3) account for most of this size difference—in many Central and Southeastern European countries these systems mirror those in higher-income countries in Europe rather than the more modest programs in non-ECA middle-income countries.

A large body of literature explores the relationship between public finance policies and economic growth. Evidence can be found for a variety of different hypotheses, occasionally conflicting. As discussed further in chapter 3, the most widely supported hypothesis is that public spending in two areas—education and infrastructure—is positively correlated with economic growth. However, contradictory evidence also exists in the case of infrastructure spending in developing countries. Moreover, most literature to date has not considered the effect of governance on public finance outcomes. It has focused primarily on Organisation for Economic Co-operation and Development (OECD) countries, where public institutions, including institutions for tax administration and public expenditure management, are more developed, have higher levels of technology and staff skills, and are embedded in overall governance systems with greater accountability and transparency than those in many developing countries. To the extent developing countries have been included in empirical work, they have tended to be countries from regions other than ECA (Latin America, Africa, and Asia), where market economies have been in place for a longer time and where, in many cases, more complete and

FIGURE 1.1
Primary Fiscal Balance of General Government, 1996–2005

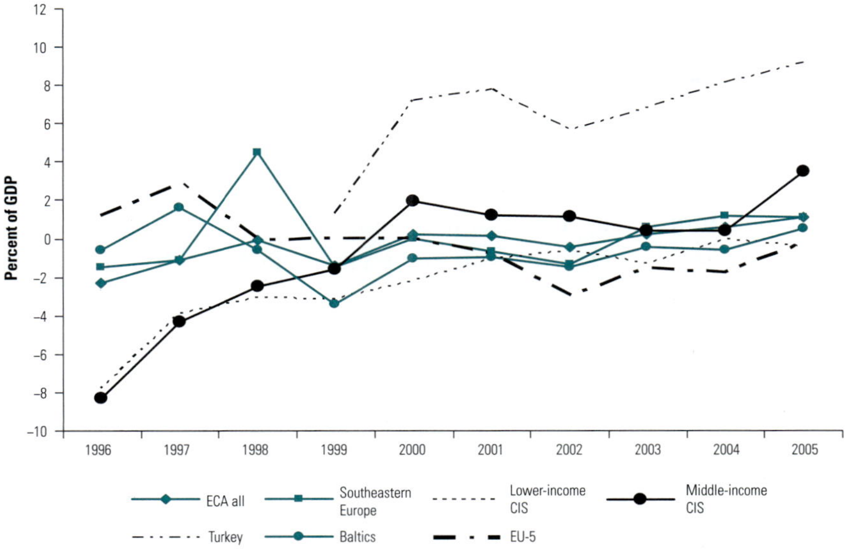

Source: ECA fiscal database.

Note: Primary fiscal balance is defined here as total revenues (including interest and privatization revenues) minus primary (noninterest) expenditures.

FIGURE 1.2
Total Public Sector Spending, by Country in ECA, 1995 and 2005

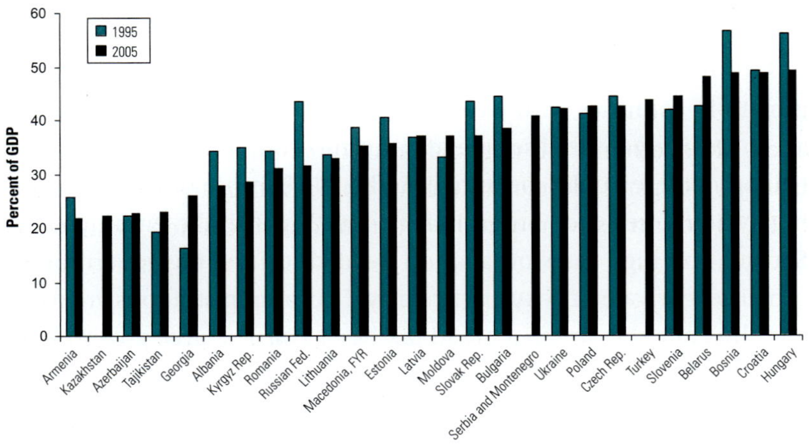

Source: ECA fiscal database.

Note: Consistent data were not available for 1995 for Kazakhstan or Turkey due to methodological concerns, or for Serbia and Montenegro due to conflict. Initial year data for Bosnia and Herzegovina are for 1996.

FIGURE 1.3

Functional Composition of Primary Expenditures, 2004

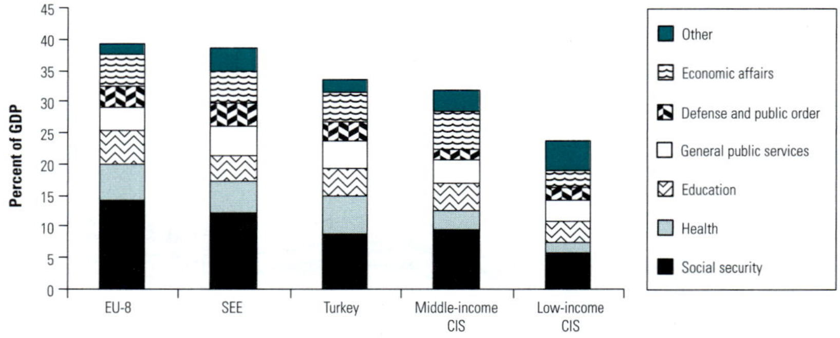

Source: ECA fiscal database.

long-term data exist. No studies have previously examined these issues in depth across the ECA region.

Detailed analysis in this study finds that the overall size of government influences economic growth rates in ECA, but that this effect depends on the state of governance. Bigger governments can hinder growth in countries with weak governance, but this effect is nonlinear: below about one-third of GDP, the size of government is not correlated with growth, but once public spending exceeds 35 percent or so of GDP, increasing government size can have a negative impact on growth. Strong governance mitigates this negative effect, which is one reason that big governments do not necessarily reduce economic growth in some higher-income OECD countries.

Multiple reasons explain why large governments can impede growth in countries with weak governance. First, large governments are more likely to run fiscal deficits during economic downturns, particularly where public spending is inflexible because of weak budgeting systems, reliance on earmarks, and high public employment. Second, the high rates of taxation needed to fund big governments can distort private activity, particularly if tax administrations are weak and thus not able to tap a broad tax base. Third, a large government presence in particular sectors may be accompanied by anticompetitive regulations on private sector participation. Finally, government spending may be misallocated as a result of corruption or poor capacity, sapping productive resources from the economy. While strong and capable governments may be able to avoid many of these problems through tight budget planning and execution and through efficient tax administration, countries with weaker governance would be well advised to keep public spending and taxation to more modest levels if they want to spur rapid rates of economic growth.

The study also finds that fiscal deficits matter for economic growth and that patterns of fiscal consolidation affect the sustainability of deficit reduction. Specifically, fiscal adjustments that lower fiscal deficits are followed by stronger economic growth, and fiscal adjustments driven by expenditure reductions are likely to be more successful and sustainable than those driven by tax increases. These findings on fiscal deficits and fiscal consolidation mirror those found elsewhere in the literature. They provide yet another reason why ECA governments should focus not only on the deficit but also on the overall level of public spending.

Although these broad patterns underline the importance of fiscal restraint and low fiscal deficits in ECA, current spending and deficit levels are low enough in a few ECA countries to provide fiscal space to enhance public spending to promote economic growth. Georgia and Kazakhstan, for example, have benefited from modest overall spending levels and strong fiscal positions in recent years. Their growth rates could thus potentially benefit from enhanced spending on health, education, and public investment.

However, economic growth is not the only goal of fiscal policy. A recent poll of citizens in ECA countries indicates wide support for public policies that promote income redistribution and help the poor (EBRD 2007), and some of the social transfer programs that lead to larger governments also help to reduce poverty. Governments need to balance these objectives and strive for efficiency in social transfers to avoid harming growth prospects.

How Can Governments Improve the Efficiency of Public Spending?

Patterns of public spending affect economic growth in at least two ways. First, broad allocations of spending among government functions may affect overall growth rates because some categories of activities appear to spur growth more than others. Second, within each broad category of spending it is possible to allocate resources more or less efficiently and effectively.

Evidence in this study supports the finding elsewhere in the literature that high levels of spending in "unproductive" areas (most notably spending on public consumption and transfers) can have a negative impact on growth, while spending in "productive" areas (investment, social sectors) can promote growth. The study also finds, however, that these results—as with those on government size more generally—depend on the state of governance. Countries with better governance are generally able to collect taxes and spend public funds more efficiently and effectively. Thus, higher spending in productive areas can lead to higher growth in countries with strong governance, and higher spending in unproductive areas is not necessarily harmful to growth. In contrast, growth in countries with weak governance tends to be slowed by higher levels of unproductive spending and the higher taxes that are required to fund it, and they do not necessarily benefit from spending in areas that are typically considered productive.

This broad characterization of spending into productive and unproductive areas is very rough, and actual spending patterns within any particular area are likely to be critical in practice. Spending in productive categories such as education can still be wasteful, while well-targeted spending in less productive categories can be beneficial. While ECA countries should try to shift spending toward productive areas to the extent possible, it is even more important that they enhance the efficiency of spending in each area, as outlined below.

Infrastructure

The quantity and quality of infrastructure is a key factor in the investment climate in any country, and most research concludes that improvements in the stock and quality of infrastructure enhance economic growth prospects. ECA countries all began the transition with good stocks of infrastructure assets but highly inefficient systems. The quality and reliability of existing infrastructure have been of growing concern, however, because the cushion of infrastructure inherited from socialism has been eroded as a result of insufficient maintenance or no longer remains relevant in a restructured, market economy. The countries whose economic growth rates have rebounded most strongly are revitalizing their asset base through new investments, especially in power, while others that are less dynamic face massive replacement and rehabilitation requirements resulting from years of undermaintenance and the effects of poor technical design. Further investments and a stronger focus on operations and maintenance are needed in many countries. Efforts are also needed to strengthen the management of public investments. For new EU member countries, for example, the availability of large amounts of structural and cohesion funds for investment provides a unique opportunity to improve infrastructure, if, indeed, the countries pursue good practices in project selection and in the budgeting of subsequent operations and maintenance expenditures.

But more infrastructure spending is unlikely to spur economic growth in a bad policy environment. A major emphasis since the start of transition has been on reforms to promote more efficient use of scarce resources through changes in ownership, pricing, collections, and safety nets to protect the poor, and the primary emphasis going forward still needs to be on policy and institutional reforms to promote efficiency and strengthen governance. Progress varies widely, and there is still a significant way to go in many ECA countries (particularly in the SEE and CIS regions). There remain significant hidden costs—or implicit subsidies—in several countries, especially for power (figure 1.4) and to a lesser extent for water, which create current or eventual contingent liabilities for the government. For example, it is estimated that Albania could save more than US$74 million annually (or 0.9 percent of GDP in 2006) if problems in the water sector, such as collection failures, underpricing, unaccounted losses, and overstaffing, were adequately addressed. Overcoming such problems should be a priority for both the sectoral and the public finance reform agendas in a wide range of ECA countries.

Looking forward, there is scope for more private sector participation in infrastructure in ECA, whether through divestiture or management contracts. Apart from telecommunications, the power sector has attracted the bulk of private participation to date, and this has led to generally beneficial results in improved collections and reliability of supply. In any case, government's role will continue to be critical. On the one hand, private sector participation is unlikely to materialize and

FIGURE 1.4
Total Hidden Costs of Power Sector, 2000–2005

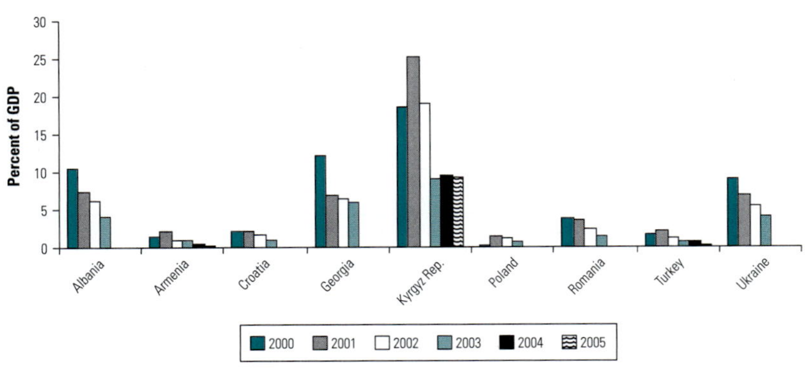

Source: World Bank staff estimates.

succeed unless policy and institutional frameworks ensure financial viability and promote fair competition. On the other hand, strong vigilance by government is required to ensure that private sector participation contributes to improved governance of the sectors and does not generate contingent public liabilities. The financing role of government will also continue to be important, because the private sector is unlikely to provide the bulk of necessary funding for infrastructure.

Education

A more educated population is clearly associated with faster economic growth, although more public spending on education is not always associated with better educational outcomes. While there is a positive correlation between per capita incomes and learning outcomes, some countries, such as Korea, Poland, and Romania, appear to have better educational outcomes than would be expected for their levels of per capita income, or, stated differently, lower per capita incomes than would be expected for their levels of educational attainment (figure 1.5). Many ECA and non-ECA high-growth comparators also have above-average school enrollment and learning outcomes given their share of public education spending in GDP, indi-

FIGURE 1.5

Imputed Learning Scores and GDP Per Capita, 2000

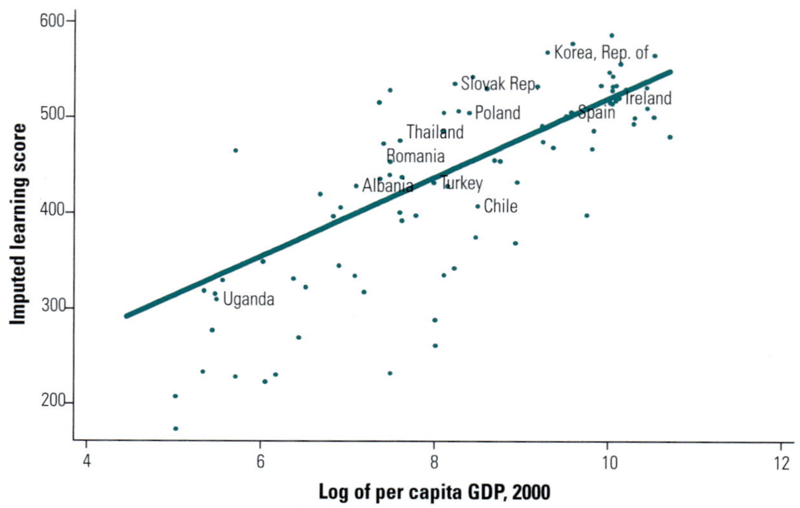

Sources: WDI; Crouch and Fasih 2004.

Note: Crouch and Fasih constructed these imputed learning scores from existing assessment scores to provide a standard measure for cross-country comparisons.

cating that public spending is achieving reasonably good results in many cases. Turkey, with significantly worse outcomes, is a notable exception to this pattern.

Although many factors other than public spending—including family background and peer influence—affect educational outcomes, the level and efficiency of public spending also matter. The ECA countries vary in their levels of efficiency, with some scoring well and others doing much worse on comparative efficiency indicators. Common problems include excessive numbers of teachers for the declining student population, combined with inflexible rules on teacher pay and employment (leading to low pay for individual teachers), as well as heavy reliance on relatively expensive technical and vocational education at the secondary level. Experience in the comparator countries, Chile and Korea in particular, indicates that ECA countries could benefit from enhanced efficiency through well-designed policy reforms, including a movement to financing on a per capita basis (capitation financing) to promote consolidation of underused facilities and better integration of technical and vocational with general education schools. In some cases, decentralization of school financing and management to subnational governments can promote accountability, although this depends on the state of governance at various levels of government and the specific design of the decentralization initiative.

Intrasectoral allocations also matter, because greater reliance on private sources of financing for tertiary education can help free up needed public funding for primary and secondary education. Korea, for example, achieves high levels of efficiency and exceptional educational outcomes with one of the lowest ratios of public spending on tertiary relative to primary education in the world. Indeed, Korea and Chile also stand out as countries with large shares (over 40 percent) of financing for education at all levels coming from private sources. In Chile, however, greater private financing has improved efficiency but has also led to greater inequity in expenditures and in the performance of students from different income groups.

Health

Determining appropriate policies and funding mechanisms for health is a difficult public finance challenge everywhere. As with education, a healthier labor force contributes to economic growth, but levels and patterns of public spending on health are not necessarily related to health outcomes. Richer countries tend to have better health outcomes than poorer countries. This is due not only to higher spending—per capita health spending is highly correlated with per capita income (figure 1.6)—but also to better governance of the health system as well as stronger complementary inputs such as education, living conditions, and environmental protection. Countries use a wide variety of models for health financing, relying on payroll taxes, general revenues, and out-of-pocket payments to various degrees, as well as a variety of health delivery systems, but cross-country evidence indicates that neither financing method nor delivery system is strongly correlated with health outcomes.

Health outcomes in ECA countries do not compare poorly in absolute terms with those in other regions, but ECA countries tend to spend more than countries elsewhere for comparable outcomes, a sign of inefficiency and poor governance in the health system. The lowest efficiency scores are in countries such as Croatia and the Slovak Republic, with good outcomes but high spending. Indeed, the size of public expenditures and the proportion of services that are publicly financed appear to be negatively associated with efficiency scores. Korea, Chile, and Thailand have the highest efficiency scores among the sample of focus countries in this study.

The primary emphasis in ECA needs to be on policy and institutional reforms to enhance the quality and efficiency of spending. Health systems in socialist times were characterized by heavy reliance on hospitals and few incentives to economize on scarce resources. This legacy is still evident in much of the ECA region. Governments in ECA have stepped up reforms in the past few years to improve efficiency—for example, by consolidating hospitals, moving toward standard basic

FIGURE 1.6
Total Health Expenditure and Per Capita GDP

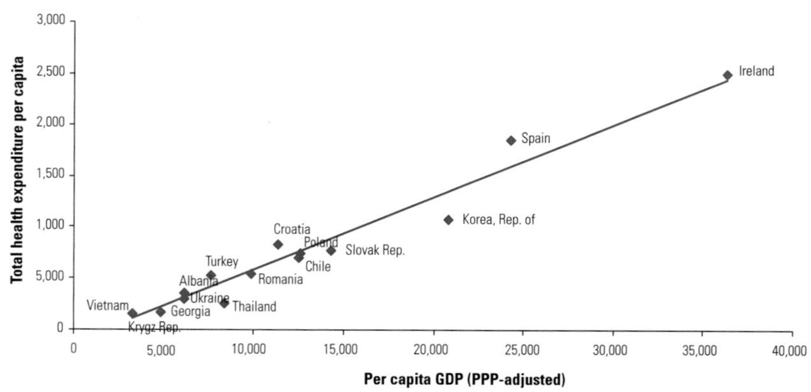

Source: WHO data.

benefits packages, and undertaking measures to contain the growth of pharmaceutical costs—but much more needs to be done. The most efficient non-ECA comparators have introduced a number of important reforms in recent years to (a) reduce systemic fragmentation in risk pooling; (b) create the right incentive frameworks for patients, insurers, and health service providers; (c) expand access while adjusting the supply of publicly provided services; and (d) increase monitoring and accountability at all levels of the health system.

Financing issues are also critical in ECA, given the effect of health contributions on labor costs in countries relying on payroll taxes to finance health services. Movement toward general revenue financing, while not necessarily affecting health outcomes, may have a positive effect on economic growth in some ECA countries through its effect on labor supply and demand, as discussed further below. Furthermore, while copayments can help to spur efficiency in health care, excessive reliance on out-of-pocket spending limits access for the poor and may deter both economic growth and poverty reduction over the medium term. Adequate mechanisms for financing and risk sharing with a reasonably modest level of copayments—defined by law and transparent to all—should be the goal of public finance policy in health.

Pensions

Pensions pose some of the most difficult and intractable issues in public finance policy in ECA, exacerbated by the legacy of socialism and demographic trends. Socialist systems were characterized by very high rates of employment and generous pension coverage—with relatively low retirement ages, high wage-replacement rates, and broad coverage for disability. Pension spending thus tends to be much higher in ECA than in fast-growing countries at similar income levels elsewhere, and such spending, while helping to alleviate poverty, may well put a drag on economic growth. As rates of formal employment have declined in ECA during transition, the share of the population paying into public pension systems has fallen relative to the share receiving benefits, leading to increasing pension fund deficits that put added pressure on fiscal balances. This trend has been aggravated by declining birth rates and the overall aging of the population. One reaction of governments has been to raise contribution rates, and ECA countries now have among the highest payroll tax rates in the world. But these high tax rates on workers in the formal sector further constrain the pension revenue base by worsening unemployment and encouraging informality in the labor market. Another reaction has been to raise retirement ages, but they still remain somewhat low (especially for women) compared to retirement ages in non-ECA countries.

Given the socialist legacy, unfavorable demographic trends, and the economic costs of high payroll taxes, most ECA countries will need to reduce public pension benefits further to tackle fiscal imbalances and provide fiscal space for growth-promoting spending. For middle-income countries, fixing the public contributory pension system and complementing it with means-tested social assistance for those who are not covered is likely to be the best option. Public contributory systems should be fully self-financing, which will generally require a reduction in benefits (whether through higher retirement ages or reduced replacement rates, or both) to allow a moderation in payroll tax rates. These can be supplemented by private contributory systems, but the key public finance criteria in all of these cases is that the system should be self-financing.

Contributory pension systems are less likely to achieve broad coverage in lower-income settings; thus, a universal or means-tested low-rate pension financed out of general revenues may be the best option. Georgia, for example, has moved to a flat-rate pension at a very low rate to provide a basic cushion for the poorest pensioners. Such universal or means-tested pensions can be supplemented by contributory pension systems for subsets of the population that can afford them (such as civil servants), but governments need to set the parameters of these contributory systems to ensure that they are self-financing, because using general revenues to subsidize such systems would be highly regressive.

How Can Governments Reduce Distortions in the Tax System?

Patterns of government financing also matter to economic growth. Taxes that distort incentives for productive investment or employment can impede growth, and analysis in this study concludes that such effect is likely to be compounded when governance is weak. In contrast, taxes that create fewer economic distortions, such as taxes on consumption, are less likely to have a negative effect on growth. Higher indirect taxes may even be associated with faster growth if the benefits of increasing expenditures outweigh the effects of increased taxation —and this is most likely to happen in countries where strong governance leads to growth-enhancing public spending. In sum, higher taxes are most likely to be harmful to growth (a) when their design is distortionary and (b) in settings where overall governance is weak.

Flat Income Tax Reforms

Many countries in ECA have adopted flat rate income taxes, motivated primarily by a desire to simplify the tax system and to lower income tax rates to spur investment and growth. The flat rates typically cover both personal and corporate income taxes, although these rates have varied widely across countries, with later adopters typically imposing lower rate levels.

The revenue impact of flat tax reforms has varied (figure 1.7), largely reflecting policy goals and resulting decisions on rate levels. In some settings, such as the Slovak Republic, rate reductions have been tempered by an expansion of the tax base and by better compliance. In other settings, such as Ukraine, the benefits of simplicity are clearly visible but the lack of reforms in other areas (such as labor taxes and tax administration) has undermined potential improvements in compliance. The specific design of the flat tax is critical in determining its revenue and overall economic impact. In addition, the experience in ECA suggests that a flat tax reform is less likely to have a negative impact on revenue collection if it is adopted during a period of strong economic growth. Revenue effects are also less severe if policy changes are complemented by strong efforts to improve tax administration.

Flat tax reforms have had another effect that is likely to be good for economic growth: they have led to a shift from direct taxes, which tax labor and capital, to less distortionary indirect taxes. Moreover, they have reduced high marginal rates and helped to reduce the overall tax burden, which is comparatively high in some of the ECA countries that have undertaken the reform. However, even though income tax rates have been lowered dramatically in many ECA countries, payroll taxes (which in ECA typically share most of their base with the personal income tax) remain high, discouraging compliance and imposing a tax wedge of 30–50 percent on employment, as discussed below.

Evidence indicates that a move to flat rate income taxes does not necessarily harm the overall progressivity of the fiscal system. If these tax systems provide generous exemptions for lower-income workers and spur tax compliance for higher-income earners, they can be more progressive in their incidence than traditional progressive income tax systems that may have more loopholes in practice. Furthermore, the overall incidence of the fiscal system can be highly progressive if revenues from flat rate income and consumption taxes are spent on public programs that enhance broadly based growth and poverty reduction.

FIGURE 1.7

Changes in Personal and Corporate Income Tax Revenue Collection after Flat Tax Reforms

a. Personal income tax revenue collection

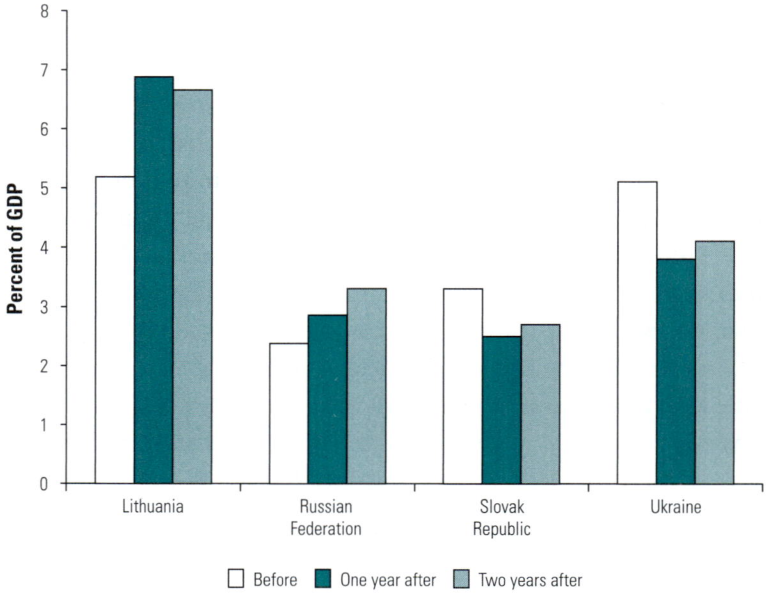

b. Corporate income tax revenue collection

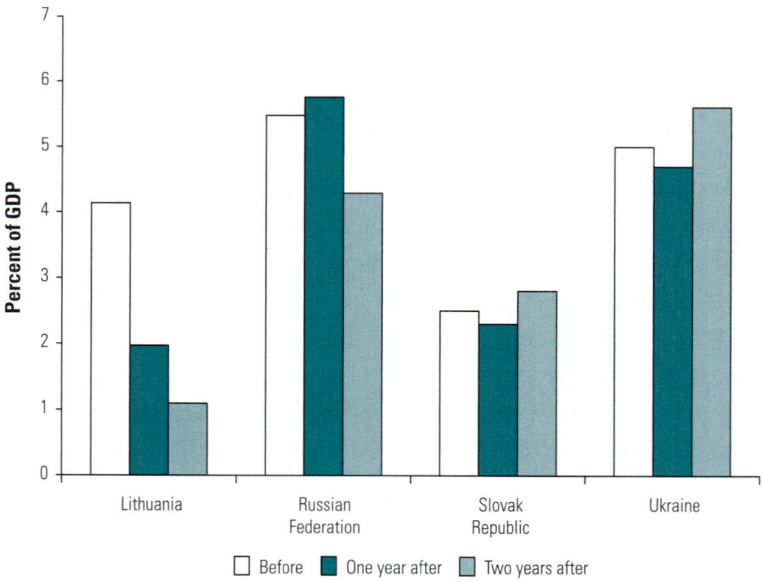

Sources: World Bank; World Bank staff calculations.

Labor Taxes

Taxes on labor are as high in ECA as in much richer countries in Western Europe and are higher in ECA than in most other regions in the world—and certainly higher than in high-growth developing countries in Asia (figure 1.8). The high taxes reflect generous social security benefits and a narrow tax base (due to lower rates of formal employment). High labor taxes have a negative effect on rates of formal employment, on the return to capital, and on growth. Whether the taxes are imposed on the employer (as typical in ECA for historical reasons) or on the employee does not appear to matter. The ultimate effect in either case is to reduce both labor demand and labor supply, with the exact division depending on the flexibility of labor demand and supply.

The best way to reduce the labor tax burden and its effect on employment is to reform the social security system (most notably pensions and health care), as discussed above. Early retirement, disability, and sickness programs are often abused and need to be tightened up in many countries, and the pensionable age needs to be raised and equalized for both sexes. An additional option in some cases may be to provide some relief from payroll taxes to those with the highest "elasticity" of labor demand, including low-skilled workers and new labor market entrants. Finally, some countries (Denmark, the United Kingdom, and Ireland, for instance) finance some

FIGURE 1.8

Tax Wedge on Labor, ECA and Selected Comparator Countries, 2006

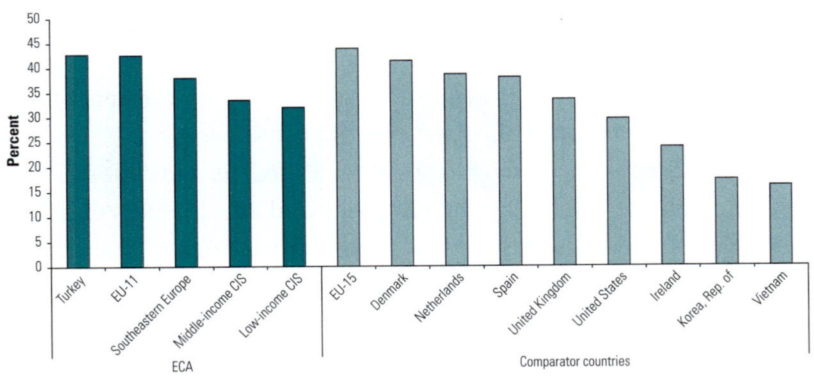

Sources: Eurostat, OECD, and World Bank data.

portions of social security out of general tax revenues, and ECA countries can also move in that direction by replacing some social insurance benefits financed by employer and employee contributions with universal benefits financed out of general taxation. Additional benefits for higher-income workers could be offered on a self-financing basis through contributory public or private systems.

Conclusion

This study illustrates the many challenges and trade-offs that policy makers inevitably face when trying to formulate public finance policies in any country. Each sector and topic involves a wide variety of highly complex issues that affect large numbers of citizens. Yet, worldwide experience offers lessons that countries can use as they try to formulate public finance policies that will promote economic growth while meeting the need for fundamental public goods. A first lesson is that macroeconomic stability is essential, because large budget deficits retard growth. A second is that moderate levels of public spending—around one-third of GDP or less—are preferable to high levels when governance and public administration are not strong. Maintaining such levels of spending while also addressing poverty concerns requires efficiency, particularly in key areas such as infrastructure, health, education, and social protection. A third lesson is that lower income and payroll tax rates can spur investment and employment. ECA countries are pioneers in adopting flat income taxes and do not appear to have generally suffered revenue losses or seriously compromised the overall progressivity of their fiscal systems as a result. But they are much further behind in addressing the problem of high payroll taxes and their effect on employment. The key to lowering payroll taxes is to improve the efficiency of social transfers (which will in some cases require a reduction in benefits) while moving toward general tax financing for some health and social assistance services.

ECA countries are moving forward with fiscal reforms but still face many hurdles in improving the efficiency and effectiveness of public spending and revenue generation. Some countries have undertaken strong fiscal consolidation and are balancing growth and poverty reduction goals with appropriate levels of public spending, while others need greater fiscal discipline and stronger reforms on the spending side. Some have undertaken bold tax reforms, but many still face daunting pressures from high labor taxes and weak tax administration. Moreover, good governance, fiscal transparency, and public accountability continue to be important challenges in most settings.

ECA countries are not alone, however—market economies everywhere are striving to enhance efficiency to compete in the global economy. Political pressures may create temporary roadblocks, but the need to enhance competitiveness, promote economic growth, and thereby raise living standards makes continued progress essential.

Note

1. Serbia and Montenegro became separate states in January 2007; however, this report refers to "Serbia and Montenegro" as one entity because the data for them reflect their joined status. Data for Serbia and Montenegro from 2000 to 2005 exclude Kosovo.

PART 1

Public Finance and Economic Growth: Trends and Interrelationships

CHAPTER 2

Public Finance Systems in Transition Countries

Tracey Lane
with contributions from
Andrzej Rzonca, Emilia Skrok, and Olga Vybornaia

The Europe and Central Asia (ECA) region comprises a diverse group of countries that have all undergone dramatic changes since the early 1990s, as they have moved from socialism toward market economies. The region suffered a major economic downturn in the early 1990s but has rebounded over the past 15 years (figure 2.1). Growth resumed in the early 1990s in Central Europe[1] and the Baltics[2]—the countries that became members of the European Union in 2004 (the EU-8)—following rapid structural reforms. Growth rebounded in Southeastern Europe (SEE)[3] following the end to regional hostilities in the mid-1990s, and in the Commonwealth of Independent States (CIS)[4] following the financial crisis in the Russian Federation in the late 1990s. The economic recovery in Russia, the favorable global trading environment, and high commodity prices have sustained high growth rates in the CIS and the Baltics, whereas growth has remained positive but not as strong in Central and Southeastern Europe. Average real GDP growth for the ECA region was 7.1 percent in 2005, which compares favorably with most other developing regions.

Are there links between these patterns of growth and public finance policies in ECA countries? This chapter examines fiscal patterns in the ECA region over the period 1995 to 2005. The analysis is followed in chapter 3 by an empirical examination of the relationship

FIGURE 2.1
ECA Regional Growth Performance, 1990–2005

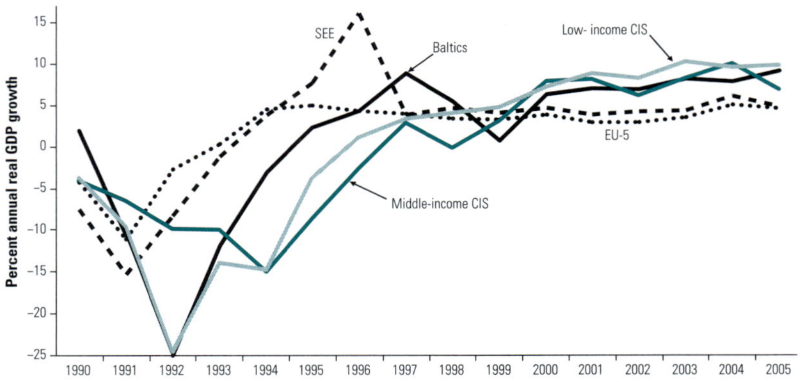

Sources: National authorities; IMF and World Bank estimates.

between fiscal policy and economic growth. While fiscal policy is not solely concerned with promoting economic growth and there are many other objectives (for example, social improvement, redistribution, and equity concerns), it is interesting to examine how far fiscal adjustment, size and composition of spending, and tax policy have changed during this dynamic period in the region, and to explore (in chapter 3) to what extent these changes were supportive of the economic growth that followed.

The economic downturns in the early years of transition led to major upheavals in intraregional fiscal transfers that contributed to large fiscal imbalances, particularly in the countries of the former Soviet Union (FSU) and former Yugoslavia. Since then, governments have undertaken macroeconomic stabilization and fiscal adjustments, and fiscal balances have been restored through a combination of reductions in public spending and increases in revenues. However, the size of government (the size of general government expenditure in proportion to GDP) and the composition of spending vary markedly across ECA countries, and significant cross-country differences in fiscal balances and the level of public debt also remain. In Central and Eastern Europe, the size and composition of public spending now approximate that of Western European members of the EU (the EU-15[5]). In the CIS, however, the economic recovery has led to increased public spending, but the size of government is much closer to that in fast-growing Asian comparators.

With the exception of low-income CIS,[6] the average size of public sector spending in ECA is significantly above international norms at similar levels of per capita income. Influenced by a history of state-sponsored provision of welfare and social security throughout the life cycle, ECA countries tend to spend more on social protection than do other countries, and this spending has increased in the past five years. Public transfers are important components of household income, especially for the poor, and play a valuable role in reducing poverty. However, high levels of spending can also threaten fiscal sustainability and impose heavy tax burdens on the private sector, which in turn can adversely affect economic growth and poverty reduction. Furthermore, most ECA countries have aging populations, and government policy will need to balance demands on public spending today with economic growth tomorrow. Poverty reduction without growth is rare, and continued growth will be critical for funding social spending in the future.

Fiscal Stabilization and Debt Dynamics

This section looks at the experience of fiscal stabilization and public debt during the transition. The early transition was characterized by a massive upheaval in public finances. Households were hit by multiple shocks, and output and incomes plummeted. With the removal of employment guarantees in state-owned enterprises, open and hidden unemployment increased rapidly, putting pressure on the state to respond with cash transfers and social assistance. At the same time, the fall in output and reforms in public enterprises led to falling government revenues. The combined effect was deterioration in fiscal performance and an increase in public debt.

Reflecting the shock of transition, fiscal deficits in ECA have on average been higher than the average in other regions, as well as higher than the average for the seven fast-growing comparator countries—Chile, Ireland, the Republic of Korea, Spain, Thailand, Uganda, and Vietnam. These countries experienced per capita growth in excess of 4 percent for the last 10 years, and examples from this group's experience are drawn upon throughout the report (table 2.1). Deficits were as high as 20 percent of GDP during the 1990s in some low-income CIS countries, many of which had previously depended on transfers from the Soviet Union. The end to these transfers led to huge declines in government revenue for these countries, with difficulties exacerbated by multiple military conflicts that broke out in the early 1990s. Deficits were lowest in the EU-8 countries, which managed to avoid prolonged fiscal crises because of better diversification and closer trade and investment links with the European Union (EU).

TABLE 2.1
Fiscal Balance in ECA Countries, 1989–2005

	Fiscal balance (% of GDP)				Primary fiscal balance (% of GDP)			
Countries	1989–2005	1989–95	1996–2001	2002–05	1989–2005	1989–95	1996–2001	2002–05
EU-8	-2.7	-2.4	-2.8	-3.1	-0.8	-0.6	-0.5	-1.3
Southeastern Europe	-4.3	-6.1	-4.4	-2.2	-0.8	-0.8	-1.1	-0.3
Middle-income CIS	-3.7	-6.9	-3.0	1.0	-1.3	-6.2	-0.9	1.9
Low-income CIS	-5.5	-9.4	-4.3	-1.1	-3.0	-9.2	-2.7	-0.1
Turkey	-	-	-15.2	-9.9	-	-	3.8	6.3
EU-15	-2.4	-4.3	-0.8	-1.4	0.8	-0.6	2.6	0.7
Non-EU high-income OECD[a]	-0.8	-2.5	0.6	0.2	1.1	-0.3	2.6	1.3
High-income OECD outside Europe[b]	-1.9	-3.0	-0.8	-1.5	0.7	0.3	1.6	-0.1
Fast-growing Asia[c]	0.1	1.5	-0.7	-1.0	2.2	3.7	1.7	1.0
Latin America[d]	-2.3	-1.7	-2.7	-2.6	1.3	1.7	0.7	1.6
Fast-growing comparators[e]	-1.0	-1.5	-0.9	-0.3	0.9	0.9	1.2	0.7

Source: IMF, World Economic Outlook database.

a. Australia, Canada, Iceland, Japan, New Zealand, Norway, Switzerland, and the United States.

b. Australia, Canada, Japan, New Zealand, and the United States.

c. China, Hong Kong (China), Indonesia, Republic of Korea, Malaysia, Singapore, Taiwan, and Thailand. The table does not include data for Korea. Primary fiscal deficit includes data for China, Indonesia, and Singapore only.

d. Argentina, Bolivia, Brazil, Chile, Mexico, Paraguay, Peru, Uruguay, and República Bolivariana de Venezuela.

e. Chile, Ireland, Spain, Thailand, Uganda, and Vietnam. The table does not include data for Korea. Primary fiscal deficit does not include data for Thailand.

Macroeconomic stabilization aimed at curbing inflation eventually resulted in large fiscal adjustments and a reduction in unsustainably high fiscal deficits. The process of stabilization was not smooth, however, and in most subregions the fiscal deficit became sustainable only at the end of the 1990s, following a period of fiscal laxity caused by financial crises, regional armed conflicts, or politically motivated spending booms (or a combination). Figure 2.2 shows the evolution of the fiscal balance, public spending, and revenue as a share of GDP for the ECA region as a whole and for five subregions: the Baltics, EU-5, middle-income CIS,[7] low-income CIS, and SEE; and for Turkey (using data as described in box 2.1). Turkey's story is different from the others, of course, because it has long been a market economy and did not experience the same transition from socialism as other countries in the ECA region.

Fiscal consolidation has advanced markedly in CIS, most of SEE, and Turkey. In the middle-income CIS, fiscal balances improved through a combination of expenditure reductions (mostly pre-2000) and gradual revenue improvements. In Azerbaijan and, to a lesser extent, Russia, post-2000 revenue improvements were buoyed by high commodity prices, which led to improvements in the fiscal balance. Low-income CIS countries have similarly seen revenues recover

FIGURE 2.2

Fiscal Balance, Total Revenues, Total Expenditures, and Primary Expenditures in ECA, 1996–2005

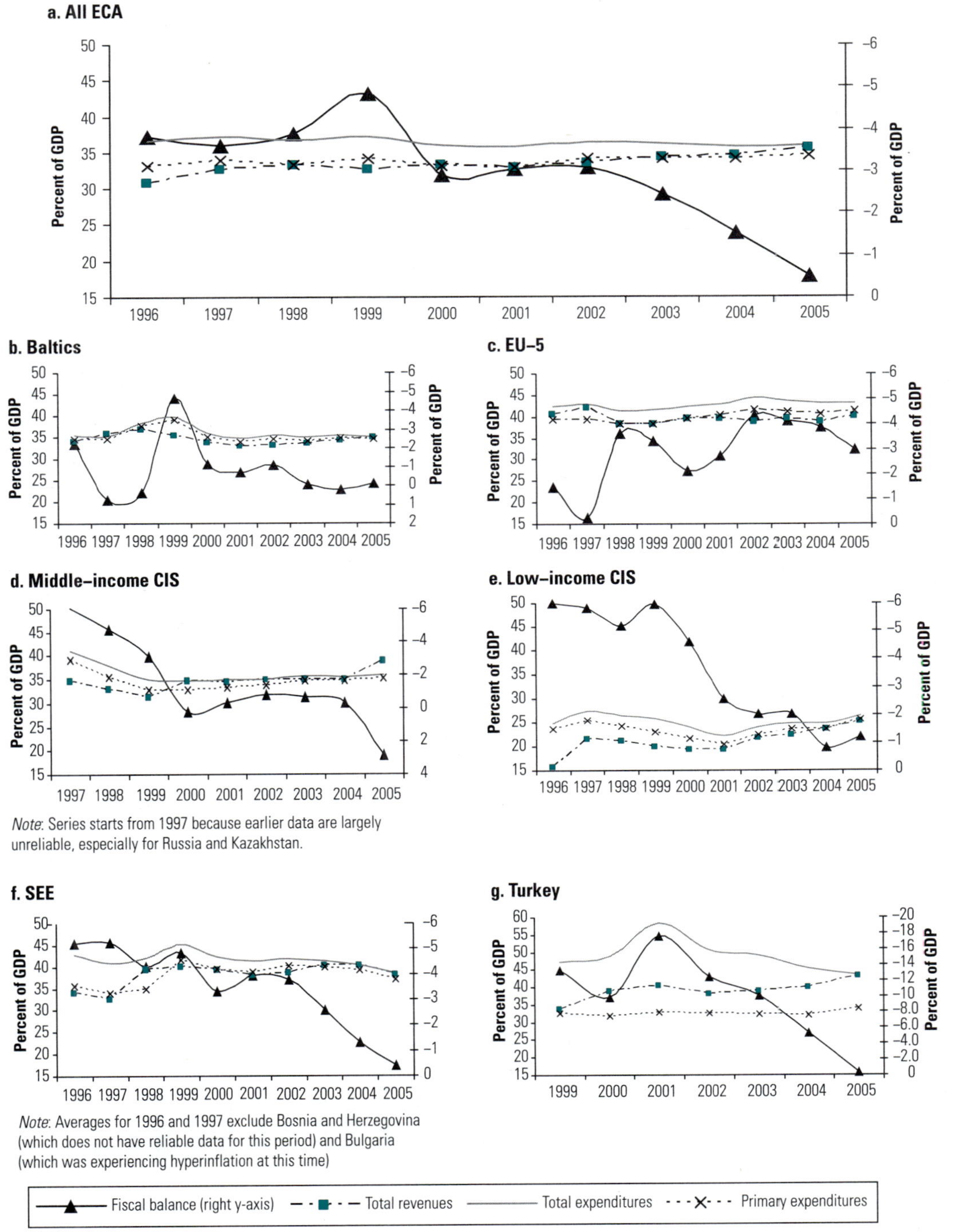

Note: Series starts from 1997 because earlier data are largely unreliable, especially for Russia and Kazakhstan.

Note: Averages for 1996 and 1997 exclude Bosnia and Herzegovina (which does not have reliable data for this period) and Bulgaria (which was experiencing hyperinflation at this time)

Source: ECA fiscal database.

Note: Data show unweighted averages.

and have even managed to increase public spending in proportion to GDP while bringing down huge fiscal deficits to less than 1 percent of GDP on average. The countries of SEE have reduced their fiscal deficits through controlled public spending and moderate increases in revenues. The deficit has been substantial (more than 4 percent of GDP) in Albania and Croatia, while most other SEE countries run surpluses. In Turkey, resolute fiscal consolidation was initiated after the 2001 crisis, with the general government primary surplus kept above 6 percent of GDP since 2002, although the overall deficit has remained significant because of large interest payments on public debt.

In the EU-8, Maastricht criteria have constrained fiscal policies, and the fiscal deficit has stabilized at around -2 percent of GDP on average, but fiscal performance has been uneven among countries. In particular, fiscal adjustment lost momentum in the early 2000s in the Central European countries that had recently joined the EU. Although these countries managed to keep public expenditure under control during the early transition recession, they did not take full advantage of the fast growth recovery to reinforce public finances. After the Russian crisis, large fiscal imbalances returned, so that fiscal deficits in Hungary, Poland, the Czech Republic, and the Slovak Republic were on average larger in the mid-2000s than the late 1990s (table 2.1).

In response to the fiscal imbalances, public-debt-to-GDP ratios increased in most of the ECA region during 1994–2001.[8] Since then, improvements in fiscal balances have brought public debt ratios down

FIGURE 2.3
Gross Public Debt as a Share of GDP and Tax Revenue, 2005

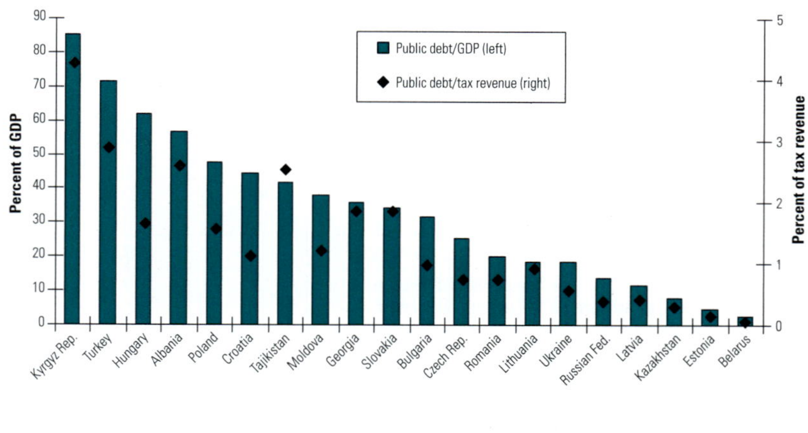

Sources: Eurostat, IMF, and World Bank ECA data set.

Note: Tax revenues include social security contributions.

to more sustainable levels. In all but four ECA countries, gross public debt in 2005 was below 50 percent of GDP (figure 2.3). Among middle-income countries in Europe, public debt ratios are highest in Turkey, Hungary, and SEE (in particular, Croatia). In low-income CIS, debt is relatively high in the Kyrgyz Republic and, to a lesser extent, Moldova. By contrast, public debt in proportion to GDP is low in middle-income CIS, the Baltic countries, and Azerbaijan.

Despite ambitious adjustment in the region, several countries still have remaining fiscal imbalances and accumulated debt stock that

BOX 2.1

Data Sources and Issues

The study used fiscal data compiled according to *A Manual on Government Financial Statistics* 1986 (GFS 1986), consolidated at the general government level by the Ministry of Finance or the IMF, as reported by World Bank country teams. For non-ECA countries, data were collected from World Bank country teams, the IMF World Economic Outlook database, and OECD publications (where applicable). Series expressed in percentage of GDP were calculated using World Development Indicators GDP numbers.

The GFS 1986 standard was selected as the common denominator for all ECA countries to ensure consistency and comparability across countries and time. Eurostat (ESA 95 reporting framework) and GFS 2001 data have been used mostly for cross-comparison purposes, because only a subsection of ECA countries report under these standards. Because of methodological issues, some discrepancies exist between GFS 1986, ESA 95, and GFS 2001 (see references in note for detailed discussion of these differences). Some data gaps in early years were not possible to fill because of national reporting constraints or unreliability of fiscal data in the early transition period, or both.

Official GDP figures in some countries (such as Bosnia and Herzegovina, Turkey, and Ukraine) are widely considered to be understated because they do not take the informal sector fully into account. A number of ECA countries have already adjusted GDP figures upward in an effort to account for the informal sector, and others are planning to do so in the near future. This study relies in all cases on official figures as reported by government authorities and makes no such additional adjustment. It should also be noted that the deflator for public expenditures may sometimes diverge from the GDP deflator, and caution should be used in interpreting expenditure-to-GDP ratios and assessing the size of the fiscal adjustment.

Note: "Government Finance Statistics Manual 2001 Companion Material: Classification of GFSM 1986 Data to *GFSM 2001* Framework," published by the IMF in 2002. "The Government Finance Statistics Manual 2001 and its Relationship with the European System of Accounts 1995," published by the IMF in 2004.

raise concerns of fiscal sustainability. Fiscal imbalances fundamentally hinder growth when they pose a risk of debt distress—that is, when the primary fiscal balance is inconsistent with the long-term sustainability of public debt under plausible circumstances. The public debt ratio will then increase, leading to rollover risk, higher real interest rates, and lower investor confidence, and eventually jeopardizing macroeconomic stability and prospects for long-run growth. Several ECA countries have generated sizeable primary fiscal surpluses that mitigate the risks of debt distress and allow for debt reduction (figure 2.4). However, in about half of ECA countries, primary fiscal balances are still in deficit. Primary fiscal deficits have been significant in recent years in four Central European countries (Hungary, Poland, the Slovak Republic, and the Czech Republic) as well as in Albania, Croatia, and the Kyrgyz Republic. In these countries, under normal circumstances (where real interest rates exceed long-term growth), the public debt ratio will have a tendency to increase—barring debt revaluations due to exchange rate appreciation or debt repayments due to one-off revenues such as privatization receipts. In countries lying below the "prudent zone" this does not necessarily imply that they should borrow more, and unfunded public sector and contingent liabilities need to be taken into consideration as well as future pressures on spending.

FIGURE 2.4
Primary Fiscal Balance, 2005

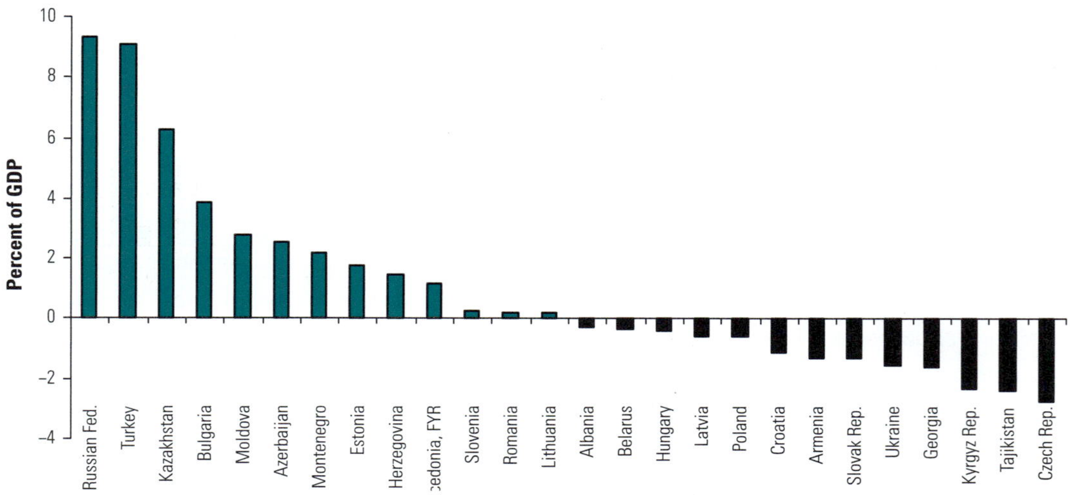

Sources: World Bank ECA data set; Eurostat.

Note: Primary fiscal balance is defined here as total revenues (including interest and privatization revenues) minus primary (noninterest) expenditures.

Debt tolerance also depends on the quality of debt management and fiscal institutions. Even in countries where measured fiscal imbalances or public debt ratios (or both) seem low in international comparison, fiscal risks may arise from poorly managed contingent liabilities of the public sector—such as unfunded pension liabilities, distressed public utilities, nonperforming assets of state-owned banks, or debt guarantees issued for various public sector entities (state-owned enterprises, local administrations, trading offices). Off-budget activities may also add to public debt.

Financing conditions have been particularly favorable in recent years, as many ECA countries managed to borrow at a cost lower than their output growth. Favorable conditions on global financial markets, reflecting subdued inflation and exceptionally large savings and liquidity, contributed to this positive outcome.[9] However, this

FIGURE 2.5

Public Sector Debt, Debt Service, and Average Public Debt Maturity for Selected Emerging Market Economies, 2006

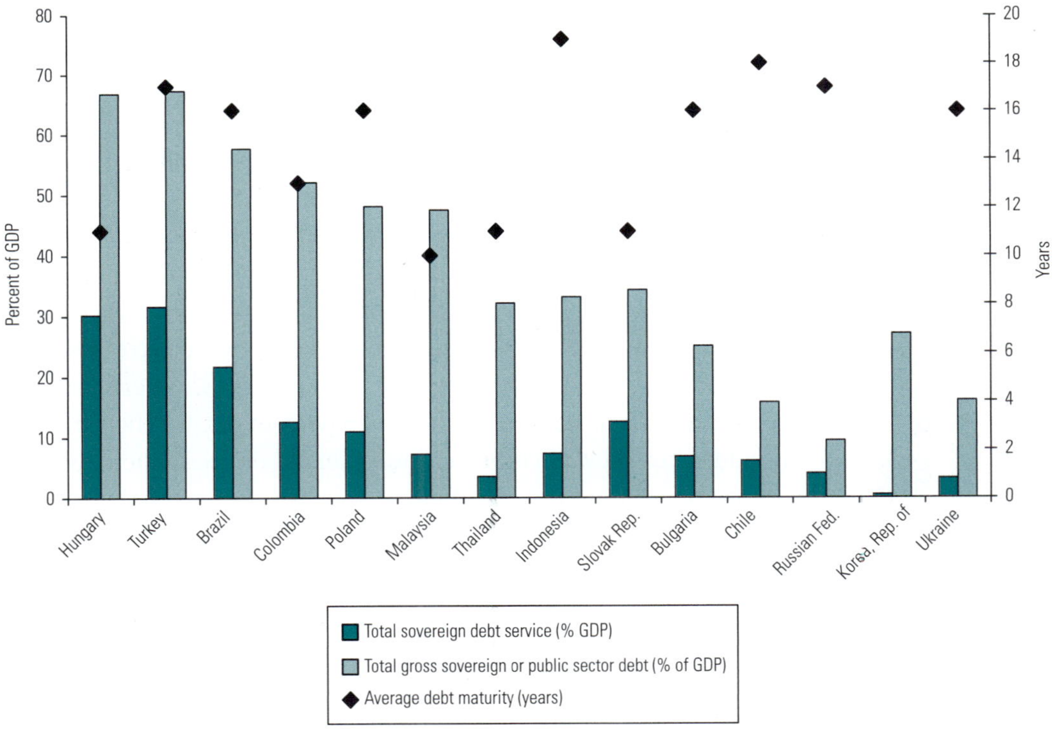

Sources: JP Morgan 2006, 2007; World Bank World Development Indicators.

Note: Public sector debt includes gross external and domestic sovereign debt. Debt service includes amortization and interest payments. Average official debt maturity is the ratio of official debt to debt amortization.

may not be sustained in the future if global liquidity conditions become tighter. Sudden reversals in capital flows could disrupt growth through higher interest rates and exchange rates, and stronger adjustments may be required to maintain fiscal sustainability. Mitigating such risks and stabilizing public debt at current levels would argue for running higher primary fiscal surpluses than those seen in recent years in several ECA countries.

In some instances, low-debt countries with strong institutions could find additional borrowing to be an attractive option to finance growth-promoting expenditure programs or tax reforms. Such debt could be serviced out of growing revenues in the future, assuming that the increased fiscal space is used wisely to finance growth-promoting expenditures in key areas such as education, infrastructure, and health care. Pension reforms that entail a transitional fiscal cost but provide long-term fiscal savings—for example, moving to a partly privately funded pension system—could also be financed by additional debt in these countries. Similarly, debt could be used to finance tax reforms that encourage investment and job creation yet entail a temporary fiscal cost. However, these are risky approaches and should be undertaken only when the likelihood of policy reforms or productivity-enhancing spending is strong, and other future claims on spending are also taken into consideration.

Patterns of Fiscal Adjustment and Public Spending

This section considers patterns of fiscal adjustment, and the success of adjustment is further considered in chapter 3. Fiscal consolidation has been achieved through a combination of cuts in public expenditure and increases in public revenues. The largest revenue increases since 1996 have occurred in low-income CIS countries, where primary expenditures have stabilized at about 25 percent of GDP (figure 2.2e). In middle-income CIS countries, public expenditure reductions have been more prominent, and primary expenditures have stabilized at a higher level of around 35 percent of GDP (figure 2.2d). Fiscal consolidation in these countries has been supported by buoyant revenues, in part reflecting high primary commodity prices. In SEE countries, expenditures and revenues both rose after 1997, with primary expenditures converging on average to around 40 percent of GDP (figure 2.2f). In Central European EU-5 countries, public expenditure in proportion to GDP has remained stable in the years following the early transition adjustment, with an upward trend in the early 2000s that worsened fiscal balances but with some recent recovery (figure 2.2c).

In contrast, in the three Baltic countries that joined the EU, general government primary expenditures are somewhat lower, at around 35 percent of GDP, and revenues have remained stable despite ambitious flat tax reforms (see discussion in chapter 8) (figure 2.2b). Turkey has been a notable exception to the overall ECA fiscal adjustment pattern. Turkey's ambitious fiscal consolidation has relied mainly on revenue-increasing measures rather than primary expenditure cuts, although steps have been taken recently to improve priority setting in public spending (figure 2.2g).

For purposes of this study, fiscal consolidation episodes were identified based on thresholds of fiscal deficit reductions. An episode of fiscal adjustment is defined as a period in which the general government primary balance improved by at least 2 percentage points of GDP within a year, or by 1.5 percentage points of GDP per year over two consecutive years (Purfield 2003).[10] Since 1991, 32 episodes fall within this definition: 5 in EU-8, 10 in SEE, 5 in middle-income CIS, 11 in low-income CIS, and 1 in Turkey. In two other episodes, improvements in primary balance were close to the threshold, and thus were added to the data set. The average size of adjustments in these episodes was 4.3 percentage points of GDP, with the 10 largest adjustments reaching an average 6.6 percentage points of GDP.

The 34 adjustment episodes are classified into four groups according to whether they were driven by (a) expenditure cuts exclusively; (b) expenditure cuts primarily; (c) tax revenue increases primarily; or (d) tax revenue increases exclusively[11] (see table 2.2):

- Fiscal adjustments were driven exclusively or primarily by expenditure cuts in the majority (19 out of 34) of identified episodes.
- Fiscal adjustments based exclusively on expenditure cuts were on average stronger than the other episodes.
- Expenditure cuts were larger when the initial primary fiscal deficit was large and the overall fiscal adjustment thus had to be ambitious. By contrast, tax revenue increases were more dominant when initial imbalances were moderate.
- Adjustments based only on expenditure reductions were more common in countries with high public spending as a share of GDP (40.3 percent on average) and a strong tax effort (see "Structure of Revenues in ECA" later in this chapter for a definition and analysis of tax effort). In contrast, exclusively tax revenue–driven adjustments prevailed in countries where the tax burden was initially low (25.2 percent of GDP on average), the tax effort was limited and public expenditures were low in proportion to GDP (27.2 percent on average).

TABLE 2.2
Features of Fiscal Adjustments in ECA, 1996–2004, percentage of GDP

Basis for adjustment	Number	Change in expenditures	Change in revenue	Fiscal adjustment	Initial primary balance	Public debt before adjustment	Expenditures before adjustment	Revenue before adjustment	Initial tax effort
Expenditure cuts only	11	-8.3	-3.2	5.1	-5.9	38.1	40.3	34.4	1.16
Expenditure cuts mostly	8	-2.4	1.1	3.5	-3.7	24.8	30.9	27.2	0.91
Revenue increases mostly	6	-1.1	3.1	4.2	-2.9	43.0	39.3	36.5	1.20
Revenue increases only	9	0.6	4.7	4.1	-2.0	41.9	27.2	25.2	0.90

Source: ECA fiscal database.

Large and sustained fiscal corrections typically resulted in sizeable reductions in primary spending in a short period. For example, primary spending as a share of GDP fell by 17.5 percentage points in Hungary and 15.8 percentage points in the former Yugoslav Republic of Macedonia between 1993 and 1997, a one-third reduction in four years. Similar adjustments took place in the CIS countries at the end of the 1990s. In Moldova, primary spending fell by over 40 percent (19.2 percentage points of GDP) between 1997 and 2001, and in Russia, spending fell by one-third (or 13.5 percentage points of GDP) between 1997 and 2000. Table 2.3 lists episodes of sustained reduction in primary expenditures, defined as reductions for three or more consecutive years.

As noted above, the extent of reduction in primary spending is positively correlated with the initial fiscal imbalance (figure 2.6). Consistent with the literature, we find that the pattern of consolidation is also determined by initial conditions. Hence, the pattern of adjustment is related to the starting condition in each country, and the biggest spending reductions are more likely to take place in economic and functional categories that are relatively high to begin with. Comparing these results with data from industrial countries during periods of fiscal adjustment in the 1980s and 1990s, further evidence is found that larger reductions occur when the initial spending levels are higher in proportion to GDP, whether for wages and salaries, transfers, health, or education (Hauptmeier, Heipertz, and Schuknecht 2006). Capital spending has been particularly prone to disruption during periods of expenditure consolidation. Given the small initial amounts involved, capital spending may not account for the majority of spending cuts, but compared with the initial year it has often been cut by more than 50 percent during periods of expenditure consolidation.[12]

TABLE 2.3

Periods of Sustained Primary Expenditure Reduction, 1994–2004

Country	Period	Decrease (percentage points of GDP)	Percentage reduction over starting year
Early expenditure reductions (initiated 1995 and earlier)			
Hungary	1993–97	17.5	29.3
Belarus	1993–96	16.6	29.1
Macedonia, FYR	1993–97	15.8	32.8
Albania	1992–94	15.7	34.7
Romania	1992–94	7.9	19.9
Kyrgyz Republic	1995–97	6.8	19.7
Ukraine	1994–96	6.2	13.8
Czech Republic	1995–98	6.2	14.2
Slovenia	1993–96	4.2	9.7
Lithuania	1994–96	3.5	9.6
Estonia	1995–97	3.3	8.1
Mid-period reductions			
Moldova	1997–2001	19.2	43.2
Bosnia and Herzegovina	1999–2001	15.3	22.8
Russian Federation	1997–2000	13.5	30.1
Ukraine	1997–99	10.6	25.1
Croatia	1999–2002	6.7	12.4
Georgia	1997–2000	6.5	29.5
Latvia	1999–2001	6.4	15.9
Estonia	1999–2001	5.3	13.3
Slovak Republic	1997–99	4.9	11.9
Kazakhstan	1997–2000	4.9	19.1
Azerbaijan	1999–2001	3.8	17.8
Armenia	1999–2002	3.6	15.3
Most recent expenditure reductions (2000 and later)			
Belarus	2000–02	4.2	9.1
Macedonia, FYR	2002–04	3.9	10.0
Hungary	2002–04	3.8	7.8
Russian Federation	2002–04	3.7	9.7
Slovak Republic	2002–04	3.6	9.5
Albania	2001–03	2.2	8.1
Romania	2000–02	0.8	2.6
Bosnia and Herzegovina	2002–04	0.8	1.4

Source: ECA fiscal database.

The Size of Government

Despite ECA's experience with fiscal adjustment and expenditure consolidation, the size of government for the ECA region as a whole (general government spending in proportion to GDP) is still large in comparison with other regions at similar levels of per capita income. Much comparative fiscal analysis in the literature tends to focus on

FIGURE 2.6
Primary Expenditure Cuts and Initial Fiscal Imbalance

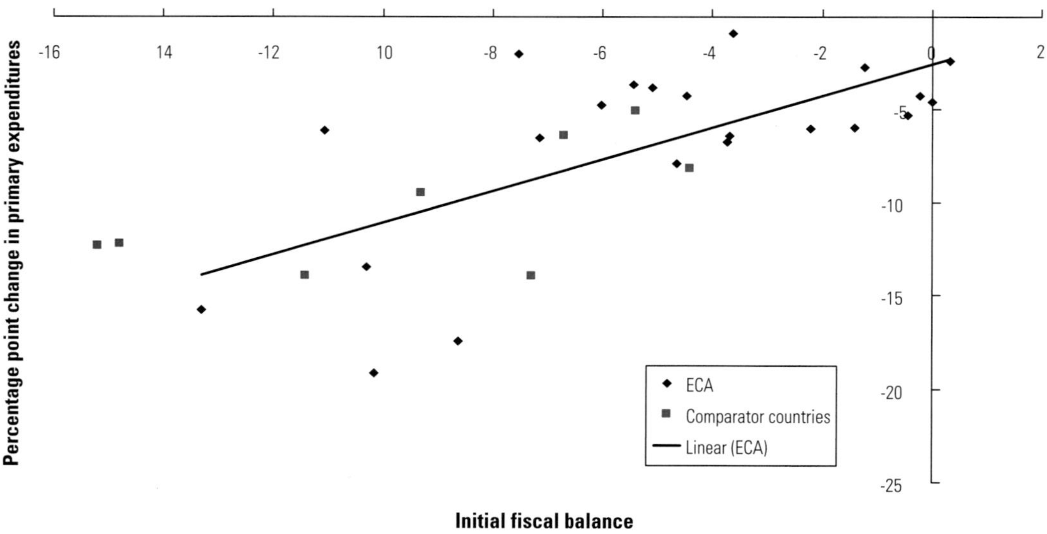

Source: ECA fiscal database.

Note: Comparator countries include Belgium, Canada, Finland, Ireland, the Netherlands, Spain, Sweden, and the United Kingdom.

Organisation for Economic Co-operation and Development (OECD) economies, given the more comprehensive data available for these countries. While on average the size of ECA's public sector primary spending is below OECD or EU-15 averages, the latter are much richer, and EU-15 countries in particular tend to have large welfare states that result in high public spending as a share of GDP. Many of the EU-15 are now struggling to reform their public finances to ensure fiscal sustainability. When compared with other middle-income regions, primary spending as a share of GDP in ECA is well above East Asian and Latin American averages (figure 2.7).

The size of public spending varies enormously across the ECA region and is strongly linked to per capita incomes and proximity to Europe. Total public spending in 2005 ranged from almost one-half of GDP in Bosnia and Herzegovina, Croatia, and Hungary to under one-fourth of GDP in Armenia, Kazakhstan, Azerbaijan, and Tajikistan (figure 2.8). Compared internationally, about half the region has an "EU-15 size" public sector, with primary spending in proportion to GDP similar to Belgium (higher even than comparators such as Ireland and Spain), and the other half approximates East Asian and

FIGURE 2.7
Primary Spending, ECA and Other Middle-Income Regions, 1994–2005

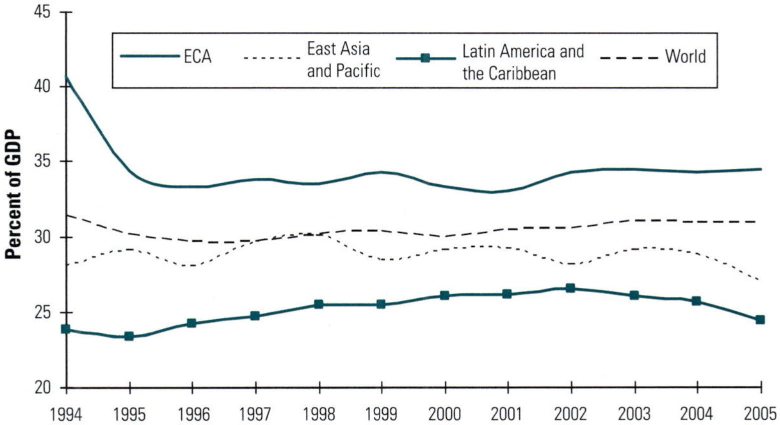

Sources: ECA fiscal database; IMF 2007.

Latin American averages, with primary spending in proportion to GDP similar to that in Chile and Korea.

Primary spending as a share of GDP is positively correlated with per capita GDP (in purchasing power parity [PPP]) for ECA countries (figure 2.9), as is the general pattern worldwide. However, most ECA subregions (EU-8, SEE, and middle-income CIS countries) lie above the international trend line, and only the low-income CIS countries lie below it. Clearly, the ECA sample group is diverse, with Croatia being a particular outlier. The high-growth comparator countries, irrespective of per capita income levels, are all below—in some cases well below—the international norm for government size. Croatia and Thailand are the two most extreme cases, with primary expenditures almost three times higher in Croatia (a difference of 30 percent of GDP) despite the two countries being at similar per capita incomes.

Composition of General Government Spending

The item of spending that stands out when ECA countries are compared with non-ECA countries is transfers (figure 2.10). Unlike comparator countries outside the region, ECA countries spend a significant amount on social protection. This is perhaps one reason

FIGURE 2.8
Total Public Sector Spending, by Country in ECA, 1995 and 2005

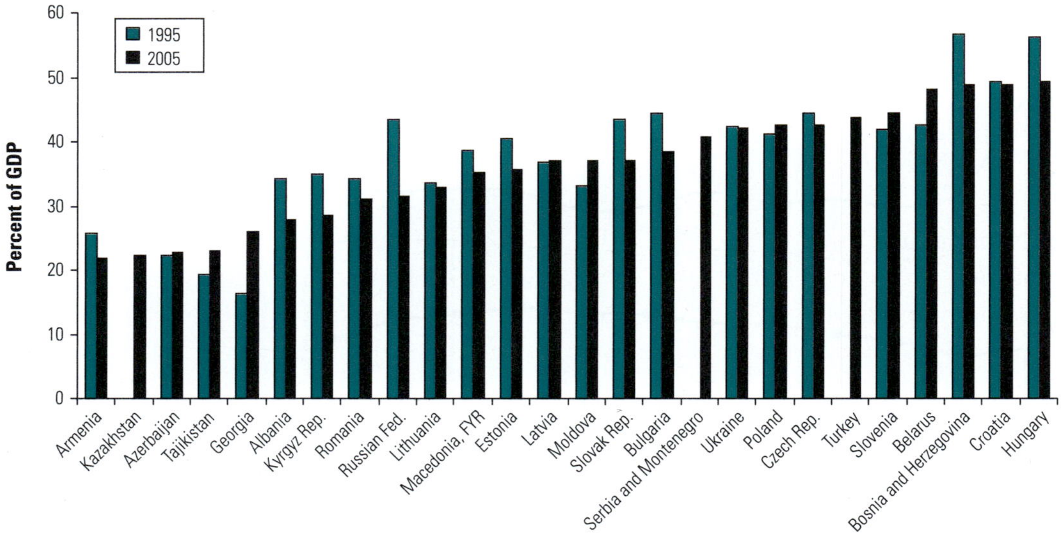

Source: ECA fiscal database.

Note: Initial year data for Bosnia and Herzegovina are 1996 and for the Russian Federation are 1997. Data for 1995 not available for Kazakhstan, Serbia and Montenegro, and Turkey.

FIGURE 2.9
Regional Primary Public Expenditures and Per Capita Incomes, Average 2000–04

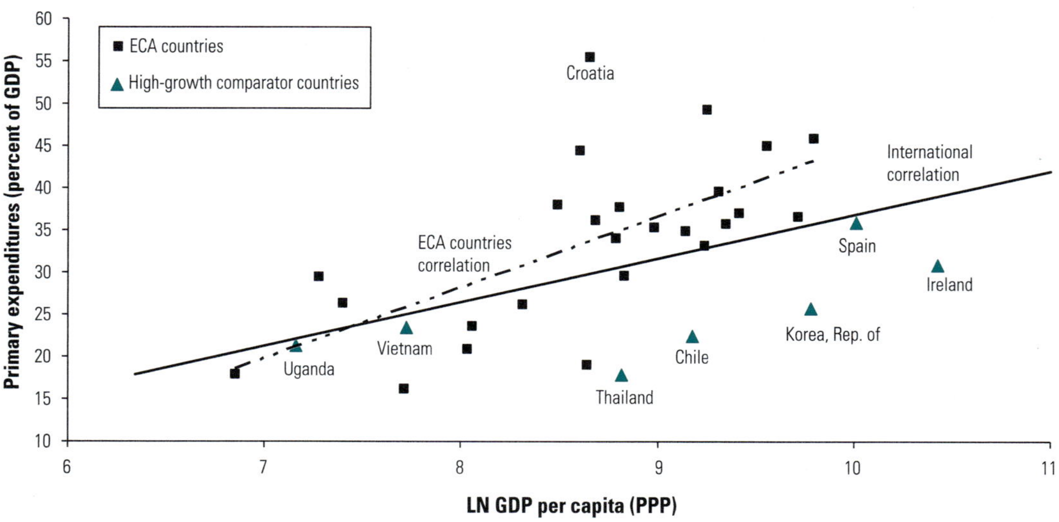

Sources: WDI, WEO, and ECA fiscal database.

Note: The solid regression line is for a sample of 48 countries (not shown) and does not include the high-growth comparators or ECA countries (shown), with an R2 of 0.42. The dashed regression line is for ECA countries only, with an R2 of 0.39, based on the 2000–04 average for 26 ECA countries.

ECA countries have a high level of spending overall and, as shown in Part 3 of this book, one reason behind the reliance on relatively high levels of distortionary taxation. There is some variation across the region. At 18 percent of GDP in 2004, transfers are much higher in the EU-8 and SEE. In the CIS, transfers averaged about 10 percent of GDP in 2004, below the international average of 13 percent of GDP although above fast-growing middle- and low-income comparator countries. From a functional classification, spending on social security and welfare in the EU8 averaged almost 15 percent of GDP in 2004, about twice that of the CIS (figure 2.11) Despite the relative immaturity of their public institutions, countries in the ECA region have quickly put in place publicly provided pensions and social assistance programs as state-owned enterprises have shed their welfare roles. In contrast, the experience in other high-growth middle-income countries has been to keep public transfers lower, even as per capita incomes have increased. In Korea, for example, public transfers are less than 5 percent of GDP, or one-third the EU8 average. Even though state-funded transfers are supplemented by relatively generous privately funded social expenditures, the combined public and private spending on social expenditures is 8 percent of GDP in Korea, still lower than the ECA average (OECD 2003b).

Much of the ECA region is demographically similar to the EU-15, in that they have high ratios of old to working-age people and hence

FIGURE 2.10

ECA Subregional Economic Composition of Primary Expenditures, 2004

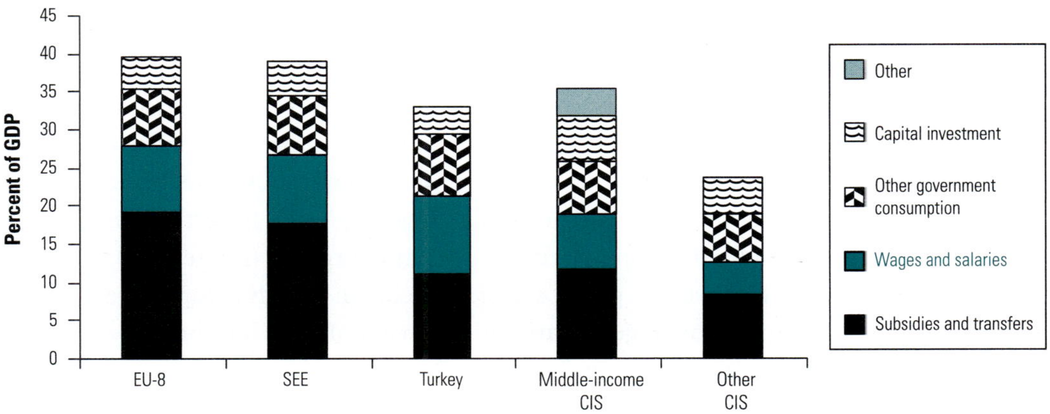

Source: ECA fiscal database.

FIGURE 2.11
ECA Subregional Functional Composition of Primary Expenditures, 2004

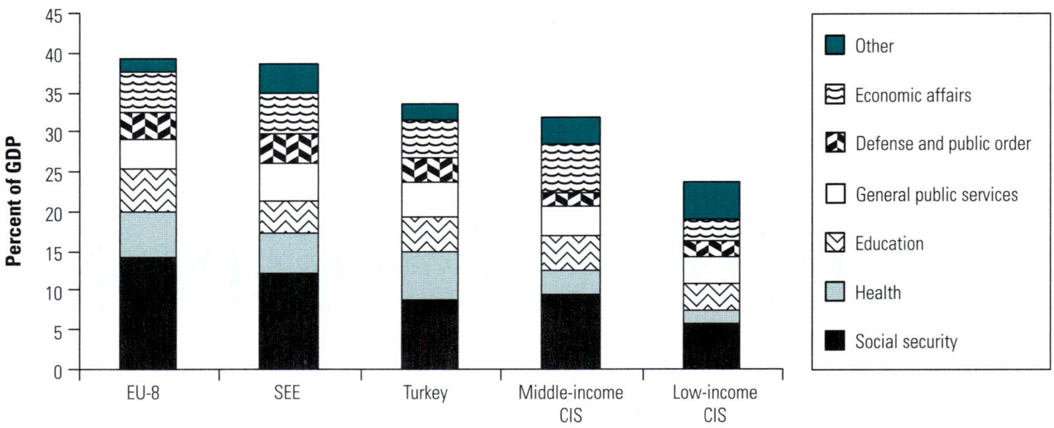

Source: ECA fiscal database.

higher outlays on health and pension spending. This demographic trend is likely to continue, because the population over age 65 is growing in all countries in the region and will exceed 20 percent of the population in many Central and Eastern European countries in the next 20 years (figure 2.12). The high share of transfers, combined with the aging population, is likely to increase pressure on future public spending. Social security and welfare spending is predominantly on pensions and shows a strong correlation with the proportion of the population over age 65.

These differences in social assistance are not the whole story, however. Spending on other categories, such as government consumption, also contribute to the higher regional average. In SEE and the EU8, spending on wages and salaries has been on the rise since 2000 (figure 2.13), reflecting in part the need to professionalize the public sector. In the CIS countries, capital expenditures have increased since 2000, reflecting the need to address neglected infrastructure and the broader development challenges in the region (figure 2.14).

The average public sector wage bill in ECA is comparable to international averages, at around 7 percent of GDP, but there is wide variation among countries (figure 2.15). Furthermore, a greater share of the labor force in ECA works for the public sector for a given wage bill— the regional average shows public sector employment is 28 percent of total employment. In Korea, in comparison, public sector

FIGURE 2.12

Percentage of Population Age 65 and Over, 2000 and 2025 (estimate)

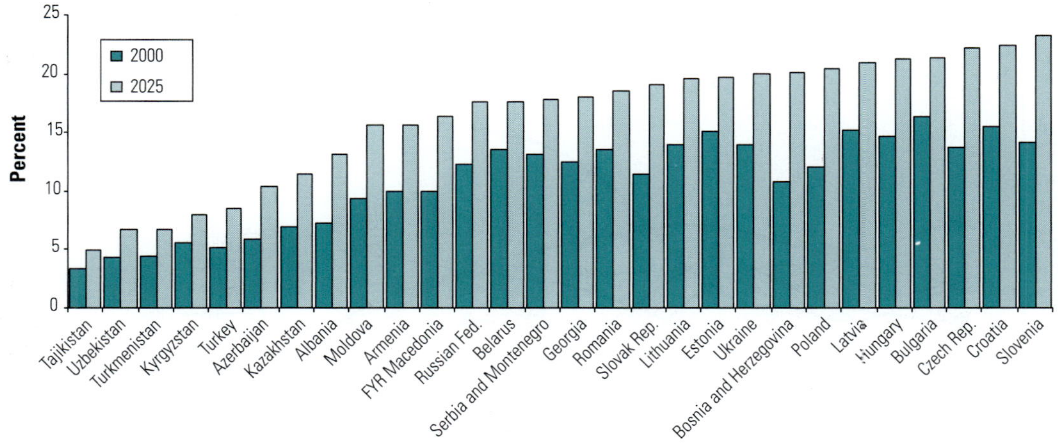

Sources: World Bank projections; World Bank 2007.

FIGURE 2.13

Trends in the Public Wage Bill in ECA, 2000–05

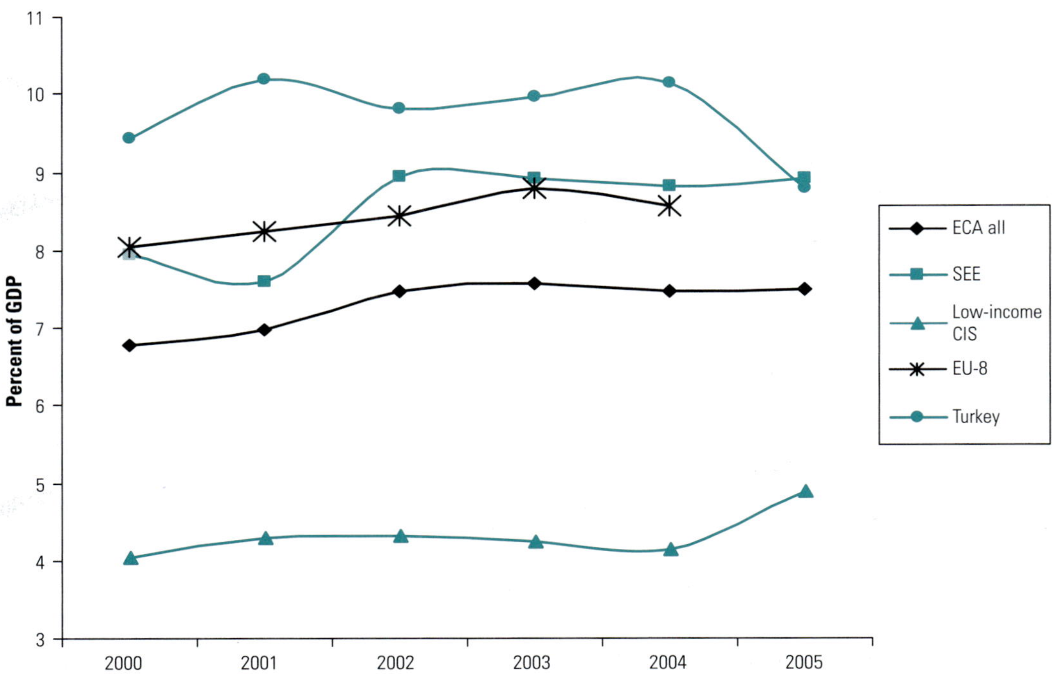

Source: ECA fiscal database.

Note: Middle-income CIS not shown here because wages and salaries expenditure data are patchy and unavailable for Russia and Ukraine for various years.

FIGURE 2.14
Trends in Capital Spending in ECA, 2000–05

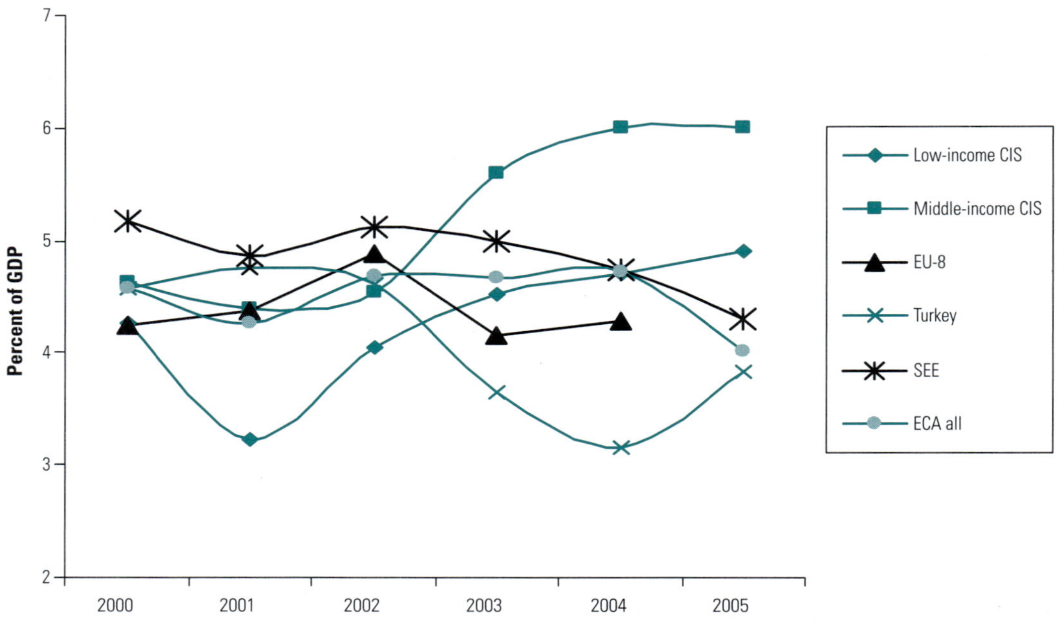

Source: ECA fiscal database.

employment is low, accounting for only 5 percent of total employment, and the wage bill tightly controlled at 6.7 percent of GDP. Spain and Ireland are spending about the same share of GDP on public sector wages and salaries as ECA countries, but public sector employment in proportion to total employment is almost half that of the ECA average.

Average capital spending in the region is consistent with international norms, at about 5 percent of GDP. While much lower in the low-income CIS countries at the beginning of the period, increases in capital spending since 2000 have brought this subregion up to the international average. Unlike spending on wages and salaries, there is little variation in capital spending in proportion to GDP, either between or within subregions. However, the outliers Croatia and Tajikistan each spent over 8 percent of GDP on public investment in 2004. In contrast, capital spending in the comparator group varies from 8 or 9 percent of GDP in the low-income countries, Uganda and Vietnam, to only 3.5 percent of GDP in Chile and Spain. Korea and

FIGURE 2.15
Public Sector Wage Bill in ECA Countries, 2004

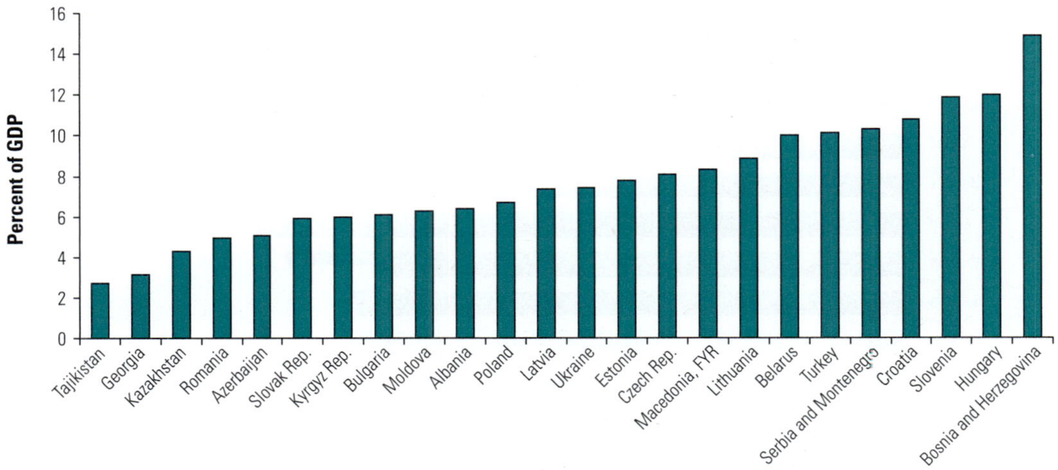

Source: ECA fiscal database.

Ireland are consistent with the international average, at 5.0 percent and 4.5 percent of GDP, respectively. Issues surrounding infrastructure spending are discussed further in chapter 4.

Trends and levels of education spending vary widely among ECA countries, both as a share of GDP (from 3 percent in Georgia to 8 percent in Slovenia) and in the extent and direction of change in the last decade. Some high spenders in the mid-1990s (Estonia and Kyrgyz Republic) have reduced education spending by several percentage points of GDP, while some moderate spenders in the mid-1990s, including Slovenia, Poland, and, to a lesser extent, Georgia and Croatia (figure 2.16), have increased education spending considerably. Demographics explain some of the variation in education spending. The positive association between the share of spending on education and the percentage of population under age 14 confirms that countries with a younger population devote a greater share of public expenditure to education. The "younger" ECA countries, with over 25 percent of the population below age 14, lie below international norms, suggesting possible underinvestment in human capital. Policies affecting education spending are discussed further in chapter 5.

There is also wide variation in public spending on health across the ECA region (figure 2.17) from the high spending in the Slovak

FIGURE 2.16

Public Education Spending in ECA Countries, 1995 and 2004

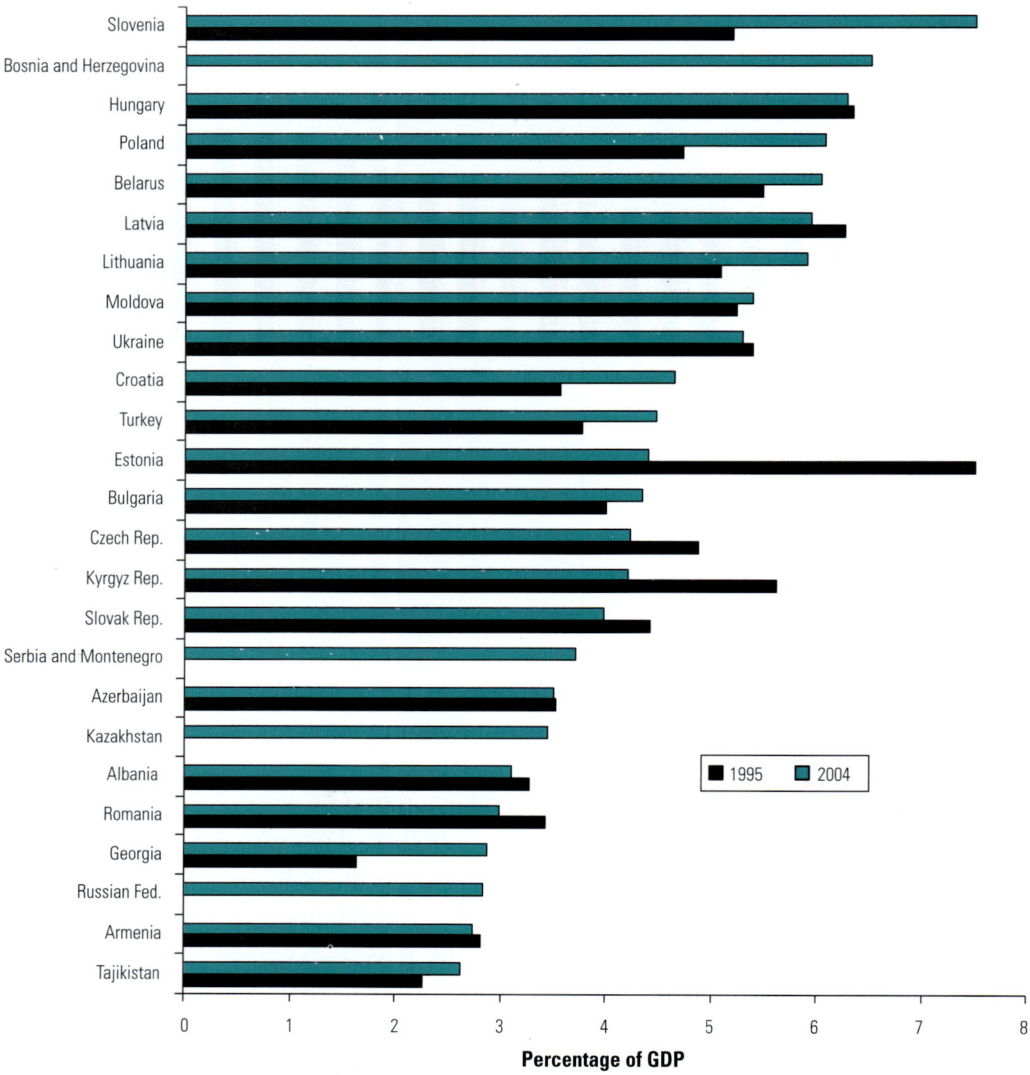

Source: ECA fiscal database.

Note: Initial year data for Slovak Republic are 1996; final year data for the Russian Federation are 2003. No 1995 data available for Bosnia and Herzegovina, Serbia and Montenegro, Kazakhstan, and the Russian Federation.

Republic (more than 9 percent of GDP) to less than 1 percent of GDP in Azerbaijan. As discussed in chapter 6, public spending on health is closely associated with per capita income level and is more stable over time than education spending.

FIGURE 2.17

Public-Sector Health Expenditures in ECA Countries, 2000 and 2004

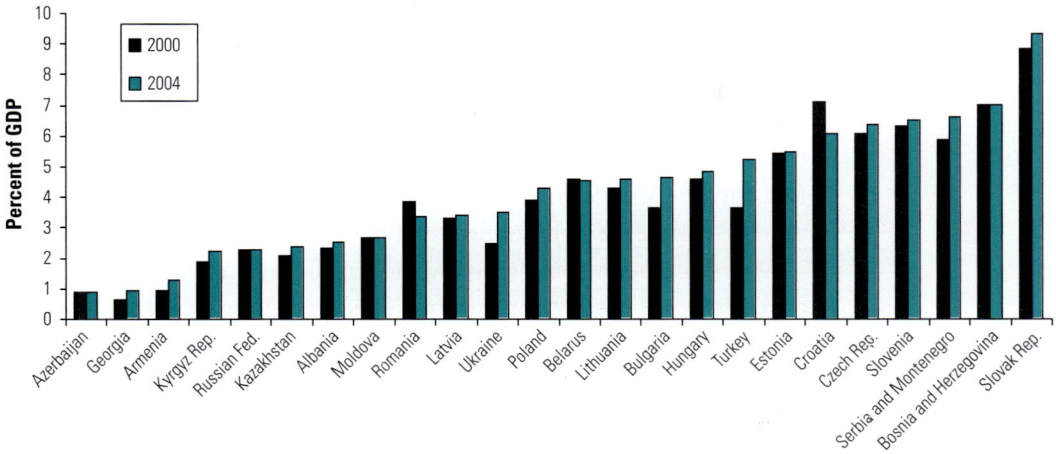

Source: ECA fiscal database.

Note:
a. Data for Russian Federation are for 2000 and 2003.

FIGURE 2.18

Total General Government Revenues, 1994–99 and 2000–04

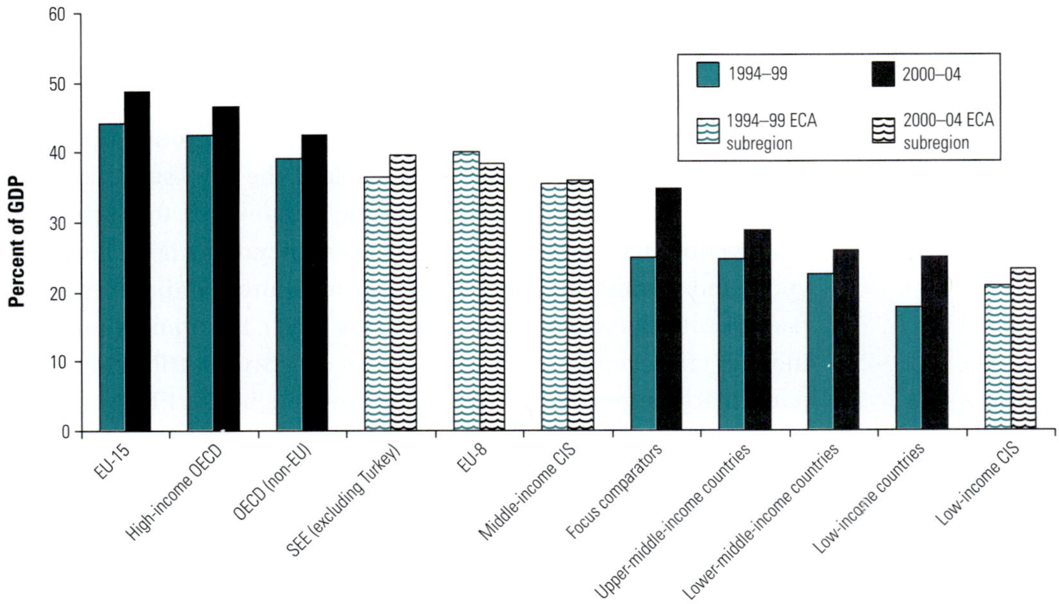

Source: ECA fiscal database; IMF 2007.

Structure of Revenues in ECA

Total revenues, including grants, ranged from approximately 40 percent of GDP in SEE and the EU-8 to 24 percent of GDP in the low-income CIS in 2004. This compares to the EU-15 average of 45 percent of GDP (figure 2.18). The share of tax revenues in most subregions is between 80 and 90 percent of total revenues, which is close to the international group and EU-15 averages. By comparison, in the low-income CIS countries, nontax revenues and grants account for almost 35 percent of revenues, and in Turkey for almost 25 percent.

There has been some convergence in the overall size of revenues, as the lower-income countries have been catching up either through an expanded tax base or resource-based revenue collections, and as several outliers in the SEE region (most notably Bosnia and Herzegovina and Croatia) have brought revenues down over time as a share of GDP. There is also considerable variation within subregions, other than the EU-8. Total revenue in proportion to GDP varies by a factor of two from the highest to lowest country within a subregion. SEE varies from 49 percent of GDP in Bosnia and Herzegovina to 25 percent of GDP in Albania, the middle-income CIS from 28 percent of GDP in Kazakhstan to 47 percent of GDP in Belarus, and the low-income CIS from 20 percent of GDP in Armenia to 36 percent of GDP in Moldova (figure 2.19).

The total revenue share is positively correlated with per capita income (figure 2.20). As with expenditures, the non-ECA focus countries lie below the trend line, because their governments are smaller than average.

Sources of tax revenue vary across ECA country groups. The composition of tax revenues is relatively stable in the EU-8 subregion (figure 2.21b). In the low-income CIS countries, however, the increase in tax revenues has come through expansion of indirect taxes levied on goods and services and international trade (figure 2.21d), reflecting in part the introduction of a value added tax (VAT), the primary source of indirect tax revenues (table 2.4). Social security contributions are a particularly important source of tax revenue in the EU-8, middle-income CIS, and SEE countries, where they are equivalent to or even exceed the share of direct income taxes. The impact of labor taxes on growth and associated reform options are examined in chapter 9.

Tax performance[13] is affected by several factors, including fiscal policies, economic structure, and institutions. Although tax ratios tend to vary by income level, some high-income countries, such as the Baltics, have chosen to levy somewhat lower taxes. Moreover, institutions are important because inefficient tax administrations and

FIGURE 2.19
Regional Variation in Revenues, 2005

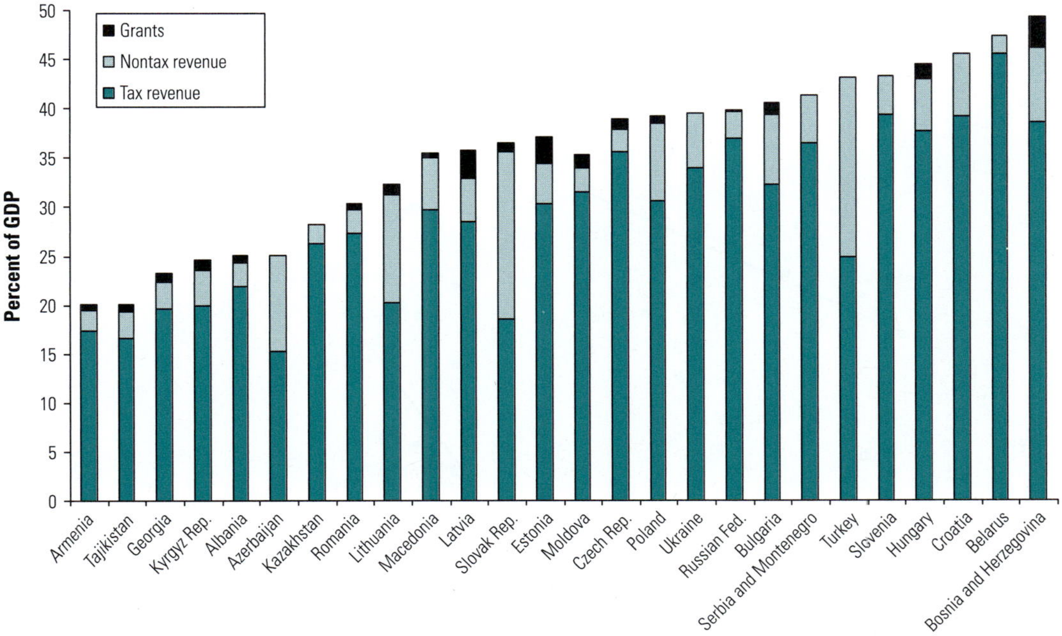

Source: ECA fiscal database.

weak domestic legal and institutional structures can create opportunities for corruption and impair efforts to raise tax revenues.

A more formal analysis of tax effort across ECA countries is outlined in annex 2A. For the period 1995–2004, the analysis confirms that per capita income, the share of agriculture in GDP, and the ratio of trade to GDP are the most consistent explanatory variables for the proportion of tax revenues to GDP.[14] A comparison of actual tax collection with that predicted by the model indicates that ECA countries have a strong tax effort overall with an index close to 1.0.[15] Tax effort in the ECA region is generally stronger than in the Latin America and East Asia regions. However, effort is uneven in ECA, ranging from high tax effort in Belarus, Bosnia and Herzegovina, Croatia, Macedonia, Moldova, Turkey, and Uzbekistan, to low tax effort in Armenia, Georgia, and Tajikistan (where the tax effort index is below 0.8).[16]

Some convergence in tax effort is observed across ECA countries (see table 2.5 for data on ECA and non-ECA focus countries). Over time those countries that had high tax efforts in 1995 generally experienced a downward trend (with the exception of Turkey and Moldova), while several of those with initially low tax efforts, includ-

FIGURE 2.20

Correlation of Revenue with Per Capita Incomes, 1995–2004 average

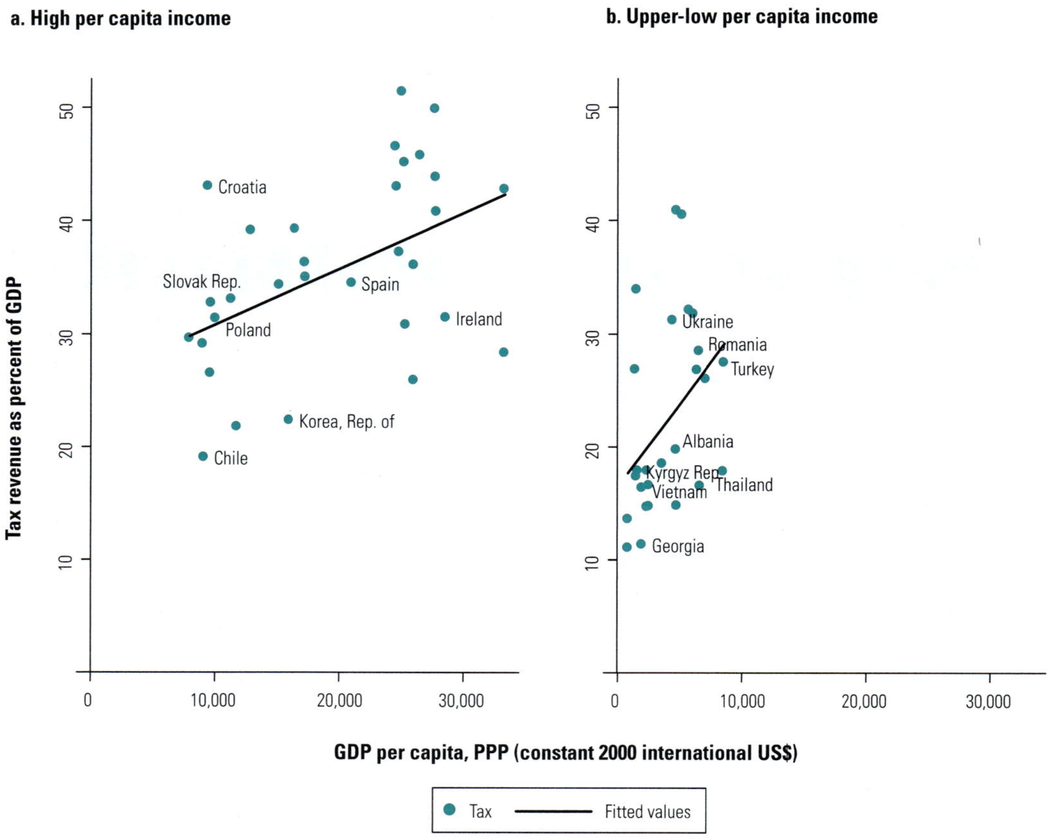

Source: WDI and ECA fiscal database.

ing Tajikistan, Georgia, Armenia, and Albania, increased their tax efforts in recent years. The non-ECA focus countries generally have low, stable, or declining tax effort indexes. The tax effort has been on the rise, particularly in Turkey, because of increases in indirect tax efforts to support fiscal consolidation (figure 2.22). In Albania the overall tax effort is now close to potential, but collection of direct taxes has outperformed other taxes. In contrast, the Slovak Republic, Ireland, and Poland have experienced downward trends in their tax effort indexes, because of sizeable declines in direct tax effort (see figure 2.23 for Slovak Republic). Where indexes of tax effort have fallen, the reduction has been more in direct than in indirect taxes, with only Hungary and Vietnam being exceptions. Where indexes have

FIGURE 2.21

Composition of Tax Revenues, 1995–2004

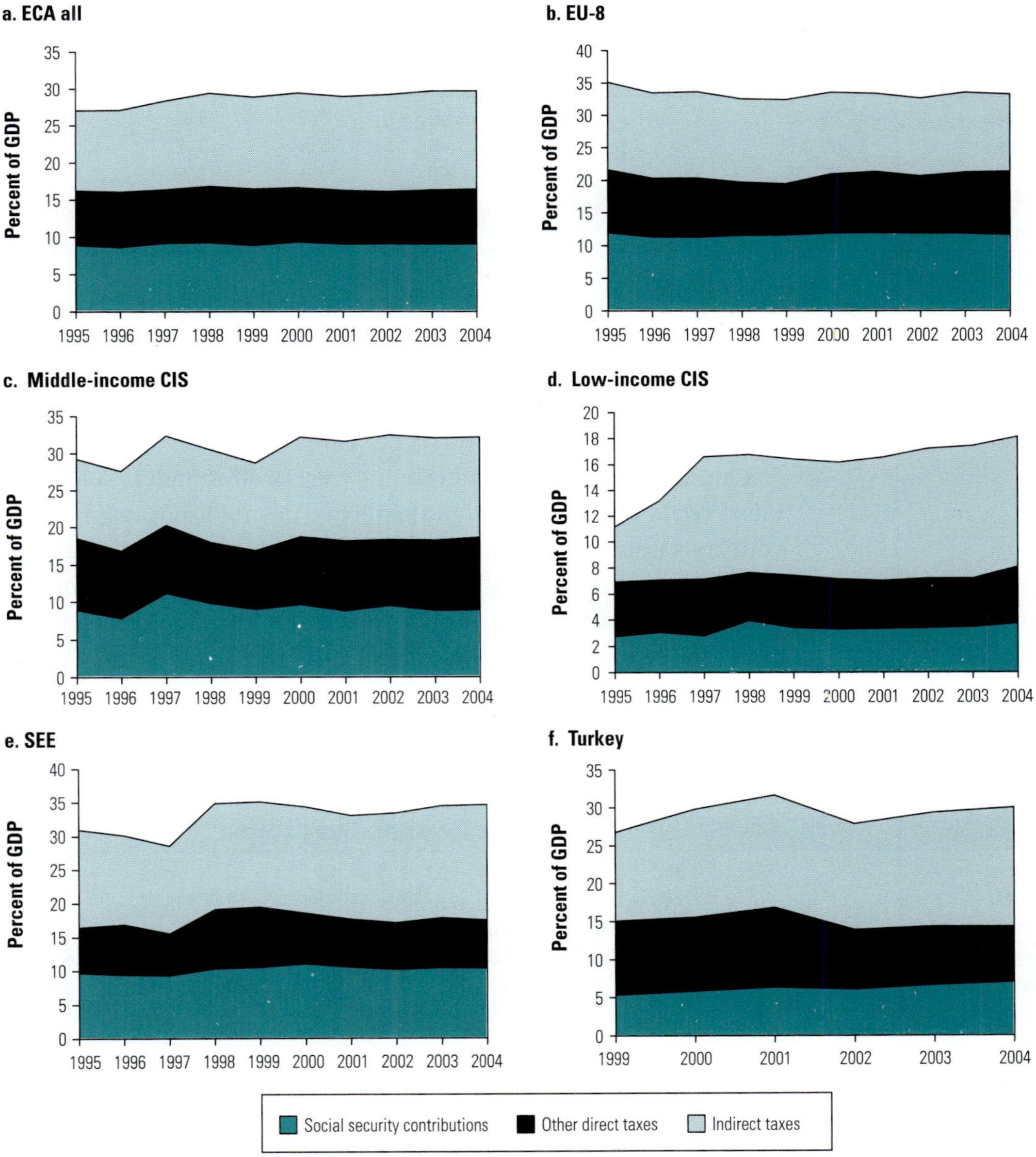

Source: ECA fiscal database.

Note: Data before 1999 not available for Turkey.

TABLE 2.4

Tax Revenue Improvements in the CIS, 1994–2004

			Tax increase components			
Country	Period	Total tax revenue increase	Tax on goods and services	Tax on trade	Social security contributions	Other taxes
Armenia	1994–99	6.71	1.27	5.13	0.89	-0.58
Georgia	1995–2001	7.49	4.15	0.42	0.88	2.46
Moldova	2001–04	5.42	2.10	0.32	0.94	2.06
Kyrgyz Republic	1994–95	1.52	1.33	0.45	0.14	-0.40
Kyrgyz Republic	2000–04	3.28	2.94	0.06	0.16	0.13

Source: ECA fiscal database.

improved, the improvement has been more balanced, with Armenia, Georgia, Tajikistan, and Turkey increasing indirect taxes and Armenia and Kazakhstan increasing direct tax effort.

Care must be taken in interpreting the tax effort index. A low tax effort could result either from ineffective or inefficient tapping of a country's potential tax base (for example, as a result of weak tax administration) or from a policy choice for smaller government and hence lower levels of taxation. In some cases it could reflect a deliberate policy to attract foreign direct investment (as in the Slovak

TABLE 2.5

Tax Effort Trends in Selected ECA and Non-ECA Countries

ECA countries	1995	1996	1997	1998	1999	2000	2001	2001	2003	2004
Albania	0.8	0.6	0.6	0.8	0.8	0.9	0.9	1.0	1.0	n.a.
Croatia	1.6	1.2	1.6	1.5	1.6	1.2	1.5	1.3	1.3	1.4
Georgia	0.3	0.5	0.6	0.6	0.6	0.6	0.6	0.6	0.6	n.a.
Kyrgyz Republic	1.3	1.2	1.1	1.2	1.0	0.9	0.9	0.9	1.1	n.a.
Poland	1.2	1.2	1.1	1.1	1.0	1.0	0.9	0.9	1.0	0.9
Romania	1.1	1.2	1.0	1.1	1.2	1.1	1.0	1.0	0.9	n.a.
Slovak Republic	1.2	1.2	1.1	1.0	1.0	0.9	0.8	0.8	0.9	0.8
Turkey	0.9	1.0	1.1	1.2	1.2	1.3	1.4	1.4	1.2	1.3
Ukraine	1.2	1.3	1.3	1.2	1.1	1.0	1.0	1.0	1.1	1.0
Non-ECA countries										
Chile	0.7	0.7	0.7	0.7	0.7	n.a.	n.a.	n.a.	n.a.	n.a.
Ireland	0.9	0.9	0.8	0.8	0.8	0.7	0.7	0.6	n.a.	n.a.
Korea	0.7	0.7	0.7	0.7	0.7	0.7	0.7	0.7	0.7	n.a.
Spain	1.0	1.0	1.0	1.0	1.0	1.0	1.0	1.0	1.0	n.a.
Thailand	0.7	0.7	0.6	0.6	0.6	0.5	0.5	0.6	0.6	n.a.
Vietnam	1.1	1.1	0.9	0.9	0.9	0.8	0.8	0.8	0.8	0.8

Source: Staff calculations.

Note: Not applicable.

FIGURE 2.22
Trends in Tax Effort Indexes in Turkey

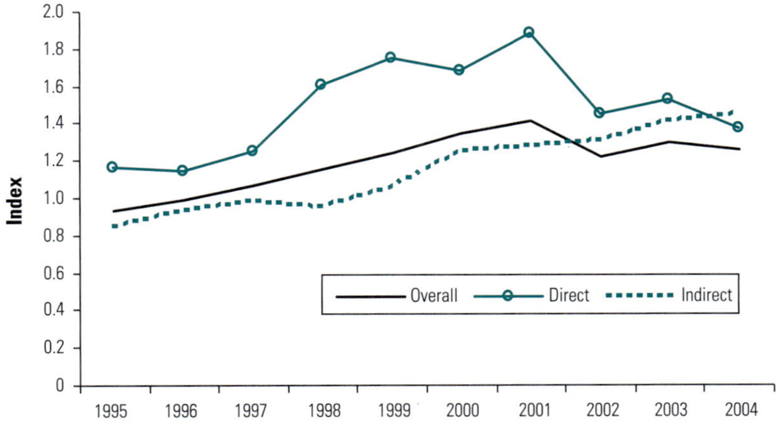

Source: Staff calculations.

Republic). A case-by-case analysis would thus be needed to draw policy-relevant conclusions. A high tax effort coupled with sound institutions (good governance) tends to suggest a high tax burden given a country's level of development and economic structure, most likely reflecting high tax rates. For a given tax effort, however, broadening the tax base can create room to lower marginal tax rates and thus lessen the harmful impact of taxes on economic growth.

Measuring the effectiveness of tax administration by comparing statutory tax rates with effective tax yields (that is, using "productivity" indexes[17]) reveals "low tax effort" countries with both relatively effective tax administrations (the Baltic countries, Ireland, Korea, the Slovak Republic, Vietnam) and weak tax administration (Armenia, Georgia, Tajikistan), as shown in figures 2.24 and 2.25 and table 2.6. For the latter countries, low tax effort may become a serious obstacle in the attempt to develop effective fiscal policy. These countries have the potential to increase tax revenues through both better use of their tax bases and strengthening of tax administration. They may also want to consider widening the tax base by subjecting previously exempt income to taxation or reducing credits and allowances, and, where possible, lowering marginal tax rates to discourage tax avoidance and evasion.

Relatively low tax effort in countries with good tax administration[18] may result from a lower social preference for publicly provided

FIGURE 2.23
Trends in Tax Effort Indexes in the Slovak Republic

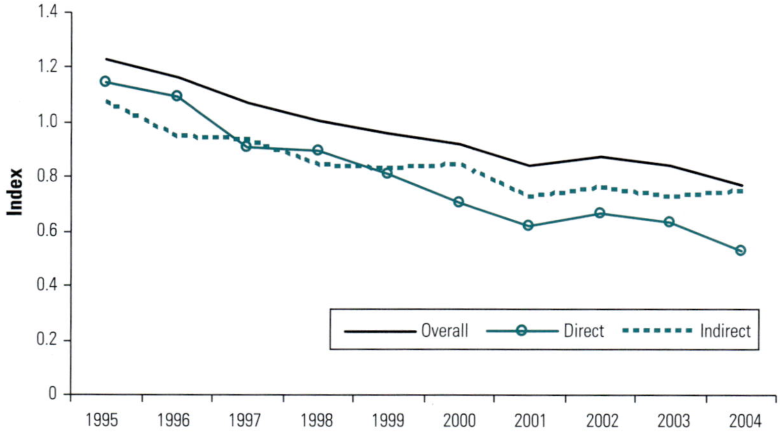

Source: Staff calculations.

goods and services, and hence a choice to expend less tax effort to boost private sector–led growth. In contrast, Belarus, Bulgaria, Croatia, Turkey, and Moldova represent countries with relatively high tax effort and stronger tax administration. Some of these countries still have fairly large untaxed sectors and high tax rates on other sectors. These countries may need to consider lowering taxes to enhance their growth rates.[19] For Hungary, Kazakhstan, the Kyrgyz Republic, Russia, and Slovenia, addressing institutional weaknesses in tax and customs administration could be a viable option to enhance the economy's tax-generating capacity. Hungary, FYR Macedonia, and Slovenia might improve compliance by reducing both tax rates and the progressivity of individual and corporate income taxes.

Measures of tax effort also help to pinpoint appropriate policies for creating fiscal space. If a country is facing a budget deficit and is already making the maximum use of its taxable capacity, as indicated by a comparatively high tax effort index, then restoring budget balance (or reducing the debt level) is likely to require expenditure rationalization and efficiency gains rather than tax increases. Several ECA countries, such as Croatia and Turkey, fall into that category (see figures 2.26 and 2.27).

The non-ECA comparator countries are generally in a favorable budget position, despite fairly low tax effort. The low tax effort appears to reflect more choice than difficulty in raising tax revenue—most of these countries are characterized by strong institutional struc-

FIGURE 2.24
VAT Revenue Productivity, 2004

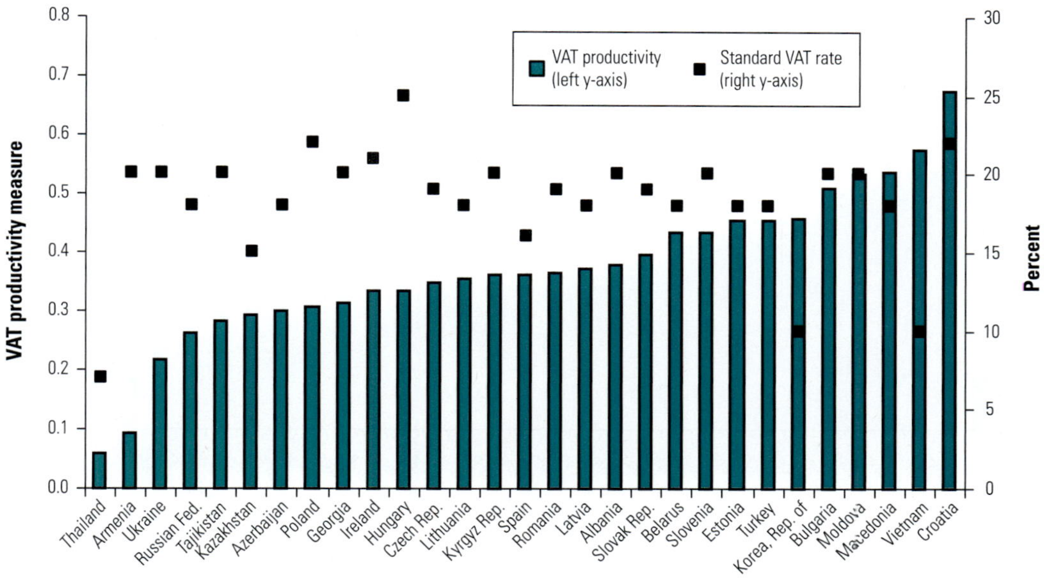

Source: World Bank staff calculations.

Note: VAT or CIT productivity is defined as VAT or CIT revenue as a share of GDP divided by the standard top rate.

tures and relatively small shadow economies. Moreover, stronger institutions can allow countries to sustain a relatively low tax effort index (Ireland, Korea) and a relatively high long-term growth rate (table 2.6).

Conclusions

The transition to a market economy has required a massive overhaul of public finance systems in ECA countries. While some common trends exist across ECA countries (especially the continued need for fiscal consolidation), the size of public expenditures, tax performance, debt levels, and risks to fiscal sustainability remain quite varied. Some key findings of this chapter are summarized below.

First, fiscal adjustment in ECA has been strong, but continued vigilance is needed. Despite ambitious efforts in many ECA countries, remaining fiscal imbalances deserve close attention to ensure a robust fiscal framework conducive to long-run growth. Although debt levels

FIGURE 2.25
Corporate Income Tax Revenue Productivity, 2004

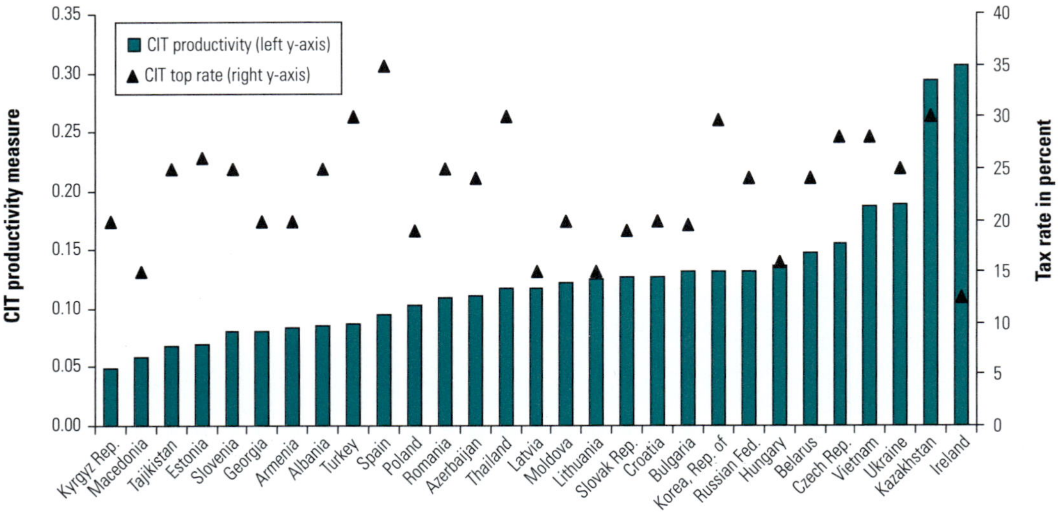

Source: World Bank staff calculations.

Note: VAT or CIT productivity is defined as VAT or CIT revenue as a share of GDP divided by the standard top rate.

remain generally low, in some ECA countries more ambitious fiscal consolidation would help to reinforce fiscal sustainability in the long run and create fiscal space for growth-promoting expenditures or for lower taxes, especially because exceptionally favorable global financial conditions may not last.

TABLE 2.6
Tax Effort and Tax Productivity, Average 1995–2004

Tax Type	High tax effort, stonger administration	High tax effort, weaker administration	Low tax effort, stonger administration	Low tax effort, weaker administration
Value added tax	Croatia, FYR Macedonia, Moldova, Turkey, Bulgaria, Belarus	Russian Fed., Kazakhstan	Vietnam, Rep. of Korea Estonia, Slovakia, Slovak Rep., Ireland	Tajikistan, Armenia Thailand
Corporate income tax	Belarus, Bulgaria Croatia, Moldova	FYR Macedonia, Kyrgyz Rep.	Ireland, Vietnam, Rep. of Korea, Slovak Rep, Lithuania	Tajikistan
Personal income tax	Turkey, Croata, FYR Macedonia	Hungary, Slovenia	Thailand, Rep. of Korea Azerbaijan	Armenia, Georgia, Vietnam Tajikistan

Source: Staff calculations.

FIGURE 2.26

Tax Effort Index versus General Government Balance, 2004

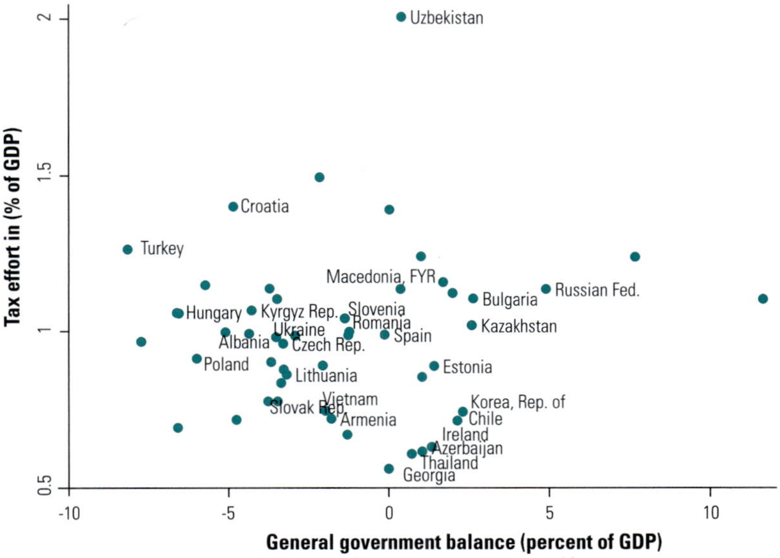

Sources: IMF WEO, staff calculations.

Second, fiscal adjustments driven by reductions in public spending have generally been more sustainable than those driven by revenue increases. Expenditure cuts were on average higher when the initial primary fiscal deficit was large and, as a result, the overall fiscal adjustment had to be ambitious. By contrast, tax revenue increases were more common when initial imbalances were moderate.

Third, governments in ECA tend to be large. With the exception of the low-income CIS countries, the average size of public sector spending in the ECA region is above international norms at similar levels of per capita income, and well above the high-growth comparator countries outside the region.

Fourth, the large size of governments in part reflects socialist legacies. Influenced by a history of state-sponsored provision of welfare security throughout the life cycle, ECA countries tend to spend more on social protection than do international comparators. Moreover, this spending has increased in the past five years, and many ECA countries have aging populations that will continue to put pressure on spending for pensions and health. But economic policy needs to be informed by the trade-off between large public sectors today and economic growth tomorrow.

FIGURE 2.27
Tax Effort Index versus Debt, 2004

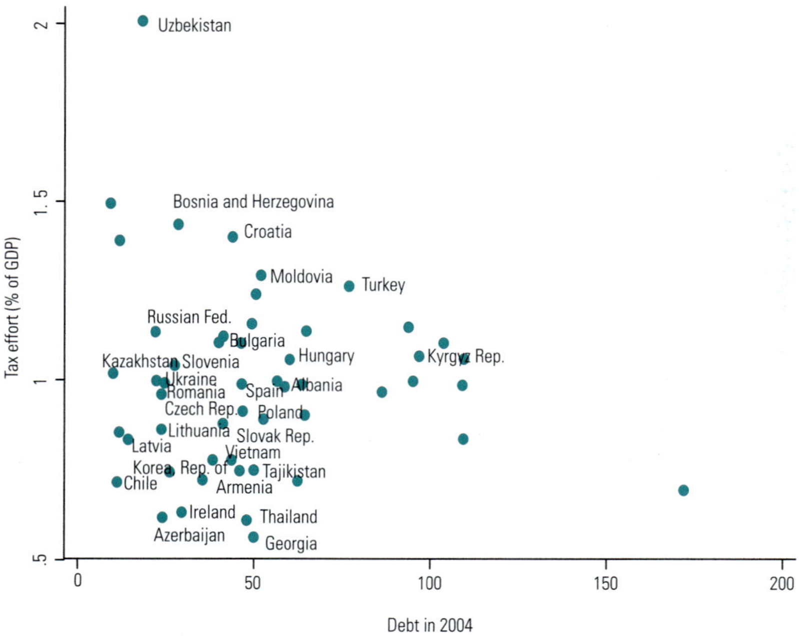

Sources: IMF WEO, staff calculations.

Fifth, the composition of spending varies across the region. EU-8 and SEE have seen increases in public-sector wages, while the CIS countries have begun to increase capital investments from, in many cases, a very low base. Other productive expenditures, such as health and education, show variation across and within subregions. These are examined further in Part 2.

Finally, tax ratios reflect spending levels, and range from 45 percent of GDP in EU-8 countries to 24 percent of GDP in low-income CIS. Tax effort in ECA countries is close to the predicted potential, and is generally higher than in the Latin America and the Caribbean and East Asia and Pacific regions. However, in some ECA countries tax performance may be overstretched, indicating that fiscal space can only be created through expenditure rationalization. The region also has several low tax effort countries with good institutions, indicating a possible preference for smaller government and policies for encouraging private sector activity in these cases.

Annex 2A Tax Performance: A Regression Model

There has been only limited effort to date to develop comprehensive tools for assessing tax performance across countries. Typically, there are two main approaches used to measure a country's tax effort. In its simplest form, comparisons can be based on differences between the effective tax rates and the standard tax yield following the methodology developed in Tanzi (1981) and Schaffer and Turley (2001). An alternative is to calculate a tax effort index as the ratio of actual tax share to the predicted (or potential) tax share. The predicted tax ratio is determined through regression relating tax shares to various explanatory variables that serve as proxies for tax bases or other factors that might affect a country's ability to tax.

Basic Model

Following recent tax effort literature (Stotsky and WoldeMariam 1997; Piancastelli 2001; Eltony and Nagy 2002; Bird, Martinez-Vazquez, and Torgler 2004; and Hudson and Teere 2004), a stochastic model was used to examine tax revenue in selected ECA and non-ECA countries, where T/Y is the tax ratio and Xi (i = 1...n) represent various independent variables expected to influence the tax ratio, while U is the error term:

$$T/Y = f(Xi \ldots Xn, U)$$

The independent variables employed in the basic model were similar to those used in the most recent literature: gross national product per capita, the ratio of trade to GDP (imports plus exports over GDP), the share of the manufacturing sector and the agricultural sector in GDP, and population growth. An overview of the variables applied in previous empirical studies is provided in table 2A.1. Other variables, such as external debt, consumer price index (CPI), rural population, and the like, were used to check the robustness of the base results. A time variable was included to capture any overall trend in taxation.

The analysis used panel data for 57 developed and developing countries, including 26 ECA and 6 non-ECA comparator countries over the period 1995–2004. The choice of sample was motivated by the need to obtain a data set composed of countries with similar characteristics to ECA and comparator countries. Data were obtained from the Bank's World Development Indicators, IMF Regional Fiscal Data Set, IMF Country Profile Chapter IV, Schneider 2005 and government finance statistics from Ministries of Finance in the countries. A set of 57 countries was used, comprising three groups: 10 in the lower-middle-income group,[20] 16 in the upper-middle-income group, and 31 in the higher-income group,[21] as defined by the World Development Indicators 2004.

The panel data model was estimated with both "fixed effects" (using the least squares dummy variable approach) and "random

TABLE 2A.1

Overview of Empirical Findings in Tax Effort Studies

Variable	Piancastelli (2001)	Bird, Martinez-Vazquez, and Torgler (2004)	Stotsky and WoldeMariam (1997)	Grigorian (2005)	Hudson and Teerea, 2004	Eltony and Nagy (2002)
1. Economic development						
GDP per capita	+	+/-	+	+	+/-	+
Population density					+	
Population growth		-				
Urban Population				+		
2. Economic structure						
Agriculture, value added as % of GDP	-	+	-	-	-	-
Manufacturing, value added as % of GDP	+		+		+/-	
Mining, value added as % of GDP			-			-
Services, value added as % of GDP GDP	+					
3. Openness						
Import, as % of GDP			+/-			+
Export, as % of GDP			+			-
Trade (eExport + iImport as % of GDP)	+	-		-	+	
4. Control variables						
External dDebt, as % of GDP					-	
Consumer pPrice iIndex				-		
Inequality		-				
Aid, as percentage to% of GDP					+	
Share of fFuel in total exports				+		
5.Institutions						
Shadow economy, as % of GDP		-		-	+/-	
Index governance		+				
Regulation to of entry		-				
Composite iInstitutional quality				+		
Tax morale		+/-				
Method of estimation	Fixed effects model	OLSOrdinary least squares	Fixed and random models	Fixed effects model	Fixed effects model, Heteroskedasticity-consistent standard errors	Fixed effects model

Source: World Bank Staff calculations.

Note: + = positive coefficient (increases tax revenues). - = negative coefficient (decreases tax revenues). +/- = non-conclusive result; the coefficients appeared to be positive or negative effects" (applying the generalized least squares [GLS] approach). The Hausman test consistently rejects the random effects model in favor of the fixed effects model.

However, in the next step the normal distribution of the error term was rejected and diagnostic tests revealed problems of cross-sectional correlation. To deal with the problem of cross-sectional correlation, the Prais-Winsten estimators[22] were employed.

The model performed generally well (table 2A.2), with estimated coefficients for the explanatory variables in line with previous findings in the literature. Higher GDP per capita is associated with a higher tax ratio. The structure of the economy seems also to matter. The tax ratio is negatively related to the share of agriculture in GDP and positively related to the share of the manufacturing sector in GDP, but the latter variable proved to be statistically insignificant (equation 1). The insignificance of manufacturing is somewhat surprising, although it may potentially be explained by a negative correlation with the agricultural share or the fact that the manufacturing share varies across countries according to the stage of development. Thus, the regression was reestimated with interactive terms between manufacturing and GDP per capita (equation 6); manufacturing then became significant. The significantly negative coefficient on the manufacturing-GDP per capita interactive term may indicate that as countries develop the importance of manufacturing as a source of tax revenue declines. Moreover, the agriculture sector is much more difficult to tax for less developed countries, as indicated by the significantly positive coefficient on the agriculture-GDP per capita interactive term. A faster rate of population growth leads to a lower tax ratio, while openness is associated with a higher tax ratio. Inclusion of dummy variables controls for differences in stage of development in the sample and reveals that the lower-middle-income countries have a statistically significant lower tax ratio than other countries in the sample. On the contrary, it is observed that high-income countries have a statistically significant higher tax ratio than other countries in the sample.

Moreover, to get a more realistic picture of a country's taxable capacity vis-à-vis its natural resource base, a dummy variable[23] for important oil producer countries was included. The ease of taxing natural resource extraction is likely to generate more tax revenue than nonfuel activities. The coefficient for the oil dummy has the predicted negative sign and is statistically significant in all equations. Finally, the trend variable is generally negative, indicating that, all else equal, tax ratios are on a downward trend, perhaps as a result of global tax competition. However, it is not statistically significant

TABLE 2A.2

Panel Regression Outcome (Prais-Winsten estimation), 1995–2004

Variable	EQ1	EQ2 Base	EQ3 Sensitivity	EQ4 Sensitivity	EQ5 Sensitivity	EQ6	EQ7
GDP per capita	.001*	.001*	.001*	.001*	.000*	.001*	.001*
	(.000)	(.000)	(.000)	(.000)	(.000)	(.000)	(.000)
Trade	.059*	.056*	.056*	.051*	.046*	.056*	.025**
	(.007)	(.006)	(.007)	(.007)	(.010)	(.009)	(.013)
Agriculture	-.137*	-.113*	-.112*	-.149*	-.185*	-.104*	-.224*
	(.048)	(.046)	(.051)	(.062)	(.049)	(.039)	(.033)
Manufacturing	.098					.161*	.222*
	(.064)					(.082)	(.091)
Population growth	-1.881*	-1.767*	-1.729*	-1.720*	-1.356*	-1.643*	-1.781*
	(.320)	(.309)	(.329)	(.342)	(.373)	(.318)	(.306)
Dummy lower middle income	-3.368*	-3.135*	-1.324*	-.719*		-3.249*	0.734
	(1.232)	(1.028)	(1.119)	(1.119)		(1.161)	(0.100)
Dummy high income	.438	1.028*	1.618*	1.691*		1.467*	1.598*
	(.432)	(.410)	(.248)	(.375)		(.539)	(.518)
Oil dummy	-5.437*	-4.742*	-5.356*	-5.147*	-6.863*	-5.410*	-3.817*
	(1.285)	(.927)	(.966)	(.966)	(.928)	(1.320)	(1.312)
Trend	-.151						
	(.099)						
Population rural			-.008*	-.008*	-.010*		
			(.001)	(.001)	(.001)		
CPI				-.039*	-.031*		
				(.015)	(.019)		
External dDebt					-.046*		
					(.012)		
GDP per capita interaction with *manufacturing.						-.00002* (2.391)	-.000* (1.750)
GDP per capita interaction with agriculture							.000*
(5.690)							
GDP per capita interaction with trade							2.740* (4.150)
Constant	324.56	20.96*	22.26*	29.59*	17.38*	(1.386)	16.51*
	(198.52)	(.867)	(.867)25.72*	(1.754)	(2.271)	(1.337)	
Observations	485	509	426	426	282	485	485
R-squared	0.59	0.59	0.59	0.60	0.44	0.60	0.63

Source: World Bank Staff calculations.

Note: External debt variable only available for developing countries.

*significant at five5 percent level.

** significant at ten 10 percent level.

(equation 1). A similar exercise was carried out with respect to indirect and direct tax collection across countries.

Modified Model: The Role of Institutional Variables

The discussion now turns to the cross-section estimates that allowed inclusion of the institutional (demand) variables such as governance indicators (government effectiveness, regulatory quality, corruption) and to control for the size of the shadow economy.[24] They had not been included in the panel estimation regression because they do not reveal much variation over time. The explanatory variables follow those employed in panel model (the basic regression corresponding to equation 2 from table 2A.2) because the regression passed the test of the omission variable (suggesting that the functional form is correct).

The empirical results, presented in table 2A.3, suggest strongly that conventional factors play a significant role in the determination of the

TABLE 2A.3

Cross-Section Results, Mean Values for Years 1995–2004 for 57 Countries

Variable	EQ1 base	EQ2	EQ3	EQ4	EQ5	EQ6	EQ4
GDP per capita	.001**	.001**	.001**	.001**	.001**	.001	.000
	(.000)	(.000)	(.000)	(.000)	(.000)	(.000)	(.000)
Trade	(.072**	.080**	.086**	.078**	.068**	.068**	.079**
	(.032)	(.032)	(.034)	(.034)	(.033)	(.033)	(.035)
Agriculture	-.118	-.226*	-.169	.016	-.182	-.168	-.016
	(.014)	(.016)	(.143)	(.163)	(.152)	(.143)	(.178)
Population growth	-2.281**	-1.966**	-2.188**	-1.863**	-2.311**	-2.440**	-1.869**
	(1.163)	(1.152)	(1.172)	(1.176)	(1.227)	(1.167)	(1.167)
Shadow economy			-.069	-.169*			-0.126
			(.095)	(.103)			(.113)
Shadow economy_1					-.019		
					(0.226)		
Corruption						2.740	1.706
						(2.337)	(2.401)
GDP per capita interaction with agriculture		.001**					.000
		(.000)					(.000)
GDP per capita interaction with shadow economy				.001**			.001**
				(.000)			(.000)
Constant	20.39	16.21**	22.63**	19.62**	21.23**	22.85**	20.24**
	(3.975)	(4.525)	(6.560)	(1.386)	(10.66)	(1.386)	(6.572)
Observations	57	57	56	56	57	57	56
R-squared	0.54	0.56	0.54	0.67	0.54	0.58	0.56

Source: World Bank staff calculations.
Note: *Significant at 10 percent level; **significant at 5 percent level.

tax ratio, while the institutional factors perform less well. Although in some cases (shadow economy, corruption index) institutional coefficients took the correct sign, they were often insignificant. The lack of significance of the institutional variables may be caused by potential causality between the level of development, the shadow economy, and the governance variables. For example, more affluent countries usually have better quality institutions and smaller shadow economies (confirmed by the significantly positive coefficient on the shadow economy-GDP per capita interactive term in equation 4). Moreover, causality may run from taxes to the informal sector (high taxes tend to encourage informality). Although the instrumental variable approach was experimented with,[25] it did not improve the estimates (equation 5).

This suggests that considerable caution should be exercised in calculating the effects of institutional variables on tax performance, and further work should seek to identify those magnitudes more reliably.

Notes

1. Central Europe is defined here as the Czech Republic, Hungary, Poland, the Slovak Republic, and Slovenia.
2. Estonia, Latvia, and Lithuania.
3. Albania, Bosnia and Herzegovina, Croatia, Bulgaria, the former Yugoslav Republic of Macedonia, Romania, and Serbia and Montenegro.
4. Armenia, Azerbaijan, Belarus, Georgia, Kazakhstan, the Kyrgyz Republic, Moldova, the Russian Federation, Tajikistan, Ukraine, and Uzbekistan.
5. Austria, Belgium, Denmark, Finland, France, Germany, Greece, Ireland, Italy, Luxembourg, the Netherlands, Portugal, Spain, Sweden, the United Kingdom.
6. Armenia, Azerbaijan, Georgia, the Kyrgyz Republic, Moldova, and Tajikistan.
7. Belarus, Kazakhstan, the Russian Federation, and Ukraine.
8. Macroeconomic imbalances at the beginning of the transition in some countries led to high inflation that wiped out the real value of debt inherited from the socialist period.
9. ECA countries have turned out to be among the largest beneficiaries of the favorable global financial environment. This environment allowed them to save about 0.8–1.4 percent of GDP on interest payments in 2005. For details, see Hauner and Kumar (2005: 13, 15). The estimates include 10 ECA countries: Bulgaria, Croatia, the Czech Republic, Hungary, Poland, Romania, Russia, the Slovak Republic, Turkey, and Ukraine.
10. Cyclically adjusted data, available for EU-8 countries, is used to verify whether these thresholds are set at levels suitable for the isolation of exclusively discretionary fiscal reductions. In the verification procedure the thresholds assumed by Alesina and Perotti (1996) were applied to

check whether in isolated periods of substantial primary deficit improvement, primary structural balance increased by at least 1.5 percentage points of GDP within one year or by 1.25 percentage points of GDP per year over a period of two years.

11. Fiscal adjustments are considered to be based "mostly on expenditure cuts" (or "mostly on tax increases") if more than 50 percent but less than 100 percent of the improvement in the primary balance reflects a curtailment in primary spending (or a rise in general government revenue).
12. Typically, the empirical literature finds four important factors influencing the consolidation process, namely macroeconomic and fiscal conditions, the composition of fiscal adjustments, and the existence of fiscal rules. See Guichard, Kennedy, Wurzel and Andrél (2007).
13. Tax performance is a government's ability to raise adequate revenue to maximize social welfare. The yield of the tax system is a function of the tax bases available (economic structure), the rates applied to these bases, and the capacity to levy taxes effectively. Given these, the success of the authorities in exploiting the tax potential and in attaining the taxation target will depend on the need and desire for government spending, or willingness to tax.
14. Generally, the findings are robust to the inclusion of additional variables that have been used to model the tax ratio in the literature (inflation, external debt, rural population).
15. Tax effort is measured by comparing the actual tax ratio of a country with that predicted by using a panel regression, equation 2 of table 2A.2. An index of 1.0 means the country's tax effort is at the expected level, given the structural factors of the country. In other words, the country is using its taxable capacity at a level consistent with the average of the other countries in the sample.
16. The following classification is used: high index (equal to or greater than 1.2), medium index (between 0.9 and 1.1), and low index (less than or equal to 0.8).
17. The VAT or CIT productivity rate is the ratio of VAT or CIT collections to GDP divided by the nominal VAT or CIT rate. The PIT productivity measure is personal income tax revenue as percent of GDP divided by the top marginal income tax rate, and multiplied by the top income tax bracket value. Measuring tax productivity is fraught with difficulties stemming from imperfect approximations of the gross tax bases (lack of data) as well as types of tax deductions and credits that are available from country to country. Thus, it should be treated with caution.
18. The following classification is proposed: stronger administration (VAT/CIT/PIT productivity is greater than average productivity in the sample) and weaker administration (VAT/CIT/PIT productivity is less than average productivity in the sample).
19. The international empirical evidence on the links between taxes and growth is inconclusive, although some findings seem relatively robust. Many studies found a significant negative relation between the aggregate tax–to-GDP ratio and growth although the size of the effect differs considerably (Engen and Skinner 1996; Cashin 1995; Fölster and Henrekson 2001; World Bank 2006h).
20. $825–$3,255 GNI per capita.

21. Above $10,065 GNI per capita (31 countries in the sample).
22. The method is an alternative to feasible generalized last squares for fitting the linear cross-sectional time series models when disturbances are not assumed to be independent and identically distributed, and it is preferable to the feasible generalized least squares when the number of observations and time span are limited.
23. OIL dummy takes value of 1 if the share of fuel (and related products) in total merchandise exports exceeds 40 percent.
24. The shadow variable reflects tax evasion.
25. Following Davoodi and Grigorian (2006) we assumed that the shadow economy is driven mainly by tax burden, quality of institutions, and GDP per capita.

CHAPTER 3

Do Public Finance Systems Matter for Growth?

Aristomene Varoudakis
with contributions from
Leszek Kasek, Taras Pushak, Andrzej Rzonca,
Emilia Skrok, and Erwin Tiongson

Governments actively use fiscal policies, whether public spending or taxation, to address market failures and achieve redistributive goals. These so-called classical functions of government—to correct externalities and ensure adequate provision of public goods and services—have a sound foundation and are conducive to higher long-run growth with social inclusion. In practice, however, it is often difficult to determine whether the optimal size of government has been reached. While the provision of public goods and services may promote growth, both the inefficient provision of these goods and revenue-raising mechanisms that distort the allocation of resources may impede growth (see, for example, Grossman 1990).

Based on evidence from countries in the Europe and Central Asia (ECA) region, the empirical analysis in this chapter explores four possible links between public finance policies and growth: (a) the effects of budget deficits and fiscal consolidation on growth; (b) the impact of the size of government on growth; (c) links with the quality of governance; and (d) the influence of the composition of expenditures and taxes on growth. In particular, the link between expenditure impact and governance has not been systematically investigated in previous empirical growth studies, although indirect evidence suggests the quality of public institutions affects the impact of key potential drivers of growth (see, for example, Burnside and Dollar 2000, 2004).

Building a strong fiscal position requires a sustained fiscal consolidation effort. As discussed in chapter 2, sizeable fiscal consolidations—sometimes recurring—have been a defining characteristic of the transition to the market. Such consolidations have been undertaken across the whole ECA region, but with varying degrees of success. Successful fiscal adjustment is an important prerequisite for growth. Unsustainable fiscal consolidations are counterproductive and may undermine investor confidence because they fail to set the government's financial position on a sound footing. Sustained fiscal adjustments are needed also to create long-term fiscal space for expenditures that promote growth. There is extensive evidence from Organisation for Economic Co-operation and Development (OECD) countries that the composition of fiscal adjustments matters for their sustainability: consolidations that have relied primarily on tax increases and cuts in public investment have not been sustainable, while those underpinned by structural reforms in public expenditure programs have had more lasting effects, because they have tackled the main types of expenditures that show a strong upward drift (Alesina and Ardagna 1998; Alesina and Perotti 1997). These results have also been confirmed for developing countries, with the difference that when fiscal consolidations are supported by better mobilization of tax revenues (through tax base broadening), the probability of sustainability increases (Gupta et al. 2003).

Beyond the fiscal deficit, the size of government spending may have an impact on economic growth. High levels of public spending can adversely affect resource allocation and growth through various channels. They may add to rigidity in the budget, making it more difficult to keep the fiscal balance under control. They also usually lead to high levels of taxation that may reduce incentives to save, invest, innovate, and participate in the labor force. Large government spending programs are often supported by intrusive regulations that may stifle private participation and investment. Moreover, as they become larger, expenditure programs may become counterproductive if they are poorly designed as a result of limited government effectiveness or if they create more opportunities for corruption and rent seeking. The effect of government expenditure programs on growth may thus be particularly sensitive to the quality of governance—a link more systematically explored in this chapter.

Empirical evidence suggests that the composition of expenditures also matters for growth. Government spending that enhances the efficiency and quantity of factors of production is considered "productive," in the sense that it contributes directly to higher growth. Similarly, spending that helps enforce the rule of law, protect property rights, and facilitate transactions can be considered productive—although views differ as to what may be a reasonable level of spending on such core government functions. In contrast, large expenditures on general public services (which may be a sign of bloated bureaucracies and low government effectiveness) and on defense are likely to be less conducive to growth and in this sense may be termed "unproductive." Similarly, sizeable spending on transfers and welfare services may create disincentives for participation in the labor force, while subsidies may distort the allocation of resources toward low-productivity activities. The evidence is still incomplete regarding the prevalence of such effects in transition economies, and one goal of this chapter is to add to our knowledge in this area.

Evidence also suggests that the structure of taxes matters for growth. Progressive personal income taxes and corporate income taxes reduce the net return to human or physical capital and thus may impair growth. High taxes on labor are particularly distorting because they deter formal employment while promoting employment in the untaxed informal sector—and thus deny the government sizeable revenues that could be used for financing productive spending.[1] By contrast, indirect taxes uniformly levied on consumption (such as the value added tax) may have less harmful impacts on growth, because they are relatively neutral toward saving and investment decisions and do not distort incentives to work.

Success in Fiscal Consolidation

Growing evidence from transition economies now shows that fiscal adjustments supported by expenditure cuts have been more successful and long-lasting than those supported by revenue-increasing measures (Purfield 2003; Afonso, Nickel, and Rother 2006). Based on the list of fiscal adjustment episodes in ECA countries over 1996–2004 identified in chapter 2, the analysis in this section looks at the characteristics of successful consolidations that have set public finances on a sustainable path.

Successful fiscal adjustments have been identified based on their duration and their effectiveness in restoring the fiscal balance and reducing the public debt.[2] Adjustments defined as successful have met three criteria simultaneously:

- Duration. In accordance with criteria adopted in previous studies, an adjustment is deemed successful if the average primary balance two years after the end of the adjustment was still lower by at least 2 percentage points of GDP relative to its level before adjustment.[3]
- Fiscal balance restored. An adjustment is deemed successful if the primary fiscal balance at the end of the adjustment is positive, or at least not significantly negative to a point that would have compromised the conditions for debt sustainability. Although the debt-stabilizing primary fiscal surplus depends on several factors that are country specific and thus difficult to assess in this exercise, a large primary fiscal deficit will not be consistent with long-term debt sustainability.
- Debt ratio effectively reduced. An adjustment is considered successful if the public debt ratio has declined in the two years after the end of the adjustment.

A majority of fiscal adjustments in ECA have been successful. According to these criteria, 18 episodes were successful, while 10 were unsuccessful. It is too early to assess whether 6 of the 34 adjustments analyzed will be successful (table 3.1). Successful fiscal adjustments were significantly bolder, amounting on average to 5 percentage points of GDP, against 3.7 percentage points when adjustments failed to deliver expected results (table 3.2). To the extent bolder adjustments indicate stronger commitment to fiscal discipline, the difference in size may explain the better outcomes from bold adjustments. Moreover, successful adjustments were based on expenditure cuts, accounting for about 85 percent of the improvement in the primary fiscal balance. By contrast, the contribution of tax revenue increases was higher when adjustments were unsuccessful.[4]

Expenditure downsizing was broadly based in episodes of sustained fiscal adjustment. Because successful adjustments were driven by expenditure cuts, these adjustments relied upon downsizing of spending across a wide array of economic categories (table 3.2). Cuts in capital spending accounted for about one-third of the expenditure adjustment effort. While such investment cuts were significant and could have a potentially harmful impact on long-term growth, the generally good infrastructure in transition economies may have mitigated these negative effects. Transfers, notably, were not cut significantly in either successful or unsuccessful adjustment efforts.

Post-adjustment, growth has been on average higher when the fiscal effort has been sustained. In both successful and unsuccessful fiscal adjustments, growth accelerated during the adjustment period compared to the year immediately preceding the start of the episode (figure 3.1). This is probably because most fiscal adjustments were

TABLE 3.1
Typology of Fiscal Adjustments in ECA, 1996–2004

Country	Initation of adjustment	Assessment	Change in primary fiscal balance (%)	% Change in primary expenditure	% Change in revenue	Balance a year before adjustment (%)	Average balance two years after adjustment (%)
Russian Federation	1999	Successful	9.1	-14.6	-5.5	-5.5	4.7
Kyrgyz Republic	1997	Unsuccessful	8.8	-10.3	-1.5	-16.1	-9.4
Albania	1998	Successful	8.0	0.5	8.5	-8.5	-2.6
Moldova	1999	Successful	7.2	-15.3	-8.0	-7.8	1.8
Lithuania	2001	Successful	5.8	-9.1	-3.4	-5.7	0.3
Turkey	2001	Successful	5.7	0.7	6.4	0.4	5.7
FYR Macedonia	2000	Unsuccessful	5.6	-1.4	4.3	-1.3	-4.1
Azerbaijan	2000	Successful	5.5	-2.7	2.7	-5.3	-0.7
FYR Macedonia	2003	Successful	5.4	-1.6	3.8	-4.4	1.4
Bosnia and Herzegovina	2003	Successful	5.0	-1.1	3.9	-2.9	0.5
Bosnia and Herzegovina	2001	Successful	4.8	-15.3	-10.5	-7.7	0.1
Georgia	2004	TBD	4.7	1.3	5.9	-1.0	—
Estonia	2001	Successful	4.6	-5.6	-0.9	-3.8	2.1
Albania	2003	Successful	4.3	-2.2	2.1	-4.7	-0.9
Armenia	2002	Successful	4.2	-2.5	1.7	-5.5	-0.9
Moldova	2001	Successful	4.1	-4.8	-0.7	-0.5	2.9
Georgia	2000	Successful	4.1	-4.3	-0.2	-4.9	0.0
Kyrgyz Republic	2002	Successful	3.9	0.3	4.3	-8.4	-3.5
Lithuania	1997	Unsuccessful	3.7	-2.1	1.6	-3.9	-4.3
Kazakhstan	2000	Successful	3.7	0.2	3.8	-0.9	4.0
Slovak Republic	2002	Unsuccessful	3.5	-0.7	2.8	-4.7	-1.5
Romania	1999	Unsuccessful	3.5	0.2	3.6	-3.1	-0.9
Armenia	1997	Unsuccessful	3.5	-4.4	-0.9	-3.2	-4.2
Serbia and Montenegro	2004	TBD	3.3	-0.9	2.4	-2.1	—
Belarus	2004	TBD	3.2	0.1	3.3	-2.7	—
Russian Federation	2004	TBD	2.8	-2.8	0.0	-0.1	—
Azerbaijan	2004	TBD	2.7	-2.5	0.2	-3.1	—
Russian Federation	2000	Unsuccessful	2.6	0.5	3.1	3.7	1.2
Czech Republic	2004	TBD	2.5	-2.1	0.4	-5.2	—
Azerbaijan	1998	Unsuccessful	2.3	-1.9	0.4	-2.0	-2.6
Romania	2001	Successful	2.3	-0.9	1.4	-2.1	-0.2
Croatia	2000	Unsuccessful	2.1	-3.7	-1.6	-6.4	-3.4
Latvia	2000	Unsuccessful	1.8	-4.4	-2.6	-3.9	-1.9
Kazakhstan	2001	Successful	1.7	1.4	3.0	2.7	3.7
Average			4.3	-3.3	1.0		

Sources: IMF World Economic Outlook database; World Bank ECA fiscal database.
Notes: — = Not available; TBD = to be determined. Primary fiscal balance excludes privatization receipts. Data on primary balance in Albania, Bosnia and Herzegovina, and FYR Macedonia in 2005, and data on interest payments in Estonia in 2003 are taken from IMF World Economic Outlook database. The primary fiscal balance in Armenia in 2004 was computed without excluding privatization receipts from revenue.

initiated in "bad times" of large fiscal imbalances, debt distress, and slow growth. Growth during adjustments was on average slightly lower in successful episodes, possibly reflecting the comparatively bolder fiscal restraint documented earlier. The most notable pattern is, however, that successful fiscal adjustments had growth rewards: on average, growth

TABLE 3.2

Basic Features of Unsuccessful and Successful Fiscal Adjustments in ECA, 1996–2004

Outcome	Composition of adjustment (in % of GDP)				
	Change in primary fiscal balance	Change in primary expenditure	Change in revenue	Balance a year before adjustment	Average balance two years after adjustment
Successful adjustments	5.0	-4.3	0.7	-4.2	1.0
Unsuccessful adjustments	3.7	-2.8	0.9	-4.1	-3.1

Outcome	Composition of expenditure cuts (economic breakdown) (in % of GDP)						
	Change in primary expenditures	Capital expenditure	Current primary expenditures	Expenditures on goods and services	Wages and salaries	Subsidies	Transfers
Successful adjustments	-4.6	-1.3	-2.8	-2.1	-0.6	-0.5	0.1
Unsuccessful adjustments	-2.6	-0.7	-1.4	-0.9	-0.2	-0.3	-.2

Source: World Bank, ECA fiscal database.

two years after the end of the adjustment was significantly higher when the fiscal effort was successful (7.6 percent per year) than when the fiscal consolidation failed (4.4 percent).

Fiscal Deficits

In ECA countries, lower fiscal imbalances have been associated with higher growth (figure 3.2a). This relationship holds even after excluding Turkey, where large fiscal imbalances have been notorious for triggering crises and sharp growth slowdowns. Obviously, the possibility of reverse causation cannot be ruled out, with stronger economic growth contributing to an improved fiscal stance as a result of independent factors, such as positive shocks in the terms of trade. And when growth is robust, government can finance more expenditure than in other circumstances, even without borrowing. However, this is unlikely to be the only causal link. The computations encompass averages over five years, a period long enough for additional revenue generated by faster-than-expected economic growth to be spent, thus removing most of the reverse causality from growth on the fiscal balance. The positive association also holds when the country-specific reverse causality between growth and the fiscal balance is removed by merging the yearly data across all ECA countries and sorting growth rates in decreasing order of magnitude. Lower fiscal imbalances are still significantly associated with higher rates of growth (figure 3.2b).

The adverse impact of deficits on growth has been abundantly investigated in theoretical and empirical studies (box 3.1). In addition

FIGURE 3.1

GDP Growth Before, During, and After Fiscal Adjustments in ECA, 1996–2004

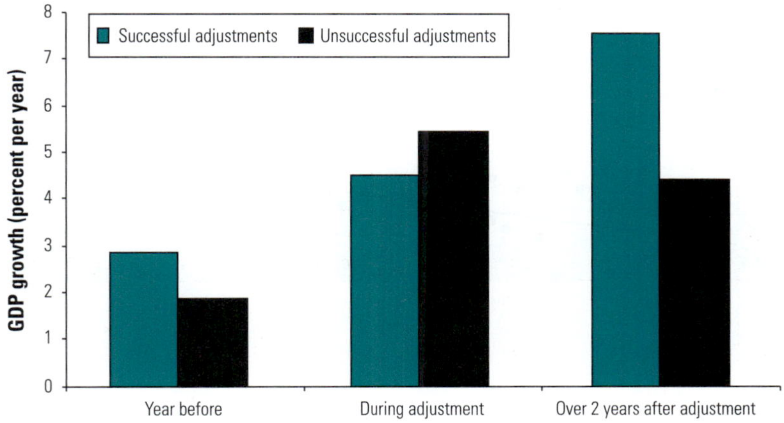

Source: Authors.

to the impact on national savings, fiscal deficits heighten business uncertainty, with a potentially damaging impact on the investment climate at a time when ECA countries are exposed to strong forces of globalization and need to continue mobilizing high domestic and foreign investment. Policy uncertainty in ECA has for years been ranked as a top business constraint, although some progress is evident from recent business surveys (table 3.3).

The fact that taxes rank highest among major business constraints in most ECA countries suggests that the large size of government is

TABLE 3.3

Policy Uncertainty as a Major Business Constraint in ECA Countries

Countries	Percentage of managers surveyed ranking policy uncertainty as a major business constraint	Rank of policy uncertainty among major business constraints	Percentage of managers surveyed ranking policy uncertainty as a major business constraint	Rank of policy uncertainty among major business constraints	Business constraint more significant than policy uncertainty
EU-8 a	24.4	2	20.8	2	tax rates
Southeastern Europe	44.7	1	31.8	1	—
Middle-income CIS	39.0	2	22.5	2	tax rates
Low-income CISb	27.7	2	20.3	2	tax rates
Turkey	53.8	1	31.5	2	tax rates

Source: World Bank, Business Environment and Enterprise Performance Survey 2005.

Note:

a. Data for EU-8 in 2002 does not include Poland.

b. Data for low-income CIS in 2002 include only Armenia, Azerbaijan, and Georgia. Data for 2005 do not include Turkmenistan.

FIGURE 3.2
Fiscal Balance and Economic Growth in ECA Countries, 1989–2005

a. Fiscal balance and economic growth, based on five-year averages (Turkey excluded)

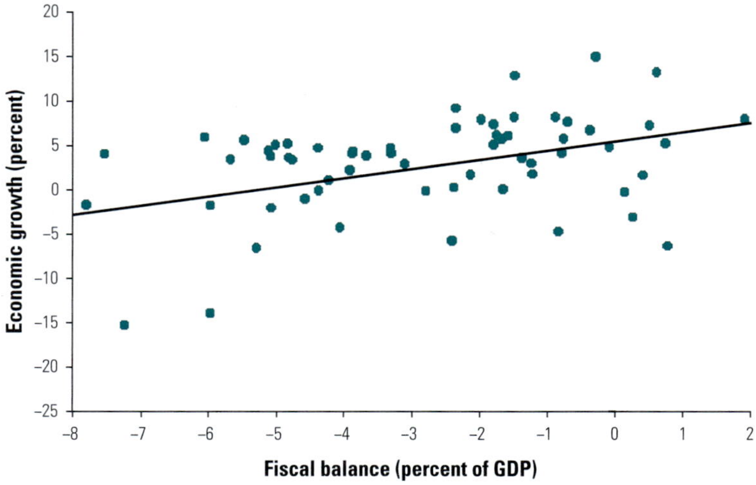

b. Fiscal balance and economic growth (based on five-year averages, with yearly data merged across countries and sorted by decreasing order of GDP growth)

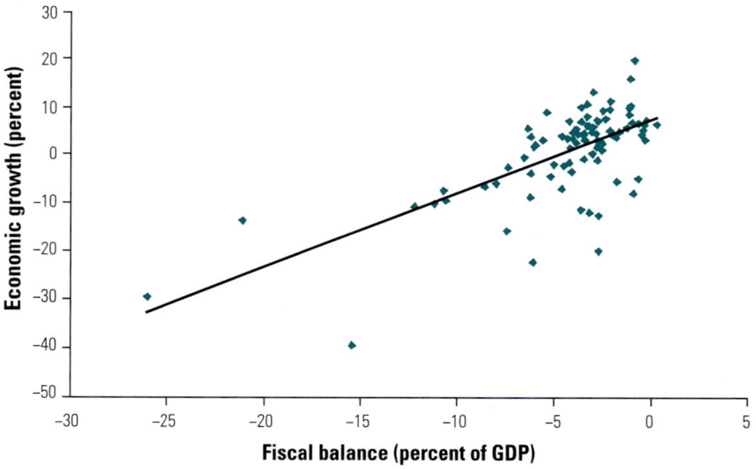

Source: IMF World Economic Outlook.

a. Fiscal balance and economic growth, based on five-year averages (Turkey excluded).

b. Fiscal balance and economic growth (based on five-year averages, with yearly data merged across countries and sorted by decreasing order of GDP growth).

FIGURE 3.3
Uncertainty as Perceived by Managers and Fiscal Balance in ECA, 2005

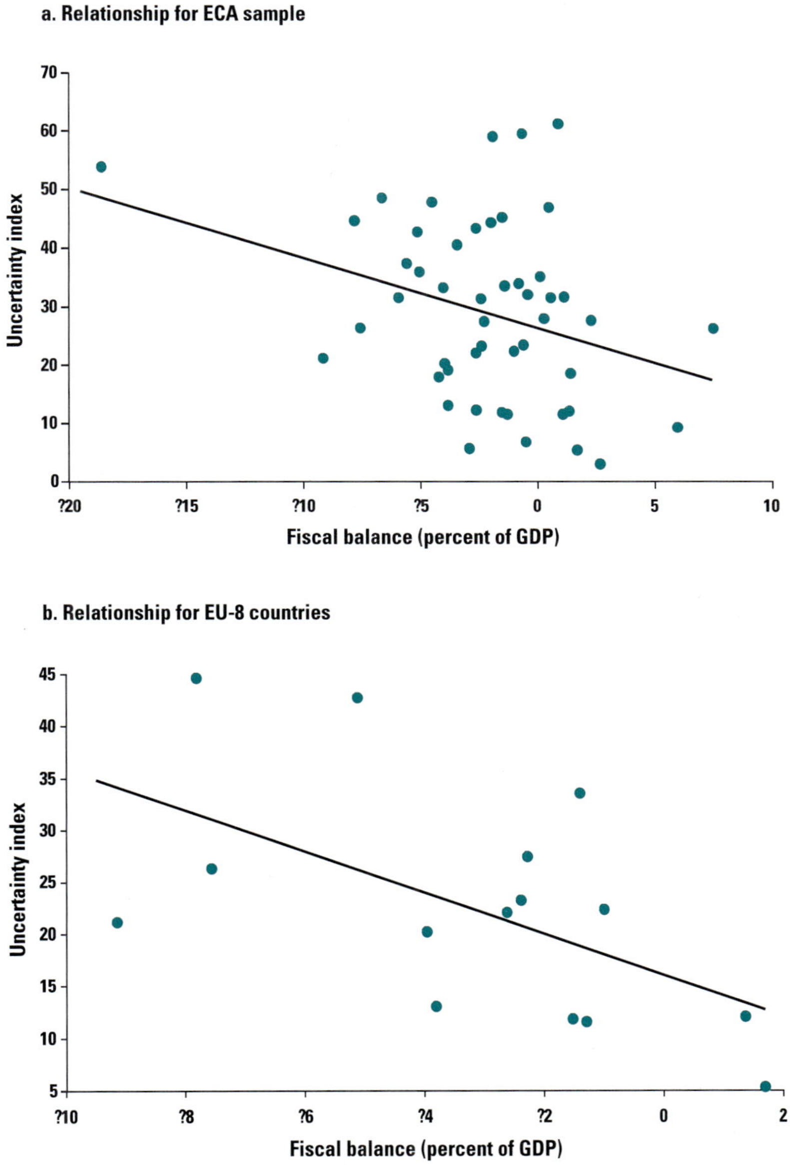

Sources: World Bank Business Environment and Enterprise Performance Survey 2005; IMF World Economic Outlook.

having an impact on growth (as discussed further below). Stronger fiscal frameworks seem to have played an important part in this decline, as shown by the negative association between perceived uncertainty and fiscal balances (figure 3.3). The correlation is most robust in EU-8,[5] the group of countries that currently face the largest fiscal tensions.

BOX 3.1

Fiscal Deficits, Private Savings, and Economic Growth

To finance a deficit, government has to borrow from the private sector. Some rational economic agents may be aware that a higher deficit today implies higher taxation in the future, and they may increase their savings today to have the means to pay those higher taxes. However, some economic agents may be subject to fiscal illusion or simply not care about higher taxes in the future. Thus, the increase in private savings may not be enough to meet additional government borrowing requirements, although empirical studies are inconclusive in this respect. A concise review of those studies can be found in Elmendorf and Mankiw (1998: 53–61).

According to neoclassical models, even if the fiscal deficit has an adverse effect on national savings, it does not reduce output growth in a lasting way, because in these models long-term economic growth is exclusively driven by technical progress, which is assumed to be exogenous. Lower savings will, however, result in a lower capital-to-labor ratio, which—due to the decreasing marginal productivity of capital—will lead to a higher real interest rate. A lower capital-to-labor ratio will also lead to lower productivity of labor and thus eventually to a lower real wage rate.

Contrary to this view, technical progress is endogenous in new growth theory (Barro and Sala-i-Martin 1995). These models rely on a broader definition of capital, incorporating positive externalities of capital accumulation (for example, learning by doing or technical progress driven by technologies embodied in new capital). As a result, in many endogenous growth models, the assumption of decreasing marginal productivity of capital is replaced by an assumption of constant marginal productivity. This enables changes in growth rates driven by changes in national savings to persist in the long run.

The negative impact of fiscal deficits on long-run growth has been empirically documented in several studies, such as Fischer (1993), Easterly and Rebelo (1993), Easterly, Rodriguez, and Schmidt-Hebbel (1994), Bleaney, Gemmell, and Kneller (2001).

Source: Authors.

The largest declines in uncertainty were in the Slovak Republic, where the fiscal deficit was reduced over this period, and in Bulgaria, where public finances were maintained more or less balanced. The fiscal burden also dropped significantly in both countries.[6] In contrast, policy uncertainty increased in the Czech Republic and Hungary, where strong tensions in public finances were left largely unresolved.

Econometric evidence strongly confirms that lower fiscal imbalances are conducive to growth.[7] Regression results underscore the broad findings from previous studies, namely that initial conditions, macroeconomic stabilization, and liberalization and structural reform

FIGURE 3.4
Fiscal Balances and Growth in ECA Countries, 1992–2004

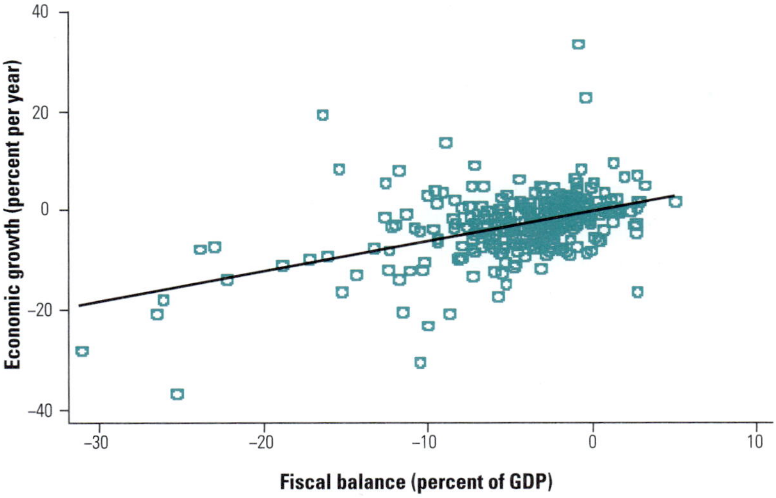

Source: World Bank staff calculations.

Note: The values on the y-axis represent economic growth after controlling for the effects of all independent variables other than the fiscal balance (in percent of GDP). Based on regression (1), table 3A.1, annex 3A.

all matter for growth, and their impact is in the expected direction. The fiscal balance turns out to be a robust positive determinant of growth after controlling for other independent variables (annex 3A and figure 3.4). An improvement in the fiscal balance of 1 percentage point of GDP is associated, on average, with a 0.4–0.5 percent increase in the rate of GDP growth, or a compounded gain over 10 years of about 4.6 percentage points of GDP. Previous studies have produced mixed evidence on the importance of fiscal consolidation to growth. The significantly stronger results obtained here are associated with the notable progress in fiscal consolidation documented in the previous section, together with the strong rebound in growth observed in recent years in several ECA countries.[8]

The Size of Government

Significant parts of public expenditure programs aim to ensure adequate provision of public goods and services, but also to promote inclusion by protecting the vulnerable through social transfers. Public goods and services in sectors such as basic education, health care, and rural infrastructure typically strengthen human and physical assets that are conducive to higher growth, while empowering lower-income people and the disadvantaged to overcome poverty. At the same time, well-designed transfers in the form of social assistance and pensions protect the vulnerable, and these safety nets have proven valuable in preventing even stronger increases in poverty during the transition. Although these functions are valuable, it is often difficult to determine whether the size of public expenditures "is right." While the provision of public goods and services, as well as social transfers, may promote growth with inclusion, the inefficient design of these expenditure programs and revenue-raising mechanisms may distort the allocation of resources and impede growth. Because this would risk making efforts to reduce poverty self-defeating, the following sections focus on the way public expenditures affect growth in relation to the quality of public sector management.

The size of government, measured here by the share of public spending in GDP, can affect economic growth in various ways. First, large public expenditures can affect growth through their impact on the fiscal balance—fiscal deficits have proven to be more difficult to control in countries with high public spending as a share of GDP. In the early 2000s, for example, deficits averaged a high 5–6 percent of GDP where public spending exceeded 40 percent of GDP (figure 3.5). This negative association may reflect the impact on the fiscal balance of more expansionary fiscal policy driven by increases in public expenditures. However, it may also reflect the impact of automatic fiscal stabilizers if the budget is rigid because of a large share of nondiscretionary expenditure such as wages, interest payments, social entitlements, and subsidies.[9] When large nondiscretionary spending prevents a swift adjustment in the budget in the face of declining fiscal revenues, a growth slowdown is likely to be reflected in larger fiscal deficits. Tensions in public finances are most evident in bad times, especially in countries where expenditure is high and rigid, nondiscretionary components are prominent.

Large public expenditures can also affect resource allocation and growth through various other channels. Large public expenditures must be financed by high levels of taxation if government solvency is to be preserved. High tax rates reduce the rate of return to saving and investment and may also distort incentives to work or create incentives to migrate, especially for highly skilled workers. The composition of spending also presumably matters, because sizeable spending on transfers and welfare services may create disincentives for participation in the labor force, while subsidies may distort the allocation of resources toward low-productivity activities. Large government spending programs in specific sectors—such as infrastructure, hous-

FIGURE 3.5

Public Expenditure and Fiscal Balance in ECA Countries, 2002–05

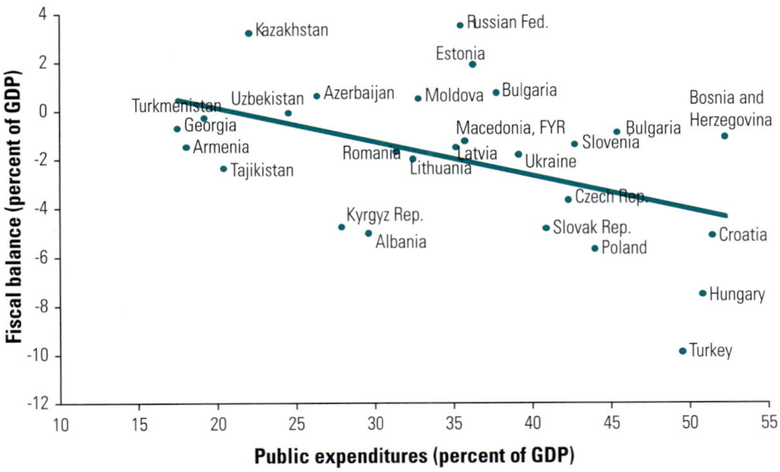

Source: World Bank staff calculations based on IMF World Economic Outlook data.

ing, or health care—are often supported by intrusive regulations that may stifle private participation and investment. Moreover, large public expenditure programs may become counterproductive if they are poorly designed as a result of limited government effectiveness or if they create more opportunities for corruption and rent seeking. Examples include poor targeting of transfer programs, inefficient selection of investment projects due to political interference, insufficient budgeting for operation and maintenance of public investments, or resource leakages owing to weak enforcement of procurement regulations. The evidence to date has been inconclusive regarding the prevalence of such effects in transition economies (box 3.2).

The impact of the size of government on economic growth is likely to be nonlinear for several reasons.

- While small governments tend to concentrate spending on the provision of key public goods (rule of law, defense, infrastructure) and efficiency-improving services (education, health care), large governments tend to spend more on "unproductive" core government functions and subsidies that are not conducive to growth (discussed further below). Large governments also spend more on social transfers, usually as part of a "social compact" to provide valued safety nets, but in many cases the design of these programs makes them fiscally unsustainable (see chapter 7 on pensions) or

BOX 3.2

Government Size and Economic Growth: Empirical Analysis to Date

Overall, the literature linking size of government and economic growth has been inconclusive. Barro (1991) found that a larger size of government negatively affects growth. However, when Levine and Renelt (1992) used extreme bounds analysis to test the sensitivity of standard empirical models of growth, they were unable to find robust and significant links between government expenditure (whether total or consumption expenditures alone) and growth, although they agreed that the relationship appears generally negative. Other researchers have argued also that there may be thresholds in the links between size of government and growth (Chen and Lee 2005) and that the composition of government expenditure matters (Devarajan, Swaroop, and Zou 1996; also see box 3.4).

The literature on transition economies to date has also generally found ambiguous links between the size of government and growth. Chu and Schwartz (1994) found little evidence linking expenditure reductions to output decline. Campos and Coricelli (2000) tested the Barro (1991) growth model using data on transition economies and found a weak impact of government consumption on growth. Conversely, Beck and Laeven (2005) found a negative but insignificant link between government consumption and average GDP per capita growth over the period 1992–2002. The limited availability of relevant data seems to have hampered empirical work. Many of the reported regression results are based on small sample sizes as, for example, the analysis in Beck and Laeven, which is based on 24 observations.

Some very recent work provides stronger evidence in support of a significant negative link between public spending and growth. Using a panel sample of 120 observations, Åslund and Jenish (2005) suggest that expenditure reductions have underpinned economic growth in the region from 1999 onward, particularly among the Commonwealth of Independent States.

Source: Authors.

requires financing through high payroll taxes that stifle employment generation (see chapter 9 on labor taxes). During 2002–04 public spending was on average 46 percent of GDP in ECA countries with large governments, compared with 28.8 percent of GDP in countries where public spending was below the average for the region as a whole. As noted in chapter 2, public spending on social security and welfare services was particularly oversized in countries with large governments—15.3 percent of GDP compared to 7.3 percent in countries with smaller governments. Core government functions (general public services, defense, public order, and safety) were also larger, representing 7.9 percent of GDP in the former countries against 5.8 percent in the latter. Because higher levels of spending are associated with larger fiscal deficits (see figure 3.5) and levels of public debt, interest payments in countries with large governments were twice as high as in countries with small governments—2.9 percent of GDP in the former compared to 1.4 percent in the latter.

- Limited administrative capacity could be another reason a threshold may exist in the way public spending affects growth. Administrative capacity improves only slowly, reflecting gradual improvements in public sector management and civil servant skills, yet expenditure programs may grow relatively swiftly, resulting in administrative bottlenecks, poor program design, and low expenditure effectiveness.
- Financing of big governments requires high levels of taxation that are likely to distort incentives for saving, investment, and work effort beyond some threshold level. The general rule of thumb is that deadweight losses from taxes increase in proportion to the square of taxation.

This study finds a nonlinear relationship between public expenditure and growth in ECA countries, using general government spending as the independent variable. The results reported in annex 3A (table 3A.2, regressions 1–3) provide evidence that public spending negatively affects growth at expenditure levels of 35 percent of GDP or higher.[10] Beyond this threshold, an increase in general government expenditures of 1 percentage point of GDP reduces growth by an estimated 0.3–0.4 percent per year. At levels below about 35 percent, public sector size has no robust measurable effect on growth.[11] Such an inflection point is to be seen as an approximate rather than an exact measure, the more so that the impact of the size of government on growth is likely to depend on public sector governance as further discussed below (see also box 3.3).

In countries where public sector governance is weak, misallocations of public expenditures and weak administrative capacity are likely to be exacerbated, making the nonlinear impact of large government programs more pronounced. In addition, taxes are likely to be more distortionary when governance is poor, with high compliance costs and bribery of tax officials adding to the impact of high and distorting tax rates. In contrast, the threshold effects of big governments on growth may be mitigated by strong public institutions.

The hypothesis that the quality of governance influences the impact of big governments on growth (see box 3.3) has been tested by using two indicators of the quality of governance. Findings are robust to the

BOX 3.3

Why Good Governance Could Mitigate the Negative Impact of Big Governments: Some Simple Analytics

It is reasonable to expect that the marginal benefits of public spending will diminish as the size of expenditure programs gets bigger, assuming a given set of public sector institutions and social preferences. Similarly, as the tax burden gets higher the marginal cost of taxation can be expected to increase, because high taxes usually distort incentives to invest and participate in the labor force. Although political factors may certainly complicate outcomes, from an economic perspective public expenditures should increase until their marginal benefits match the marginal cost of taxes needed for their financing (see figure below, point A).

Better public sector governance would affect both determinants of government size. The marginal benefit of a given level of public expenditures would increase, because better program design and resource management would improve outcomes, for example, in health care or education. At the same time, the marginal cost of a given level of taxes would decrease, because better tax administration and tax design could help raise revenues in less distorting ways. With better than average governance (as in high-income OECD countries), the optimal size of government—as measured by the size of public expenditures and taxes—could thus increase compared to the typical country (see figure below, point A*). A bigger size of government would not necessarily exert a negative impact on efficiency and growth.

(continued)

use of alternative indicators of governance: (a) the World Bank's Country Policy and Institutional Assessment (CPIA) ratings for public sector management and institutions, 1992–2004; and (b) an indicator of government effectiveness compiled by the World Bank.[12]

The analysis confirms that strong governance mitigates the negative impact of public sector size on growth. The ECA country sample was split into two broad country groups, one with relatively poor quality of public sector management (or weak government effectiveness) and another with relatively good quality of public sector management (or high government effectiveness). The results in annex 3A, table 3A.2, indicate that public sector size—above the indicative threshold of 35 percent of GDP—exerts a strong negative impact on growth in countries with weak government effectiveness. However, public sector size does not have a significant negative impact in countries with good government effectiveness. Results using the CPIA indicator (annex 3A, table 3A.3) consistently indicate a strong negative impact of "big government" in countries with relatively weak

BOX 3.3. CONTINUED

Suppose, however, that public expenditures and taxes were to rise in the typical country (with average quality of governance) up to the levels indicated by E* and T*. This would create a gap between a higher marginal cost of taxes (point C) and a lower marginal benefit of expenditures (point B). Misalignment of marginal cost and benefits would create an efficiency loss (or deadweight loss), measured by the familiar "Harberger triangle" ABC. The larger the efficiency loss, the more negative the impact of government size on growth. By contrast, efficiency losses would not be felt unless the size of government exceeded the optimal size. The association of large public expenditure with lower growth in countries with weak governance—but only beyond a certain threshold of expenditure—is corroborated by the empirical findings in this study.

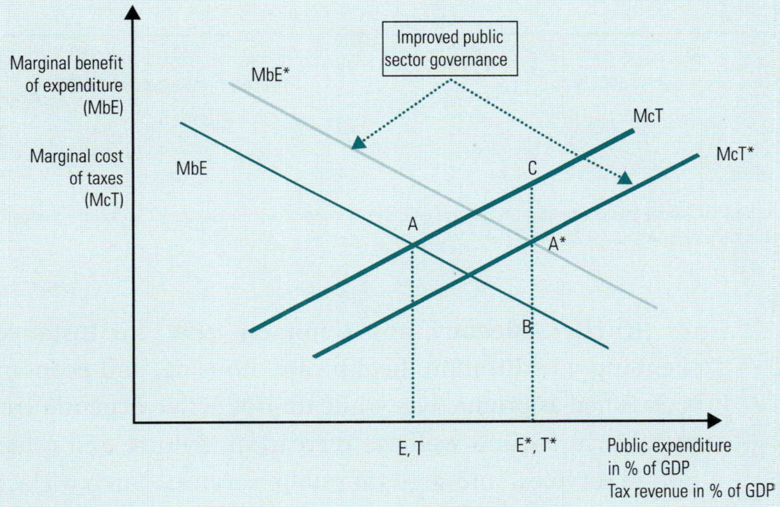

Source: Authors.

public management and institutions but do not reveal a consistent pattern for countries where public management is strong. The differential impact of the size of government in the two groups of countries is depicted in figures 3.6a and 3.6b.

The Composition of Expenditures and Structure of Taxes

For this study, the growth effects of "distorting" and "nondistorting" taxes and of "productive" and "unproductive" expenditures were analyzed, while accounting for the government's budget constraint. There is, indeed, empirical evidence that productive expenditures are conducive to growth, particularly when financed with nondistorting taxes (box 3.4). Departing only slightly from previous stud-

FIGURE 3.6

Economic Growth and the Size of Government by Relative Government Effectiveness in ECA Countries, 1992–2004

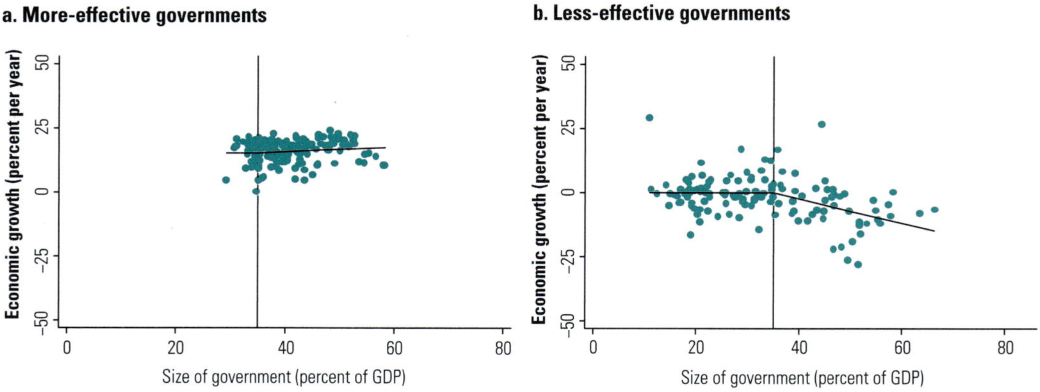

Source: World Bank staff calculations.

Note: The values on the y-axis represent economic growth after controlling for the effects of all independent variables other than the size of government (in percent of GDP). Based on regressions (4) and (7), table 3A.2, annex 3A.

ies (Kneller, Bleaney, and Gemmell 1999, for instance) public spending on education, health care, housing, and economic affairs is classified as productive, while unproductive expenditures include social security and welfare, recreation, culture and religion, economic services, and general public services. Such a classification should not be taken as a value judgment, because social transfers are usually part of a "social compact" to provide valued safety nets. However, if the design of these programs makes them fiscally unsustainable, or requires financing through high labor taxes that impede employment, their unwanted consequences for growth may offset their intended redistributive impacts. Distorting taxes include personal and corporate taxes, payroll taxes, social security contributions, and property taxes. Taxes on domestic goods and services are considered nondistorting. The analysis covers 20 ECA countries during the period 1995–2004, a relatively short estimation period because of limitations in the available data on general government expenditures by function.

The empirical results (annex 3B) once again confirm that a larger fiscal surplus promotes growth (table 3B.2, regressions 5–8). Moreover, a larger fiscal surplus (or a smaller deficit) appears to have a stronger impact on growth when achieved through a cut in unproductive expenditures, with the impact being slightly lower in the case

BOX 3.4

Public Expenditure Composition, Tax Structure, and Economic Growth: Empirical Analysis to Date

Since the blossoming of empirical growth literature in the late 1980s, several studies have examined the impact of key expenditure components on growth. Aschauer (1989) found that spending on core infrastructure (streets, highways, airports, mass transit, and so forth) had a positive impact on private sector productivity. Several other studies have found positive growth effects of public investment (Nourzad and Vrieze 1995; Sanchez-Robles 1998; Kamps 2004), with some evidence supporting the law of diminishing returns (De la Fuente 1997). Furthermore, several studies have presented evidence that public investment can be productive if it creates infrastructure that serves as input to private investment (Devarajan, Swaroop, and Zou 1996).

The literature strongly supports the growth-enhancing effect of expenditure on human capital if it is well-targeted (Guellec and van Pottelsberghe 1999; Diamond 1999; De la Fuente and Doménech 2000; Heitger 2001). Some studies, however, emphasize that public spending (in particular, on research and development) must complement rather than crowd out private spending (David, Hall, and Toole 2000). Consumption and social security spending have generally been found to have either no effect or a negative effect on growth (Aschauer 1989; Barro 1990, 1991; Grier and Tullock 1989), although some (Cashin 1995) found a positive growth impact from welfare spending. For other categories of public spending, the evidence is even less conclusive.

Regarding tax structure, using a panel of 23 OECD countries, Widmalm (2001) found that different taxes have different growth effects and that tax progressivity is bad for growth. The harmful effects of a progressive income tax structure were also noted by Padovano and Galli (2001, 2002), and Lee and Gordon (2005). The latter found that the marginal corporate tax rate is negatively correlated with economic growth in a cross-section of 70 countries during 1970–97, while other tax variables, including the average tax rate on labor income, are not significantly associated with economic growth. Kneller, Bleaney, and Gemmell (1999) found that an increase in productive expenditures enhances growth when financed by nondistorting taxation, provided the overall size of government remains relatively limited, while an increase in distorting taxes sig-

of financing through an increase in nondistorting taxes. Although differences are small, the impact is further reduced when the increase in the surplus is financed by an increase in distorting taxes or a cut in productive expenditures.

Large unproductive expenditures lead to lower growth, especially when financed with debt or higher taxes. The negative impact of unproductive expenditures on growth is robust across all empirical specifications (annex 3B, table 3B.2, regressions 4–5 and 7–8). This harmful effect is even larger when an increase in unproductive spending is debt-financed (that is, accompanied by an increase in the fiscal deficit) or financed by an increase in distorting taxes. Financing through nondistorting taxes appears to be almost equally harmful. Although estimated differences are again small, the least negative impact is seen when taxes (whether actual or future, if more debt is issued) are held constant, with higher unproductive spending thus financed through cuts in productive expenditure.[13]

Evidence regarding the impact of productive expenditures and the structure of taxes is mixed. The results indicate that productive expenditures always have a positive (though not always significant) impact on growth, in contrast to the harmful incidence of unproductive expenditures. It is, however, counterintuitive that the impact of larger productive spending is not significant when matched by lower unproductive spending (annex 3B, table 3B.2, regression 6). This may reflect the threshold effects of overall spending and the quality of governance discussed earlier. Distorting taxes exert a negative, but generally not significant, incidence on growth unless they finance an increase in unproductive spending, in which case their impact is significantly negative (table 3B.2, regression 6). Finally, the growth impact of nondistorting taxes does not appear to be significant.

The negative impact of unproductive expenditures on growth is particularly strong where governance is weak. This has been tested again by splitting the ECA country group into two subgroups according to the quality of governance, using the same indicators discussed in the previous section—the CPIA average rating on "public sector management and institutions" and the "government effectiveness" indicator. The empirical findings are detailed in annex 3B (table 3B.4) and summarized in table 3.4. Results indicate that unproductive expenditures are indeed harmful for growth when public sector management or government effectiveness (or both) is weak, but their impact is mitigated when government effectiveness is strong. Moreover, productive expenditures promote growth (when tax-financed) in countries where governance is good, but have no significant impact where governance is poor. In countries where government effectiveness is weak, identifying and cutting unproductive spending would make a strong contribution to growth and poverty reduction in the short run. This should indeed be as a short-term policy priority, because building capacity for better governance and institutions requires time and brings a development benefit only over the longer run.

TABLE 3.4

Summary of Empirical Findings on Growth Impact of Public Expenditure Composition and Tax Structure

	Good governance	Poor governance
"Unproductive" expenditures	No measurable impact	Negative impact
"Productive" expenditures	Positive impact	No measurable impact
"Distorting" taxes	Negative impact	No measurable impact
"Nondistorting" taxes	Positive impact	No measurable impact

Source: Based on annex 3B, tables 3B.1 and 3B.4

The structure of taxes appears to matter for growth only where governance is strong. When governance is relatively effective, the impact of big government is mitigated but the structure of financing matters. Distorting taxes have a significantly negative impact on growth, while nondistorting taxes seem to have a positive incidence—presumably because the effective use of revenues raised by these taxes outweighs their costs. In contrast, when governance is weak, what seems to matter is the overall size of government and the resulting total tax burden, rather than the structure of taxes. It is more likely that all types of taxes have high compliance costs that outweigh any benefits from less-distorting tax design.

Creating Fiscal Space

Fiscal space is the government's ability to increase expenditure or reduce taxes without impairing the sustainability of its financial position (see Heller 2005). This requires that the primary fiscal surplus be consistent with a stable public debt ratio over the long run (annex 3C). On the expenditure side, fiscal space can be created by (a) reallocating expenditures from low-value programs toward programs with a higher effect on growth or (b) improving the efficiency of public expenditures to get better value from particular programs. On the financing side, fiscal space can be created by (a) broadening the tax base, (b) increasing tax rates, or (c) mobilizing grant aid. Moreover, fiscal space can be created by accelerating the reduction of public debt—or using one-off revenues (such as privatization revenues) to pay back public debt—to reduce the primary fiscal surplus required for debt solvency. The analysis below focuses on the expenditure side of the budget.

Expenditure Allocations and Fiscal Space

The differences between the actual primary balance over 2002–05 in ECA countries and the primary fiscal balance required to stabilize the public debt ratio in the long run can be considered an approximate indicator of fiscal space. A positive difference indicates that fiscal space is potentially available for increased spending or for lower taxes, while a negative difference signals that fiscal space would need to be created before any decision to increase expenditures or reduce taxes. Illustrative estimations of the primary fiscal surplus needed to stabilize the debt ratio in the long run have been carried out for ECA countries based on the methodology outlined in annex 3C. At least three caveats apply: (a) more conservative assumptions regarding future financing conditions would imply much lower estimates of fiscal space; (b) mitigating surrounding risks (such as debt rollover risks due to short debt maturities or interest rate and exchange risks) would call in many countries for reducing the public debt ratio, thus further limiting fiscal space; (c) the threshold of public debt consistent with a low risk of insolvency depends on the quality of public debt and budget management institutions, which is uneven across countries. Weak institutions would call for a higher primary fiscal surplus (which would thus be equivalent to lower fiscal space) to achieve a reduction in public debt in proportion to GDP.

Despite ambitious fiscal consolidation, fiscal space appears to be still limited in many ECA countries. Four groups of countries can be identified:

- Countries where fiscal space seems to be available but public spending in growth-promoting sectors is below the group average
- Countries where fiscal space seems to be available but public spending in those growth-promoting sectors is above average for the whole group
- Countries where additional fiscal space needs to be created to ensure long-run solvency and public spending in growth-promoting areas is below the group average
- Countries where additional fiscal space needs to be created to ensure long-run solvency and public spending in these growth-promoting areas is relatively oversized

Estimates of fiscal space and the size of growth-promoting expenditures on public investment and social sectors are shown in figure 3.7

Policy priorities vary in each country group. Expenditure increases could be considered in countries where fiscal space is available and

FIGURE 3.7

Potentially Growth-Promoting Expenditure and Fiscal Space in ECA Countries

a. Capital expenditure

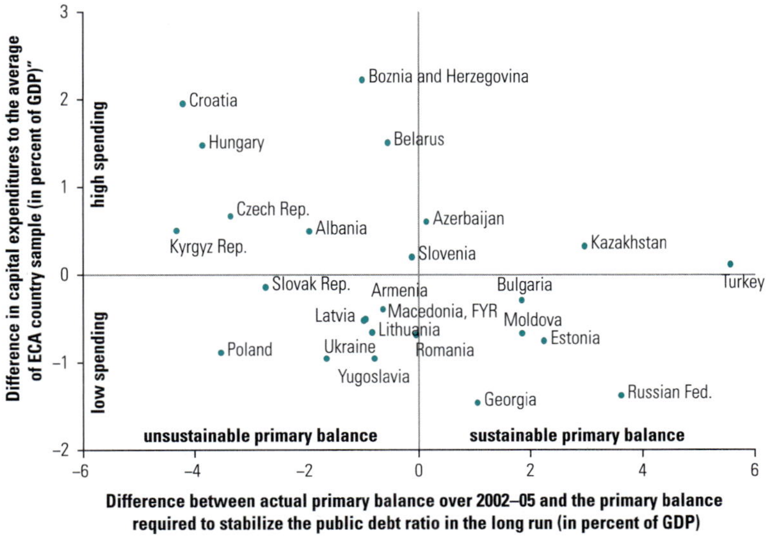

b. Expenditure oneducation and health care

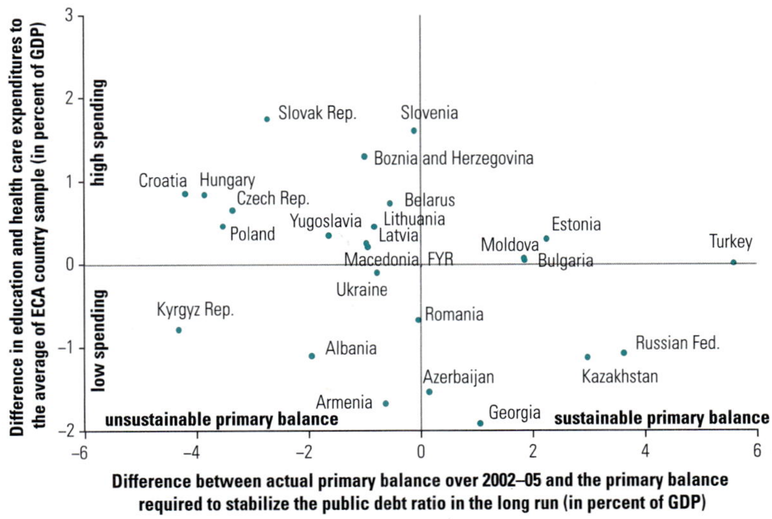

Sources: IMF, Eurostat, and ECA fiscal database.

Note: Averages for 2002–04. Differences in expenditures in proportion to GDP are normalized to the sample average.

expenditures in a specific category seem to be relatively low (the lower right quadrant in figure 3.7)—subject to the caveats mentioned above and to careful selection of projects. In countries where fiscal space is available but expenditures appear to be high (the upper right quadrant), it would seem more appropriate to try to improve efficiency than to increase spending. In countries where public spending is below average but fiscal space is lacking (the lower left quadrant), the emphasis should be on expenditure reallocations, because they represent the only viable means of increasing potentially growth-promoting spending without impairing solvency. Finally, in countries where fiscal space needs to be created but public expenditures are oversized relative to comparators (the upper left quadrant), mostly EU-8 and Southeastern Europe[14] countries, measures are needed to improve expenditure efficiency and reduce spending because expenditure increases would compromise debt sustainability.

Oversized core government functions and social security and welfare services are associated with relatively low levels of potentially growth-promoting expenditures. As documented earlier, large fiscal imbalances are the main reason for lack of fiscal space and are associated with high levels of public spending in proportion to GDP (figure 3.5). In turn, large public expenditures often reflect oversized core government functions and sizeable payments for social security and welfare. Expenditures for education and infrastructure—typically considered growth-promoting because they enhance the efficiency of production factors—appear to be on average lower in countries with large expenditures for core government functions, social security, and welfare (figure 3.8). In these countries, expenditures for education and capital spending are lower by about 1.5–2.5 percentage points of total general government expenditures—the equivalent of 0.7–1.1 percentage points of GDP for each expenditure category. Similarly, higher interest payments on public debt seem to crowd out spending on education and capital spending.

Thus, when fiscal space is lacking, a key goal should be to reduce potentially unproductive spending. As noted above, large unproductive expenditures come at the expense of potentially productive spending, especially in education and infrastructure. Changing the composition of expenditures for a given total amount of spending would thus improve prospects for long-term growth. In addition, as indicated by empirical evidence reviewed earlier, an improvement in the fiscal balance seems to be more beneficial for growth when financed by a curtailment in unproductive spending. Creating needed fiscal space for debt sustainability by reducing unproductive expenditures thus has a mutually reinforcing impact on growth.

FIGURE 3.8
"Productive" versus "Unproductive" Expenditure Allocations in ECA Countries, Average, 2002–04

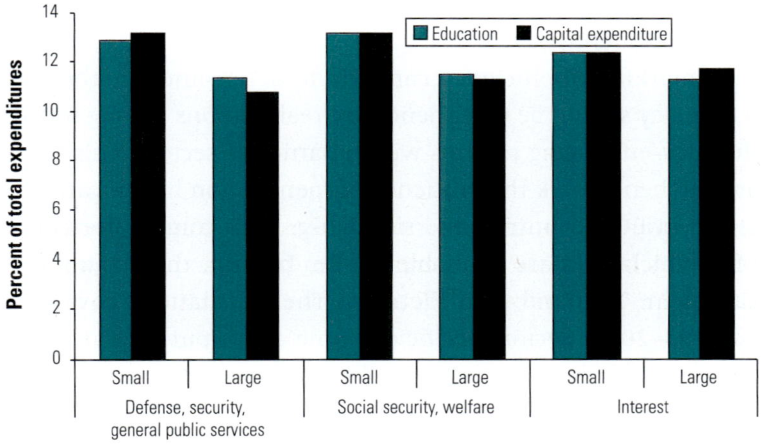

Source: ECA fiscal database.

Efficiency of Expenditures and Fiscal Space

Better expenditure efficiency also increases available fiscal space. Improved efficiency delivers better results out of a given amount of resources—or, equivalently, makes it possible to save on resources necessary to achieve policy goals. Indeed, ensuring expenditure efficiency in a sector should be a precondition for committing additional scarce public resources in that sector. Education, health care, and some infrastructure services are also provided in part through private financing. Efficiency in public service delivery is also important to complement private spending in these sectors.

Expenditure efficiency depends on both sector-specific and cross-cutting factors. Fundamentally, efficiency depends on sector-specific institutional arrangements, addressed in Part 2 of this study. For example, efficiency in health care depends on incentives for responsible use of pharmaceuticals and medical services, operational autonomy and accountability of hospitals, and incentives for cost containment created by provider payment systems. Expenditure efficiency may also depend on the composition of expenditures—for example, the amount of resources spent on preventive care or the share of expenditures on educational equipment such as computers and scientific instruments. However, as indicated by the empirical findings discussed above, expenditure efficiency may also depend on broader factors that affect the quality of public sector governance—such as the incentives (or disincentives) for results-oriented performance in the civil service, the control of corruption, and the quality of public procurement systems.

Benchmarking of efficiency can help to determine whether the focus of policy should be on expenditure reallocations among sectors or efficiency-enhancing reforms within particular sectors. This study attempts to benchmark the efficiency of spending on health care and education in ECA countries and six high-growth comparator countries for which data are available: Chile, Ireland, the Republic of Korea, Spain, Thailand, and Vietnam. The calculations cover the period 1995–2004. Sector-specific outcome and input indicators are summarized in table 3.5, and overall performance has been calculated as the average value of the outcome indicators for each sector.[15]

Sector outcomes depend both on the quantity of inputs used, as measured by expenditure per student in education and expenditure per capita in health care, and on the efficiency of such spending. All else equal, higher levels of spending would be expected to improve outcomes through, for example, more advanced equipment or better training of personnel (or both). Indeed, a positive relationship exists between performance in a sector (as measured by the combined outcome indicator) and the level of public spending (figures 3.9 and 3.10).[16] But expenditure efficiency also matters, as measured by the difference between actual performance and the average level predicted by the level of public spending in the sector.

Four groups of countries can be identified with regard to relative expenditure efficiency:

- Low-spending countries with above-average performance based on their level of expenditure (that is, those above the regression line)

TABLE 3.5

Performance and Input Indicators for Expenditures in Health Care and Education

Outcomes	Health care	Education
	• Life expectancy at birth (years)	• Imputed learning scores calculated by Crouch and Fasih (2004)
	• Infant survival rate (per 1,000 births) • Maternal survival rate (per 100,000 births)	• Youth employment rate (% of total labor force ages 15–24 years) • School life expectancy (years), total
	• Immunization, average measles and DPT (% of children ages 12–23 months)	• School enrollment, tertiary (% gross) • Literacy rate, youth female (% of females ages 15–24)
Inputs	• Health expenditure, public (US$ per capita, PPP, constant prices from 2000)	• Public spending on education (US$ per capita, PPP, constant prices from 2000), adjusted by share of school-age population

Source: World Bank staff.

Note: DPT = Diptththeria, pertusis, tetanus vaccine. PPP = Purchasing power parity.

FIGURE 3.9

Health Care Performance Compared with Public Spending Per Capita, Average, 1995–2004

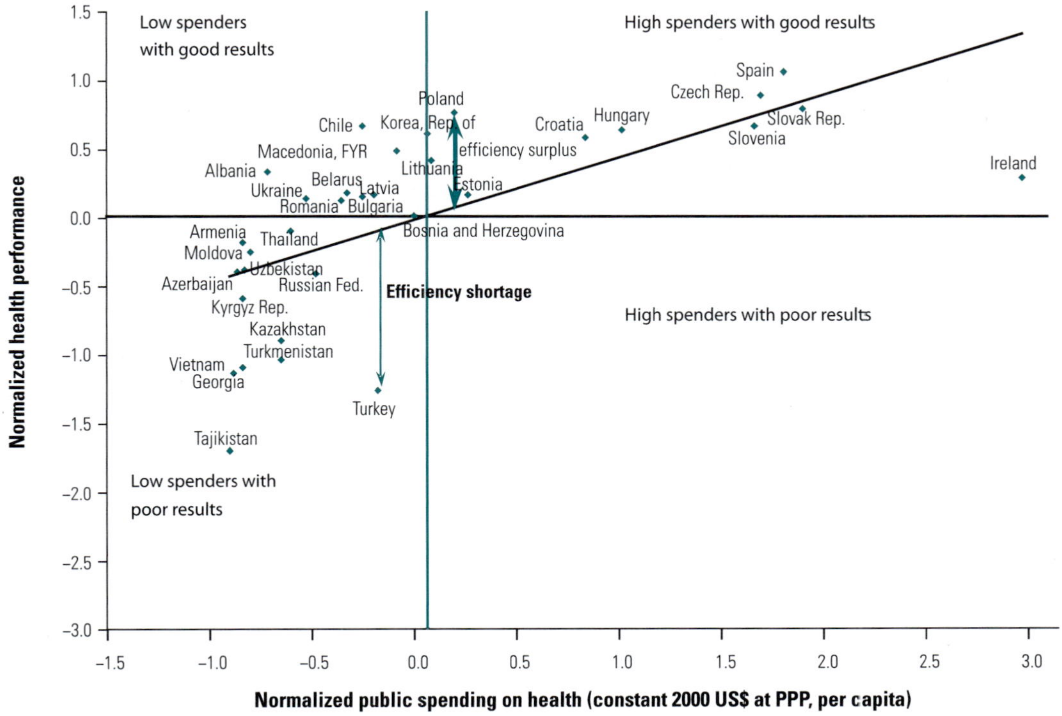

Source: World Bank staff.

- High-spending countries with above-average performance based on their level of expenditure (mostly higher-income countries)
- Low-spending countries with performance below the predicted average (below the regression line)
- High-spending countries with performance below the predicted average

The calculations support the finding that better public sector governance contributes to improved expenditure efficiency in health care and education. The quality of public sector governance was measured by the CPIA indicator of the quality of public sector management—one key indicator used in the econometric estimations in the previous section.[17] Efficiency gaps (as measured by the difference between actual and predicted performance) in both health and education are positively correlated with the quality of governance in ECA countries (figure 3.11).

FIGURE 3.10

Education Performance Compared with Public Spending Per Capita of School-Age Population, Average, 1995–2004

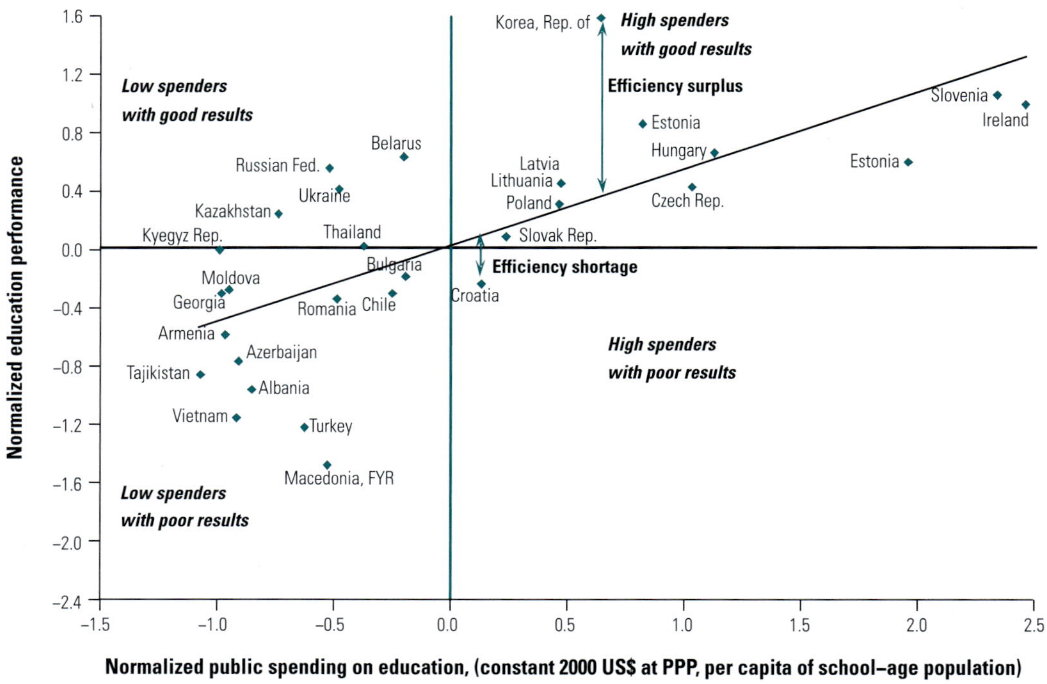

Source: World Bank staff.

Policy priorities depend on a country's relative efficiency position. In low-spending countries that achieve relatively poor results in a specific sector, improving efficiency should be a precondition to increased spending in that sector. Improving efficiency is even more critical in high-spending countries where results are relatively poor, because higher spending is even less of an option. In contrast, low-spending countries with relatively good performance in a sector may be able to improve outcomes still further through expenditure reallocations that increase the amount of resources spent in that sector, as long as the additional resources are also spent productively. In all countries, broadly based improvements in public sector governance can reinforce the positive impacts of sector expenditure reforms.

FIGURE 3.11

Efficiency Gaps in Health Care and Education and the Quality of Governance

a. Health care

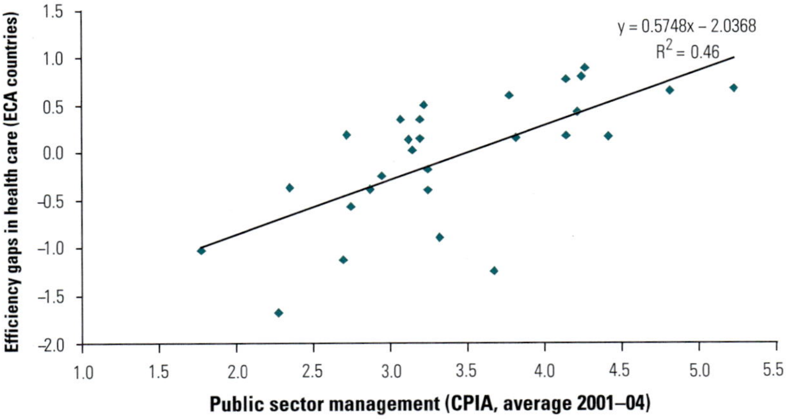

b. Education

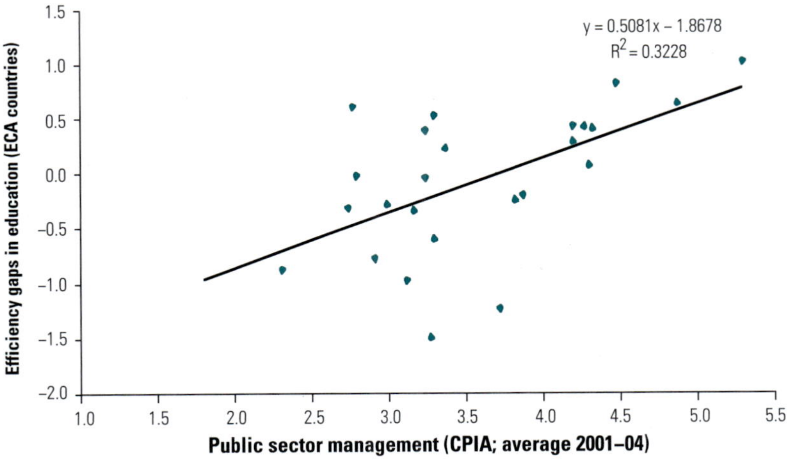

Source: World Bank staff.

Note: The sample includes only ECA countries using the efficiency gaps portrayed in figures 3.9 and 3.10.

Conclusions

What types of adjustments have been successful? A majority of fiscal adjustments in ECA have been successful—that is, they have been sustained over a sufficient period to restore fiscal balances to levels consistent with solvency and reduction in the public debt ratio. Most successful deficit reductions were driven by expenditure cuts across a vast array of economic categories. In the aftermath of fiscal consolidations, growth has been higher when the fiscal effort has been successful than when adjustments have failed.

Does the fiscal deficit matter for growth? A sound fiscal position appears to be a key prerequisite for higher growth in ECA. Lower fiscal imbalances are associated with greater macroeconomic stability, less business uncertainty, and a stronger investment climate.

Does the size of government matter for growth? The size of government affects economic growth in a nonlinear manner, with the impact also depending on the quality of governance. At expenditure levels of roughly 35 percent of GDP or higher, public spending negatively affects growth, while at levels below that threshold government size has no robust measurable effect on growth. The quality of governance mitigates the negative impact of public sector size on growth—public sector size strongly impairs growth in countries with weak government effectiveness, but there is no significant evidence of a negative impact when government is effective.

Does growth depend on the composition of expenditures and the structure of taxes? Large "unproductive" spending leads to lower growth when government effectiveness is weak, but its impact is insignificant when governance is relatively strong. Productive spending promotes growth in countries where governance is good, but has no significant impact where governance is poor. When governance is effective, the structure of financing also matters for growth. Distorting taxes have a significantly negative impact on growth but nondistorting taxes seem to have a positive affect, presumably because the effective use of revenues outweighs their costs. In contrast, what seems to matter when governance is weak is the overall size of government, which determines the total tax burden, rather than the structure of taxes.

Are productive expenditures constrained by unproductive spending? Lack of fiscal space for productive spending is often associated with large government size, which in turn reflects oversized core government functions (general public services, defense, and security), transfer payments for social security and welfare services, and interest payments on public debt. Potentially growth-promoting expenditures, especially for education and public investment, are thus crowded out.

What trade-offs exist between levels of spending and expenditure efficiency? Improving expenditure efficiency can provide benefits at very low cost. The efficiency of public spending varies considerably across ECA countries, as discussed further in chapters 4–7. Before considering increases in spending, countries with serious efficiency gaps should focus on institutional reforms to strengthen the impact of public spending.

Annex 3A Determinants of Growth in Transition Economies, 1992–2004; Econometric Evidence

Baseline Empirical Model

The regression model draws on Fischer and Sahay (2000). The baseline specification is of the following general form:

$$Gr_{i,t} = \beta_0 + \beta_1 WD_{i,t} + \beta_2 INF_{i,t} + \beta_3 FIS_{i,t} + \beta_6 IRP_{i,t}$$

where $Gr_{i,t}$ is the real GDP per capita growth rate; $WD_{i,t}$ is a war dummy or an index of armed conflict; $INF_{i,t}$ is the natural log of inflation; $FIS_{i,t}$ is the fiscal balance in percent of GDP, with positive values denoting fiscal surpluses; and IRPit is the overall index of reform progress, which is the unweighted sum of the European Bank for Reconstruction and Development indexes of small-scale privatization and price liberalization, with higher values indicating greater progress in structural reform; and *i* and *t* are country and year indexes, respectively. Ordinary least squares (OLS) is used to estimate equation (1). To test the robustness of the baseline results and account for cross-country heterogeneity, we also utilize other econometric methods, such as fixed effects and random effects estimators. Estimation results are provided in tables 3A.1, 3A.2, and 3A.3.

TABLE 3A.1

Determinants of Economic Growth, 1992–2004

Variable	OLS (1)	Fixed effects (2)	Random effects (3)
War dummy	-5.70*	-5.86***	-5.83***
	(1.90)	(3.15)	(3.30)
Ln(inflation) (IMF)	-2.09***	-1.73***	-1.91***
	(7.32)	(4.92)	(6.44)
Fiscal balance (% of GDP)	0.61***	0.74***	0.70***
	(5.78)	(8.37)	(8.56)
Overall index of reform	-0.10	0.01	-0.07
	(0.91)	(0.05)	(0.58)
Constant	13.76***	10.55**	12.96***
	(3.76)	(2.11)	(3.53)
Observations	295	295	295
R-squared	0.53	0.57	
Number of countries		25	25

Source: World Bank staff calculations.

Note: OLS = Ordinary least squares. *Significant at 10 percent level. ** Significant at 5 percent level. *** Significant at 1 percent level. Robust t-statistics in parentheses.

TABLE 3A.2

Economic Growth and the Size of Government By Government Effectiveness, 1992–2004 WB Governance Indicator for Government Effectiveness

	All Countries			Relatively more effective government			Relatively less effective government		
Variables	OLS (1)	Fixed effects (2)	Random effects (3)	OLS (4)	Fixed effects (5)	Random effects (6)	OLS (7)	Fixed effects (8)	Random effects (9)
War dummy	-5.45*	-5.92***	-5.67***	-3.16	-1.69	-2.66*	-5.74	-4.7	-5.34*
	(1.86)	(3.18)	(3.27)	(1.55)	(0.89)	(1.66)	(1.25)	(1.48)	(1.81)
Ln(inflation) (IMF)	-1.91***	-1.83***	-1.85***	-0.88***	-1.06***	-1.00***	-2.97***	-2.38***	-2.72***
	(5.95)	(5.32)	(6.30)	(3.37)	(3.89)	(4.18)	(4.80)	(3.43)	(4.48)
Fiscal balance (% of GDP)	0.51***	0.38***	0.49***	0.71***	0.73***	0.70***	0.47***	0.32	0.44***
	(4.75)	(3.24)	(5.22)	(7.20)	(6.31)	(7.01)	(3.38)	(1.64)	(2.83)
Overall index of reform	-0.01	-0.11	-0.05	0.34***	0.36***	0.34***	-0.59*	-0.52	-0.62**
	(0.08)	(0.68)	(0.40)	(3.94)	(2.90)	(3.49)	(1.66)	(1.41)	(1.99)
Expenditure (percent of GDP) (<35%)	-0.14	-0.25	-0.17*	-0.08	-0.11	-0.12	0.00	-0.2	-0.08
	(1.26)	(1.65)	(1.67)	(0.15)	(0.27)	(0.29)	(0.00)	(0.85)	(0.45)
Expenditure (percent of GDP) (≥35%)	-0.13*	-0.41***	-0.26***	0.13**	0.19*	0.14*	-0.48***	-0.67***	-0.55***
	(1.68)	(3.85)	(2.87)	(2.16)	(1.74)	(1.84)	(2.87)	(3.60)	(3.36)
Dummy (expenditure) ≥≥35%	-0.52	0.12	0.09	-1.18	-0.62	-0.81	0.08	-0.93	-0.45
	(0.43)	(0.09)	(0.08)	(0.88)	(0.60)	(0.82)	(0.03)	(0.30)	(0.15)
Constant	16.10***	22.29***	18.14***	0.8	0.96	2.13	28.71***	31.18***	31.43***
	(3.42)	(3.34)	(4.41)	(0.04)	(0.07)	(0.16)	(2.66)	(2.71)	(3.41)
Observations	295	295	295	160	160	160	135	135	135
R-squared	0.56	0.6		0.61	0.61		0.6	0.63	
Number of countries		25	25		13	13		12	12

Source: World Bank staff calculations.

Note: * Significant at 10 percent level. ** Significant at 5 percent level. *** Significant at 1 percent level.

TABLE 3A.3

Economic Growth and the Size of Government by Government Effectiveness CPIA Indicator for Public Sector Management

	All Countries			Relatively more effective government			Relatively less effective government		
	OLS	Fixed effects	Random effects	OLS	Fixed effects	Random effects	OLS	Fixed effects	Random effects
Variables	(1)	(2)	(3)	(4)	(5)	(6)	(7)	(8)	(9)
War dummy	-5.45*	-5.92***	-5.67***	4.00	4.79*	4.22*	-11.55***	-9.74***	-10.85***
	(1.86)	(3.18)	(3.27)	(1.06)	(1.93)	(1.89)	(4.15)	(3.81)	(4.49)
Ln(inflation) (IMF)	-1.91***	-1.83***	-1.85***	-1.16***	-0.80*	-1.11***	-2.51***	-2.01***	-2.36***
	(5.95)	(5.32)	(6.30)	(3.54)	(1.93)	(3.01)	(5.42)	(3.79)	(5.26)
Fiscal balance (% of GDP)	0.51***	0.38***	0.49***	0.42**	0.72***	0.50***	0.44***	0.15	0.37***
	(4.75)	(3.24)	(5.22)	(2.41)	(4.68)	(3.67)	(3.90)	(0.94)	(2.91)
Overall index of reform	-0.01	-0.11	-0.05	0.18	0.41**	0.17	-0.38	-0.2	-0.33
	(0.08)	(0.68)	(0.40)	(1.22)	(2.18)	(1.14)	(1.56)	(0.75)	(1.47)
Expenditure (percentof GDP) (< 35%)	-0.14	-0.25	-0.17*	-0.51***	-0.02	-0.47***	0.13	-0.24	-0.01
	(1.26)	(1.65)	(1.67)	(2.80)	(0.09)	(3.84)	(1.17)	(1.22)	(0.08)
Expenditure (percent of GDP) (?3 5%)	-0.13*	-0.41***	-0.26***	0.03	0.38**	0.13	-0.30**	-0.57***	-0.38***
	(1.68)	(3.85)	(2.87)	(0.39)	(2.27)	(1.04)	(2.21)	(3.89)	(3.07)
Dummy (expenditur e ? 35%)	-0.52	0.12	0.09	1.92	1.15	1.65	-2.49	-2.23	-2.09
	(0.43)	(0.09)	(0.08)	(1.07)	(0.75)	(1.15)	(1.50)	(1.15)	(1.12)
Constant	16.10***	22.29***	18.14***	17.90**	-5.55	16.83***	19.00***	24.41***	21.58***
	(3.42)	(3.34)	(4.41)	(2.13)	(0.61)	(3.54)	(3.19)	(2.64)	(3.05)
Observations	295	295	295	152	152	152	143	143	143
R-squared	0.56	0.6		0.39	0.4		0.68	0.72	
Number of countries		25	25		13	13		12	12

Source: World Bank staff calculations.

Note: CPIA = Country Policy and Institutional Assessment. * Significant at 10 percent level. ** Significant at 5 percent level. *** Significant at 1 percent level.

Annex 3B Composition of Public Expenditures, Structure of Taxes, and Growth in ECA Countries, 1995–2004: Econometric Evidence

Empirical Model and Data

Taxes are classified as distorting and nondistorting and expenditures are classified as productive and unproductive as shown in table 3B.1.

The empirical model draws on the specification used in Barro and Sala-i-Martin (1992) and Barro (1997) and is similar to the specification proposed by Bleaney, Gemmell, and Kneller (2001) and Kneller, Bleaney, and Gemmell (1999). The following growth equation is estimated:

$$g_{it} = \alpha + \sum_{i=1}^{k} \beta_i I_{it} + \sum_{i=1}^{m} \gamma_i M_{it} + \sum_{i=1}^{n} \theta_i Z_{it} + \varepsilon_{it}$$

where g_{it} is per capita real GDP growth in country *i* at time *t*, and I_{it} is a vector of variables often included in growth regressions surveyed by Levine and Renelt (1992): the initial level of income and the investment ratio. M_{it} is a vector of fiscal variables that includes revenues *(rev)*, expenditures *(exp)*, and budget surplus *(surplus)*, that is, $M = [rev, exp, surplus]$. Furthermore, the model accounts for the government's budget constraint, thus .

TABLE 3B.1

Classification of Taxes and Expenditures

Classification for estimation purposes	Functional classifications
Distorting taxes	Taxation on income and profit (personal income tax, corporate income tax)
	Social security contributions
	Taxation on payroll and manpower
	Taxation on property
Nondistorting taxes	Taxation on domestic goods and services
Other revenues	Taxation on international trade
	Nontax revenues
	Other tax revenues
Productive expenditures	Educational expenditure
	Health expenditure
	Housing expenditure
	Economic affairs (includes transport)
Unproductive expenditures	Social security and welfare expenditure
	Expenditure on recreation, culture, and religion
	Expenditure on economic services
	General public services expenditure
Other expenditures	Other expenditure (unclassified)
	Defense expenditure
	Public order and safety

Source: World Bank staff.

$$\sum_{i=1}^{m} \gamma_i M_{it} = 0$$

Given that the sum of revenues, expenditures, and the budget balance equals zero, one element must be omitted in the estimation to exclude perfect collinearity. The variable omitted is assumed to be an implicit financing element. Finally, Z_{it} is a vector of variables identified by past studies as potentially important explanatory variables of growth (for example, proxies for country openness to international trade, institutional variables, or inflation). A transition dummy (for negative GDP growth periods caused by transition) is also included. The panel regression is estimated with the Prais-Winsten method. Estimation results are in table 3B.2.

TABLE 3B.2

Public Expenditure Composition, Taxation Structure, and GDP Growth, 1995–2004
Dependent variable: Growth of GDP per Capita Estimation Technique: Linear Regression, Heteroskedastic Panels Corrected Standard Errors

Omitted fiscal variable	Surplus (1)	Spending (2)	Revenue (3)	Surplus (4)	Non-distortionary taxation (5)	Non-productive spending (6)	distortionary taxation (7)	Productive spending (8)
Explanatory variable - eq (1)								
Initial level of income	0	-0.000***	-0.001***	0	0	0	-0.000**	0
	-1.59	-3.03	-5.67	-0.8	-0.62	-0.61	-2.31	-0.28
Investment ratio	0.059*	0.038	0.032	0.054**	0.034	0.036	0.031	0.039*
	-1.84	-1.47	-1.13	-2.05	-1.24	-1.41	-1.14	-1.76
Population growth	-0.1	-0.021	0.037	-0.083	-0.031	-0.031	-0.01	-0.039
	-1	-0.23	-0.28	-0.87	-0.36	-0.33	-0.11	-0.5
Recession dummy	-11.606***	-9.244***	-8.684***	-10.864***	-8.980***	-8.960***	-8.962***	-9.101***
	-11.57	-6.39	-6.25	-7.1	-4.69	-6.21	-4.78	-4.84
Revenue	-0.136**	-0.101***						
	-2.35	-4.49						
Expenditure	0.052		0					
	-0.71		-0.01					
Fiscal surplus		0.463***	0.435***		0.437***	0.484***	0.407***	0.406***
		-5.85	-6.5		-5.14	-6.22	-5.26	-4.97
Distorting taxes				-0.016	-0.101*	-0.180***		-0.105*
				-0.37	-1.95	-3.11		-1.8
Productive expenditure				0.047	0.150**	0.031	0.144**	
				-0.85	-2.28	-0.51	-2.22	
Non-distorting taxes				0.055		-0.054	-0.026	0.059
				-1.17		-1.02	-0.58	-1.2
Unproductive expenditure				-0.339***	-0.284***		-0.310***	-0.229***
				-8.22	-7.43		-8.89	-7.37
Observations	181	171	171	181	171	171	171	171
Number of cty_id	21	20	20	21	20	20	20	20

Source: World Bank staff calculations.
Note: * Significant at 10 percent level. ** Significant at 5 percent level. *** Significant at 1 percent level.

Robustness tests have been conducted through extreme bound analyses (EBA) as proposed by Levine and Renelt (1992), following the methodology elaborated by Leamer (1985). Generally, the findings in table 3B.2 are robust to the inclusion of additional variables that have been linked to growth in the literature (openness, progress in privatization, and inflation). However, among the fiscal variables only the budget surplus and unproductive spending have a robust impact on growth in *all* specifications, as required by the stringent EBA criterion. Increase in government unproductive spending financed by increase in distorting taxes or deficit seems to have a most harmful growth effect. Moreover, the expenditure-financed reduction in the government deficit has a larger effect than the tax-financed reduction. EBA results are summarized in table 3B.3.

Results based on country groups, depending on the quality of governance, are shown in table 3B.4.

The findings should be interpreted with caution, given a number of problems that are commonly encountered in this type of cross-section regression. The most important of these may be a potentially severe simultaneity problem, arising from business cycle effects and Wagner's law (the tendency for government expenditure to be higher at higher levels of per capita GDP). There may also be concerns about

TABLE 3B.3

Robustness Test for the ECA Country Sample with Three Conditioning Variables

Financed by: Coefficient	Distortionary	Nondistortionary	Productive spending	Unproductive spending	Surplus
Distortionary					
EBA lower bound	n.a.	-.013	-0.19	-0.26	-0.07
EBA higher bound	n.a.	-.07	-0.10	-0.18	-0.01
Robust		No	No	Yes*	No
Productive spending					
EBA lower bound	0.18	0.09	n.a.	-0.09	-0.08
EBA higher bound	0.57	0.19	n.a.	0.04	0.06
Robust	No	No		No	No
Unproductive spending					
EBA lower bound	-0.35	-0.31	-0.27	n.a.	-0.37
EBA higher bound	-0.31	-0.23	-0.22	n.a.	-0.31
Robust	Yes	Yes*	Yes		Yes
Surplus					
EBA lower bound	0.40	0.43	0.41	0.48	n.a.
EBA higher bound	0.48	0.51	0.52	0.57	n.a.
Robust	Yes	Yes	Yes	Yes	

Source: World Bank staff calculations.

Notes: Results significant at the 5% level, three conditioning variables

* At the 10% level, three conditioning variables, model specification as in Table A2.5.

TABLE 3B.4

Expenditure Composition, Tax Structure, and Growth in ECA, 1995–2004 Estimations by Government Effectiveness (WB Governance Indicator for Government Effectiveness)

	High government effectiveness					Less government effectiveness				
Variables	(1)	(2)	(3)	(4)	(5)	(6)	(7)	(8)	(9)	(10)
Initial level of	0.000*	0	0	-0.000*	0	-0.001*	-0.001***	-0.000**	-0.001***	-0.001***
income	-1.73	-1.07	-0.42	-1.75	-0.3	-1.84	-2.75	-1.97	-2.68	-2.89
Investment	0.025	0.077	0.122	-0.079	0.186***	0.082**	0.077***	0.063**	0.075**	0.077***
ratio	-0.32	-0.92	-1.55	-0.65	-2.71	-2.49	-2.72	-2.38	-2.43	-2.85
Population	-0.275	-0.205	-0.088	-0.207	-0.129	-0.043	-0.025	-0.024	-0.046	-0.031
growth	-0.79	-0.72	-0.35	-0.54	-0.45	-0.57	-0.3	-0.24	-0.75	-0.4
Recession	0	0	0	0	0	3.034	4.304	6.168**	4.388	4.202
dummy	(.)	(.)	(.)	(.)	(.)	-0.6	-1.09	-2.46	-1.05	-0.99
Productive	0.106*	0.167***	0.113	0.229**		-0.169	0.023	-0.200***	-0.037	
expenditure	-1.79	-2.83	-1.32	-2.57		-1.29	-0.24	-3.12	-0.29	
Unproductive	-0.14	0.065		-0.192*	0.085	-0.346***	-0.318***		-0.356***	-0.369***
expenditure	-1.23	-0.8		-1.8	-0.85	-2.79	-3.78		-3.73	-3.93
Distorting taxes	-0.431***	-0.464***	-0.566***		-0.608***	0.161	0.105	0.037		0.053
	-3.86	-4.45	-4.94		-4.91	-1.33	-1.27	-0.28		-0.46
Nondistorting	0.165***		0.181***	-0.077	0.214***	0.156		-0.032	0.172	0.13
taxes	-3.25		-3.06	-1.21	-4.63	-0.8	-0.24	-1.17	-0.87	
Fiscal surplus		0.743***	0.752***	0.610***	0.765***		0.283**	0.264***	0.295***	0.292**
		-6.22	-7.12	-3.82	-6.81		-2.48	-2.59	-2.7	-2.51
Observations	92	82	82	82	82	89	89	89	89	89
Number of cty_id	10	9	9	9	9	11	11	11	11	11

Source: World Bank staff calculations.

Note: CPIA = Country Policy and Institutional Assessment. * Significant at 10 percent level. ** Significant at 5 percent level. *** Significant at 1 percent level.

data quality and measurement errors. While the possible simultaneity effect is an argument in favor of panel regressions with shorter time spans (as used in this exercise), it at the same time limits the room for including potentially important lags of the explanatory variables. Additional regressions (not reported here but available upon request) tried to tackle the potential endogeneity problem in three ways. First, regressions were run with (moving) five-year averages of the data, which eliminates some of the short-run cyclical simultaneity between growth and fiscal performance. Second, the empirical model was respecified so that fiscal factors affect growth with a lag. Finally, a dynamic panel model was estimated using the Arellano and Bond (1991) Generalized Method of Moments (GMM) technique, which uses lags of the endogenous variables as instruments. The alternative specification does not change the point estimates radically, although there is a marked reduction in the statistical significance and precision of the estimates given the small and unbalanced nature of the panel.

Annex 3C Calculating a Sustainable Primary Fiscal Balance in ECA Countries—A Note on Methodology

A sustainable primary fiscal balance can be defined as the primary balance that stabilizes public debt in proportion to GDP. This can be computed starting from the general government budget constraint:

$$\Delta\left(\frac{D}{Y}\right)=\frac{D_t}{Y_t}-\frac{D_{t-1}}{Y_{t-1}}=\frac{D_t}{Y_t}-\frac{D_{t-1}\left(1+\frac{\Delta Y}{Y_{t-1}}\right)}{Y_{t-1}\left(1+\frac{\Delta Y}{Y_{t-1}}\right)}=\frac{D_t-D_{t-1}-D_{t-1}\frac{\Delta Y}{Y_{t-1}}}{Y_t}=\frac{\Delta D-D_{t-1}g}{Y_t}$$

where b is primary balance, i is nominal interest rate on public debt, D is public debt, and t denotes time.

Expressing a change in public debt to GDP ratio as a function of GDP growth rate and imposing a constant public debt ratio condition:

$$\frac{\Delta D-D_{t-1}g}{Y_t}=\frac{-b_t+iD_{t-1}-D_{t-1}g}{Y_t}=\frac{-b_t+(i-g)D_{t-1}}{Y_t}=\frac{-b_t}{Y_t}+\frac{(i-g)D_{t-1}}{Y_{t-1}(1+g)}=0\Leftrightarrow\frac{b}{Y}=\left(\frac{i-g}{1+g}\right)\frac{D}{Y}$$

where Y is nominal GDP and g is its growth rate.

This condition implies that as long as the interest rate exceeds economic growth, governments have to run a primary surplus to rein in public debt growth relative to output. A primary deficit can be sustained only if the interest rate is permanently lower than the rate of economic growth, which is unlikely for several reasons.

First, economic agents have to be remunerated for deferring consumption; if "spenders" could consume more than "savers" both in the current period and in the future, no one would want to save. In such a situation, the resulting shortage of savings would result in an increase in the interest rate sufficient to create adequate incentives for deferring consumption over time. Second, excessive borrowing and investment at low interest rates would eventually lower the growth rate, given the decreasing marginal productivity of capital and possible efficiency bottlenecks in the use of inputs.

Theoretically, a government with high credibility could run a primary deficit permanently and not go bankrupt, if such a government could borrow at a lower interest rate than output growth. This would require economic agents to be excessively risk averse (with a strong preference for low but stable returns on government debt) and returns on public debt to be much less uncertain than economic growth. However, even in these circumstances, taking excessive advantage of the opportunity to run a primary deficit and roll over public debt might push a government into a situation where a growth slowdown would force higher taxes on a generation already hit by slower growth (Ball, Elmendorf, and Mankiw 1995).

Estimations of the fiscal primary surplus needed to stabilize the debt ratio in the long run are based on the assumption that the difference between real interest rates and economic growth in ECA countries in the long run will be similar to the average observed in the member countries of the euro area over the last two decades. Obviously this is a favorable assumption, given that country risk in ECA is in general higher, as reflected in risk premiums on interest rates for foreign currency–denominated sovereign bonds. Moreover, in some countries, poorly managed contingent liabilities of the public sector may periodically add to public debt.

Notes

1. Extensive evidence indicates that high taxes on labor use negatively affect labor market outcomes in OECD countries. Evidence is more limited in ECA countries, but tends to confirm findings from OECD countries (see World Bank 2005b, and chapter 9 in this report).
2. Thus, according to the criterion used here, whether an adjustment is successful will not depend on its eventual impact on the long-term growth potential of the economy but only on its contribution to fiscal solvency. It is conceivable that, although successful fiscal consolidations may ensure fiscal solvency in the short term, they may impede long-term growth if the brunt of adjustment falls onto public investment programs or calls for education and health expenditure compression. The impact of the composition of public expenditures on growth is examined as a separate question later in this chapter.
3. This definition implies that the improvement in the primary balance is sustained once the adjustment episode has ended because the primary balance does not drop below the level that qualified it as an adjustment (see Purfield 2003). An alternative, much more demanding, definition of successful adjustment, more suitable to the study of fiscal adjustments in developed countries, has been proposed by Alesina and Perotti (1997).
4. The low number of unsuccessful adjustments in ECA and their heterogeneity with respect to composition make it difficult to estimate a logit model of sufficient quality to explain in a more quantitative way what factors made adjustments successful or unsuccessful. Moreover, the

calculation of the contribution of changes in revenue should be adjusted for changes in hydrocarbon revenue to correct for swings in energy prices. Unfortunately, disentangling oil and non-oil revenues is not always possible using Government Finance Statistics international fiscal data.

5. The Czech Republic, Estonia, Hungary, Latvia, Lithuania, Poland, the Slovak Republic, and Slovenia.
6. The Heritage Foundation's index of fiscal burden takes into account the top marginal income tax rate, top marginal corporate tax rate, and a change in government expenditure as a percentage of GDP.
7. A parsimonious empirical model has been used (Fischer and Sahay 2000) where growth is modeled as a function of stabilization, structural reform, and exogenous shocks related to conflict. Specification details and estimation results are provided in annex 3A. The sample consists of an annual panel for 24 ECA countries over the period 1992–2004. Macroeconomic stabilization is measured by the annual inflation rate and the fiscal balance as a percentage of GDP. An indicator is also used to account for disruptions caused by armed conflict. Structural reform is measured by the overall index of reform progress elaborated by the European Bank for Reconstruction and Development. This measure follows Sachs (1996).
8. It should be noted that the findings are robust to changes in the specification of the empirical model. They hold true in a more standard specification using the Barro and Sala-i-Martin empirical growth regressions, as further analyzed below and in annex 3B.
9. However, the economies in these high-deficit countries did not generally experience a cyclical slowdown in the early 2000s (except for Poland), which would be expected if automatic fiscal stabilizers were functioning.
10. The method proposed by Hansen (1999, 2000) for testing the existence of threshold effects in the relationship between growth and total expenditure provides similar results.
11. The baseline results on the nonlinear relationship between size of government and growth, and how governance affects this relationship, are robust to the use of data from 1995–2004. The use of this shorter, more recent period effectively excludes the early transition period characterized by very large governments and a deep economic recession in the region. These additional results are available in Pushak, Tiongson, and Varoudakis (2007). The findings are also valid regardless of whether the regression model also controls for the impact of the fiscal balance. Results excluding the fiscal balance are not reported in annex 3A.
12. This indicator measures "the competence of the bureaucracy and the quality of public service delivery." See Kaufmann, Kraay, and Mastruzzi (2006).
13. By reallocating spending, the negative impact of higher unproductive spending in such a case is not exacerbated by a larger overall size of government, which—according to the results presented in the previous section—is detrimental to long-run growth, especially when governance is weak. It should be noted that the negative growth impacts of unproduc-

tive spending and larger fiscal deficits are robust after accounting for specification bias due to the possible omission of other pertinent determinants of growth from the empirical model. This has been confirmed through "Extreme Bound Analysis" (EBA), the results of which are reported in annex 3B, table 3B.3. By contrast, the impact of distorting and nondistorting taxes, as well as of productive expenditures, was not confirmed to be robust in EBA.

14. Albania, Bosnia and Herzegovina, Croatia, Bulgaria, the former Yugoslav Republic of Macedonia, Romania, and Serbia and Montenegro.
15. Values of the outcome and input indicators have been normalized by subtracting the sample average from the individual country values and dividing by the standard deviation for the entire sample.
16. This relationship does not portray an efficiency frontier (an international best practice) in a sector but an average level of efficiency across ECA countries and the six comparators after controlling for expenditures. Measures of expenditure efficiency based on an international efficiency frontier can be found in Herrera and Pang (2005). It could also be claimed that a relationship incorporating diminishing returns to government spending may represent a better specification than a linear relationship because many of the performance indicators considered are bounded.
17. The average value of the indicator over 2001–04 was used to ensure consistency in its definition.

PART 2

Selected Issues in Public Expenditure

CHAPTER 4

Infrastructure

Christine Kessides and Shaheena Khan

This chapter looks at trends and issues in the main sectors of economic infrastructure—power, water, and transport (railways and roads)[1]—and their implications for the Europe and Central Asia (ECA) region's prospects for continued growth and fiscal sustainability. From a public finance perspective, infrastructure occupies an important share of public investment as well as of recurrent expenditure, either through the government budget or through publicly owned enterprises that depend to various degrees on fiscal funding. The relationship between public finance and infrastructure is inherently different for roads (which are public goods)[2] than for the utility subsectors (power and water) and railways, which are tariff-based. For utilities, the basic public finance commitment should be to (a) compensate for operational expenses that cannot be funded by tariffs—namely, public service obligations and essential service to users genuinely unable to pay, and (b) create fiscal space for necessary investments where these also cannot be covered by tariffs, ideally through medium- or long-term loans to be repaid by the utility revenues, or through loan guarantees. However, governments often assume greater public finance commitments to infrastructure than appropriate on these terms because operators fail to achieve standards of commercial viability or because of weak governance (including political pressure and corruption) in the public agencies and ministries involved.

At the outset of transition in ECA (with the partial exception of Turkey), all infrastructure facilities were owned and operated by the public sector, with little commercial orientation and weak incentives for cost recovery. In most of the countries the systems have come a very long way in 15 years toward a more economically rational relationship to public finance. Public finance data on infrastructure sectors (recurrent and investment expenditure and tax revenues) are rather unreliable in ECA countries, as indeed in most regions. Interpretation of such data requires knowledge of the performance and reform status of sectors to determine if public expenditures are appropriate given the demand and supply situation, operational efficiency, and financial viability of operations. Therefore, the analysis here focuses on the conditions, performance, and policy and institutional frameworks for the sectors as essential background to understanding their public finance implications. Because comparisons of public expenditure over time or across countries are largely unreliable, the chapter relies mainly on real sector indicators as available and on more qualitative and anecdotal evidence,[3] with particular attention to the 10 focus countries in ECA.[4]

This chapter argues that while infrastructure was not a significant constraint to growth in the early transition years, it is becoming a bottleneck for growth in the future. Of greatest concern is the need for rehabilitation and for enhancements in service quality, as well as for more adequate supply in some countries. These requirements will entail additional improvements in the governance and management of systems to further increase efficiency, as well as new investments. Although most countries have initiated reforms to strengthen the financial viability of utilities, important contingent liabilities remain that, if not addressed, could threaten both the sustainability of services and fiscal stability in the future.

Infrastructure and Economic Growth

A large and diverse literature has arisen in recent decades on the relationship between infrastructure development and economic outcomes (Estache 2006; IMF 2004b; Poot 2000). There are major methodological issues in empirical estimation (for example, to separate two-way causality), and many differences in sectors covered (usually telecommunications, electricity, and transport) and in identification of the independent variables (public investment or real stocks). Data limitations dictate that most studies look at physical assets (stocks) rather than the flow of services, and expenditure-based measures have yielded less conclusive results than physical measures in determining growth effects (Serven 2006). However, on the whole, this global research—especially the studies focusing on developing countries—confirms that infrastructure contributes positively to economic output, growth, or productivity (or all three) (Briceño-Garmendia, Estache, and Shafik 2004).

Among the more robust studies, Calderon and Serven (2004) use a large global panel data set covering 40 years that takes account of both quantity and quality measures and controls for potential endogeneity of infrastructure. They find that growth is positively affected by the stock of infrastructure assets, and that higher infrastructure quantity and quality also reduce income inequality. The positive effects of infrastructure appear stronger in low- or lower-middle-income countries and subregions, such as found in ECA, than in more highly developed economies (Canning and Bennathan 2000). However, careful analysis of infrastructure investment in Spain during the early stages of accession to the European Union (EU) indicates that infrastructure spending was a major determinant of growth and productivity convergence across regions of the country (de la Fuente 2002). Ireland has also invested in infrastructure strategically with positive effects for national growth (Davies and Hallet 2002).

Relatively few of the published empirical studies include many of the ECA countries or give them special focus. Preliminary findings of an ongoing research effort applying the Calderon and Serven (2004) methodology to the ECA countries suggest a robust relationship between infrastructure stock and quality and productivity growth (box 4.1). A review of social rates of return from World Bank projects completed between 1960 and 2000 finds especially high rates in transport (25 percent), telecommunications (22 percent), and energy and mining (18 percent), with the highest rates observed in Eastern Europe (Briceño-Garmendia, Estache, and Shafik 2004). In short, there is every reason to believe from the available research evidence that infrastructure matters for growth in countries of the ECA region.

There are several important methodological shortcomings in most existing analyses, however. Impacts depend on the efficiency with which facilities are used and the quality and reliability of services actually delivered, and stock data do not measure these aspects. Furthermore, past stocks do not indicate effective demand where supply is inelastic and prices misspecified or little used. Affordability constraints mean that services may be underconsumed, especially by the poor. In ECA countries during socialism and in the early period of

BOX 4.1

Economic Impacts of Infrastructure in ECA

An ongoing research study looks at trends in access and quality of three infrastructure sectors (telecommunications, electricity, and roads) in a sample of 18 ECA countries[a] from 1991 to 2005 to assess impacts on output per worker, using the methodology developed in Calderon and Serven (2004) and comparing with a global database. The study has developed composite indexes of the stock and quality of the three sectors (figures below).[b] These illustrate that the ECA countries were close to the seven East Asia "miracle" countries (EAP-7)[c] in stock indicators in the beginning of transition and well above Latin America, although ECA lost ground relative to EAP-7 by 2005, mainly because of Asia's investment push. For quality, however, the ECA sample started off much worse than EAP and remains far behind, closer to the average for Latin America and other developing countries.

Aggregate Index of Infrastructure Stock and Quality

(Aggregate Indices Obtained using Principal Components Analysis)

a. Aggregate Infrastructure Stock, 1991–2005

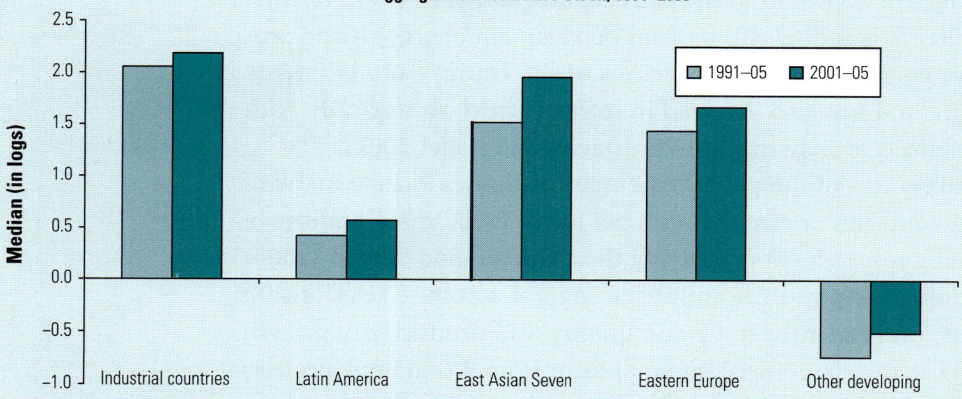

(continued)

transition, the quantities of services supplied had little relation to cost (especially of energy), and prices to users were suppressed and distorted by heavy state subsidies or internal cross-subsidies. While input prices and tariffs have been adjusting closer to market levels in most countries in the last several years, pervasive issues of poor governance and weak financial sustainability continue, resulting in inadequate or worsening levels of service and problems of affordability, especially in certain countries and secondary cities.

BOX 4.1 (continued)

The econometric analysis finds a positive and robust relationship between aggregate indexes of infrastructure stock and quality and growth in real output per worker. The model estimates changes in productivity growth due to the evolution of infrastructure over 2001–05 relative to 1991–95 for the ECA countries, breaking down the effect of changes in the accumulation of infrastructure assets as compared with changes in quality. Although the impacts are heterogeneous between the two indexes, it seems clear that for the EU-8 countries both stock accumulation and quality improvements contributed to productivity growth, whereas in the Kyrgyz Republic and Ukraine a worsening of infrastructure quantity and quality seem to explain a decline in productivity growth.[d] The study also calculates the potential payoff of infrastructure improvement for the productivity growth premium that could be gained by raising sector performance to certain benchmark levels. Achieving the infrastructure levels of the ECA leader,[e] for example, would raise the average productivity growth rate of the ECA sample countries by 1.8 percent per year. The benefit would be even larger for the ECA countries currently lagging behind, such as Ukraine. The potential payoff to ECA countries of reaching the infrastructure stock and quality levels of the EAP-7 leader would be a productivity growth premium of 1.3 percent per year.

Source: Calderon (2007) .

a. The sample includes the EU-10 (Bulgaria, the Czech Republic, Estonia, Hungary, Latvia, Lithuania, Poland, Romania, the Slovak Republic, and Slovenia); Croatia and Serbia and Montenegro in SEE; four middle-income CIS (Belarus, Kazakhstan, the Russian Federation, Ukraine); the Kyrgyz Republic; and Turkey (of current ECA focus countries, Albania, Armenia, and Georgia are not included). The quality indicators reflect quality of access (waiting time for phone installation, share of paved roads) and efficiency of operation (power transmission and distribution losses) rather than quality of service flows to users.

b. To construct the aggregate indexes of infrastructure stock and quality of infrastructure services, principal components analysis is used (Theil 1970). This method takes n specific indicators and yields new indexes ("principal components") that capture information of the different dimensions of the data and that are mutually uncorrelated.

c. Including Hong Kong (China), Indonesia, Republic of Korea, Malaysia, Singapore, Taiwan, and Thailand.

d. Most of the contribution of infrastructure development to growth is related to improvements in the quality of telecommunications.

The Legacy of Transition and Recent Performance

Even after disinvestment during the turbulent 1990s, ECA countries enjoyed high rates of access to most categories of infrastructure. Table 4.1 compares ECA's nearly universal access to electricity, water, and sanitation to that of regions with comparable or greater average income (especially Latin America and the Caribbean). ECA's rural access remains notably better than that of the comparator countries, with the exception of Thailand.

TABLE 4.1

Percentage of Households with Access to Electricity, Water, and Sanitation

Region and focus countries	GDP per capita (constant 2000 US$)	Electricity				Improved water supply				Improved sanitation			
		Urban		Rural		Urban		Rural		Urban		Rural	
		2000	2002	2000	2002	1990	2004	1990	2004	1990	2004	1990	2004
East Asia and Pacific	*1,352*	*99*	*96*	*81*	*83*	*97*	*92*	*61*	*69.8*	*65*	*72*	*15*	*36.1*
Korea, Repub. of	13,210	—	—	—	—	97	97	—	71.0	—	—	—	—
Thailand	2,440	—	—	—	—	98	98	94	100.0	95	98	74	99.0
Vietnam	539	—	—	—	—	90	99	59	80.0	58	92	30	50.0
Europe and Central Asia	*2,604*	*100*[a]	*100*	*97*[a]	*99*	*97*	*99*	*85*	*80.4*	*94*	*93*	*72*	*71.1*
Albania	1,535	—	100	—	100	99	99	94	94.0	99	99	—	84.0
Armenia	1,128	—	99	—	98	99	99	—	80.0	96	96	—	61.0
Croatia	5,138	—	—	—	—	100	100	100	100.0	100	100	100	100.0
Georgia	971	—	100	—	100	91	96	67	67.0	99	96	94	91.0
Kyrgyz Republic	319	—	98	—	100	98	98	66	66.0	75	75	51	51.0
Poland	5,194	—	100	—	100	100	100	—	—	—	—	—	—
Romania	2,259	—	99	—	94	—	91	—	16.0	—	89	—	—
Slovak Republic	4,761	—	—	—	—	100	100	99	99.0	100	100	98	98.0
Turkey	3,390	—	100	—	100	92	98	74	93.0	96	96	70	72.0
Ukraine	959	—	96	—	98	99	99	90	91.0	98	98	92	93.0
Latin America	*4,037*	*98*	*98*	*52*	*61*	*93*	*96*	*60*	*73.2*	*81*	*86*	*36*	*49.2*
Chile	5,747	—	—	—	—	98	100	49	58.0	91	95	52	62.0
Middle East and North Africa	*1,790*	*99*	*99*	*79*	*83*	*96*	*96*	*79*	*80.7*	*87*	*92*	*52*	*57.9*
South Asia	*562*	*68*	*69*	*30*	*33*	*89*	*94*	*65*	*81.3*	*50*	*63*	*6*	*26.6*
Sub-Saharan Africa	*560*	*51*	*52*	*8*	*8*	*82*	*80*	*36*	*42.5*	*52*	*53*	*24*	*28.1*
Uganda	267	—	—	—	—	80	87	40	56.0	54	54	41	41.0
Developing and Transition countries		*86*	*85*	*51*	*52*	*92*	*93*	*64*	*71.0*	*72*	*77*	*34*	*45*

Sources: World Bank, World Development Indicators, 2006; for electricity, IEA, World Energy Outlook, 2002 and 2004. Figures on ECA from World Bank, "People and Power, Electricity Sector Reforrms and the Poor in Europe and Central Asia," November 2006.

a. World Bank, "Infrastructure in Europe and Central Asia," June 2006.

At the start of transition, natural gas supply networks extended to both urban and rural areas wherever trunk pipelines existed. Most large urban areas had district heating services (an option that is feasible only in relatively dense settlements). Telephone connections were sparse in rural areas but available to most urban households, especially in capital cities. Rail networks were vast and designed mainly for hauling raw materials and heavy goods across long distances, especially to support the intraregional trading arrangements of the Council of Mutual Economic Assistance. Most communities had access to an all-weather road, and about 89 percent of the network was paved, even though it was not designed (especially in the Commonwealth of Independent States [CIS]) to serve substantial transport of goods.

However, this physical legacy created problems and challenges during transition that remain a struggle for many countries, especially in the CIS. The initial contraction in output and demand caused overcapacity, making it difficult to maintain the systems or to pay for imported fuel—still an issue for countries suffering the longest recessions, such as Ukraine. Systems were oversized relative to effective economic demand, especially in electricity and district heating and, to some extent, in gas supply. Water facilities were overdimensioned and inefficiently designed, and wastewater treatment was highly inadequate relative to modern environmental standards. District heating, gas, and water consumption levels per customer far exceeded averages in market economies because the distribution was not metered and leakage was typically high.

The imbalances at the time of transition were more qualitative in transport, reflecting the need for adjustments to respond to the changing nature of demand. The shift of production away from heavy freight and changes in the direction of trading relationships required restructuring and rationalization of rail networks, while primary and secondary roads had to absorb rapidly growing truck and private car traffic.

Excess capacity is less an issue now that most of the ECA countries have undergone considerable structural change in their production and have resumed economic growth. However, the inability to fund normal operations and widespread neglect of maintenance during the early transition years has left much of the stock, already heavily depreciated and outmoded, in a dismal state. In some countries, especially the low-income CIS[5] and the southeast Europe[6] subregions, shortages of electricity are a growing concern, as evidenced by blackouts or reduced periods of service even in the capital city (figure 4.1).[7] Because much of the inherited stock has outlived its useful life or deteriorated badly, expenditure priorities include rehabilitation and modernization or upgrading, and, in some cases, even expansion of facilities (especially in power generation and gas networks). In the CIS, district heating plants have become almost unusable or require major investment to improve their energy efficiency. In Ukraine, heat production in 2002 was 42 percent of its 1990 level, and even in Poland the figure was only 47 percent (IEA 2004).

In the water sector, problems of access, reduced reliability, and less frequent service have emerged, especially outside capital cities. In Albania less than 40 percent, and in Armenia less than 20 percent of urban settlements had water 24 hours a day in 2000. In Armenia and Georgia, the capital cities were more than twice as likely to have full water service as other urban areas (World Bank 2006d). However, much progress has been made in recent years in both countries, and continuous water supply was available to more than 50 percent of the population in 2005.

In the road sector the recession led to neglect of maintenance as public funding dried up, while increased traffic of heavy vehicles and private cars placed new burdens on the existing stock. Lack of regular maintenance led to accelerated degeneration of roads and worsening safety in the face of growing traffic.

With the return to growth and the adoption of sectoral reforms, which have permitted improvements in operational efficiency and revenue mobilization as discussed below, problems of intermittent availability and poor quality of service have lessened. The 2005 Business Environment and Enterprise Performance surveys (BEEPS) found improvements, albeit modest, in electricity services in most

FIGURE 4.1
Reliability of Infrastructure and Energy Services in ECA in Early 2000

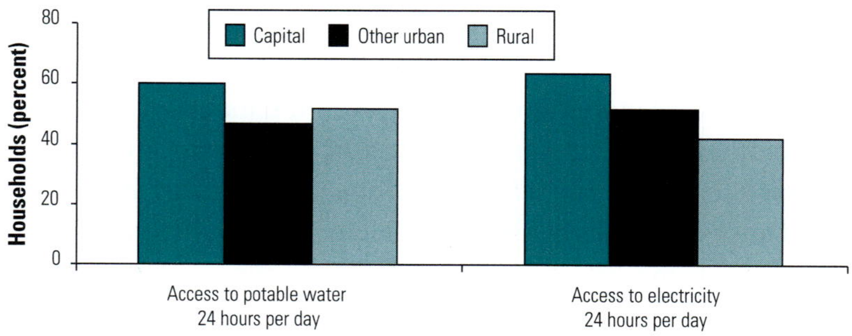

Source: Household survey data (World Bank 2006b).

Note: Average among eight ECA countries for potable water; eight for electricity.

countries and subregions, with the worst ratings for Albania, Georgia, and Turkey (table 4.2). Transport services were considered unchanged or somewhat worse, especially in Armenia and Georgia, probably reflecting the declining road quality and congestion. However, the BEEPS reported dramatic improvements in regulatory certainty and the prevalence of unofficial payments. Significant problems remained in 2005 with prevalence of power outages or surges in Albania (194 days in previous 12 months on average), Georgia (57 days), and the Kyrgyz Republic (14 days), although only Albania's figure had increased since 2002.[8] The problems of intermittent or insufficient water supply had sharply declined in all countries except Albania.

To conclude, the installed infrastructure at the start of transition permitted the ECA countries to withstand the early years of recession and structural transformation without major new investment, and in fact many facilities were mothballed or simply run down. It was not infrastructure that impeded growth in this early transition period,

TABLE 4.2

Percentage of Businesses Reporting Problems, 2002 and 2005

Subregion / and country	Problems with electricity services		Problems with transport services		Regulatory uncertainty		Unofficial payments for electricity & water	
	2002 (%)	2005 (%)	2002 (%)	2005 (%)	2002 (%)	2005 (%)	2002 (%)	2005 (%)
Baltics	13	11	11	11	60	45	1	1
Central and Eastern Europe	10	12	12	14	59	62	3	3
Poland	14	11	15	13	84	66	3	2
Slovak Republic	15	7	17	7	67	39	3	1
Middle-income CIS-MI	10	8	9	9	64	49	6	4
Ukraine	14	11	9	10	76	58	8	4
Low-income CIS-LI	27	22	15	14	58	45	8	7
Armenia	30	10	19	13	63	36	2	6
Georgia	49	48	16	27	76	73	11	5
Kyrgyz Republic	21	15	13	9	57	69	9	11
Southeastern Europe	25	23	19	18	72	59	10	7
Albania	76	57	35	26	71	55	14	17
Croatia	6	4	11	8	67	45	3	5
Romania	19	18	19	19	73	64	5	2
Turkey	32	23	19	21	79	60	13	5
ECA average	19	17	14	14	63	51	7	5
Non-ECA (ICAs)								
Uganda	45	--	23	--	28	--	22	

Sources: EBRD-World Bank Business Environment and Enterprise Performance Surveys (BEEPS) for the ECA countries. Uganda Investment Climate Survey, 2004.
Note: "Problems with electricity," "Problems with transport services" and "Regulatory uncertainty" shown as the sum of "Moderate obstacle" and "Major obstacle." "Unofficial payments" is sum of "Frequently," "Usually," and "Always." For Uganda, "Unofficial payments" figure is for electricity only. Comparable information for other non-ECA Investment Climate Assessments not found in BankWB Investment Climate Assessment database.

although the rapid unraveling of services to households certainly added to their personal hardships. However, as most of the countries return to a more favorable output trend, the problems of service quality and reliability are becoming more evident and could hamper competitiveness. The EU accession countries[9] and the rest of southeast Europe in particular are now facing the challenge familiar to the rest of the developing world: how to find the financial means to expand and modernize infrastructure to support durable economic growth. This task will require continued efforts to reform the management and governance of the sectors, as discussed below.

Financial Sustainability: Hidden Costs and Priorities for Structural Reform

The financial performance of utilities has important implications for fiscal and macroeconomic stability in a country. Power and water systems in transition economies have relied heavily on the public budget to sustain operations. They generally have had low technical efficiency, centralized controls on tariff levels, and low rates of bill collection, especially from other state enterprises. If the sector is operated by public sector agencies, commercial practices to recover costs have often not been implemented because such services have been treated as vehicles for promoting political interests, and in the socialist context underpriced services were a supplement to low wages and considered a social entitlement. Violations of commercial and economic principles have led to nonviable financial performance with direct impacts on state budgets in the form of utility bailouts and accumulation of tax arrears. It also has had repercussions for the sustainability of services, reflected in reduced access and deteriorating service quality.

This section discusses three dimensions of the problem: the extent of (a) unaccounted losses (in excess of normal technical losses of power or water distributed through the network), (b) low efficiency of bill collection, and (c) tariffs below cost recovery. Together these problems comprise hidden costs or implicit subsidies that result in indirect or eventual claims on public budgets, as well as burdens to consumers through reduced or deteriorated service (box 4.2). The stringent fiscal restraints needed for macroeconomic stability led governments in the late 1990s to recognize the importance of commercializing the infrastructure sectors. In each country, reforms have been made along each of these dimensions, leading to generally improving trends in hidden costs, but there is still a way to go for many of them.

BOX 4.2

Assessing the Economic and Fiscal Burden of Poor Infrastructure Management

High losses, nonpayment of bills, and tariffs set below cost recovery hurt the financial performance of a utility sector, creating direct and indirect—or hidden (implicit)—subsidies that raise demands for eventual bailouts by government.[a] These hidden subsidies are not usually recorded or made transparent, but their impact is felt in the form of reduced investments, delay of essential maintenance, and deterioration of service. Postponed maintenance leads to further deterioration in the value of assets, increased per unit cost of service provided, and h gher technical losses in the systems. Inefficient service delivery and high losses result in greater electricity and fuel consumption, increasing fuel imports and thus the debt burden of a country.

International partners, the International Monetary Fund (IMF), and the World Bank, have devised a model called the Hidden Cost Calculator. Hidden costs refer to the difference between actual and potential collected revenue, determined as the sum of three subsidy components:

- Excessive system losses (difference between actual system losses and normative losses, multiplied by the economic price of the service)
- Collection inefficiency (the difference between billed revenue and actual collected revenue)
- Pricing inefficiency (the difference between the cost recovery price and the actual price or tariff charged, multiplied by the billed quantity of service)

These calculations take account of normative losses and collection rates prevailing in comparable, well-run utility systems. The economic or cost recovery price is determined on the basis of long-run marginal cost, or on-border prices adjusted for delivery costs.

The Hidden Cost Calculator Model draws on data compiled by Bank staff for a four year period, 2000–03.[b] The sources of data include Enerdata; ERRANET; existing World Bank publications and reports; and data obtained from country experts, World Bank staff, and IMF staff. The model has been applied to the power, water, and gas sectors.

Sources: Ebinger 2006; World Bank 2006f.

a. The total hidden subsidies form part of quasi-fiscal deficit. This term implies that the hidden cost is effectively covered by the state budget in some form eventually, although much of it is borne in reality by consumers, through reduction or deterioration in service, for indefinite periods.

b. See World Bank (2006f) and Ebinger (2006) for a more detailed explanation. By mid-2007 the model is scheduled to be updated for 2004 and 2005.

Power

Electricity has been by far the largest recipient of implicit subsidies among the infrastructure sectors in ECA countries, because of its sheer size and the degree of disparity between the cost recovery price and weighted average tariff. The energy intensity of growth in the ECA region ranges from four times (in the CEE) to 13 times (in the CIS) the average for Organisation for Economic Co-operation and Development (OECD) countries.[10] Power (as well as water and gas) networks in ECA during the first decade of transition were typically characterized by high system losses (output generated and not billed) caused by poor design and inadequate upkeep of facilities, theft, or unofficial connections, and the absence of metering. The total hidden costs in the power sector as a share of GDP were as high as 18 percent in some countries in the mid-1990s.

Hidden costs have been declining in almost all ECA countries in recent years as a result of tariff adjustments and improved efficiency in managing losses, and in billing and collections, as well as increases in GDP. Technical losses have been reduced through better maintenance, rehabilitation, and, where necessary, decommissioning of facilities. Metering and vigilance against illegal connections have reduced commercial losses. Improvements in collections have been achieved by reforms in utility governance and legal and administrative changes that have made it easier to pursue nonpayment claims and to disconnect services. Tariff restructuring has also been pursued, reducing cross-subsidies of residential tariffs by industrial users. As of 2003, the weighted average end-user tariffs[11] in Armenia, Croatia, and Turkey approached the level of medium-term cost recovery—that is, not only covering operation and maintenance costs but also contributing to investment needs (at least for rehabilitation and meter installation).[12]

Because demand is reemerging strongly in the CEE and SEE countries, the targeted cost recovery tariff will need to rise to permit adequate investment in rehabilitation and new generating capacity. In countries where appropriate fiscal space has been created by reducing the public debt ratio and the fiscal deficit, investment to meet growing demand could also be partly financed through borrowing—that is, by taxation of future incomes. The situation in the CIS countries varies. Because most of them still have excess generating capacity and modest demand forecasts (remaining below their 1990 levels) for the next 5–10 years, the cost recovery tariff levels presently estimated are less than in the more buoyant economies. However, in parts of the CIS, notably the Kyrgyz Republic, tariffs have not even reached short-term financial viability (covering costs of fuel, operation, and basic maintenance).

Figure 4.2 shows total hidden costs in the power sector (that is, the sum of unaccounted losses, collection failure, and tariffs below cost recovery price) as a percentage of GDP across the focus countries during 2000–05. In Armenia, Turkey, Poland, and Croatia, total hidden costs had been almost eliminated by 2003. The Kyrgyz Republic has maintained the highest share of hidden costs among the sample, although its 9.4 percent of GDP in 2003–05 was still much lower than in earlier years. Albania, Georgia, and Ukraine also more than halved their shares of hidden costs from 2000 to 2003. Armenia has gained through improved sector efficiency promoted by power sector reforms (box 4.3). This reduced hidden costs or implicit subsidies to less than 0.5 percent of GDP in 2005.

In the composition among the three components, inadequate tariffs account for the bulk of the hidden costs estimated in Ukraine, Romania, and Poland. The potential revenue losses from tariffs below cost recovery alone amounted to 3 percent of GDP in Ukraine and the Kyrgyz Republic in 2003 (down to 2 percent in the Kyrgyz Republic in 2005). Unaccounted losses were the biggest share of hidden costs in Turkey, the Kyrgyz Republic, Georgia, Armenia, and Albania. Although each country made considerable improvements, unaccounted losses still represented over 3 percent of GDP in Georgia in 2003 and 2.4 percent in the Kyrgyz Republic in 2005. Losses

FIGURE 4.2
Total Hidden Costs of Power Sector, 2000–05

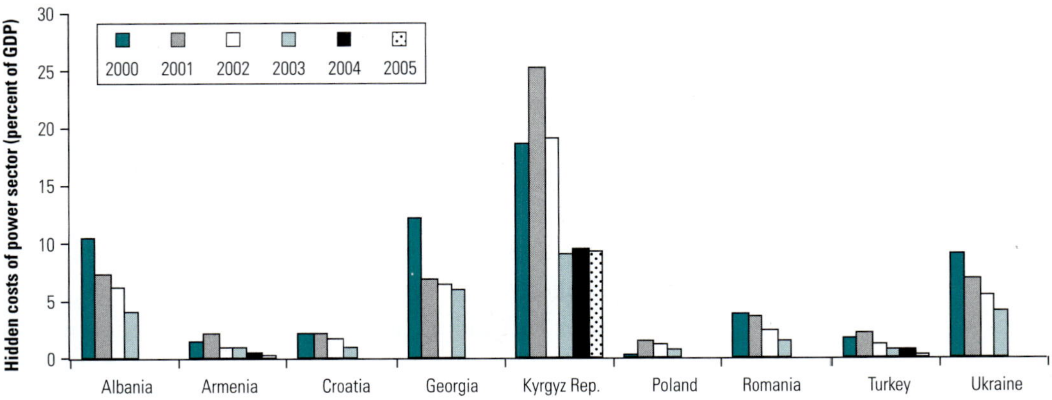

Source: World Bank 2006f and updated staff estimates.

from poor collections were the smallest component of hidden subsidies, yet in 2003 remained an unacceptable 1.0–1.5 percent of GDP in the Kyrgyz Republic and Georgia. Only in Croatia did collection failures dominate.

Lower hidden costs indicate progress in sector reform but do not necessarily mean that the contribution of infrastructure services to growth is maximized. The reduction of hidden costs means that tariffs are better aligned with costs as a result of tariff increases and cost savings, reflecting better efficiency in the provision of services. However, if costs remain uncompetitive, higher tariffs may detract from competitiveness and deter growth. For example, despite Turkey's progress in reducing hidden costs, electricity prices for industrial users are higher than the average in OECD countries, which is a potential obstacle to competitiveness and higher growth (World Bank 2006i).

Water

Transition also brought major shifts in public policies with respect to water services. At the outset of transition, consumption levels in the region were three times as high as in OECD countries. Reform had to start with promoting the public image of water supply as an economic good rather than a social privilege.

In the early years of transition, water services were decentralized and assets transferred to the municipal level throughout the ECA region, with the exception of the Slovak Republic and Bulgaria. However, most countries (other than the Czech Republic) have reversed or modified this trend in recent years. Recent moves have aggregated municipal water services, dramatically reducing the number of utilities and creating regional water companies. The intent has been to simplify tariff regulation, introduce economies of scale, and ease mechanisms for public investment in the sector (World Bank 2006d).

Wide regional disparities characterize ECA water systems. In Poland and the Slovak Republic, water is supplied largely by commercialized utilities that offer high-quality water and sanitation services. The new entrants have a high level of institutional capacity, tariff levels sufficient to cover operating and maintenance costs, and sufficient market scale to attract domestic and external capital. The key institutional challenge will be meeting high EU standards, especially for wastewater treatment, which requires substantial investment. For Romania and the EU pre-accession countries Croatia and Turkey, tariffs may be covering operation and maintenance costs but sector efficiency is not yet high enough to attract large inflows of domestic and foreign capital. Moreover, issues related to wastewater

BOX 4.3

Armenia: The Long Road to Success in Power Sector Reform

Armenia suffered extreme collapse of output and electricity generation during the early 1990s, when the only source of oil and gas for the national thermal power grid was cut off by the economic blockade imposed by Azerbaijan and Turkey. Gas supply from the pipeline built in 1993 through neighboring Georgia was regularly interrupted by sabotage. The massive earthquake in 1988 had already prompted the closure of the Medzamor nuclear plant. Dependence on Lake Seven for hydro power led to its depletion, because it was also providing irrigation and drinking water. Despite brutal winters, electricity supply was reduced to only two hours per day. Financial performance of the sector suffered, with bill collection of less than 50 percent and commercial losses of at least 25 percent. Fiscal and quasi-fiscal subsidies to the power sector reached roughly 11 percent of Armenia's GDP by 1995.

The adverse conditions strengthened the government's commitment to power sector reform. By late 1996, 24-hour supply was restored with the reopening of the Medzamor nuclear plant, abatement of the gas pipeline sabotage, and enhanced generation through improvements in the hydrology of Lake Seven. The government also initiated a campaign aimed at establishing a link between service quality and payment discipline, while gradually adjusting tariffs for all customers to remove cross-subsidies among users and to achieve cost recovery. A targeted family benefit program was introduced to provide a social safety net to needy households through cash transfers, replacing previous subsidy schemes. Donors also provided needed financial support for the reform agenda.

Unbundling of the sector into generation, transmission, and distribution companies in 1995 was accompanied by establishment of an independent regulator, the Armenian Energy Regulatory Commission, which became the champion of reform. The government also initiated privatization of the distribution company as part of the reform program, although two tenders offered in 2001 failed. Thereafter, the government altered the privatization plan to seek a management contractor rather than a private owner. Midland Resources Holding, a small strategic investor, took control of Armenia's distribution system at the end of 2002.

Bill collection and theft were addressed by installation of new tamper-proof meters. An automated metering and data acquisition system established customer information that helped to identify the source and extent of unaccounted losses and other systemic problems. Enforcement of payment discipline has resulted in a collection rate above 96 percent.

The power utility turned around its deficit of 2.4 percent of GDP in 1995 to a surplus of 3.3 percent of GDP in 2002. Financial flows are starting to move from the power sector to the government, freeing up fiscal space for social spending. Behind all these achievements has been a strong government commitment to ensuring a financially viable sector.

Source: Sargsyan, Balabanyan, and Hankinson 2006.

treatment pose a particular challenge for their acceptance in the EU. The southeast European countries[13] have competent human resources in the sector but need institutional reorganization and modern management methods. Armenia, Georgia, the Kyrgyz Republic, and Ukraine face severe challenges with declining service levels, low institutional capacities, and very limited ability to mobilize additional resources by tapping government budgets.

Hidden costs have been estimated for the water sector as a function of system losses, tariffs below cost recovery, and collection performance.[14] Nonrevenue water (NRW) is a good summary measure of sector inefficiency. It measures the percentage of water produced that is not actually invoiced and is a combination of technical losses (leaks) and administrative losses, such as from illegal connections.

Figure 4.3 presents NRW in 2002 for a sample of ECA countries, including eight of the focus countries: Albania, Armenia, Croatia, Georgia, the Kyrgyz Republic, Poland, Romania, and Ukraine. Six of these, all but Romania and Ukraine, had NRW above the ECA average of 38 percent in 2002. The international benchmark for unaccounted losses is about 20 percent, representing unavoidable (technical) loss in the distribution system.

An adequate level and structure of tariffs is a key policy instrument to promote demand management and financial sustainability of utilities. Despite the urgent need for adjustments, raising the level of tariffs is one of the most politically controversial aspects of infrastructure

FIGURE 4.3
Nonrevenue Water in ECA Countries, 2002

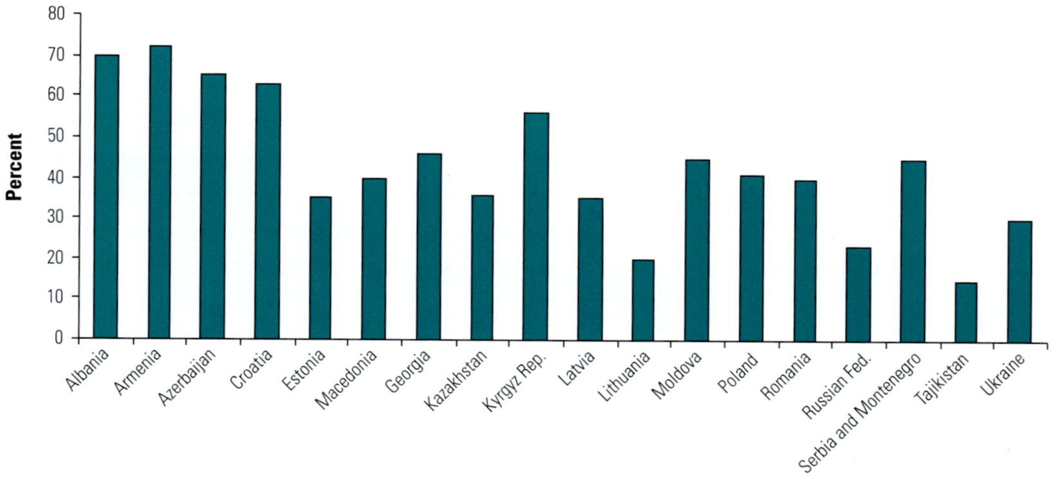

Source: Global Water Intelligence 2005.

reform, especially in the water sector. In most CIS countries municipalities are responsible for setting tariffs. Tariffs often do not cover operational costs, let alone required maintenance and capital costs. As a result, investment may fall short by a factor of five to ten times the level that would be required to maintain and renew existing water infrastructure.

Table 4.3 presents water tariffs in US$ per cubic meter in the selected countries, for the most recent available years.[15] With the exception of Armenia, average industrial tariffs were higher than average residential tariffs in 2003, indicating in most cases a continuation of internal cross-subsidies. Average tariffs (2004 data) were the highest in Croatia, followed by Turkey. The average water supply tariff was US$0.70 per cubic meter in metropolitan areas but considerably less in the smaller municipalities in Turkey (population below 100,000), which were less able to fully cover their costs.

Table 4.3 also presents estimates of the tariff required for cost recovery. The cost recovery tariff has been defined as the cost of supplying 24 hours of water,[16] including the cost of operation, maintenance,[17] and necessary investments. The cost recovery tariff acts as a benchmark for assessing the financial gap that needs to be recovered either by further raising tariffs or reducing the cost of supply. If operational inefficiencies were reduced, reflected in falling NRW and energy and labor costs, the pressure to raise tariffs could be eased, at least in the short run. However, EU standards require major investments by EU accession countries and may make the cost recovery tariff unaffordable for large segments of users.

Unlike in Romania and Poland, tariffs in many other countries do not account for environmental charges. Tariffs have increased in

TABLE 4.3

Average Water Tariffs in Selected Countries (US$/cubic meter)

Selected countries	Residential	Industrial	Weighted tariffs	Cost recovery tariff
Albania (2005)	0.30	1.08	0.44	0.65
Armenia (2005)	0.24	0.24	0.24	0.35
Croatia (2004)	0.47	2.02	0.87	0.65
Georgia (2005)	0.04	0.41	0.08	0.12
Kyrgyz Republic (2003)	0.03	0.14	0.08	0.08
Poland (2003)	0.55	0.62	0.56	0.68
Romania (2004)	0.15	0.62	0.39	0.65
Turkey (2004)	--	--	0.70	0.70
Ukraine (2003)	0.08	0.17	0.11	0.13

Source: World Bank ECA database.
Note: -- = Not available.

recent years in most countries, but production costs have also increased at the same or a higher pace. Ukraine introduced a law on Communal and Housing Services in 2004 that requires the regulator to compensate utilities for below-cost tariffs. This policy has provided incentives to local authorities to effectively implement cost-recovery tariffs.

For countries that are still a long way from cost recovery, a carefully planned phasing of tariff increases would ease the burden on poor households. While each country needs to assess this trade-off, the optimum approach would be to provide an effective social safety net to underpin relatively rapid tariff reform. ECA countries have introduced various social protection schemes during the transition period to replace the earlier reliance on general subsidies, internal cross-subsidies, and lax collection (box 4.4).

Cost recovery also requires payment discipline and metering. Most ECA countries are now approaching the international benchmark of an average of three months between the billing and collection of payments (OECD 2005). Metering used to be considered an infringement of basic rights, especially in CIS countries. Recently, some countries, such as Georgia and Armenia, have achieved high levels of metering. In Armenia, tariffs increased substantially in 2004, and collection rates have been improving over time with the Household Arrears Restructuring Program. In 2002, a legal framework was introduced that provided incentives for bill collection. Consumers were allowed some write-off of their past arrears if they agreed to meter installation. By 2005, collection ratios improved to 100 percent. Households have been willing to accept metering because it reduces billing amounts and has raised public confidence in the bills issued. Not only the financial viability of Armenian utilities but also transparency and sector governance have improved.

Albania has traditionally had the worst collection rate and lowest operating cost ratio among the focus countries, though the collection ratio improved to 74 percent[18] in 2006 (World Bank 2006a). Utilities rarely resort to cutting off illegal connections and nonpaying customers, although an existing policy allows for disconnections. Despite very low residential tariffs in Albania, domestic customers are the worst payers.

Table 4.4 indicates that the share in GDP of total hidden subsidies for water declined in Georgia between 2000 and 2003 but rose in Ukraine and Armenia (improving again in Armenia in 2004 and 2005). The share was much lower than in the power sector, however (figure 4.2). Water subsidies in Ukraine and Poland represented less than 0.5 percent of GDP in the period 2000 to 2003.

BOX 4.4

Ensuring a Social Safety Net for Infrastructure Pricing Reform

Safety nets in ECA countries vary in their targeting effectiveness, fiscal cost, and efficiency impacts. The Kyrgyz Republic and Ukraine still rely on poorly targeted budget transfers that are fiscally costly. In Ukraine, utility subsidies in recent years have represented almost 0.8 percent of GDP and are biased against the poor, and are one of the most expensive means of reducing poverty. Armenia and Georgia have implemented better-targeted family benefit programs to provide cash transfers to poor households, although the administrative requirements have been formidable. Poland has supported unemployment benefits and lump sum housing allowances from the general budget in place of energy price subsidies, thus setting the practice of transparent allocation from the budget. In mid-2006, Albania decided to replace the compensation of consumers unable to pay utility bills with a direct cash transfer to socially vulnerable households. The introduction of lifeline tariffs (a low rate applied to a quantity of basic consumption) for electricity in Romania has provided a relatively effective means of targeting the poor and supporting energy efficiency.

Social protection policies have also been critical for labor retrenchment, especially in railway restructuring. Poland has made successful strides in improving labor productivity in the railway sector in the period between 1998 and 2005 through a 58 percent reduction in employment achieved without labor tension, as consensus with key stakeholders was made part of the labor restructuring process. Social protection (severance pay, preretirement benefits, leave, labor redeployment services including training, labor mediation) and social monitoring became the core elements of the program. Labor productivity rose 19 percent despite traffic decline of 32 percent during this period.

Source: Authors' summary from various documents.

The recent "Public Expenditure and Institutional Review" in Albania (World Bank 2006a) determined potential savings from eliminating annual hidden costs in the water systems. If problems with collection failures, underpricing, unaccounted losses, and other inefficiencies such as overstaffing were addressed, Albania could save more than US$74 million annually—or 0.9 percent of GDP in 2006. The unaccounted losses alone absorb US$51 million annually. It should be noted, however, that upfront expenditure would be needed for metering to improve billing and collections, even though metering is expensive and not easily justified everywhere. Adequate investment in rehabilitation is urgently needed to reduce enormous losses in the systems from leakage.

TABLE 4.4
Share of Total Hidden Cost for Water in GDP

	Total hidden costs as % of GDP (2001 US$)					
	2000	2001	2002	2003	2004	2005
Armenia		0.88	1.55	1.59	1.09	0.69
Georgia	1.35	1.62	1.28	1.06	0.86	0.57
Poland	0.15	0.15	0.17	0.16	--	--
Ukraine	0.11	0.28	0.34	0.32	--	--

Source: World Bank 2006c,
Note: -- = Not available.

Land-Based Transport

Given the geographical location of ECA countries between the large EU markets and rapidly growing East Asia, land-based transport services are important for growth. Efficient and cost-effective transport is a key requirement for deepening the integration of ECA countries into transnational production networks and global markets. Railways and road transport are the two principal land-based transport modes where outcomes are to a large extent interdependent, reflecting evolving competition in network use.

Many of the transition countries face the challenge of sustaining a railway system of similar network density as Western Europe with less than half the traffic density, around a third of the total labor productivity, and a fraction of per capita income. The railway network density (rail route kilometers per thousand square kilometers) varies greatly among the ECA countries, from a high of 74 in the Slovak Republic to 2 in the Kyrgyz Republic. The economic importance varies as well. Except in the CIS countries of Armenia, Georgia, the Kyrgyz Republic, and Ukraine, the share of railways in surface transport has declined over the transition, most notably in Poland, the Slovak Republic, and Romania. The growth rate of rail traffic in 1999–2003 exceeded GDP growth only in Georgia and Ukraine. Both countries have also maintained a much higher share of freight (which is most related to economic activity) in total rail traffic. With sustained economic recovery, it is envisaged that the declining trend in traffic will end.

The road sector has seen increased traffic from both passengers and freight. The rising private ownership of vehicles resulting from higher per capita incomes and the liberalization of trucking (responding to the increased demand for just-in-time movement of high-value goods over short distances) have been the main factors behind the new motorization. Shifting trade relationships have also created new regional opportunities for transit traffic, mainly toward the West. The modal shift toward road transport intensifies the need for sufficient budgets to ensure that the existing network is maintained in a sustainable manner.

Railways. To observe the use of railway network capacity in each country and evaluate financial implications, *traffic density*[19] has been determined for the selected countries and compared with *traffic mix* (the share of passenger traffic in total traffic volumes). Together, they provide an important indication of yield per traffic unit (table 4.5). The higher the traffic density, the higher the network utilization to cover the operating costs of running the railways. However, railways with a higher share of passengers in the traffic mix may not be recovering all their operating costs, even with financial support for discounted passenger travel by the governments, given that passenger traffic units are more resource intensive than freight traffic units.

Traffic density in Ukraine has remained by far the highest among all countries, although Georgia's grew most rapidly from 1999 to 2003. In contrast, traffic density in Poland and Romania declined by 2–5 percent per year on average. This may be at least partly the result of a modal shift of traffic with industrial restructuring during the period. Despite signs of improvement in traffic densities, it is envisaged that in none of the countries are railways likely to recover the share of traffic they had in the 1980s.

Georgian railways, with a relatively lower proportion of passenger traffic and higher intensity of use than some other countries, have

TABLE 4.5

Railways: Trends in Total Activity, Density, and Traffic Mix (1999 and 2003)

	Total traffic units (passenger-km + freight tonne-km, -millions)		Traffic density (traffic units /route-km , thousands-'000) (A)		Traffic mix (% of passenger kms in total traffic units) (B)	
	1999	2003	1999	2003	1999	2003
Albania	147	144	329	327	82	85
Armenia	370	500	434	703	13	10
Croatia	2,985	3,911	1,095	1,435	38	30
Georgia	3,573	5,476	2,217	3,584	10	7
Kyrgyz Republic	433[a]	612	1,038	1,050	--	10
Poland	81,647	67,056	4,082	3,353	32	29
Romania	28,231	25,100	2,470	2,282	44	34
Slovak Republic	12,830	13,065	3,498	3,573	23	21
Turkey	14,592	14,545	1,695	1,678	42	40
Ukraine	203,936	243,685	9,075	11,037	23	21

Source: 1999 data collated from various sources; 2003 data from Amos (2005) and other Bank reports.

a. 1995.

been less vulnerable to financial distress during the transition period and have required no government subsidies.[20] In countries where traffic density is low and share of passenger traffic is high, such as Turkey, Croatia, and Romania, railways have faced financial difficulties. In Albania, the decline in total traffic units and an unusually high and growing share of passengers in the traffic mix (85 percent in 2003) result in extremely low yields per traffic unit, leading to a precarious financial state in the railways.[21] In Ukraine, most of the transit traffic is from the Russian Federation to the Black Sea ports and involves heavy commodities (oil and iron ore).

Railway reform entails tailoring of physical infrastructure to expected demand, through selling obsolete assets, closing railway units, outsourcing and privatizing noncore activities, and reducing remaining operational costs, especially of labor. EU membership further requires harmonizing with the directives of the acquis communautaire, which involve separating rail infrastructure from operations, imposing a track access fee, and establishing commercialized operations with defined public service obligations for socially necessary but unprofitable services. As a further direction of reform, cross-country initiatives are being promoted to address declining traffic density and continuing deterioration of national railways and to focus resources in market segments where railways have a viable future. Studies have been undertaken to establish regional "core" networks and priorities for investment on those networks, such as the Transport Infrastructure Regional Study (Berger 2002) and Regional Balkans Infrastructure Study (REBIS) completed in 2003 (COWI 2003).

A recent report ranked the countries of the region into high, medium, and low reformers as of yearend 2004 (Amos 2005). Among the focus countries, Poland, Romania, and the Slovak Republic were ranked as high reformers, though they had not completed all reforms in the sector. Medium reformers included Armenia, Croatia, and Georgia, which had achieved some commercial orientation and undergone some labor adjustment. Albania, the Kyrgyz Republic, and Ukraine were ranked as low reformers.

Table 4.6 presents financial and fiscal performance indicators in selected countries in the most recent available years. As already noted, the increasing share of rail freight due to buoyant commodity trade has brought financial health to railways in Georgia and Armenia, and to some extent in the Kyrgyz Republic and Ukraine. Georgia and Armenia have shown short-term financial viability as reflected by the working ratio less than unity.[22] The working ratio in Albania, Croatia, and Turkey is higher than 2.0, indicating extreme financial distress. In Romania, the working ratio is also more than unity.Even

TABLE 4.6

Railways: Financial Performance and Government Subsidy in Selected Countries

Country	Subsidy (% of GDP)		Subsidy (US$ millions)	Working ratio excluding subsidy	
	2002	2004	2004	2000/01/02	2004/05
Albania	0.10	0.10	8	—	2.52
Armenia	None	None	None	1.35	0.79
Croatia	1.00	2.20[a]	544	1.87	2.22
Georgia	None	None	None	0.62	0.69
Kyrgyz Republic	—	None	None	—	—
Poland	0.10	0.13	304	0.99	0.93
Romania	0.60	0.50[a]	501[a]	1.16	1.12[a]
Slovak Republic	0.68	—	166[b]	0.92	—
Turkey	0.20	0.40[a]	1,410[a]	3.85	3.20[a]

Source: Data collated from various World Bank data reports.
Note: — = Not available.
a. 2005 data.
b. 2001 data.

a low ratio, however, does not imply that these systems have been working efficiently and require no substantial reforms[23] or that they can pay for needed investment. Maintenance programs may have been delayed, contributing to the loss of asset value of railway companies through obsolescence and depreciation. Although Armenia and Georgia have been modest in their reform efforts, they continue (in 2007) to require no budget support from the government. Information on subsidies is incomplete in the Kyrgyz Republic and Ukraine, which have been even slower to reform.[24]

When reform measures to rationalize the size, infrastructure, and labor force do not keep pace with declining traffic density, operating costs increase and the financial health of railways deteriorates. Turkey and Croatia have initiated restructuring and modernization of their railways. In Croatia, traffic density has increased with modest growth in freight volumes. With a hike in tariff charges, share of revenues rose from 0.7 percent of GDP in 2002 to 1.1 percent in 2005, albeit the share of subsidies more than doubled in this period to 2.2 percent of GDP—the highest among the focus countries with data. In absolute terms, subsidies are the highest in Turkey but form only about 0.4 percent of GDP. Poland has managed to keep the share of subsidies in GDP constant and the working ratio fairly low, due to improvements in sector performance. However, driven by the downward spiral of the railway's output together with inadequate compensation for the socially necessary but unprofitable passenger services and high access charges, the main challenges facing the Polish railway include a liquidity crisis and the need to fund investment in rail infrastructure, facilities, and equipment.

When subsidies are compared with the length of the network, the allocation appears highest in Croatia with US$200,000 per route km, followed by US$172,000 in Turkey and $46,000 in Romania, in 2005. The subsidy levels in these countries also reflect high borrowing and debt servicing requirements for the implementation of ongoing reforms.

Roads. This study looked at national or state roads (including motorways and trunk roads), which are by definition lengthy, carry relatively high volumes of traffic, and compete for public resources from the central government.[25] Table 4.7 presents the network density (total length of the road network per thousand square kilometers of land area) in the selected countries compared to regional averages. Coverage rates vary considerably for historical, political, and locational reasons. Poland, the Slovak Republic, and Romania have higher densities than others in the sample, with Poland leading at 1.4 km per thousand square kilometers. Road network densities in Romania and the Slovak Republic (at about 0.9) are higher than the ECA regional average, though fall short of the comparator average for upper-middle-income countries. The road network density in Turkey is below the regional average and that of other upper-middle-income countries, while Albania has relatively high density (though not necessarily better quality road facilities overall) compared to its neighbor, Croatia. Countries in the CIS also fall below the ECA average but have road densities similar to lower-middle-income countries in other parts of the world, and access to the main urban centers has been considered adequate. The Kyrgyz Republic has the lowest road density among the focus countries.

The portion of roads that are paved indicates the degree of access and mobility and general efficiency of the road network. Poland and

TABLE 4.7
Road Network Densities

Country	Road network density (km/1,000 sq. km)	Country	Road network density (km/1,000 sq. km)
Albania	0.66	Turkey	0.46
Armenia	0.27	Ukraine	0.29
Croatia	0.51	France	1.50
Georgia	0.29	Germany	2.00
Kyrgyz Republic	0.10	Europe & Central Asia	0.60
Poland	1.38	Upper middle income (UMI)	1.10
Romania	0.86	Lower middle income (LMI)	0.30
Slovak Republic	0.89	High-income OECD	1.30

Sources: Collated from Vvarious Bank reports and the International Road Federation (IRF).

the Slovak Republic lead the focus sample in paved road length per 1,000 people, with eight and seven kms/1,000 residents, respectively, while Georgia and Turkey fall at the low end of the sample (each with about 2 kms/1,000 people). Scaling the paved road length against economic output gives yet a different picture of adequacy. Using this criterion, the CIS countries Armenia, Georgia, and Ukraine, with about 2–3 km per US$ million GDP, exceed figures for the EU member and candidate sample, while the Kyrgyz Republic comes in far above all, at 8 km per US$ million GDP. These higher rates indicate a greater burden of maintenance relative to the size of the economy.

Virtually all the ECA countries have seen growth in total road traffic (for example, 10 percent per year in Albania). Ukraine has relatively low road utilization and experienced a sharp decline in road freight traffic during the 1990s. This trend, which reflected the slow and comparatively prolonged transition period, has recently reversed. However, fierce competition from the railway industry, which continues to dominate in Ukraine as well as in Georgia, is likely to continue.

Despite increases in traffic volumes, road network density in ECA countries is considered adequate for the foreseeable future. Overall, the poor quality of the network rather than its extent has been an impending issue for the region, because poor quality has negative effects on competitiveness and economic growth. Economies need coherent and properly maintained road networks that allow for flow of traffic, both passenger and freight, with reduced time, less congestion, and greater safety. Increasingly, high volumes of passenger cars and heavy truck freights are adding stress to the existing network structures, whose maintenance and rehabilitation needs have been long neglected. Proper road maintenance contributes to reliable transport at reduced cost, because there is a direct link between road condition and vehicle operating costs that have to be borne by the users. According to studies undertaken in the region, poor or limited road quality can raise transport costs by 28–56 percent (World Bank 2003c).

Consistent and adequate allocation of expenditures for annual and periodic maintenance would also promote efficiency in public investment by protecting public assets and reducing needs for rebuilding. Heggie and Vickers (1998) report that rehabilitation of a paved road is three times more expensive than maintaining it if measured in current terms, and around 35 percent more if measured in net present value. The importance of timeliness in road maintenance has been illustrated by research conducted in Turkey based on 20 years of historical data (cited in World Bank [2003c]). It found that if road maintenance is not completed by the end of the 12th year, roads start deteriorating eight times faster than in the first few years of their lifetimes.

Many countries have started to rationalize their national road networks by reclassifying and devolving segments to local authorities. The transfer of responsibility for secondary roads to local governments can scale down maintenance requirements and promote expenditure efficiencies in the maintenance of main roads.[26] Poland reduced its national road network by 61 percent, retaining for high-level maintenance the segments with highest traffic volumes that involve international transit and most directly affect economic activity. In Albania, Georgia, and the Kyrgyz Republic, the road networks are also being realigned among levels of government, although it is unclear how well municipalities can meet the necessary costs.

Expenditure priorities remain an issue in many countries, with implications for road quality and for public sector financing. During the early 1990s, most road investments funded by external donors were in the form of piecemeal project support, as emergency measures to rebuild the most deteriorated infrastructure. It is increasingly recognized that institutional reforms for good management of road infrastructure is the key challenge for the public sector. For example, the EU's Stabilization and Accession Process imposes a requirement that capacity of the public sector for planning and budgeting road maintenance expenditures be strengthened, along with improvement in road safety, encouragement of private sector participation, and use of modern road technologies.

However, many countries continue to prioritize new investment over maintenance. In Albania, the expansion of the Durres-Kukes-Morine road link has detracted from maintenance expenditures, while the share of roads rated in poor condition remains at 67 percent and the share in good condition is only 16 percent World Bank 2006a. Croatia spends one of the highest shares of GDP on roads among the ECA focus countries (3.4 percent in 2001–04), but 75 percent of this amount is allocated to motorways, such as the Zagreb-Karlovac-Rijeka highway that is part of the Trans-European Highway network. This ambitious program was initiated despite a 1999 survey's finding that Croatia's motorway traffic density was only about a third of the Western Europe average and insufficient to economically justify a four-lane motorway. While traffic has picked up in recent years, above the levels projected at the time, the current focus on motorways has resulted in a serious maintenance backlog, deteriorating road conditions, and a growing burden of sovereign- and subsovereign-guaranteed debt.

Toward Better Management of Public Investment in Infrastructure

The design and management of public investment programs in infrastructure can be a major factor determining the impact of public investment on sector performance. Key issues include

- the need for realistic design of the investment program, in the context of a medium-term framework, to insulate infrastructure from expenditure cuts forced by fiscal stabilization;
- adequate budgeting for operations and maintenance expenditures over time;
- selection of projects based on sound cost-benefit analysis; and
- ensuring value for money in public procurement.

Such measures depend not only on good technical and strategic analysis but also on good governance, including transparency in decision making about priorities and oversight of public investment.

Because of the need to restore fiscal sustainability, many ECA countries (especially in the CIS) have been affected by a dramatic decline in the overall level of public investment as well as a residual approach to investment budgeting. Turkey is an example where public investment has been clearly pro-cyclical as a result of weak portfolio management, overprogramming, and lack of a realistic medium-term perspective. The brunt of fiscal adjustment from 2000 to 2004 was borne by investment in infrastructure. Total public investment (inclusive of local administrations and state-owned enterprises) was cut to 4.2 percent of GNP in 2004 from 6.8 percent in 2000 (World Bank 2006i). Excluding local administrations, the annual allocation for infrastructure investment fell from above 3 percent of GNP in 2000 to below 2 percent in 2004.[27] Total maintenance expenditures were also hit hard, declining from 0.5 percent of GNP in 2000 to 0.3 percent in 2004. With progress on fiscal adjustment, public investment in 2005 rebounded by close to 1 percent of GNP. In Turkey and other ECA countries, the volatility of annual investment allocations has hampered implementation and increased total costs and average completion times of projects.

Ensuring sustainability in medium-term infrastructure investment calls for strengthening the budgetary and investment planning process. A prerequisite to achieving stable and foreseeable annual investment allocations is macroeconomic stability and sustained fiscal discipline. A medium-term expenditure framework can help to insulate infrastructure investment from pro-cyclical volatility. Replacing the annual process of budgetary allocations with a rolling medium-

BOX 4.5

ECA Experiences with Road Funds

Starting in the 1990s, a number of ECA countries created road funds, following practices in other regions, in an attempt to sequester road user charges and ensure their allocation to necessary road expenditures without competition from other sectors. A strong governance mechanism, such as a board representing road users and other stakeholders, was typically favored by advocates of road funds, although not consistently implemented in practice. Critics of road funds, in contrast, argued that further earmarking of proceeds from road funds would reduce the fiscal flexibility and prioritization of expenditures in accordance with sector needs (Gwilliam and Shalizi 1999).

Several ECA countries found that road funds did not bypass difficult resource allocation questions and fell victim to underlying governance problems. Collections of the road fund in Georgia steadily declined from 1999 after governance issues started to emerge. The government attempted to move the fund's management toward a more commercial orientation as well as to improve the governance structure, but the outcome was unsatisfactory because of lack of commitment. The new government abolished the road fund in 2003 and decided to increase funding for maintenance through direct budget transfers. The commitment to a multiyear program and direct budget transfers have helped raise revenues threefold, and have been a stable alternative to the road fund in Georgia (World Bank 2004d).

(continued)

term (usually three-year) process can smooth out cash flows for multiyear projects. Sound cost-benefit analysis and realistic programming are important for ensuring that economically justified projects are indeed selected and, once included in the public investment program, are completed on time. For new EU member countries, the availability of large amounts of structural and cohesion funds for investment provides a unique opportunity to improve infrastructure, if indeed the countries pursue good practices in project selection and in budgeting subsequent operations and maintenance expenditures.

Along with general improvements in investment planning and budgeting, good practices within sectors in prioritizing investments and providing adequate operations and maintenance funding are just as important. In the power sector, for example, investment planning should begin with the identification of a least-cost expansion program. In the water sector, the environmental agenda is beginning to drive the allocation of investment and rehabilitation expenditures as

BOX 4.5 (continued)

Croatia and Romania also are no longer depending on road funds as a vehicle for resource mobilization to meet the annual cost of maintenance. Romania abolished the road fund and has resorted to short-term commercial loans for maintenance and new investments. Increasing reliance on commercial loans and declining state budgets implies a rising level of debt service obligations, and it has become evident that there is still a need to identify a mechanism for raising user revenues. To improve the transparency of financial control in the General Directorate of Roads, Albania has considered some sort of commercial road fund for maintenance, which would be managed by an independent board of public and private stakeholders.[a]

In an interesting departure from the recent regional experience, Poland established a new road fund, called the National Road Fund (KFD), in January 2004. The objective of KFD is to enhance the transparent allocation of resources for upgrading and modernization of the road network. KFD is subject to annual audit and is expected to generate €250 million (US$330million) per year from a special fuel surcharge. Collection of KFD revenues is entrusted to the customs department, and administration and management of EU grant funds to the Polish Central Bank with terms and conditions defined by the Ministry of Finance. Revenues from the fund are used as collateral for floating bonds and raising loans from international financial institutions. Other qualifying expenditures include loans to concessionaires, shadow tolls, and costs of administering the road fund. In the future, the fund may also finance road safety interventions. The Road Administration prepares an approved list of funded projects each year and disburses payments to contractors and concessionaires directly. With strong attention to governance and transparency, Poland's KFD has a better chance of success than the road funds of its neighbors.

Source: Authors, from various sources.

a. The Public Expenditure and Institutional Review on Albania has cautioned against the establishment of the road fund (World Bank 2006a).

a result of growing concerns with water quality, especially for countries joining or hoping to join the EU. In the roads sector, investment strategy sometimes starts with rationalization of the road network, as in Poland. Georgia has established a multiyear framework for maintenance of secondary roads. Planning tools to predict traffic volumes and assess maintenance requirements are being used in some cases. Bosnia and Herzegovina, for example, has a functioning and established asset-management system in the road sector that prioritizes expenditure requirements using the Highway Design and Maintenance-4 highway design decision model. Poland has pursued a consistent increase in its budget for road maintenance in the last few years, with corresponding improvements in the road network. Institutional innovations have also been introduced to increase transparency through annual public disclosure of maintenance expenditures and of technical road quality.

Alignment with the EU *acquis* has been a guiding and motivating factor as EU accession countries strive to improve investment programming and procurement. As part of preaccession negotiations, these countries have to prepare sector operating plans (SOPs) for the use of structural funds, with multiyear investment frameworks. These efforts are still evolving—in Romania, for example, the capacity to program, prioritize, and implement investments remains below EU benchmarks. For both the railway and road sectors, expenditure plans need to be rationalized, particularly to reflect implementation capacity constraints. For the water sector, EU funds require cofinancing from national sources, and these amounts are not currently visible in Romania's medium-term expenditure framework. As experience progresses, the SOP approach may be useful for other ECA countries, especially those in the EU neighborhood who also have some access to associated funding.

Ideally, road maintenance and rehabilitation costs should be met with a combination of budget allocations and cost recovery measures that generate resources from the network users. Road user charges should be linked to the costs of road maintenance, and the social costs of road use. In other words, the user pays principle should form the basis of charges imposed on road users to cover cost of wear and tear in infrastructure, and promote competition between modes of inland transport. The difficulty has often been less with charges to users than with management of the revenues collected. Funding from road user charges has typically covered 30 to 40 percent of maintenance expenditure. Albania and Croatia, for example, have raised significant revenues from user charges, including a fuel levy, but these funds have not ensured an adequate flow of maintenance expenditures. Several countries have experimented with road funds, but these have not often solved fundamental problems of governance (box 4.5).

Building Partnerships with the Private Sector

In the early to mid-1990s, many governments in the region thought that the private sector would be willing to finance and operate major components of the infrastructure sectors, and this hope motivated much of the initial reform effort. Private sector participation can be valuable, not only as a source of cash, technology, and management expertise, but also as a way of transforming the paradigm of service provision from social entitlement to economic good. However, governments need first to set policies to ensure a minimum of financial viability and establish confidence for both investors and consumers.

From 1990 through 2004, private funding flowed predominantly into telecommunications, with energy attracting about one-quarter of the investment and transport and water together obtaining less than 10 percent of the total regional inflow. The majority of transactions took the form of divestiture, with greenfield projects (such as build-own-operate) a close second. Concessions, leases, and management contracts were rarer (6 percent of the total). Half of the private investments in infrastructure were in the CEE countries.

Power generation and distribution attracted much of the private involvement. Among the focus countries, Armenia, Poland, and Georgia privatized significant portions of their generation assets. Only the Slovak Republic privatized its entire power distribution system, although Poland, Romania, and Ukraine have done so for portions of the distribution network. In Albania, the state-owned utility is operated under a management contract, an arrangement that does not involve private risk capital. Management contracts are also being used in Georgia for both distribution and transmission.

On the whole, private sector participation in the power sector has produced beneficial results because private operators have succeeded in improving collections and the reliability of supply. Tariff-related disagreements have been more troublesome in the CIS, and in two cases resulted in disinvestment. A decision by the Georgian regulatory authority in 2002 to raise tariffs, in line with a contractual agreement between the private distribution company and the government, was reversed by the constitutional court, which ordered a rollback. This created conflicts between the company and the government and resulted (together with systemic problems of nonpayment) in departure of the private investor.

The experience with private participation in power has provided some useful lessons. Countries have learned that their emphasis on seeking strategic (mainly Western) investors will not produce major turnarounds in performance in the absence of credible reforms in the basic conditions for financial sustainability. It has become clear that creating payment discipline, bringing tariffs close to at least medium-term cost-recovery levels, and putting in place credible regulatory arrangements are preconditions for success and should be ensured before divestiture, as with Armenia (box 4.3). Setting appropriate conditions for competition is also critical. Unbundling is often called for, and vertically integrated monopolies need to be dismantled before sale. Competition and transparency in the awarding of contracts, such as leases and concessions, are also critical to their success, as well as to public acceptance. Care is also needed to mitigate the risk of contingent liabilities resulting from poorly designed concessions to private operators. In Turkey the government provided guarantees to private operators in electricity generation that subsequently led to legal challenges, arbitration, and further liabilities for the budget.

The water supply and sewerage sector has received only 3 percent of total private investment in the region. Among the focus countries, privately owned and operated water systems are now found in some cities in Poland, the Slovak Republic, and Romania, although they are nowhere as extensive as those in the Czech Republic. A water concession is under way in one city in Albania. Management contracts are the more common of the various forms of private sector provision and are found in Albania, Armenia, Turkey, and Ukraine. Under a management contract the private operator receives a fee with incentives for achieving good performance, but does not finance investment. The Armenian (Yerevan) experience has been so good that the government has decided to make the subsequent arrangement a lease, implying more extensive responsibility for the private partner. A concession is much longer term (at least 15 years) and the contractor finances agreed on investment; the benefits can be much greater but so are the risks if the government (as regulator) does not live up to commitments regarding tariff approvals or associated investments. The results from two high-profile water and wastewater system concessions, one in the Czech Republic and the other in Sofia, Bulgaria, have been quite positive. However, private sector participation in water is not spreading widely throughout ECA, in part because of global retrenchment by the major private water investors. Creditworthy municipal governments are beginning to look at opportunities for borrowing directly on domestic or international capital markets for their needed water investments, provided basic utility performance is satisfactory.

The transport sector has absorbed only about 4 percent of the privately financed investment in the region since 1990. Among the focus countries, the largest recipients have been toll roads in Croatia, Hungary, and Poland. In Hungary, the toll road concessions proved overoptimistic in projecting market demand, and they have been revised to protect the toll operators from traffic risk by transferring the risk to the state. This provides a cautionary note to the Croatian motorway program mentioned earlier, 60 percent of which is funded by sovereign- and subsovereign-guaranteed debt. This experience with private sector participation in major road programs underscores the critical importance of realistic demand forecasts and of risk-sharing arrangements between the public and private sectors, to ensure that the expected benefits for the country are sustainable without undue burden on the government. The road sector has had broader but less visible private sector participation for periodic maintenance, through competitive awarding of contracts. The shift from reliance on government maintenance units to contracting out to the private sector has improved efficiency, although possibly less than could be achieved if legal frameworks and contracts were more transparent (Willoughby 2006).

For most of the region the challenge for railways is to establish commercialization as a basic prerequisite to attract more private involvement. Poland and the Slovak Republic have separated the railways' lines of business, and Romania has converted the three major business lines into legally independent companies (for track infrastructure, freight, and passenger operations) and is investigating privatization of the freight company. In response to EU influence, these three countries have also opened track access for third-party railway operators to allow for competition. Georgia features some private competition in rail supply industries (Amos 2005), and the government in Armenia has recently decided to seek a private concessionaire for its railway.

Conclusions

Adequate infrastructure is essential to economic growth. This overview of status and reform progress in four infrastructure sectors in ECA leads to several conclusions with implications for public finance policy. First, transition countries in ECA inherited more infrastructure stocks than typical in countries at similar levels of per capita income. Thus, they did not face pressures for investment in expansion or suffer absolute supply constraints in the 1990s. However, this cushion—which was much softer and deeper for some countries than others—is no longer evident in most economies. The countries where growth rebounded most strongly are now outgrowing much of their asset base, especially in power, while the less dynamic countries face massive replacement and rehabilitation requirements as a result of years of undermaintenance and the effects of poor technical design (which have contributed to system losses). Quality and reliability of infrastructure are a persistent concern throughout ECA, and past neglect of environmental impacts has also created a backlog of investments in such areas as wastewater treatment.

Second, most ECA countries have adopted policy reforms designed to enhance operational efficiency, financial sustainability, and commercial orientation. The record and results are generally better in the CEE countries of the sample than in the SEE or low-income CIS countries (with the exception of Armenia, which has followed some notable good practices to date). This suggests that an overall environment of better governance and prospects for EU accession are also helpful in spurring reform. The major investment funding becoming availability in the prospective EU member countries can greatly enhance their infrastructure, provided the recipients pursue sound project selection and operations and maintenance practices.

Third, significant hidden costs or implicit subsidies remain in several ECA countries, especially for power and, to a lesser extent, for water, and they create current or contingent liabilities for the public sector. Addressing unaccounted losses, low collection rates, and tariffs below cost recovery should be a priority for both the sectoral and the broader public finance reform agendas.

Fourth, although tariffs set at cost-recovery levels appear to be affordable in the CEE countries,[28] full and rapid adjustment to full cost recovery might be less affordable in many of the SEE and CIS countries, particularly for the lowest income group. Most countries will need to make further improvements in social safety nets to enhance targeting and strengthen administrative efficiency to ensure access of poor households to basic infrastructure services. Such safety nets obviously have fiscal implications, but these can be less burdensome to the general budget and more effective in protecting vulnerable users than the traditional tariff subsidies that persist in many of the countries.

Fifth, governments need to ensure adequate funding not only for needed investments but also for ongoing maintenance. Although experience with dedicated road funds has been largely disappointing to date, institutional arrangements are needed to facilitate user funding to the extent possible and allocate that funding between maintenance and new investment.

Sixth, most ECA countries have transferred responsibility for managing certain types of infrastructure to municipal governments. However, it is unclear whether municipalities have the capacity to enforce financial and operational discipline and to provide appropriate levels of fiscal support. The incentives for municipal investment and the capacity and creditworthiness of municipal governments are becoming increasingly important issues for the public finance agenda.

Finally, scope exists for greater private sector participation in infrastructure, which has expanded rather slowly in recent years. But private sector participation is unlikely to materialize and succeed unless the policy framework ensures financial viability and promotes fair competition. Furthermore, some transactions and contractual arrangements undertaken to date indicate the need for strong vigilance to ensure that private sector participation contributes to improved governance. In any case, the private sector is unlikely to provide the bulk of necessary funding, and provision of infrastructure services will continue to claim an important share of the public budget.

Notes

The authors gratefully acknowledge contributions from Jane Ebinger, Martin Humphreys, Jonathan Kamkwalala, Henry Kerali, Martha Lawrence, Michael Webster, and other staff of the Sustainable Development Department. The chapter also draws from two previous departmental reports (World Bank 2006d, 2006f).

1. Telecommunications, ports and airports, and gas networks are also economic infrastructure but are not discussed here. These are all tariff-based and amenable to fully commercialized operation as well as to private sector provision, and therefore less of a concern to public finance analysis. The chapter also refers only briefly to sewerage, district heating, solid waste disposal, or public transport systems—activities that generate tariff revenues but are typically not fully cost covering even under efficient operation, and generate social externalities. Many of the infrastructure services delivered to households (often called "communal services" in the region) fall under the jurisdiction of municipalities, which bear the public finance responsibility.
2. Toll roads are an exception, although they occupy a very small share of the total road network in most countries.
3. The public expenditure data series collected for the present study has figures on "Transport" or "Transport and Communications" and on "Fuel and Energy." Aside from the fact that these categories are too imprecise to permit sectoral analysis, comparisons across countries or over time, even as shares of GDP, are not likely to be accurate for several reasons. There may be differences in whether the accounts of publicly owned utilities are included in government budgets. If so, whatever costs are recovered from users should not be considered public expenditures. Countries also differ in the extent to which infrastructure providers are privatized or are decentralized to local governments, making it difficult to define comparable expenditure aggregates from the reported public sector data. In countries of most regions, including ECA, water utilities, local roads, and suburban passenger rail services have been largely devolved to local authorities. However, information on municipal budgets tends to be incomplete or missing in national level data sources. It is safe to say that during the socialist period in the ECA transition countries, virtually all infrastructure was developed by centralized public expenditure with little attempt at cost recovery, and that this situation

has been changing at a varied pace in all the focus countries as discussed here. Of the non-ECA focus countries, only Vietnam and possibly Uganda have a similar recent history.

4. Albania, Armenia, Croatia, Georgia, the Kyrgyz Republic, Poland, Romania, the Slovak Republic, Turkey, and Ukraine.
5. The Kyrgyz Republic, Moldova, Tajikistan, and Uzbekistan.
6. Albania, Bosnia and Herzegovina, Croatia, FYR Macedonia, and Serbia and Montenegro.
7. All of the ECA focus countries are energy resource–short, so meeting necessary demands requires imports of fuels or electricity.
8. Power supply in Albania shows effects of constraints in hydropower output from drought, high costs of imported fuel, and lack of adequate investment in new generating capacity to keep up with economic growth.
9. The transition countries of central and eastern Europe that have joined the European Union to date include Bulgaria, the Czech Republic, Estonia, Hungary, Latvia, Lithuania, Poland, Romania, Slovenia, and the Slovak Republic.
10. EBRD *Transition Report* 2001, cited in World Bank 2006d (p. 36, table 43.2). The ratio of per capita annual kWh of electricity consumed to per capita GDP is about 0.8 in middle-income countries, versus 1.4 in Armenia, 1.6 in Georgia, 2.9 in Ukraine, and 4.4 in the Kyrgyz Republic.
11. The weighted average end-user tariff (WAET) is the average tariff rate actually charged taking into account differences in residential and non-residential tariff rates and respective quantities consumed.
12. Turkey will require major energy sector investments (estimated by the Ministry of Energy at US$4 billion annually) to meet its future electricity needs. The cost recovery tariff of US$07.74/kWh estimated in 2003 was actually slightly below the actual 2003 WAET.
13. Albania, Bosnia and Herzegovina, Croatia, FYR Macedonia, and Serbia and Montenegro.
14. Available data are reported for individual utilities, often comprising less than the complete number of utilities in the country. This makes it difficult to compare data over time and across countries because samples may not be consistent. Illustrations provided are based on utility-specific data in each country sample that may not be representative of conditions in the national water sector.
15. The figures for the Kyrgyz Republic represent only Bishkek and Osh, and should not be interpreted as reflecting sector efficiency in the country overall. Only 10 percent of water service in the country is metered.
16. Assumed savings incurred through interrupted water supplies are equal to one-quarter of the cost of maintaining supplies around the clock. Savings reflect reduced need for short-term maintenance and energy consumption. A reduction in the duration of water supplies does not necessarily mean a reduction in consumption.
17. To ensure service standards, necessary maintenance is assumed to be based on the value of assets, at 4 percent per year, based on asset life span of 25 years. This is also consistent with the standard under Soviet rule.
18. Average 2006 figure for 62 utilities, based on the Monitoring and Bench-

marking Program Results in the Water Supply and Sewerage Sector in Albania.

19. Traffic density is measured by the ratio of total traffic units (freight tons-km + passenger-km) to total network capacity.
20. The Georgian railway does not receive any government subsidy, although it is requesting that the government end the cross-subsidization of passenger service from freight and provide a public service obligation fiscal subsidy for passenger services. Georgia railway is profitable and has growing traffic because it carries large volumes of oil and oil products from Kazakhstan and Turkmenistan for onward movement to Europe.
21. World Bank 2006a, chapter on Transport.
22. Working ratio is defined as operating expenses (excluding depreciation) divided by operating revenues (including other operating and nonmonetary income, but excluding government subsidies and privatization proceeds). The higher the working ratio, the higher the degree of financial distress.
23. At least until recently, Armenia Railway has been a very poor example of a railway taking action to downsize and cut costs. The railway may be operating a sharply reduced network (from 800 km down to 350 km), but they keep open facilities on the whole network, including staff for stations that have no traffic. While the railway is modestly profitable, cash flow from operations—US$200,000–400,000 per year in recent years—could fund only US$3–6 million of US$400 million in investment needed to replace or rehabilitate severely deteriorated assets. The Armenian government has recently decided to concession the railway to a private operator, which may make a difference in performance. A better example of a railway in the region (although not in the present sample) that has done well at cutting costs and putting operation on a business footing is Kosovo.
24. World Bank (2004e) reported that no public funds were allocated to railways as of that year.
25. Regional (provincial or secondary roads) and communal roads often have significant social functions compared to their economic functions; they are mostly access roads in either rural or urban areas, span relatively shorter lengths than major roads, and carry low levels of motorized traffic. These roads are usually the financial responsibility of provincial or local governments.
26. Maintenance of secondary roads will be at lower standards and hence lower cost, because of lower traffic density.
27. Some of these infrastructure investment cuts were probably overdue and occurred in the context of the rationalization of the public investment portfolio. In the past, the investment program seems to have been overloaded with low-priority projects. Unclear criteria and processing rules had resulted in "overprogramming" of the public investment program. As a result, the stock of approved but unfinished projects grew to an average of more than 5,000 during the latter half of the 1990s, and the average completion time increased to about 10 years. Many projects received "trace" allocations, that is, amounts nowhere near enough to implement the project, but assigned merely to keep it in the PIP. Ratio-

nalization of the investment portfolio initiated in 2001 has been quite effective, by eliminating about 1,000 projects in the 2001 program (mostly transport, energy, and agriculture projects) and by reducing the number of multiyear projects. The total number of projects further declined from over 5,000 in 2001 to 2,627 in 2005, while the average completion times (based on actual annual investment spending) was reduced to 5.5 years in 2006.

28. At least before taking account of the EU-required environmental investments (for wastewater treatment, for instance).

CHAPTER 5

Education

Dina Abu-Ghaida

Providing educational opportunities to the population is a critical task for all governments and is essential for economic growth. Indeed, education is the one category of spending that is confirmed by all empirical studies to be positively associated with growth rates. However, more spending is not the answer by itself—the efficiency of spending is as important as the amount of spending. While research is clear that a more educated population leads to rapid economic growth, higher levels of public spending are not always associated with better educational outcomes. The efficiency and effectiveness of education spending varies widely among countries. Some of the Europe and Central Asia (ECA) region and non-ECA comparator countries covered in this study have better educational outcomes (whether enrollment rates, average years of schooling, or learning scores) than would be expected given their levels of per capita income or public spending on education, while others have worse outcomes than would be expected.

Although many factors other than public spending influence educational outcomes, clear policy choices also affect the efficiency of public spending. As discussed in greater detail in this chapter, many ECA countries need to deal with excessive numbers of teachers and classrooms as well as low pay scales for teachers, both of which skew public spending toward salaries and away from complementary inputs such as books and supplies while also demotivating teachers. A move toward capitation financing can help spur school consolidation, but it needs to be accompanied by a loosening of labor and wage regulations to facilitate needed restructuring of expenditures. ECA countries have also inherited from socialism a legacy of expensive technical and vocational education at the secondary level, while the trend in other high-growth countries is to move toward greater integration of technical and vocational education with general education streams. Moreover, ECA countries are seeking to enhance efficiency by taking decentralization further than the deconcentration of the socialist era, as well as by greater reliance on private delivery of education services and on private financing, particularly at the tertiary level.

Education and Economic Growth

An extensive body of research exists on the links between education and economic growth. For individuals, research on the value of schooling focuses on the economic returns to differing levels of school attainment, following the analyses of human capital by Mincer (1970, 1974), which consider how investing in differing amounts of schooling affects individual earnings. Over the past 30 years, hundreds of such studies have been conducted around the world (Hanushek and Wössmann 2007) and they have shown that more schooling is associated with higher individual earnings, with a rate of return across countries of roughly 10 percent per additional year of schooling (Psacharopoulos and Patrinos 2004). These basic estimates of the Mincerian earnings models are typically interpreted as the private returns to schooling, with social returns exceeding the private returns as a result of positive externalities, for example, the positive effects of education on crime reduction (Lochner and Moretti 2004), improved health (Currie and Moretti 2003), and increased citizenship participation (Dee 2004).

Moving beyond the microeconomic evidence of the productivity-enhancing effects of education to the macroeconomic perspective of long-run economic growth of countries, there are at least three mechanisms through which education may affect economic growth (Hanushek and Wössmann 2007). First, education increases the human capital in the labor force, which increases labor productivity and thus transitional growth toward a higher equilibrium level of output (as in the augmented neoclassical growth theories, for example, Mankiw, Romer, and Weil [1992]). Second, education may increase the innovative capacity of the economy, and additional knowledge on new technologies, products, and processes promotes growth (as in theories of endogenous growth, for example, Lucas [1988]). Third, education may facilitate the diffusion and transmission of knowledge needed to understand and process new information and to successfully implement new technologies devised by others, which again promotes economic growth (for example, Benhabib and Spiegel [2005]).

Thus, most cross-country empirical studies of long-run economic growth now include some proxy for human capital, and these are invariably significant. The standard method to estimate the effect of education on economic growth is to estimate cross-country growth regressions where countries' average annual growth in GDP per capita over several decades is expressed as a function of measures of schooling and a set of other variables deemed to be important for economic growth (Hanushek and Wössmann 2007). Following the classical contributions by Barro (1991, 1997), a vast early literature of cross-country growth regressions has tended to find a significant positive association between quantitative measures of schooling and economic growth (for an extensive review, see Sianesi and Van Reenen [2003]). Indeed, an extensive robustness analysis by Sala-i-Martin, Doppelhofer, and Miller (2004) of 67 explanatory variables in growth regressions on a sample of 88 countries finds primary schooling to be the most robust influence factor (after an East Asian dummy) on growth in GDP per capita during 1960–96.

Yet questions persist about the interpretation of such relationships. A substantial controversy has emerged in the economics literature about whether it is the *level* of years of schooling (as would be predicted by several models of endogenous growth) or the *change* in years of schooling (as would be predicted by basic neoclassical models) that is the more important driver of economic growth (Hanushek and Wössmann 2007). While recent research tends to find a positive effect of schooling quantity on economic growth, it seems beyond the scope of current data to draw strong conclusions about the relative importance of different mechanisms for school quantity to affect economic growth. Even so, several recent studies suggest that education is important in facilitating research and development and the diffusion of technologies, with initial phases of education more important for imitation, and higher education more important for innovation (Vandenbussche et al. 2006).[16] But reverse causation running from higher economic growth to additional education may be at least as important as the causal effect of education on growth in the cross-country association (Bils and Klenow 2000). It is also important—for economic growth—to get other things right as well, particularly the institutional framework of the economy (Pritchett 2001, 2006).

Investigations of growth have employed various measures of formal schooling activities as proxies for relevant human capital, the most frequently used measures being either the primary- or secondary-school enrollment rate (Barro 1991; Mankiw, Romer, and Weil 1992; Levine and Renelt 1992).[1] See table 5.1. Generally speaking, both the ECA and non-ECA countries demonstrate near-universal primary enrollment rates (only Croatia, Turkey , and Ukraine have primary net enrollment rates below 90 percent); secondary enrollment rates are slightly lower but remain high, and tertiary enrollment shows a wider variation.

The share of secondary enrollments in the academic versus the vocational or technical track provides an interesting insight. As table 5.2 shows, of the ECA focus countries, only Poland and Ukraine have secondary enrollments roughly evenly split between the academic and the vocational tracks. Among the other countries, Albania, Armenia, Georgia, and the Kyrgyz Republic have a substantially higher

TABLE 5.1
Enrollment Rates, 2004

Country	Primary		Secondary		Tertiary
	Gross	Net	Gross	Net	Gross
ECA focus countries					
Albania[a]	104.2	95.6	77.8	73.9	16.4
Armenia	100.9	93.7	91.4	88.7	26.2
Croatiaa	94.4	87.3	88.2	85.0	38.7
Georgia	95.1	92.8	82.3	80.7	41.5
Kyrgyz Republic	98.0	90.1	88.0	—	39.7
Poland	98.9	97.3	96.7	90.0	61.0
Romania	106.5	91.9	85.1	80.8	40.2
Slovak Republic	99.1	—	94.2	—	36.1
Turkey	93.3	89.3	79.2	—	29.0
Ukraine	94.8	82.1	92.9	83.5	65.5
ECA average[b]	103.6	90.4	90.5	—	49.8
Comparator countries					
Chile	103.7	—	89.1	—	43.0
Ireland	106.5	96.4	111.6	86.5	58.5
Korea, Republic of	105.1	99.6	90.9	88.3	88.5
Spain	107.7	99.4	119.1	96.7	65.7
Thailand	98.5	—	77.3	—	41.0
Uganda	125.4	—	18.6	15.1	3.4
Vietnam	98.0	—	73.5	—	10.2

Source: World Development Indicators.
Note: — = Not available.
a. 2003 data.
b. Includes all ECA countries (not only the focus countries) where 2004 data are available.

TABLE 5.2

Upper Secondary Education Enrollment, Percentage Share of Gross Rate, 2004

Country	General or academic	Vocational or technical	Country	General or academic	Vocational or technical
ECA focus countries			*Comparator countries*		
Albania	83.3	16.7	Chile	—	—
Armenia	75.8	24.2	Ireland (2001–02)	100.0	0
Croatia	26.6	73.4	Korea, Republic of	—	—
Georgia	2.8	27.2	Spain (2001–02)	62.0	38.0
Kyrgyz Republic	72.1	27.9	Thailand	—	—
Poland	46.7	53.3	Uganda	—	—
Romania	34.5	65.5	Vietnam	—	—
Slovak Republic	38.2	61.8			
Turkey	—	—			
Ukraine	52.7	47.3			

Sources: TransMONEE 2006 Database, UNICEF IRC, Florence; European Commission 2005.
Note: — = Not available. The gross enrollment rate for ECA countries is calculated using the population ages 15–18,except in the case of the Slovak Republic, where it is those ages 14–17.

share of enrollments in the academic track, while the opposite is true for Croatia, Romania, and the Slovak Republic. The two European comparator countries are yet different: Ireland has no vocational or technical track in upper secondary, and in Spain the academic track accounts for roughly two-thirds of upper secondary enrollment.

Bearing in mind the above-cited evidence on the link between education and growth, a simple scatter plot of secondary net enrollment rate against GDP per capita for 116 countries (figure 5.1) shows the expected positive correlation. All ECA focus and most comparator countries (with the exception of Ireland and Uganda) lie above the regression line, that is, they demonstrate relatively high secondary net enrollment rates for the level of GDP per capita. However, thinking about causality flowing in the opposite direction, that is, the effect of education on growth, then countries above the regression line have relatively low GDP per capita for their level of secondary enrollment. In other words, they do poorly in translating their secondary education into economic growth. Furthermore, among the ECA focus countries, Ukraine, Armenia, and Georgia, all countries where secondary enrollments are more biased to the academic track, have the largest gap between their enrollment rates and GDP per capita. This would imply a tighter link between enrollment in vocational and technical education and economic growth than enrollment in the academic track. A similar scatter plot of tertiary gross enrollment rate against GDP per capita (figure 5.2) shows again a positive relationship between the two but this time the performance of the ECA focus countries is closer to the regression line. That is, the ECA focus countries do better in translating their tertiary education into economic growth.

Notwithstanding the fact that growth regressions tend to include schooling flow variables such as net or gross enrollments rates as proxies for human capital, arguably these do not accurately represent the relevant stock of human capital. To deal with this problem Barro and Lee (1993) pioneered the development of better schooling stock variables through the use of individual country survey and census data. A plot of the mean years of education of the population ages 25 years and older against per capita GDP (figure 5.3) shows the familiar positive correlation again. Although data are only available for five of the ECA focus countries, Romania and Turkey are farthest from the regression line, with Romania demonstrating lower than expected GDP per capita, and Turkey higher than expected, given their populations' mean years of education.

A challenging problem made clear by the alternative of using mean years of education, however, comes from the lack of adjustment for schooling quality. It seems beyond doubt that the amount of knowledge acquired in one year of schooling is not independent of the qual-

FIGURE 5.1

Secondary Net Enrollment Rate and Per Capita GDP, 2000

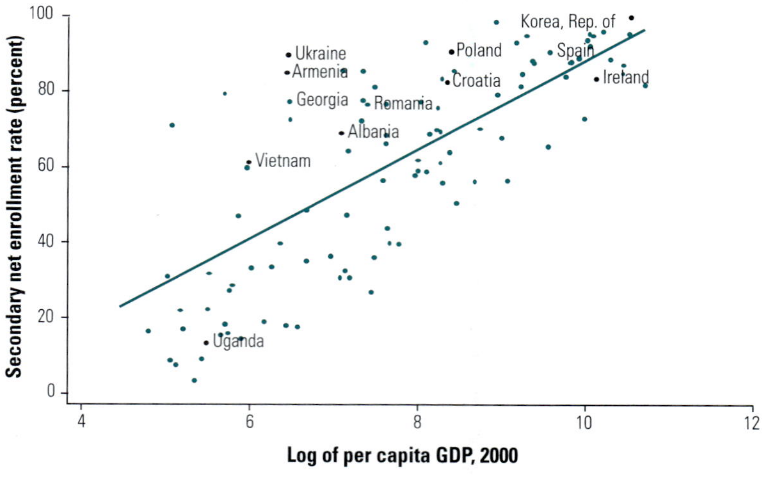

Source: World Development Indicators.

Note: The line corresponds to the predicted enrollment rate from a weighted regression on log per capita GDP and a constant, with the weights given by population in a country. The sample size for the regression is 105 countries. Only the ECA focus and comparator country names are included. Data are provided for 2000 for consistency purposes because the latest data on mean years of education available from Barro and Lee (2001), which will be used in figure 5.2, are for 2000.

FIGURE 5.2
Tertiary Gross Enrollment Rate and Per Capita GDP, 2000

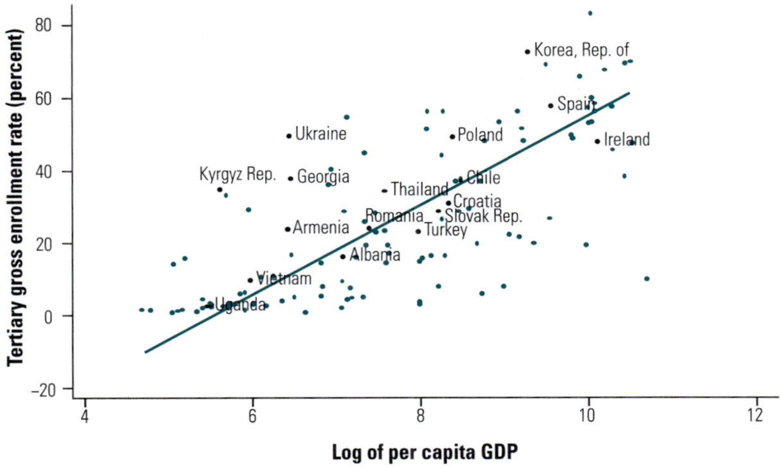

Source: World Development Indicators.

Note: The line corresponds to the predicted enrollment rate from a weighted regression on log per capita GDP and a constant, with the weights given by population in a country. The sample size for the regression is 120 countries. Only the ECA focus and comparator country names are included.

FIGURE 5.3
Mean Years of Education and Per Capita GDP, 2000

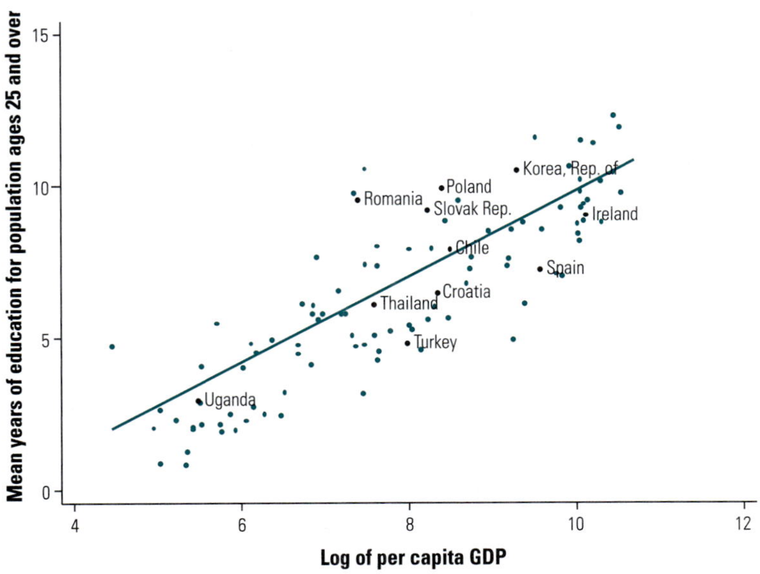

Sources: WDI; Barro and Lee 2001.

Note: The line corresponds to the predicted years of education from a weighted regression on log per capita GDP and a constant, with the weights given by population in a country. The sample size for the regression is 106 countries. Only the ECA focus and comparator country names are included.

ity of the education system in which it takes place. Different increases in skills depend on the efficiency of the education system in which the schooling takes place, the quality of teaching, the educational infrastructure, and the curriculum. Thus, rather than counting how long students have sat in school, how much students have learned while in school would seem to determine the effect of education on economic growth. Indeed, when using data from international student achievement tests through 1991 to build a measure of educational quality, Hanushek and Kimko (2000) find a statistically and economically significant positive effect of the quality of education on economic growth over 1960–90 that dwarfs the association between quantity of education and growth.

Crouch and Fasih (2004) address lack of a common measure of learning (and therefore education quality) across many developing countries by constructing an imputed learning score that uses the overlap between various international assessments to assign a likely value to those countries that only participated in one assessment on a scale equivalent to the 1999 application of the Trends in International Mathematics and Science Study. Figure 5.4 shows the positive correlation between this imputed learning score and GDP per capita.

FIGURE 5.4

Correlation Between Imputed Learning Score and GDP Per Capita, 2000

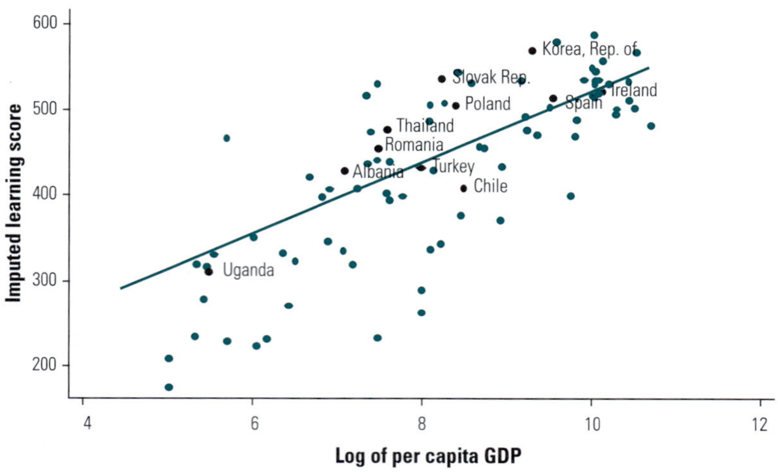

Sources: World Development Indicators; Crouch and Fasih 2004.

Note: The line corresponds to the predicted learning score from a weighted regression on log per capita GDP and a constant, with the weights given by population in a country. The sample size for the regression is 86 countries. Only the ECA focus and comparator country names are included.

Although again the coverage of ECA focus countries is limited, it is arguably the case that both the focus and comparator countries are quite clustered around the regression line. Turkey, in particular, lies far closer to the regression line than when mean years of education alone were considered, so that correcting this stock variable for its quality leads to a smaller gap between education and expected GDP per capita.

Turning to the comparator countries, the Republic of Korea represents a clear outlier with higher education outcomes than its GDP per capita would predict, or conversely, lower GDP per capita than its education measures would predict. The other countries lie close to the regression line, with the exception of Ireland and Chile, which demonstrate somewhat higher GDP per capita than their education measures would indicate. Indeed, OECD (2000) reports that the improvement in human capital seems to be a common factor behind the growth process of the past decades in all Organisation for Economic Co-operation and Development (OECD) countries, but especially so in Italy, Greece, Ireland, and Spain, where the increase in human capital accounted for more than half a percentage point acceleration in growth in the 1990s compared with the previous decade.

Public Education Spending and Education Outcomes

Given the link between education outcomes and economic growth outlined above, the issue of how to achieve better education outcomes—and the role public education expenditures play—becomes important. Indeed, public education expenditures constitute a significant outlay on the part of governments, averaging 5.5 percent of GDP and 13.3 percent of total public spending in OECD countries in 2003 (OECD 2006a). Turning to the ECA focus and comparator countries, with the exception of Poland and Ukraine, the percentage shares of public education expenditures in GDP are lower than the 2003 OECD average (table 5.3). The shares for Armenia and Georgia are particularly low at 2.1 and 2.9 percent, respectively. However, the OECD share of public education expenditures in total government expenditures is surpassed by several of the focus and comparator countries, including Chile, Korea, Thailand, Uganda, and Ukraine.

In contrast to the general finding that education has a positive effect on growth, many studies show that the relationship between public spending for education and measures of education attainment is weak (Flug, Spilimbergo, and Wachtenheim 1998; Landau 1986; Mingat and Tan 1992, 1998; Noss 1991). Instead, other variables have

TABLE 5.3
Total Public Education Expenditure, 2003

Country	GDP	Total public expenditure	Country	General or GDP	Total public expenditure
ECA focus countries			*Comparator countries*		
Albania	3.1	—	Chile	4.1	19.1
Armenia	2.1	—	Ireland (2001–02)	4.4	13.2
Croatia	4.7	—	Korea, Republic of	4.6	16.1
Georgia	2.9	13.1	Spain (2001–02)	4.5	11.2
Kyrgyz Republic	4.4	—	Thailand	4.2	27.5
Poland	5.8	12.7	Uganda	5.2	18.3
Romania	3.6	—	Vietnam	—	—
Slovak Republic	4.4	11.0			
Turkey	3.7	—			
Ukraine	5.6	19.8			
Europe and Central Asia	4.4	—			

Sources: World Development Indicators, Eurostat, and TransMONEE databases.
Note: — = Not available.

been found to be important in explaining education attainment, including per capita income (Flug, Spilimbergo, and Wachtenheim 1998; Mingat and Tan 1992), the age distribution of the population (Mingat and Tan 1992), and family background or parental education (Appleton and Mackinnon 1996). As figures 5.5 and 5.6 show, the correlation between different education outcomes and the share of public education expenditure in GDP is weak (the scatter plots do not reveal a clear pattern). This is true when considering secondary net enrollment or tertiary gross enrollment rates. Nonetheless, insofar as one is able to comment on the performance of the ECA focus and comparator countries in these figures, it is the case that, with the exception of Uganda, they tend to show better enrollment rates than would be expected given their levels of expenditure.

While Hanushek and Kimko (2000) find that labor-force quality has a strong relationship with economic growth, they further find that quality differences are not necessarily related to the resources devoted by a country to schooling. Indeed, the scatter plot for imputed learning score (Crouch and Fasih 2004) and public education expenditures as a share of GDP (figure 5.7) reveals no relationship between the two. Nonetheless, most of the ECA focus and comparator countries, with the exception of Turkey, Chile, and Uganda, are in the upper hemisphere of the scatter plot.

In the United States, the Coleman Report (Coleman et al. 1966) is credited with launching an explosion of studies estimating the relationship between educational outcomes and school inputs, including

FIGURE 5.5

Correlation Between Secondary Net Enrollment Rate and Public Education Expenditure as Share of GDP, 2000

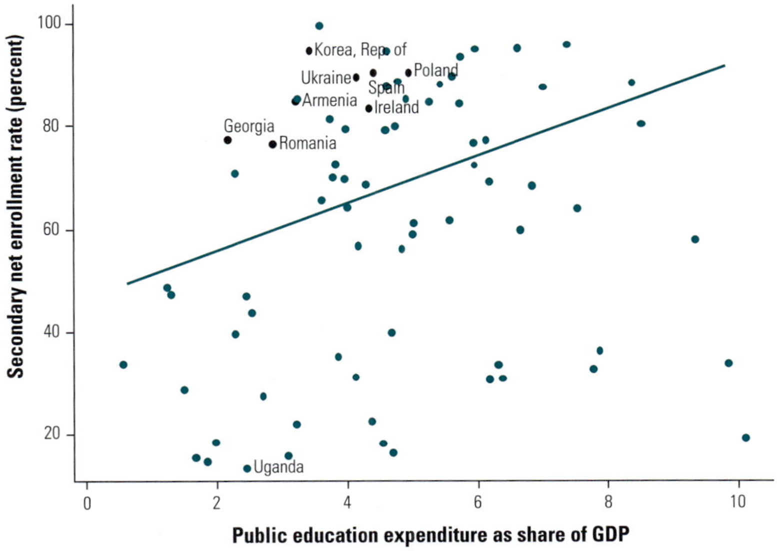

Source: World Development Indicators.

Note: The line corresponds to the predicted enrollment rate from a weighted regression on percentage share of public education expenditure in GDP and a constant, with the weights given by population in a country. The sample size for the regression is 76 countries. Only the ECA focus and comparator country names are included.

resources. The general objective was to sort out the causal impacts of school factors (that is, aspects that can potentially be influenced by policy) from other influences on student achievement, including family background, peers, neighborhood influences, and the like. The report was broadly interpreted to find that schools do not matter and that family background and peers explained most of the variation in education outcomes. By the mid-1980s, Hanushek (1986) included 147 studies in a survey of the literature relating educational outcomes to school inputs. Ten years later, Hanushek (1996) found more than double the number of studies to survey. The reviews and conclusions of Hanushek's analyses reinforced the findings of the Coleman Report. As Hanushek (1997) wrote, "Simple resource policies hold little hope for improving student outcomes."

However, using more sophisticated meta-analytical techniques than Hanushek's simple "vote counting," Hedges and Greenwald (1996) concluded that among the studies surveyed in Hanushek (1989), per pupil expenditures, teacher experience, and teacher-pupil

FIGURE 5.6

Correlation Between Tertiary Gross Enrollment Rate and Public Education Expenditure as Share of GDP, 2000

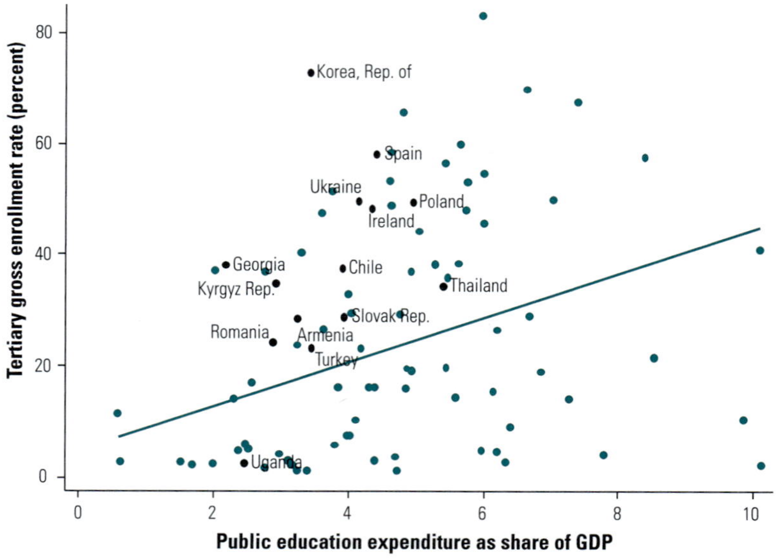

Source: World Development Indicators.

Note: The line corresponds to the predicted enrollment rate from a weighted regression on percentage share of public education expenditure in GDP and a constant, with the weights given by population in a country. The sample size for the regression is 90 countries. Only the ECA focus and comparator country names are included.

ratios are positively related to student outcomes. They also found that the sizes of the effect of per pupil expenditures were large and educationally important. Other analyses of the link between public education expenditures and education outcomes highlight the importance of one or more of the following attributes of education spending: (a) efficiency of public spending, (b) intrasectoral allocation of public spending, (c) private education spending, and (d) governance.

Enhancing the Efficiency of Education Spending

Governments of developing and transition countries typically spend resources equivalent to between 15 and 40 percent of GDP. Hence, small changes in the efficiency of public spending could have a significant impact on GDP and the attainment of the government's objectives. The first challenge faced by stakeholders is measuring and

FIGURE 5.7

Correlation Between Imputed Learning Score and Public Education Expenditure as Share of GDP, 2000

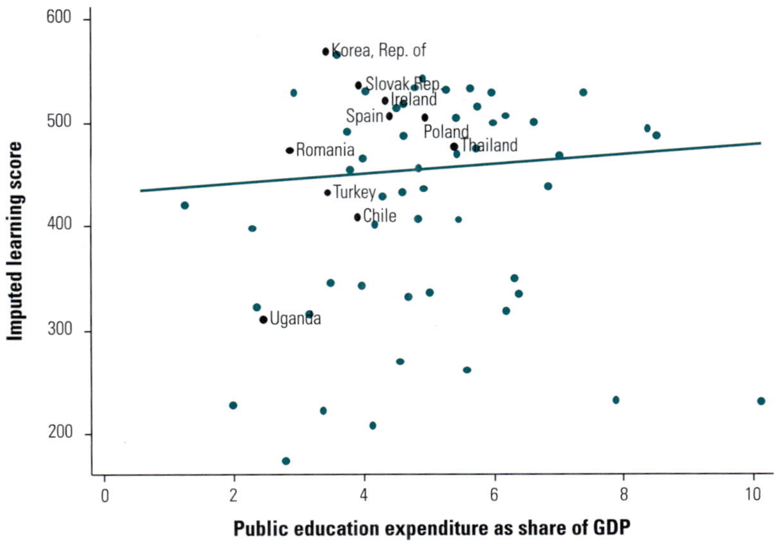

Sources: World Development Indicators; Crouch and Fasih 2004.

Note: The line corresponds to the predicted learning score from a weighted regression on percentage share of public education expenditure in GDP and a constant, with the weights given by population in a country. The sample size for the regression is 62 countries. Only the ECA focus and comparator country names are included.

scoring efficiency. A study by Herrera and Pang (2005) estimates efficiency of public spending on education as the distance between observed input-output combinations and an efficiency frontier (defined as the maximum attainable output for a given level of inputs). Both input inefficiency (excess input consumption to achieve a level of output) and output inefficiency (output shortfall for a given level of inputs) are scored in a sample of 140 countries using data from 1975 to 2002. The study uses nine indicators of education output: primary school enrollment (gross and net), secondary school enrollment (gross and net), literacy of youth, average years of school, first level complete and second level complete (as a share of those ages 15 years and older), and learning scores (the Crouch and Fasih [2004] dataset discussed above).

When the analysis is conducted for learning scores on a sample of developing and transition countries only, several ECA countries appear on the efficiency frontier (Bulgaria, the Czech Republic,

Hungary, and Russia) as well as the comparator country Chile (see figure 5.8). However, when the sample includes developed countries, as in figure 5.9, this is no longer the case. And though Chile appears to be efficient, with learning scores of about 400 points, the country could still achieve higher learning scores of over 500 points at the cost of additional public spending, assuming it moved along the efficiency frontier to the higher target output level. In other words, the fact that Chile is spending efficiently does not necessarily imply that it is achieving high-quality education.

Decentralization

In 1980, Chile's military government (1973–90) launched a profound market-based education reform (Delannoy 2000). Its objective was to promote greater efficiency through administrative decentralization, capitation-based financing, labor deregulation, and open competition between public and privately administered schools. The expected

FIGURE 5.8
Learning Scores Efficiency Frontier: Developing and Transition Countries Sample

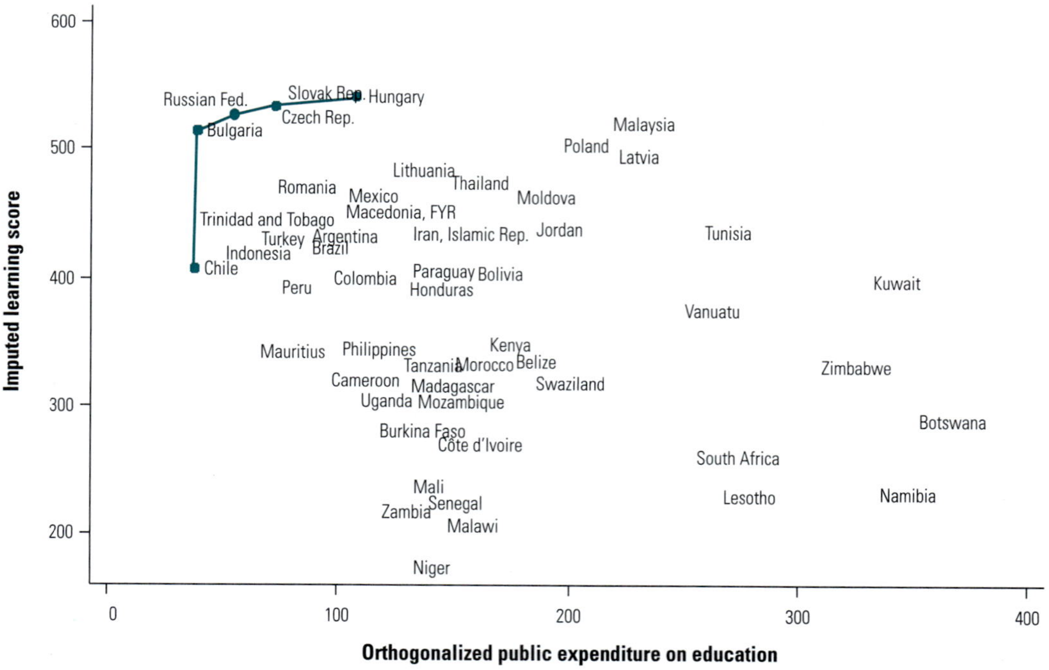

Source: Herrera and Pang 2005.

benefits of decentralization included increased efficiency in the production of services, improved decision making with the use of local information, greater accountability, and improved responsiveness to local needs and conditions. Some evidence indicates that Chile may have increased public sector efficiency through implementing decentralization policies, because total expenditures fell while output measured by average achievement scores did not decline (Parry 1997; also see below).

Subnational governments are an important part of the public sector in ECA countries. They provide basic public services both in the social sectors (education, health, and social assistance) and in infrastructure (water supply, sewerage, and transport). For example, they account for about one-quarter of government spending in the EU-8 countries[2] (Dillinger 2006). According to conventional economic theory, the primary aim of a system of local government finance is to promote efficiency in the allocation of resources. Theory argues that if the benefits of particular services are largely confined to local juris-

FIGURE 5.9

Learning Scores Efficiency Frontier: Developing, Transition, and Developed Countries Sample

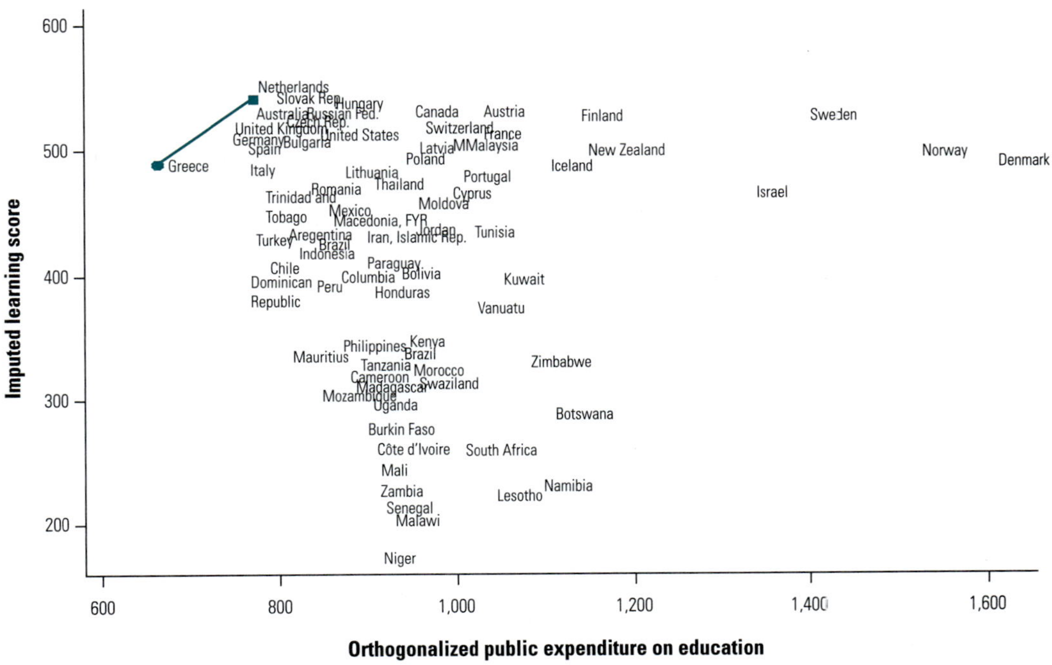

Source: Herrera and Pang 2005.

dictions, welfare gains can be achieved by permitting the level and mix of such services to vary according to local preferences.

In ECA countries, education is the largest single item of local government expenditure. It accounts for one-quarter to one-half of total local government expenditure in the EU-8 countries, for example. By the same token, local governments dominate the provision of primary and secondary education. As table 5.4 shows, local governments account for roughly two-thirds of total public spending on education in all ECA focus countries (where data are available) with the exception of Croatia. This is not true for the comparator countries for which data are available, with Ireland's and Spain's shares at 25 percent and 4 percent, respectively.

However, despite the prominence of local governments in financing primary and secondary education, the incentives of the pretransition period were such that planners determined wages, subsidies, and prices using a complex system of centrally mandated input norms that were in many instances adopted in the 1930s (Berryman 2000). Space norms resulted in wasted space—for example, large lobbies and highly specialized laboratories and workshops that were and remain underutilized. Staffing norms encouraged inefficiencies: for example, resources were allocated by classroom with each class getting a teacher and teaching aids. Schools were therefore encouraged to minimize class size to maximize the number of teachers and teaching aids. As a result, the fact that local governments generally accounted for the majority of public sector spending on primary and secondary education did not translate into improved efficiency of spending.

The post–socialist era systems of education financing, therefore, reflect an acute desire to encourage efficiency in the use of education funding, often by taking decentralization further than the deconcen-

TABLE 5.4
Share of Local Government in Total Public Education Spending

Country	Local share of total public education spending (%)	Country	Local share of total public education spending (%)
ECA focus countries:		*Comparator countries:*	
Croatia (2003)	24	Ireland (2004)	25
Georgia (2005)	73	Korea, Republic of	—
Poland (2005)	72	Spain (2004)	4
Romania (2002)	56		
Slovak Republic (2005)	67		
Turkey	—		
Ukraine (2005)	63		

Source: Government Finance Statistics Yearbook 2006.
Note: — = Not available.

tration of the socialist era. All the EU-8 countries, for example, use some method to constrain the demand for transfers for central government support. One particular focus has been on spending on underenrolled schools. In the case of the EU-8 countries, an overdimensioned system of primary and secondary education is part of the inheritance from the Soviet era. Schools were designed for an expanding population and one that was still to a large extent rural, but the number of school-age children has dropped precipitously in the EU-8 countries, and in rural areas more so than in urban ones. As a result, ministries of education confront an oversupply of school rooms and teachers. The education financing system of most EU-8 countries now reflects attempts to address this problem using fiscal instruments.

Capitation Financing

Hungary, Lithuania, the Czech Republic, as well as the focus countries Poland and the Slovak Republic, now employ some form of capitation-based financing for primary education.[3] The distribution of funding for education on a per pupil (capitation) basis allows local governments considerable discretion over how these funds are used. In theory, this approach has several advantages. It ensures a minimum level of education financing in all jurisdictions while allowing the central government to ration the level of such spending through its control over the per capita amount. At the same time, it permits local governments to find the most efficient means of providing education within this overall spending envelope. In particular, it imposes efficiency measures on jurisdictions with underenrolled schools. Under a capitation-based formula, falling enrollment will cause a drop in school funding, forcing local governments to close schools they can no longer afford.

None of the five countries employs a single, nationally uniform amount. Instead, capitation rates are adjusted to reflect ostensible differences in the costs of providing education. In Poland, for example, rural schools receive a 33 percent supplement over the basic per capita amount. Towns with populations under 5,000 receive an 18 percent supplement. Hungary also supplements its standard per capita amount with additional funding for primary education in villages with populations of 3,000–3,500 and those with fewer than 3,000 inhabitants. In the Czech Republic, capitation figures distinguish among different levels and forms of education as well as among regions. Regional variations are intended to reflect variations in labor costs, and therefore favor rather than discriminate against Prague. These differentials have been used, in part, to soften the impact of the switch to capitation-based financing in rural areas. Additional transitional arrangements have had to be introduced to smooth the adjustment process. In Poland, for example, the initial weights reflected teacher characteristics so that places with unusually high wage levels did not experience extreme cuts (this provision has since been phased out).

An important issue threatens the success of capitation-based financing: the inability of local governments to dismiss staff. While falling enrollment triggers a drop in funding, local governments often lack the legal authority or political will to make corresponding cuts in staff. In Poland, for example, school directors are, in theory, free to make their own decisions about staffing levels. However, regulations constrain dismissals: although a teacher may be dismissed when a school is totally or partially liquidated, a municipality must provide six month's severance pay and re-employ the teacher at the first opportunity (see box 5.1). Similar constraints on downsizing exist in Lithuania and Hungary. Political constraints appear to be particularly acute in municipalities where downsizing implies the closure of entire schools. It is therefore arguably the case that attempts to use the system of intergovernmental relations to encourage greater efficiency in the production of public services have not been very successful. While the majority of the EU-8 countries now finance education on a capitation basis, this has often not been sufficient to prompt the closure of underenrolled classrooms or schools.

Teaching Wage Bill

The ability to right-size the teaching force is particularly important given the finding that spending tends to be more inefficient in countries in which the wage bill represents a higher fraction of total expenditure (Herrera and Pang 2005). Mingat and Tan (1998) also point to the importance of teachers' salaries in increasing the cost of education in low-income countries. They estimate that 50 percent of the difference in education attainment between high-income and low-income countries can be attributed to lower teachers' salaries in high-income countries, which release resources for nonwage inputs such as textbooks.

Table 5.5 shows that staff costs represent roughly 70 percent of total education expenditures in several ECA focus as well as comparator countries. This share is on the low end compared with the salary bill for teachers across a sample of 47 countries in six regions, including ECA (Bruns, Mingat, and Rakatomalala 2003). In that study, the teaching bill represented more than 70 percent of recurrent

BOX 5.1

Poland: The First Decade of Capitation Financing in Education

Between the fall of communism in 1989 and 2000, Poland transferred responsibility for the management of some 35,000 preschools, primary schools, and secondary schools to democratically elected local governments. At the same time, the national government significantly changed the structure and content of primary and secondary education, and reformed the way it regulated and financed the sector. However, the assignment of managerial and financial responsibilities to local governments remained confused. It was unclear who was responsible for setting and financing teachers' wages (the national government or local governments) and who was responsible for hiring and firing them (local governments or school directors). Initially, amendments to the Teachers' Charter made in 1990 simply transferred the national government's wage and benefit obligations to teachers to local governments. The only significant right given to local governments with respect to teacher employment was the right to provide teachers with motivational bonuses beyond those mandated by the law. But the charter did not specify employment standards for teachers such as pupil-teacher ratios or class sizes. Instead, these kinds of norms were contained in a variety of other ordinances and expressed as pedagogical minimums, not employment standards. This meant that while it was possible to determine the minimum number of teachers needed to teach any given grade level, there was no easy way to determine the maximum number of teachers that should be employed in any given school or, for that matter, in any given jurisdiction. At the same time, the law guaranteed that the national government would provide local governments with the financial resources necessary to realize their education responsibilities, including teachers' pay and the maintenance of schools. Without the specification of employment norms, this legal guarantee became an unconditional promise by the national government to fully fund the hiring practices of school directors and local governments.

This division of labor worked reasonably well during the first half of the 1990s, because transfers by national to local governments for education were generally in line with the basic operating costs of schools and local governments were, in fact, primarily concerned with improving school infrastructure. With time, however, the division of labor became an increasing problem for three reasons. First and most important, the demographic decline radically increased the per pupil costs of small rural schools, costs that the national government was unwilling to finance fully. Second, the national government increased teachers' wages without increasing commensurately the transfers it provided to local governments. Third, popular pressure on local governments to improve and restructure their school systems not only forced them, given falling state transfers, to contribute increasingly significant shares of their general revenues to the sector, but also to become concerned with what their resources were actually buying in the way of educational quality.

Source: Levitas and Herczynski 2002.

spending in the education sector in virtually all countries and as much as 95 percent in some. In addition, a wide variation in average annual salaries was observed across the 47 countries, ranging from 0.6 times to 9.6 times per capita GDP. In the Sahelian African countries, for example, the average is more than six times per capita GDP, while in ECA countries the average is less than per capita GDP. The observed average in the highest primary-completion countries in the sample is, by contrast, 3.3. times per capita GDP. Thus, the fact that the teaching wage bill is at roughly 70 percent in ECA countries, despite the relatively low average teacher salary, is a reflection of the excess numbers of teachers.

Indeed, Bruns, Mingat, and Rakatomalala (2003) document that the core service delivery parameters in Armenia, Georgia, and Moldova (the three ECA low-income countries that had not achieved universal primary completion) all deviate sharply from the benchmarks in a pattern common to ECA countries: the number of teachers employed (relative to the student population) is far higher than in other countries and the average teacher salary is far lower. In a simulation for determining the Education For All financing gap conducted by, Bruns, Mingat, and Rakatomalala, that takes into account improving both quality and efficiency of service delivery, the average teacher salary in Armenia would increase dramatically, from 0.6 to 3.5 times per capita GDP, as a quality measure in the simulation. As a corresponding efficiency measure, the 13:1 pupil-teacher ratio would rise to 40:1, also a tremendous adjustment. Given the projected low growth of the school-age population, the clear implication is that the number of teachers employed would decline significantly. The authors acknowledge that the realism of such dramatic shifts is questionable, but they point out that "the simulation serves to illuminate

TABLE 5.5

Distribution of Total Annual Expenditure in Public-Sector Education Institutions by Functional Classification (Preprimary through Tertiary), 2001

Country	Capital expenditure	Current expenditure	
		Staff	Other
ECA focus countries			
Poland	6.7	68.6	24.7
Romania	8.6	66.0	25.4
Slovak Republic	6.2	68.1	25.7
Comparator countries			
Ireland	12.6	68.0	19.4
Spain	8.9	77.7	13.4

Source: European Commission 2005.

the root causes of Armenia's key educational issues: excess staffing, low teacher motivation, absenteeism, and informal shifting of costs to families, linked to inadequate salaries; and high operating and maintenance costs for an inefficient number of schools and classrooms, which divert resources from other needed areas such as modernization of curriculum and learning materials, teacher retraining, and system management" (Bruns, Mingat, and Rakatomalala 2003: 79).

Nor has the move to capitation financing necessarily facilitated the process of increasing teachers' salaries. While the post–socialist era systems of education financing sought to improve efficiency of expenditures, a first priority was to ensure a basic level of education financing in all jurisdictions, regardless of the strength of their local tax bases. This resulted, for example, in countries financing the largest component of education spending—teachers' salaries—through some form of intergovernmental transfer. At the same time, with the implementation of capitation financing, central governments showed unwillingness or inability to increase the level of capitation transfers to reflect centrally mandated increases in costs. For example, the principal determinant of costs—the wage level—is largely determined by the central government in the EU-8 countries. In Lithuania, the national civil service laws sets out a structure of pay scales for municipal employees, based on grade, years of employment, and—in the case of teachers—class size and number of classes taught. The pay structure is expressed as a multiple of the so-called basic wage. As a result, government changes in the basic wage trigger automatic increases in salaries. In Poland, similarly, teachers' salaries are determined on the basis of the Teacher's Charter and annual ministerial regulations on the remuneration of teachers (Fiszbein 2001). Yet, the level of central funding is determined as a fixed percentage of total projected government expenditure.

Vocational versus Academic Upper Secondary Track

Table 5.2 showed that vocational education plays a varying but important role in upper secondary education in all of the ECA focus countries. A key issue in the efficient delivery of secondary education is the balance between academic and vocational education. Fewer technical tracks, more emphasis on general skills, and better links with higher technical education can make vocational education more cost effective (Di Gropello 2006). A review of 24 studies on 20 countries in Africa, Asia, Latin America, and the United States shows that unit costs of vocational and technical schools are 1.14 to 7.20 times higher than those of academic schools (Tsang 1997). Middleton,

Ziderman, and Van Adams (1993) described why the unit costs in vocational and technical education are generally higher than unit costs in academic schooling. First, student-teacher ratios tend to be smaller in vocational and technical schools because of a more segmented curriculum and smaller classes due to training workshops. Second, though this varies across countries, the policy in most countries requires a certain level of experience or license-based skills to teach vocational and technical courses, and thus schools compete against industry to hire qualified teachers, which leads to increases in teachers' salaries. Third, vocational and technical education requires specialized equipment and facilities to meet the level of technology that is used in industries, and the need for up-to-date equipment and facilities increases the costs of vocational and technical education continuously.

However, current technical and vocational education trends can potentially decrease unit costs and improve quality and relevance. In particular, a more integrated general-technical curriculum could result in less separation between tracks and schools and therefore improve economies of scale in the use of teachers and equipment, as well as yield higher-quality technical education. A recent comparison of mean efficiency scores across technical-vocational and general education schools in the comparator country Korea shows no or little difference in cost effectiveness (Di Gropello 2006). The good efficiency results of the Korean vocational schools, at least concerning human resources, can be related to the country's successful vocational education framework. In 1991, the government pushed forward new policies to increase the share of students attending vocational schools to half of total upper secondary enrollment. Subsequently, the country made substantial efforts to improve curricula (with an emphasis on general skills) and link vocational high schools with technical colleges so that rather than providing terminal degrees, vocational high school became a prerequisite for advanced studies.

Another efficient and innovative case of reform of vocational education occurred in the comparator country Chile (Di Gropello 2006). The reform proceeded gradually by education level (starting with primary in 1992 and extending to higher education in 1998). It is now fully framed in a lifelong learning perspective, providing strong links between secondary and higher education levels, and these levels and the productive sector (through formal and informal training), which allows continuity and flexibility in the delivery of technical education. The Chilean vocational education system is also an efficient one, composed now of only 13 vocational categories compared with 400 training specialties before the 1980s.

The Intrasectoral Allocation of Public Spending

Gupta, Verhoeven, and Tiongson (2002) reassess whether increased public spending on education matters using a comprehensive data set of public spending and social indicators for 50 developing and transition countries. Their results indicate that in education, both the overall level of public spending and intrasectoral allocation matter. In particular, shifting spending toward primary and secondary education is associated with improvements in widely used measures of education attainment. The authors argue that if expenditure allocations for education are to boost economic growth and promote the well-being of the poor, policy makers in many developing and transition countries need to pay greater attention to allocations within the sector. Baldacci, Guin-Siu, and de Mello (2003) find that the ratio of public spending per pupil in tertiary education to that in primary education, measuring the intrasectoral composition of education spending, correlates negatively with both primary and secondary enrollment rates.

Table 5.6 shows expenditures per tertiary student as a percentage share of expenditures per primary student, both measured as a percent of GDP per capita. Comparator countries have ratios that are close to or smaller than the OECD average (with the exception of Uganda), and ECA focus countries have ratios higher than the OECD average (with the exception of Poland and Croatia). Korea has one of the lowest ratios worldwide of public expenditure per tertiary student to primary student. In most of the economies of East Asia, the excess demand for secondary and tertiary education (generated by rapid attainment of universal primary education) has been met largely by a combination of expansion in the public secondary system, meritocratic entrance requirements, and a self-financed private system (World Bank 1993). This stands in stark contrast to many other low- and middle-income economies, which have stressed public subsidies to university education. Indeed, as table 5.6 further shows, there is a clear correlation between the ratio of expenditures on tertiary relative to primary students and the share of public funds in expenditures on tertiary education: the lower the ratio, the lower the share of public funds. For the two ECA focus countries where data are available, Poland and the Slovak Republic, the difference is between 69 percent of expenditures on tertiary education being publicly funded in Poland versus 86 percent in the Slovak Republic.

A recent World Bank report on reforms in the financing of higher education in the countries of Central and Eastern Europe and the Baltics (Canning, Godfrey, and Holzer-Zelazewska 2006) documents how participation rates in higher education began to rise immediately following transition, fueled by evidence that a university degree offered a greater chance of employment in an increasingly uncertain labor market. Expansion of access to higher education became a priority for governments. Throughout the 1990s, the difficulty of centrally managing a growing and more diversified higher education system became increasingly clear. Inevitably, increased participation began to raise questions about the sustainability, equity, and quality of the systems. In most countries, private provision of higher education services emerged in response to the need for system expansion. By the middle of the 1990s, new forms of allocating finances to universities had emerged, such as block grants (Czech Republic), normative financing based on the number of students and on norms for research and maintenance (Hungary), and performance-related financing (Estonia). The economic reality of the need to attract more private financing into the system to offset the limitations in state funding had become clear.

Canning, Godfrey, and Holzer-Zelazewska (2006) further report on the share of financial aid to students as a percentage of total public expenditure on education. Poland stands out in this regard, with merely 0.4–0.5 percent of education expenditures in 2001 dedicated

TABLE 5.6
Intrasectoral Composition of Public Education Spending

Country	Tertiary student expenditure as % of primary student expenditure (average for 1998–2004)	Share of public sources in expenditures for tertiary education (2003)
Korea, Republic of	42	23.2
Poland	80	69.0
Spain	118	76.9
Chile	128	—
2003 EU-19 average	129	84.3
Croatia	144	
2003 OECD average	148	76.4
Thailand	189	—
Ireland	247	83.8
Slovak Republic	275	86.2
Romania	281	—
Kyrgyz Republic	320	—
Ukraine	364	—
Turkey	393	95.2
Albania	470	—
Armenia	639	—
Uganda	1,675	—

Sources: World Development Indicators; OECD 2006.
Note: — = Not available.

to financial aid in primary, secondary, and higher education. This compares to an EU-8 average of 5.8 percent for primary and secondary students, and 12.8 percent for students in higher education institutions. At the same time, Poland is an outlier among the EU-8 countries with regard to its share of its university students in private institutions (close to 30 percent). Although the Polish constitution guarantees free higher education to all who achieve entry level qualifications, in fact over 50 percent of all students pay some form of tuition fees, including both those attending private higher education institutions and extra-mural, part-time, or evening students who can be charged tuition fees. As a result, there is a 17 percentage point difference between the education enrollment rates of 19–24 year-olds of the richest and poorest consumption quintiles (table 5.7) although the level is still quite high for the latter. Thus, although Poland's intrasectoral allocation of resources in education may indicate the highest impact on growth, there are equity considerations that must also be taken into account.

The Role of Private Spending

Herrera and Pang (2005) find that countries in which public financing is a larger share of total expenditure on health services also register lower efficiency scores. However, the data set available for the health sector is not available for education, so they do not provide parallel analysis for the education sector. Nonetheless, table 5.8 shows that for both ECA and comparator countries where data are available, the overwhelming share of education expenditures are public, except in Korea, where expenditures are more evenly distributed between public and private.

TABLE 5.7

Poland: Age-Specific Enrollment Rate by Household Consumption Quintile, 2003 (percent)

	Age group				
Quintile	3–6	7–10	11–15	16–18	19–25
Poorest quintile	4.6	94.7	99.6	90.9	36.2
II	3.8	95.0	99.7	96.1	46.6
III	4.2	95.2	99.9	97.2	52.6
IV	2.0	94.1	99.4	97.9	55.0
Richest quintile	3.3	96.4	100.0	97.3	52.6
Overall	4.1	94.9	99.7	94.7	47.4

Source: Canning, Godfrey, and Holzer-Zelazewska 2006.

TABLE 5.8

Public and Private Education Expenditure, 2002

Country	Public	Private	Country	Public	Private
ECA countries			*Comparator countries*		
Poland	89.2	10.8	Ireland	93.5	6.5
Slovak Republic	95.3	4.7	Korea, Republic of	59.2	40.8
Turkey	88.8	11.2	Spain	88.9	11.1

Source: OECD 2006.

Most developing countries provide public education without charge or at minimal cost to their citizens (Glewwe and Patrinos 1999). Fiscal constraints, however, prevent many developing countries from relying solely on government revenues to finance desired educational expansion. To solve this problem, many countries adopt policies to (a) charge tuition fees to recoup part of the cost of providing public education services or (b) encourage development of private schools to handle at least part of the expansion. There are several potential advantages to increased user fees. In principle, charging fees can increase educational spending per student enrolled. It can also improve equity by allowing the public sector to target subsidies more effectively to students from poor families. Moreover, increased cost recovery can improve school accountability to parents. Finally, selective charges on some learning inputs can increase the effectiveness of service delivery. For example, charging for books improves the on-time delivery of materials.

In Asia, the more that costs are financed through student fees, the greater is the overall coverage (as measured by the gross enrollment rate) of the education system (Mingat and Tan 1992). In other words, private funds can increase enrollment, whether they are used at private or publicly provided institutions. Focusing on the comparator country Korea in particular, Mingat and Tan (1992) find that Korea's mid-1980s average of 3.4 percent of GNP spent on public education was in line with the regional average, as it had been in previous decades. What differentiated Korea from other Asian economies (except for the Philippines) was the amount of private spending on education: 2.5 times more than the Asian average, according to Mingat and Tan's index of private financing in higher education. Thus, according to data collected by the Korean Education Development Institute, when private spending on education is included, the country's total was 10 percent of GNP in 1990.

The comparator country Chile is also of particular interest. While evidence on the extensive voucher system in Chile is less uniform,

BOX 5.2

Chile and Privatization

The Chilean education system features a high degree of private sector participation (see table below). Out of a total of 10,600 schools in 1998, parents had the option of placing their children in (a) public schools managed since 1980 by the municipalities (55.1 percent of 1998 enrollment); (b) private schools subsidized by the government on the basis of enrollment (34.1 percent); (c) fully private schools (9.2 percent); and (d) private technical-vocational schools run by private businesses or corporations (1.5 percent).

Chilean spending on education (percent)

	1990	1991	1992	1993	1994	1995	1996	1997	1998
Public education spending/GDP	2.6	2.7	2.9	3.0	3.1	3.1	3.4	3.5	3.9
Private education spending/GDP	2.0	2.0	2.2	2.4	2.5	2.5	2.8	2.9	3.1
Total education spending/GDP	4.6	4.7	5.1	5.4	5.6	5.6	6.2	6.4	7.0

Source: Table I, page 2, Delannoy 2000.

The primary motive for privatization is to improve responsiveness in service delivery and to raise the quality of output by forcing providers to survive in a competitive market. In addition, the profit motive in the private sector is expected to improve efficiency as entrepreneurs search for lower cost production. Private schools are in much greater supply in urban, upper-middle-income areas and are relatively rare in rural areas. Not only do low-income students have less opportunity to attend private schools, but many schools have also raised entrance barriers. Private schools have always been more likely to use entrance exams or minimum grades to select their students, and the better public schools have also succumbed to this practice. Furthermore, although it is difficult to make reliable comparisons across time, national average scores have not risen even though private provision of education has expanded dramatically while public education has waned. Both decentralization and privatization have resulted in greater inequity in expenditures and in the performance of students from different income groups.

Sources: Delannoy 2000; Parry 1997.

BOX 5.3

A New Beginning for Georgia's University Admissions

Transparency International's Corruption Perception Index 2004 listed Georgia among 60 countries suffering from serious corruption. The government that came to power after the Rose Revolution of November 2003 declared that the fight against corruption was one of its central priorities. The education sector, where corruption had previously been widespread, was among the first sectors to be targeted for reform. The higher education system in Georgia has traditionally been plagued by corruption. Until 2004, students were able to purchase not only their university admissions, but also passing grades and eventually a diploma. Individual universities administered their own admissions exams. Admissions bodies, composed of university lecturers, would sit in on oral exams and grade written papers. No independent observers were allowed to monitor the process. Previously, there were two ways of obtaining a university place. The first involved students in their final year of secondary school taking private classes offered by the same lecturers who sat on the admissions body at his or her chosen university. The second required the parents of a university applicant simply to bribe the admissions body before the entrance exams. In both instances, students would be asked previously agreed on questions in the oral exam and given advance warning of the subjects in the written exam.

Corruption in Georgia's education system is commonly associated with Soviet and post-Soviet styles of governance and was partly the result of the low salaries paid to administrators and teachers. There is now a strong desire to return to an educational system that commands respect and truly facilitates future employment prospects. It was in this context that parliament adopted a new Law on Higher Education in 2004. The law targets specific reforms in the higher education system:

- Improvements in administration and governance at all levels (including removing elements of corruption lingering from the previous system)
- Decentralization to address the diversity of local needs and promote fiscal and administrative accountability

(continued)

the most elaborate studies tend to suggest that it had positive effects on students' performance. Mizala, Romaguera, and Farren (2002) find that private fee-paying schools are the most technically efficient ones in Chile, followed by private subsidized and public schools. However, as box 5.2 highlights, the equity implications of Chile's privatization of its education system were adverse. In addition, it is not clear that privatization leads to better quality education as a result of the presumed higher accountability of educators to parents.

BOX 5.3 (continued)

- In-service training for teachers and administrators to reform instruction
- Parent education to encourage community engagement
- Ongoing student assessment and program evaluation for multilevel accountability
- Standardization in testing toward grade promotion, 11th grade graduation, and university admission

In 1999, the Ministry of Education began to implement the Georgian Education System Realignment and Strengthening Program, as part of which the National Assessment and Examination Center (NAEC) was established in July 2002 to develop new exams for university admission that guarantee objectivity in selecting entrants and reduce corruption. In 2005 for the first time, 31,174 applicants sat for the new university admission exam, which consisted of three mandatory exams and one optional exam, all administered nationwide. To assess the transparency of the new process, Transparency International Georgia conducted a monitoring project during the period May–August 2005. Its monitors were present during the exam at all 14 sites for the first two days of the examination process, on July 11 and 12. The NAEC and the Ministry of Education were found to have invested significant effort into informing university entrants, parents, teachers, and exam administrators about the new examination process. The examinations were well-organized and transparent, and the appeal process was meticulously planned and objective.

Source: Karosadnize and Christensen 2005.

Governance

Given that the proportion of the national budget devoted to education is significant for both developed and developing countries, it is essential that public funds be directed effectively and used for the purposes for which they are allocated. Rajkumar and Swaroop (2002) find that public health spending lowers child and infant mortality rates in countries with good governance, and that as countries improve their governance, public spending on primary education becomes effective in increasing primary education attainment. In addition, several studies conducted in the last decade have clearly emphasized the negative impact of corruption on the economic, political, and social development of countries. It has been observed that corruption increases transaction costs, reduces the efficiency and quality of services, distorts the decision-making process, and undermines social values. Recent surveys conducted on the impact of corruption on the provision of social services—including education—suggest that illegal payments for school entrance and other hidden costs help explain low school enrollment and drop-out rates in developing countries, and that bribes and payoffs in teacher recruitment and promotion tend to lower the quality of public school teachers (Hallak and Poisson 2005). On the one hand, ongoing trends such as decentralization and privatization in education may help to reduce corrupt practices (box 5.3). On the other hand, increased complexity in the sector may create new opportunities for corruption.

The move to capitation financing in ECA should help to improve governance because a funding formula is an agreed-on rule for allocating resources to operational units such as schools that is universally applied to all schools of a given type within an education jurisdiction. In a study focusing on school funding formulae used as part of a decentralized system of school finance for public schools, Ross and Levacic (1999) identify the main features of formula funding that should reduce opportunities for corruption as

- transparency, because the amount each school should receive is calculated objectively and can be made available to the public and openly published; and
- incentives at school level to manage resources efficiently, which can be enhanced by parental choice of school.

However, formula funding can create its own opportunities for corruption unless measures are put in place to minimize these. Schools have an incentive to inflate data that trigger funding in the formula, although this can be prevented by external checks and sanctions and by selecting indicators that the school cannot influence. Managing finances at the school level also gives more people the opportunity to misuse small sums of money, compared to a centralized system where fewer officials have scope to misuse larger sums. Financial management at schools must, therefore, be accompanied by comprehensive and enforced financial regulations and external auditing of school accounts.

The study findings indicate the importance of legal requirements for publication of financial information and training in financial management for school personnel if formula funding is to gain its full potential for enhanced transparency. Furthermore, the trade-off between the more complex formulae required for equitable allocations among schools and simpler formulae for greater understanding and hence greater transparency is not easily resolved. This is illustrated by the example of Poland, where simple per pupil formulae require differential school funding outside the formula to tackle school-based cost differentials, which does not aid transparency.

However, no such funding outside the formula is needed in Victoria, Australia, but the formula itself is very difficult for most education stakeholders to understand, so that transparency is also not fully achieved.

The Polish example sheds further light on the complex relationship between formula funding of schools and transparency. Indeed, there are two sides to transparency: public availability of information and public scrutiny of school finances as well as the simplicity and transparency of the financing mechanisms themselves. The introduction of formula funding alone is not sufficient to ensure transparency and the involvement of local education stakeholders in the budgeting process. Two Polish cities that did introduce a radically simple voucher system failed to fully involve teachers and parents. One of them did not even routinely publish school budgets. While they proudly present their innovative budgeting procedures at the national level, for instance, to the Association of Polish Cities, their message does not get through to their electorates.

Conclusions

This chapter has surveyed the relationships between educational outcomes, public spending on education, and economic growth, and it has explored how transition countries might enhance the impact of public spending on education levels and thus economic growth. Several key points emerge. First, better education in a population clearly leads to faster economic growth, but more spending on education does not necessarily lead to better educational outcomes. The latter link depends on several attributes of the spending itself.

Second, transition countries compare favorably in educational outcomes and efficiency indicators with developing countries, but they have a way to go to match OECD levels.

Third, transition countries have undertaken a variety of reforms to enhance the efficiency of public spending on education, including taking decentralization further than the deconcentration of the socialist era and adoption of per capita financing formulae that provide incentives for efficient use of facilities. However, these reforms have not yet gone far enough in most countries. As a result of rigid salary rules, most systems still have too many teachers with salaries that are too low to motivate good performance. Too high a share of spending tends to be allocated to tertiary as opposed to primary and secondary levels, in part reflecting insufficient reliance on private financing at the tertiary level. And vocational education, which has a far higher unit cost than the academic track, is not adequately integrated with general education or with tertiary and lifelong learning opportunities.

In sum, further reforms in education policy and in resulting patterns of public education spending are needed to improve education outcomes and foster continued economic growth. Although details vary from country to country, the general direction of needed reforms is similar across the ECA region. Fast-growing countries in other regions, most notably Korea and Chile, offer valuable lessons for ECA.

Notes

The author is grateful for the research assistance provided by Qing Wu, Elena Rydralova, and Shweta Jain.

1. Education systems in ECA countries generally are not classified into a primary and secondary cycle but rather into a basic and upper secondary cycle. However, to be able to make comparisons with countries in other regions, the more common terms of "primary" and "secondary" are used here.
2. The Czech Republic, Estonia, Hungary, Latvia, Lithuania, Poland, the Slovak Republic, and Slovenia.
3. The discussion in this section relies heavily on Dillinger (2006).

CHAPTER 6

Health

Daniel Dulitzky and Xiaohui Hou

Following the dissolution of central planning, most Europe and Central Asia (ECA) region countries began to implement a series of health care reforms. The reforms represented a move away from the traditional "Semashko" health care model prevalent in the former Soviet Union—centrally planned, hospital based, with virtually free universal access to most services and central financing through general revenues. Some countries successfully implemented social health insurance (SHI) schemes with reforms in health care financing and delivery systems, while others maintained the old state-budget financing formula. Not all reforms to date have been fully successful, however. Some health care systems have become financially unsustainable, and others have failed to improve health outcomes or provide increased access to the majority of the population at affordable prices.

This chapter has four objectives: (a) to address the relationship between health spending and economic growth; (b) to describe current patterns of health care financing and spending, the prevailing funding models for health care, and the relationship of these variables to health outcomes; (c) to consider the influence of efficiency and governance on the link between public spending and health outcomes; and (d) to identify some of the challenges that ECA countries face in the health arena and draw lessons from international experience. The analysis in the chapter concentrates on the sample of ECA and high-growth comparator countries selected for particular focus in the overall study.

Consistent with the literature, the analysis in this chapter finds that there is no systematic relationship between the particular model of health care financing and the level of public health spending or health outcomes in the sample of countries considered. The level of public health spending is only tenuously related to health outcomes, and other factors such as governance and efficiency greatly influence the relationship. International focus countries have initiated various reforms to improve governance and efficiency, from which ECA countries can draw lessons. ECA countries face other challenges as well, including improving access to health care, handling aging populations, and ensuring financial sustainability in health care provision; international comparator countries also provide successful examples of dealing with these issues.

Health Outcomes and Economic Growth

The modern growth literature shows the importance of human capital in determining the pace and character of economic growth (Barro 1991; Benhabib and Speigel 1994; Van Zon and Muysken 2001). However, human capital is usually broadly defined, and most of the research has focused on education. The relationship between health and economic growth has recently regained attention, both theoretically and empirically. Bloom and Canning (2000) propose a model in which economic growth is driven by knowledge accumulation and labor services by healthy people. They argue that the share of healthy people in the population determines the extent to which potential labor services embodied in the population can be used effectively, and healthy hours spent for knowledge accumulation lead to economic growth. Howitt (2005) lays out a theoretical model based on the recent Schumpeterian growth theory and identifies different channels through which an improvement in a country's population health will affect its long-run growth. Improved health increases productive efficiency, life expectancy, learning capacity, creativity, and coping skills, which all contribute to productivity improvement. More specifically, this study underscores the beneficial effects of childhood health and maternal health on various dimensions of human capital, such as learning capacity, creativity, and coping skills. Of course, there is also likely to be some degree of reverse causation because economic growth provides more resources to be spent on health care and other factors that affect the health status of a population.

Gyimah-Bremponga and Wilson (2004) investigate the effects of health human capital on the growth rate of per capita income in Sub-Saharan African and Organisation for Economic Co-operation and Development (OECD) countries. They find that the stock of human capital has a positive and statistically significant effect on growth of per capita income, 22 percent in Sub-Saharan African countries and 30 percent in OECD countries, respectively. In addition, the effect is quadratic: increases in health human capital increase the growth of per capita income at a decreasing rate. Bloom, Canning, and Sevilla (2001) use panel data from 104 countries and conclude that good health has a positive, sizeable, and statistically significant effect on economic growth, suggesting that a one-year improvement in a population's life expectancy contributes to an increase of 4 percent in output. At the micro level, evidence from household surveys from Ghana, Côte d'Ivoire, and Brazil suggest that health human capital has a large effect on wages as well (Schultz 2005). The analysis of the impact of health on economic growth in ECA countries is limited.

Models of Health Care Financing

Health systems have been classified historically along many different dimensions. Kutzin (2001), for example, provides a framework to analyze the typology of health systems that includes how funds are collected and pooled, how services are purchased and provided, and how responsibilities are allocated across the different levels of government and health facilities. One aspect of this typology is the prevailing financing scheme—"Bismarck" or "Beveridge" models being the pure and opposite models. In a Bismarckian system, the main source of financing for health is derived from employee and employer contributions calculated as a proportion of payroll, with pooled funds managed by a quasi-state SHI agency. SHI systems usually come with a defined package of benefits for their members, who are entitled because of their contributions (Gottret and Schieber 2006). Under pure Beveridge models, health care is funded from general revenues, with at least theoretical universal coverage for a comprehensive scope of services.

Very few systems fall into one of the two pure schemes because a health sector usually has multiple sources of funding. In some cases, neither source is predominant because of poor implementation and governance, and out-of-pocket spending becomes the main source of financing for health services. Risk-pooling is very limited and applies only at the household level. For that reason this section follows Preker, Jakab, and Schneider (2002) and categorizes the countries into three groups based on the relative strength of these various health care financing methods.

The clustering is depicted in figure 6.1. The first group, organized along the Beveridge model with health care predominantly financed by general tax revenues, includes only Ukraine (among the ECA focus countries). The second group has moved toward a Bismarckian model, with health care predominantly financed by payroll taxes. This group includes Croatia, Poland, Romania, and the Slovak Republic. In the third group, out-of-pocket payments are the predominant mode of health financing, amounting to 50–80 percent of total health revenue. This group includes Armenia, Georgia, and the Kyrgyz Republic.

As many ECA countries moved to a SHI scheme, among the ECA focus group, only Ukraine retained the tax-based health-financing approach. Government budgets remain the major official source of

FIGURE 6.1

Percentage of Total Public Expenditures on Health Financed by Taxes and Social Health Insurance, 2004 or Latest Year Available

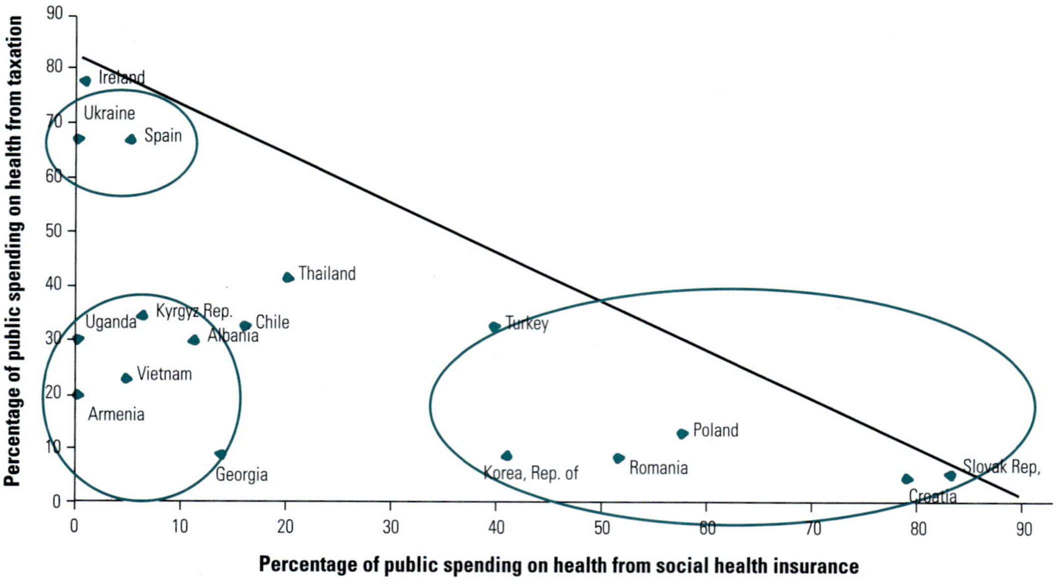

Source: Adapted from Preker, Jakab, Schneider (2002), updated using World Health Organization European Health for All Database and World Health Statistics 2006.

health care financing, with 80 percent based on local budgets and the remaining 20 percent on state budgets, supervised by regional authorities and the Ministry of Health, respectively. The services were free of charge until 1996, when official user fees were introduced. Since then, the public share of health care financing has been reduced from 80 percent in 1996 to about 66 percent in 2004 (European Observatory on Health Care Systems 2005).

The majority of ECA focus countries fall into the SHI group, as those countries have introduced that mechanism as complementary to, or as, the main health care financing method. Table 6.1 shows the introduction year of SHI in some ECA countries and the respective contribution rates. Many of these reforms are less than 10 years old, and contributions vary greatly, from 2 percent in the Kyrgyz Republic to 18 percent in Croatia. Several reasons have been offered for the move toward payroll taxes for health care funding in many ECA countries. First, payroll tax financing is less dependent on yearly budgetary negotiations than general revenue financing, and thus is regarded as a more stable source of revenue. Second, the introduction of payroll taxes breaks the monopoly of government, particularly the Ministry of Finance, over the ownership and financing of health services. Third, SHI puts more responsibility on individuals to finance their own health care through labor market participation (Preker, Jakab, and Schneider 2002; Saltman 2004). Fourth, SHI can be used as an instrument to redistribute income through cross-subsidization from high-income to low-income participants and from low-risk to

TABLE 6.1

The Introduction of Social Health Insurance in the ECA Region

Country	Source	Year introduced	Contribution rate for salaried workers (%)	Employer share (%)	Employee share (%)
Albania	HIT (Health in Transition)	1995	3.40	1.70	1.70
Croatia	Preker, Jakab, and Schneider 2002	1993	18.00	18.00	0.00
Georgia	HIT 2002	1995	4.00	3.00	1.00
Kyrgyz Republic	HIT Dixon et al				
Poland		1997	2.00	2.00	0.00
		1999	7.75	0.00	7.75
Romania	Preker, Jakab, and Schneider 2002	1999	14.00	7.00	7.00
Slovak Republic	Preker, Jakab, and Schneider 2002	1994	13.70	10.00	3.70
Turkey	World Bank 2006g	1945	11.00	6.00	5.00

Source: Author's compilation.

BOX 6.1

Albania: Social Health Insurance

SHI was introduced in Albania in 1995, with a 3.4 percent payroll contribution divided equally between employers and employees. The system is not yet deemed financially sustainable and is not providing the services it was intended to. The system developed very slowly—in 2002, active contributors only accounted for one-third of the total active labor force while the number covered by the state was uncertain. Currently, only 7 percent of public sector spending on health comes from nonbudgetary contributions to health insurance, and coverage is still very low. Between 1995 and 2004, funding from payroll taxes increased slowly, while funding from general budget revenues declined drastically—from 71 percent in 1995 to 30 percent in 2004—and out-of-pocket spending increased from 23 percent in 1995 to 59 percent in 2004. About two-thirds of public funding for Health Insurance Institute (HII) activities comes from general revenues (in the form of contributions for dependent populations). The HII scheme provides somewhat limited benefits and does not appear to decrease out-of-pocket expenditures for outpatient care or affect the likelihood of having to pay for health care. Despite being mandatory, the latest household survey suggests that only about 40–45 percent of the population is covered by health insurance. There are also significant regional differences in health insurance coverage.

Various reasons help to explain the lack of progress in implementing a full SHI system. A large share of the active labor force works in the informal sector and thus avoids contributions. Anecdotal evidence suggests that knowledge about health insurance benefits appears to be limited for a significant part of the population. The lines of accountability and the allocation of responsibilities between the Ministry of Health and the HII are blurred, and the financing of health is fragmented among the ministry, HII, local governments, and other institutions, which creates uncertainty in funding levels and potential for corruption. Finally, administrative capacity to enforce contributions is weak, and few regulatory and oversight structures exist.

(continued)

high-risk participants.[1] Finally, many ECA countries have moved to SHI schemes either for historical reasons (to return to systems prevailing in the past) or for political reasons (to match systems prevailing in neighboring countries).

Some caveats apply, however, to the above arguments for SHI. First, the introduction of single treasury accounts in many ECA countries reduces the extent to which SHI funding is isolated from general revenues and thus from budget negotiations. Second, general subsidies supplement payroll taxes as a funding source for SHI systems in many countries in the region. Finally, payroll contributions can have

BOX 6.1 (continued)

The Albanian government recently proposed an increase in the payroll contribution rate to increase revenues. However, concerns remain that further increasing payroll tax contributions will push some workers to the informal sector, thus the net gain from the increase in the contribution rate will be minimal. Advisors have recommended that the Albanian government shift public health financing from a partial payroll tax system to full funding from general tax revenues. However, the amount of public sector resources allocated to health will stil be limited in the medium term, and user fees will inevitably continue to be an important complementary source of financing.

The case of Albania is not unique. Three common problems afflict lower-middle-income countries that rely on payroll tax financing for health care:

- Greater inequity in access than systems relying on general tax financing, especially where a large fraction of the labor force is in the informal sector or unsalaried
- Greater inequity in financing burden, as beneficiaries seek exemptions from contributions, for example, by registering as unemployed
- Higher labor costs, reduced competitiveness, and greater incentives for the labor force to move into the informal sector because of the high payroll tax burden (see chapter 9)

Source: World Bank 2006e.

the same degree of volatility as other fiscal revenues, and evasion and informality can become serious issues.

Not every country in the sample has been successful in implementing SHI schemes because some countries have not been able to achieve financial sustainability while at the same time securing universal access to basic care. In Albania, Georgia, and the Kyrgyz Republic, out-of-pocket spending is still the major source of financing, long after the introduction of SHI. Administering an SHI system requires regulatory and administrative capacity to raise revenues from payroll taxes, and this can take time to develop. In addition, the presence of a large proportion of unemployed, self-employed, and informal workers contributes to the problem, as the case of Albania illustrates (box 6.1).

High out-of-pocket payments are not associated with a particular health-financing scheme. Armenia retained a general tax–funded system but has also experienced problems in successfully pooling risks associated with health shocks. In contrast to Albania and the Kyrgyz Republic, high out-of-pocket spending on health in Armenia is mainly a result of severe economic problems following its independence. Public spending on health was limited to a minimum, forcing the introduction of a predominantly private out-of-pocket payment system of health care financing (European Observatory on Health Care Systems 2002).

Countries in the international comparator group also provide a wide range of financial models. Health care in Ireland and Spain is largely financed by general taxes. The Republic of Korea's health care is financed by mandatory SHI and the Medical Aid Program, a social assistance program for the poor financed though general taxation. Thailand's health care financing has three pillars—a Universal Coverage Scheme, a Civil Servant Medical Benefit Scheme, and a social security scheme—with the first two financed through the general budget and the third financed by mandatory contributions. Private health insurance has emerged in Chile and cofinances health care with public health insurance. Finally, user fees still constitute an important source of health care financing in Vietnam.

Patterns of Health Care Spending

The last section showed that very few countries exhibit pure Bismarckian or Beveridge systems. Most fall into hybrid categories, and many rely on private out-of-pocket spending to finance a significant portion of health expenditures. Based on the typology laid out above, this section examines the relationship between the various health-financing models and health spending.

Total Spending

The main driver of total health spending in a country is the level of GDP. According to most estimates, the income elasticity of total health expenditure is at or around unity (Gerdtham and Jonsson 1991). The sample of ECA and comparator countries used in this study confirms this trend. Figure 6.2 shows the correlation between per capita GDP and total health expenditure in the sample countries. There is a large variation in total spending on health, and clearly countries spend more as they become richer. There does not appear to be systematic over- or underspending for ECA or comparator countries. Some ECA countries, such as Croatia and Turkey, spend slightly more on health relative to their income levels. The same applies to some international comparator countries, such as Spain. Thailand, Korea, and Chile,

FIGURE 6.2

The Correlation Between Per Capita GDP and Per Capita Total Expenditure on Health, 2004 or Latest Year Available

PPP-adjusted dollars

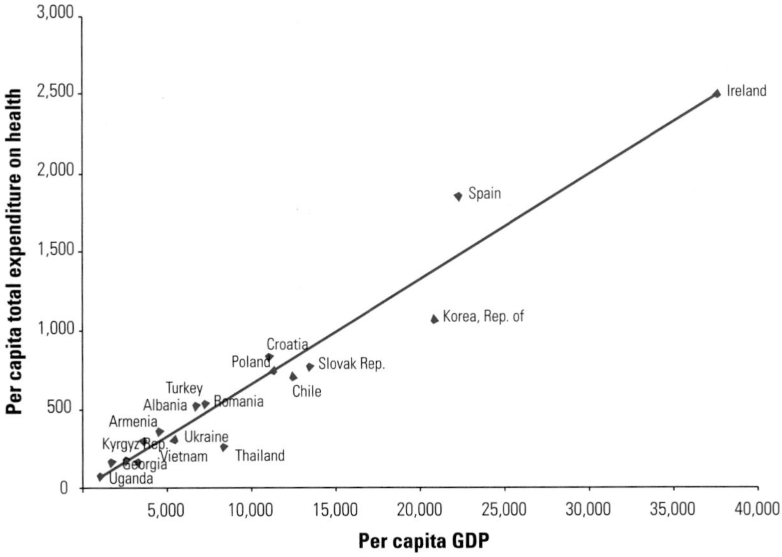

Source: World Health Organization European Health for All Database and World Health Statistics 2006.

however, tend to spend less than the levels predicted by their per capita GDP.

Public Spending

Table 6.2 shows public spending on health for ECA and comparator countries, using the clustering described in the Models of Health Care Financing section. Among ECA focus countries, the middle-income countries in Central and Eastern Europe[2] have Bismarckian systems and have the largest percentage of health spending coming from public sources. In the comparator countries, the higher-income countries in the group—Ireland and Spain—also have the largest share of public to total health spending but have Beveridge rather than Bismarckian systems. The lowest levels of public spending on health are in the lower-income countries in both groups, where out-of-pocket payments are the primary mode of financing. On average, the ECA and comparator countries spend a similar percentage of GDP on health (approximately 6.1 percent).

TABLE 6.2

Health Expenditures in ECA and Comparator Countries, 2003

Country	Total health expenditures (% of GDP)	Public expenditure on health (% of total health expenditures)	Public expenditure on health (% of GDP)	Public expenditure on health (% of total government expenditures)
ECA countries				
Group A				
Ukraine	5.7	65.9	3.8	10.2
Group B				
Croatia	7.8	83.6	6.5	13.8
Poland	6.5	69.9	4.5	9.8
Romania	6.1	62.9	3.8	10.9
Slovak Republic	5.9	88.3	5.2	13.2
Turkey	7.6	71.6	5.4	13.9
Average	*6.8*	*75.3*	*5.1*	*12.3*
Group C				
Albania	6.5	41.7	2.7	9.2
Armenia	6.0	20.2	1.2	5.4
Georgia	4.0	23.9	1.0	4.7
Kyrgyz Republic	5.3	40.8	2.2	9.0
Average	*5.5*	*31.7*	*1.8*	*7.1*
Comparator countries				
Group A				
Ireland	7.3	78.9	5.8	17.2
Spain	7.7	71.3	5.5	13.7
Average	*7.5*	*75.1*	*5.6*	*15.5*
Group B				
Thailand	3.3	61.6	2.0	13.6
Chile	6.1	48.8	3.0	12.7
Korea, Republic of	5.6	49.4	2.8	8.9
Average	*5.0*	*53.3*	*2.6*	*11.7*
Group C				
Vietnam	5.4	27.8	1.5	5.6
Uganda	7.3	30.4	2.2	10.7
Average	*6.4*	*29.1*	*1.9*	*8.2*
Average of ECA countries	**6.1**	**56.9**	**3.6**	**10.0**
Average of comparator countries	**6.1**	**52.6**	**3.2**	**11.8**

Source: For non-European countries, WHO country profile; for European countries, WHO European Health for All database.

A review of the literature on the determinants of health spending shows that (a) income (proxied by GDP per capita) seems to be the most significant explanatory variable; (b) the age structure of the population is a significant variable in some studies (proportion of population over age 65) but not in others; (c) some health care risk factors, such as tobacco use, tend to be significant; and (d) institutional characteristics also explain health spending but are not always significant (for example, public provision is associated with lower spending, a higher ratio of inpatient care spending is associated with higher spending).[3] Other factors that have not been systematically explored in the literature are cultural (for example, seeking health care as a social activity) or political-historical (strong traditions of seeking care in hospitals or of offering generous benefits, for instance). Many of the countries with low public spending on health have gone through reforms that limited the benefit package (Korea) or increased private participation through supplementary insurance (Chile) or user fees (Vietnam).

Countries in the sample also allocate a varying proportion of the government's budget to health care. Richer countries in the sample allocate a large proportion (15.5 percent on average) while poorer countries tend to spend a smaller share of government resources on health (10.2 percent in Ukraine, 10.7 percent in Uganda, and 5.6 percent in Vietnam). The influence of health care financing models on public health expenditure as a percentage of government expenditure is not obvious.

Private Out-of-Pocket Spending

Out-of-pocket payments include a range of charges that individuals must pay at the point of service, including copayments, initial deductibles, and payments for uncovered medical services, supplies, and drugs. Bribes are also a significant share of out-of-pocket payments in many countries, but may not be well-captured in statistics. Figure 6.3 shows an estimate of the share of out-of-pocket payments in total health spending in ECA and comparator countries. Georgia is the highest among the focus countries, where out-of-pocket accounts for 76 percent of total health expenditures (see box 6.2). Out-of-pocket spending is 64 percent in Armenia and 59 percent in the Kyrgyz Republic and Albania. Among the comparator countries, Vietnam and Uganda have the largest share of out-of-pocket payments, 53.6 percent and 52.8 percent, respectively. Out-of-pocket spending in Korea is 41.9 percent, mostly directed to high levels of care (such as inpatient care and pharmaceuticals) because Korea has universal coverage of primary health care.

Out-of-pocket spending is often required as an explicit government policy, with the intention of reducing unnecessary demand by relating payments directly to use. In such cases, copayments for certain services are required, especially for inpatient care and pharmaceuticals. Countries with SHI systems tend to exempt certain groups

FIGURE 6.3

Out-of-Pocket Spending as a Percentage of Total Health Expenditures, 2004 or Latest Year Available

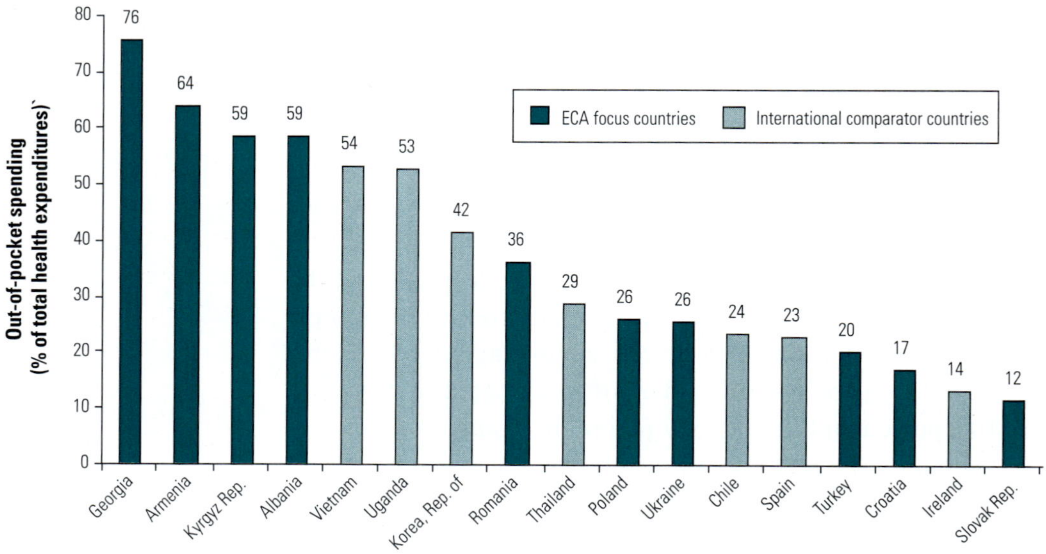

Sources: World Health Organization European Health for All Database and World Health Statistics 2006.

from copayments to improve equity and influence use. For this reason, many countries have a different insurance policy to cover three population groups: unemployed, pensioners, and low-income. A general trend, however, is to move away from categorical eligibility for copay exemption to broadly based eligibility tied to income or other means. In the United Kingdom, for example, prescription charges cover about 40 percent of average prescription costs, but only 12 percent of prescriptions are actually charged because of exemptions for patients with specific chronic diseases or for the elderly or those with very low income. In the United States, the Medicare scheme, which covers elderly people, reimburses only certain drugs, and Medicaid, which covers some of the poor, reimburses only drugs that are on the approved list in a state.

However, high out-of-pocket spending on health care signals a failure in risk-pooling because the risk is pooled only at the household level. One of the goals of an SHI system is to provide protection to households against large catastrophic health shocks. When out-of-pocket spending becomes an important source of revenues for the

BOX 6.2

Georgia: High Out-of-Pocket Spending

Before the introduction of health sector reforms in 1995, the Georgian health care system was financed primarily from the central budget. However, unable to maintain its role as the sole financier of health care following the economic crisis in 1991, the government introduced three additional sources of financing in 1995: payroll-based SHI, municipal financing, and official copayments. For the next decade, in part because of successive economic crises, the government was consistently unable to meet its revenue and expenditure targets, leading to across-the-board expenditure cuts in the 1998, 1999, and 2000 budgets; the continued accumulation of large arrears in health, wages, and pensions; and increasing reliance on private out-of-pocket payments to finance health care.

A 1995 household survey estimated private expenditure on health to be almost 272.7 million laris (US$221.7 million in 1995[a]). Since then, several national household surveys have been conducted, and the range of out-of-pocket spending has been estimated at between 65 and 87 percent of total health spending. For example, a study by the Georgia Department of Statistics found that out-of-pocket payments were approximately US$28 per capita, or 73 percent of total health expenditures. In 2000, according to the Tbilisi Household Survey, total out-of-pocket expenditures amounted to 132 million laris (US$68 million in 2000[b]), or about 66 percent of total spending on health.

One of the drivers of large out-of-pocket payments is the presence of informal payments for care. With the collapse of the economy in the early 1990s, informal payments became the main source of income for many health staff. Under the 1995 reforms, payments for certain health services not covered by the Basic Benefit Package (BBP), which is free, were legalized, with the expectation that formal payments would reduce informal payments in the health sector. Partly because of relatively low salary levels, informal payments continued to supplement the actual cost of care in the system. However, in some selectively contracted and well-managed health programs, such as hemodialysis, cardiac surgery, and, to some extent, maternity care, informal payments are reported to have decreased, and in some cases are not demanded.

Under the BBP concept, all services included in the BBP list are either free or partially subsidized. Patients must pay the hospital or doctor directly (or through private insurance, if applicable) for services not included in the BBP. Copayments are retained by the facilities and used to fund recurrent costs. However, patients have typically not been well-informed of their entitlements, and providers could manipulate the cost of treatments because public information campaigns were largely absent.

(continued)

BOX 6.2 (continued)

Constraints in public funding and problems related to budget execution exacerbated the problem of out-of-pocket payments. Household surveys conducted since 1995 found that the cost of health care was a serious impediment to seeking care. The surveys also noted that a high percentage of the population self treats, which partly reflects the response of households to the costs of seeking care. Most of the out-of-pocket payments have gone toward the purchase of drugs (45 percent), followed by hospitalization (26 percent), and outpatient services (17 percent).

Source: World Bank 2004c.

a. The calculation is based on exchange rate US$1= 1.23 GEL in 1996 (CIA World Factbook).

b. The calculation is based on exchange rate US$1=1.98 GEL in 2000 (CIA World Factbook).

health system or represents a large percentage of household spending on health, this objective may not be achieved. High out-of-pocket spending may affect equity and access to health care by discouraging poor households from seeking care.[4] Informal payments are also a significant element of out-of-pocket expenses. Although Albanian legislation provides for free inpatient hospital care for all, out-of-pocket expenditures in the event of hospitalization are substantial, and a large share of those payments are informal. The system of informal payments is partly encouraged by an ill-defined and poorly enforced copayment policy (World Bank 2006e). The current copayment system blurs the distinction between formal and informal payments. For example, if a patient requires certain treatments and the supplies are not available at the providing institution, patients may be required either to purchase their own supplies or to reimburse the attending physician or nurse for the supplies. This may be considered to be an informal payment by some.

The experience of the Kyrgyz Republic shows that it is possible to reduce informal payments if the problem is addressed as part of overall health finance reforms. All public resources allocated to health—state budget, local government budget, and health insurance funding—are now pooled into the Health Insurance Fund (HIF), which has become the sole purchaser of health services. A basic package of benefits covering primary care through family physicians contracted by the HIF is available free of charge to the entire population. Those who contribute to the HIF are entitled to lower copayments and outpatient drug benefit coverage. The reform also introduced copayments for inpatient care. Revenues are collected and stay in the hospital, which can use them according to certain guidelines. In addition, the HIF provides exemptions or reduced copayments for those covered under HIF, including low-income vulnerable groups. By formalizing payments, hospital revenues through this source become subject to policy management directives. Preliminary analysis of the impact of these policies shows that even though overall out-of-pocket payments have not decreased, the share of patients with knowledge of the amounts to be paid for use of hospitals has tripled, out-of-pocket expenditures for drugs and medical supplies for hospital care have decreased over 90 percent, and informal payments made to hospital staff have decreased 70 percent (World Bank 2006e).

Health Care Spending and Health Outcomes

One interesting question for health policy makers is whether additional health spending will lead to better health outcomes. The section below describes the pattern of health care spending and health outcomes among the ECA focus countries and international comparator countries from the lens of both financing mechanism and public spending. It then reviews the literature and draws conclusions on the relationship between health spending and health outcomes.

Does the Method of Financing Matter?

ECA and comparator countries show surprisingly similar average health outcomes. However, these averages hide wide intragroup variation. Infant mortality, for example, stands at 22.3 deaths per 1,000 live births in ECA countries and 19.7 in comparator countries, but it varies from 81 (Uganda) to 4 (Spain) in comparator countries and 58 (the Kyrgyz Republic) to 6 (Croatia) in ECA countries. A similar phenomenon is observed with other outcome indicators. Healthy life expectancy values are close for the two groups (65.0 years for ECA countries and 65.2 years for comparator countries for females), but in the ECA countries it varies between 69.4 years (the Slovak Republic and Croatia) and 58.4 years (the Kyrgyz Republic) while in comparator countries it reaches 75.3 years for Spain but is only 43.7 years in Uganda.

The countries in table 6.3 have been clustered according to their prevailing financing arrangement, as described in the Models of Health Care Financing section. The literature on the link between health outcomes and the organizational framework of health care financing is rather limited. Figueras et al. (2004) compare the per-

TABLE 6.3

Health Care Financing Models and Population Health Status, 2003 or Latest Year Available

Country	Healthy life expectancy, male (years)	Healthy life expectancy, female (years)	Infant mortality rate (per 1,000 live births)	Three doses of DTP vaccine (% of 1-year olds)	Standardized death rates for cancer of the cervix (per 100,000 population)
ECA countries					
Group A					
Ukraine	54.9	63.6	14.0	99.0	6.8
Group B					
Croatia	63.8	69.3	6.0	96.0	5.2
Poland	63.1	68.5	7.0	99.0	1.5
Romania	61.0	65.2	17.0	—	4.7
Slovak Republic	63.0	69.4	7.0	99.0	4.2
Turkey	61.2	62.8	28.0	—	2.2
Average	*62.4*	*67.0*	*13.0*	*98.0*	*3.6*
Group C					
Albania	59.5	63.3	16.0	97.0	1.2
Armenia	59.4	62.6	29.0	91.0	3.5
Georgia	62.2	66.6	41.0	78.0	1.5
Kyrgyz Republic	52.2	58.4	58.0	99.0	2.4
Average	*58.3*	*62.7*	*36.0*	*91.3*	*2.2*
Comparator counties					
Group A					
Ireland	68.1	71.5	5.0	89.0	1.1
Spain	69.9	75.3	4.0	96.0	1.1
Average	*69.0*	*73.4*	*4.5*	*92.5*	*1.1*
Group B					
Thailand	57.7	62.4	18.0	98.0	13.2
Chile	64.9	69.7	8.0	94.0	3.1
Korea, Republic of	64.8	70.8	5.0	88.0	7.1
Average	*62.5*	*67.6*	*10.3*	*93.3*	*7.8*
Group C					
Vietnam	59.8	62.9	17.0	96.0	6.7
Uganda	41.7	43.7	81.0	—	3.9
Average	*50.8*	*53.3*	*49.0*	*96.0*	*5.3*
Average ECA countries	60.0	65.0	22.3	94.8	3.3
Average comparator countries	61.0	65.2	19.7	93.5	5.2

Source: WHO data.
Note: — = Not available.

formance of SHI in Western European countries with the performance of tax-financed systems in the same region. They analyze three dimensions: outcomes, equity, and patient satisfaction with responsiveness of health systems. For health outcomes, they find no discernible pattern to distinguish SHI from tax-funded systems. For example, the average life expectancy is 78.6 years in sample countries with SHI compared to 78.1 in sample countries with tax-funded systems. The difference in healthy life expectancy between the two groups is also negligible—70.4 years in SHI systems versus 69.9 years in general tax–financed systems. Other measures like standardized death rates (SDRs) from "amenable conditions"[5] offer similar results. They do find that SHI systems are slightly less equitable but more responsive to patients' needs.

Baeza and Packard (2006) look at Latin American countries and find that there are some differences in health outcomes among countries with different health-financing strategies, but these differences are related more to specific internal institutional and functional characteristics than to whether financing schemes are Bismarckian or Beveridge. Healthy life expectancy for males and females in the Bismarckian cluster of ECA countries is higher than in the other two groups in the region, but the opposite pattern arises among countries in the comparator group, where the Beveridge cluster has better outcomes than the other groups. Overall, it is apparent that richer countries show better results irrespective of their financing mechanism for health. However, in both ECA and comparator countries health outcomes are significantly worse where out-of-pocket spending is the main source of financing.

Important caveats have to be considered when discussing health outcomes and their links to health spending or health financing, including the choice of outcome indicators and the link between outcomes and inputs. Two indicators—infant and maternal mortality—can play an important role in comparative health system research and provide the basic indicators for monitoring and evaluating changes. However, definitions of these variables can differ. Some ECA countries still follow the definition of infant mortality rate used in the former Soviet Union, which gives a rate well below the one used by the World Health Organization (Anderson and Silver 1986; World Bank 2004g). Furthermore, these indicators reflect the impact of a variety of factors that contribute to good health apart from proper health care, including clean water, good nutrition, and positive lifestyles. Therefore, a good outcome cannot be attributed exclusively to health system performance.[6]

Does the Level of Public Spending Matter?

Figure 6.4 shows the correlation between public expenditure on health (PPP adjusted) and the infant mortality rate. As most of the existing literature suggests, this correlation is negative, that is, an increase in spending is associated with a reduction in infant mortality.

FIGURE 6.4

Infant Mortality and Public Expenditure on Health, 2004 or Latest Year Available

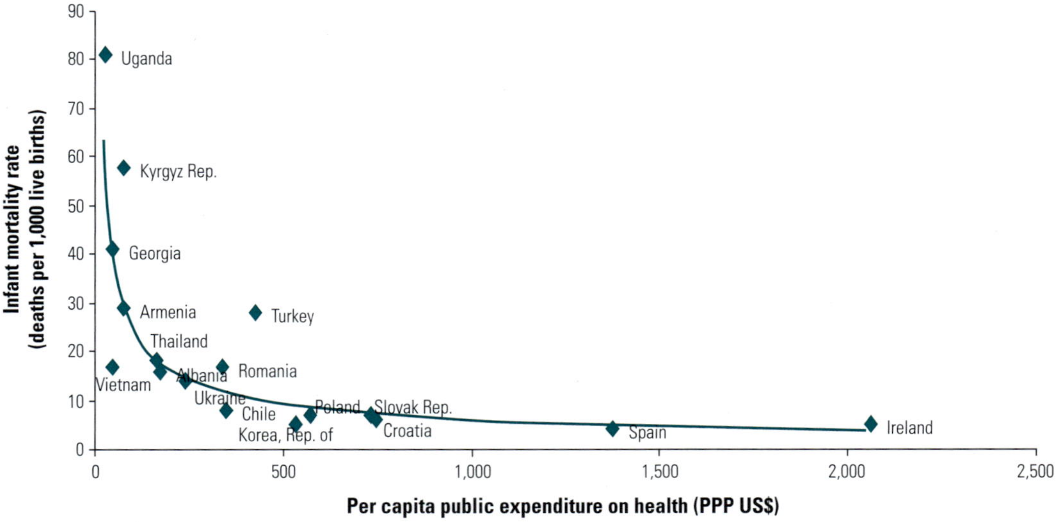

Sources: World Health Organization European Health for All Database and World Health Statistics 2006.

The majority of comparator focus countries—Vietnam, Chile, Korea, and Spain—are below the line, suggesting that public health spending may be more efficient in these countries. Although Vietnam, Armenia, Georgia, and the Kyrgyz Republic have similar spending levels, Vietnam has a much lower infant mortality rate than the other three countries. The correlations between public expenditure on health and other outcome indicators, such as healthy adjusted life years, show a similar pattern.

The strong correlation between spending and outcomes may be hiding other factors with more direct impacts on outcomes. In fact, the consensus on this matter is that public spending on health has a very limited impact on health outcomes after controlling for other factors. Filmer and Pritchett (1999), for example, use a cross-section of countries to look at the impact of public health spending on child (under-5) and infant mortality. They find that the impact of public spending on health is quite small, while other factors, such as income per capita, inequality in income distributions, and female education, are more important determinants. They point out at least three variables that affect that relationship: (a) institutional capacity; (b) the relationship between public and private service providers (because under certain circumstances the expansion of public provision may crowd out private provision, resulting in overall constant provision); and (c) changes in the demand for health services resulting from additional funding for health.[7]

The general consensus is that public spending on health and health outcomes are tenuously related. Baldacci et al. (2004) show that an increase in health spending of 1 percentage point of GDP is associated with a rise in the under-5 survival rate of 0.2 percentage points. At the same time, governance issues have a direct impact on this relationship. Filmer, Hammer, and Pritchett (2000) argue that public spending may have little impact because the efficacy of government in delivering services is low. The *World Development Report 2004* (World Bank 2004g) suggests that the efficiency (the organization and allocation of spending) and effectiveness (capacity and governance) of public spending are two issues that shape the relationship between public spending on health and health outcomes.

The discussion above on methods of health financing and levels of public spending on health are focused primarily on curative services within the health care system. However, public health may also play a role in determining health outcomes. The scope of public health is very wide, ranging from anti-smoking and anti-alcohol public campaigns to safety belt law enforcement, public education on HIV/AIDS prevention, and immunization services. Although the cost effectiveness of preventive interventions in public health is well-known, few studies have been done to investigate the correlation or causality between different health-financing methods and government spending on public health, whether the level of spending on public health or health outcomes. More research and policy discussion on these topics should be encouraged by policy makers.

Policy Reforms to Enhance Efficiency and Governance

Because the amount of money spent by a government on health is at best as important as how that money is spent, the "transmission mechanisms" from funding to outcomes and service delivery are essential for determining the effectiveness of service provision. The organization of service delivery, monitoring, and accountability mechanisms are critical in determining quality of care and accessibility of services. Delivery mechanisms do not depend on financing model, because strong delivery mechanisms in tax-funded systems can be mimicked in health insurance schemes and vice versa. In addition, SHI is neither better nor worse than tax-funded systems for health outcomes.

Indicators of Efficiency

Many countries in ECA implemented structural reforms to their health care systems with the objective of improving outcomes and achieving a sustainable financing path. However, after a decade of reforms some of them have not achieved their goals, and many reforms meant to enhance efficiency have not resulted in cost containment). Some countries, such as Croatia, have very good health outcomes, but public spending on health is above average and some argue unsustainable. Other countries, such as Georgia, spend very little on health, and outcomes are worse than average. This is clearly seen in figure 6.5, where a normalized health performance index for the ECA and comparator countries is plotted against public spending on health. The performance index is a simple average of five outcome indicators: healthy life expectancy for males and females, infant mortality rate, immunization rate for DPT3, and SDRs of cancer of the cervix. Countries are divided into four quadrants. Poland and Croatia—in the upper right quadrant—are higher spenders and better performers; Armenia, Georgia, and the Kyrgyz Republic—in the lower left quadrant—are lower spenders and worse performers; and countries in the upper left quadrant—like Chile—are lower spenders and better performers.[8]

FIGURE 6.5

Health Performance Index and Public Spending on Health, ECA and Comparator Countries, 2003 or Latest Year Available

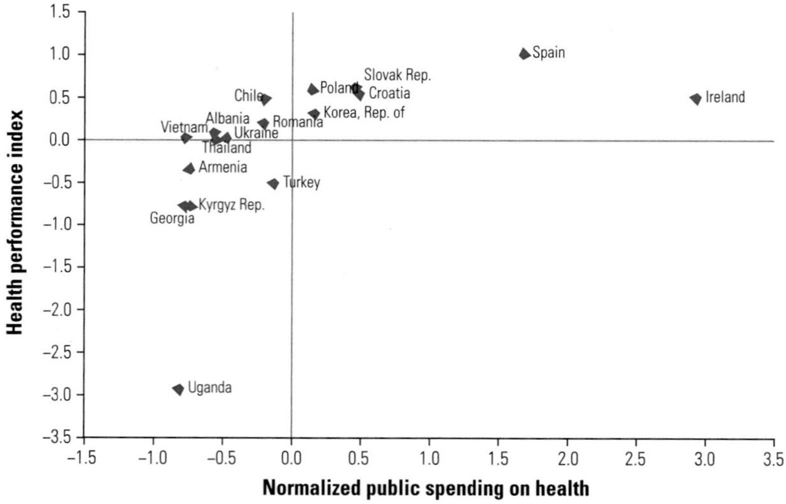

Sources: WHO and World Bank data.

Figures 6.6 and 6.7 describe the input efficiency score for life expectancy at birth and for DPT immunization, respectively, calculated using a large sample of countries.[9] Herrera and Pang (2005) estimate efficiency as the distance between the observed input-output combinations and an efficiency frontier, defined as the maximum attainable output for a given level of inputs and estimated for several health and education output indicators using two different methodologies. The three most efficient countries in the sample are in the comparator group: Chile, Korea, and Thailand. They have higher efficiency scores using various methods and output indicators. From the ECA focus countries, Albania, Ukraine, and the Kyrgyz Republic have the highest efficiency scores. This is true in spite of the somewhat poor health outcomes observed, particularly in the Kyrgyz Republic. The high relative score is due largely to the low spending level. For those countries it is critical to expand spending along the efficient frontier. The lowest efficiency scores are in countries such as Croatia, the Slovak Republic, and Poland, with good outcomes but high spending. Herrera and Pang (2005) find that the size of public expenditures and the proportion of services that are publicly financed are negatively associated with efficiency scores.

FIGURE 6.6
Input Efficiency Score for Life Expectancy at Birth

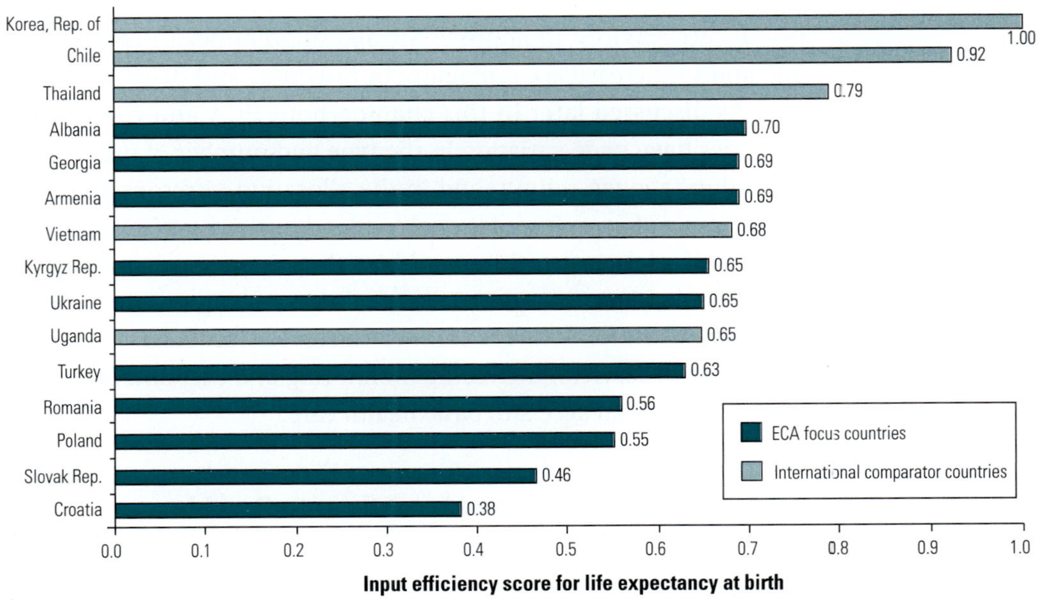

Source: Herrera and Pang 2005.

FIGURE 6.7
Input Efficiency Score for DPT Immunization

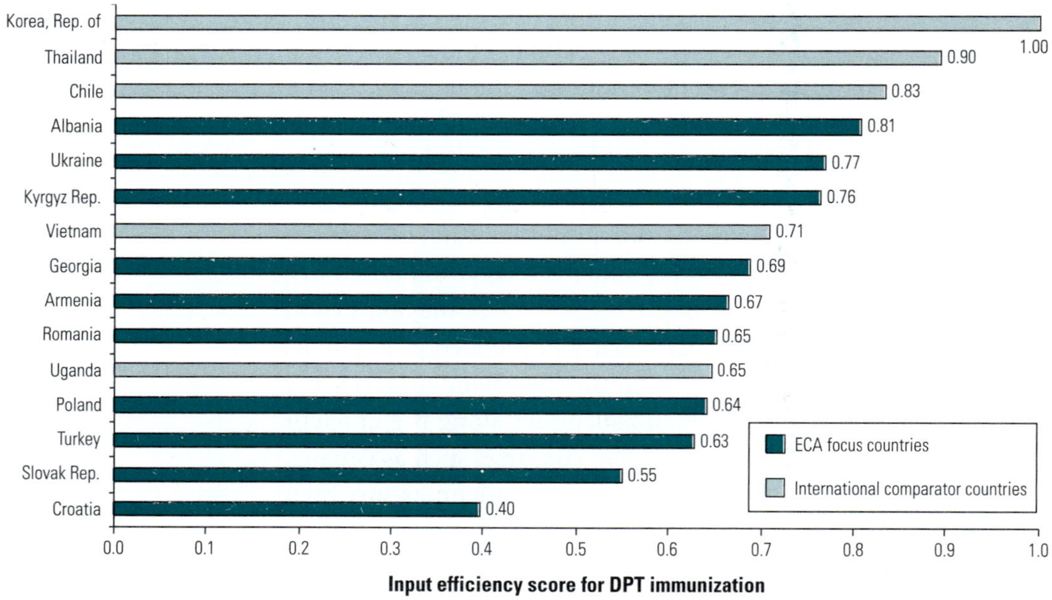

Source: Herrera and Pang 2005.

Maximizing outputs and outcomes with available resources requires coordinated policies to manage the supply of and demand for health care services, to improve the allocation of health care financing, and to increase accountability of providers and oversight agencies. As discussed later in this chapter, both ECA and comparator countries have wide variation in the type and number of inputs used to produce a given output, and in the allocation of resources to different levels of care. International focus countries have introduced a number of reforms over time to address these issues, including reducing systemic fragmentation in risk-pooling, creating the right incentive framework for insurers and health services providers, adjusting the supply of services, increasing monitoring and accountability, and securing universal access to basic health care.

Payment Mechanisms and Incentives to Providers

Two common reforms to increase efficiency in health care provision have been instituting primary care physicians as gatekeepers and changing payment mechanisms to providers. The bias toward hospital care relative to outpatient treatment is characteristic of many ECA countries and has contributed to high spending. According to Langenbrunner and Wiley (2002), referral rates to hospitals in the former Soviet Union countries were about 25–30 percent of first visits to clinics in the early 1990s, compared to 8.6 percent in the United Kingdom and 5.2 percent in the United States. Hospital admission rates as a percentage of population were also relatively high. Changing payment mechanisms for both primary physicians and hospitals is one way to create incentives to reduce unnecessary referrals and shift resources from hospitals to primary care. Pay for primary physicians becomes a combination of capitation payments (to control spending) and fees for services provided (to stimulate implementation of certain procedures or prevention activities), and regulatory agencies impose a maximum number of authorized referrals to hospitals with penalties for unjustified referrals above the statutory number. The implementation of such measures in ECA has been met with differing degrees of success, in part because the changes are recent or have never been fully implemented. Table 6.4 lists the prevailing hospital payment mechanisms in the sample of ECA countries.

Many countries have also introduced changes in payment mechanisms to hospitals to increase the efficiency of spending within hospitals. The most popular cost-minimization payment schemes are the "case-mix" systems, of which the Diagnosis-Related Group (DRG) is the most common application (see box 6.3 for examples). Payment is based on a discharge that has been corrected by the type of case treated. This payment mechanism tends to minimize unnecessary procedures to treat a given case and therefore minimizes the cost of treatment, but if inadequately monitored it may generate distortions, such as an increase in the number of cases treated and changes in coding toward more expensive cases.[10] Table 6.4 shows that case mix (or per case) payments have been implemented or are in the process of being

TABLE 6.4

Prevailing Hospital Payment Mechanisms in Sampled ECA Countries

Country	Line item	Per day	Per case	Country	Line item	Per day	Per case
Albania	X			Poland		X	X
Armenia	X		Developing	Romania			Developing
Croatia		X	Developing	Slovak Republic	X	X	
Georgia			X	Turkey	X		
Kyrgyz Republic	X		X	Ukraine	X		

Source: Langenbrunner and Wiley 2002 (with updates).

Note: No sample countries use the pure global budget or capitation mechanisms for hospital payment.

BOX 6.3

Introducing Mixed Payment Systems

Korea. Until 1997, health providers in Korea were reimbursed on a fee-for-service basis. This generated some distortions, such as an increase in the overall number of procedures and in the amount of out-of-pocket payments in spite of the additional coverage of the benefit package, due to a supply-induced shift in procedures toward those that were not insured and thus reimbursed more generously (for example, Korea was the country with third highest number of CT scanners in the world and cesarean deliveries increased from 6 percent in 1985 to 43 percent in 1999, partly due to the way providers were paid for them). To reduce the distortions among service provision by specialty, a resource-based relative value scale was introduced in 2001, which rated procedures according to relative complexity and cost and made payment contingent upon the resources needed to supply the services. The purpose was to discourage overprovision by some providers of a given specialty. In 1997 the government launched a DRG pilot in 54 medical facilities, extended to 132 in the second year and to 798 in the third year. The initial introduction of DRGs was facilitated by the overall increase in payments to providers, because the DRG payment was about 23.8 percent higher on average than the comparable regulated fee for service. The pilot covered nine disease categories and 25 DRG codes depending on the severity and age of the patient, and accounted for 25 percent of inpatient cases. The initial evaluation of the system shows that medical care cost declined on average 8.3 percent and Average Length of Stay dropped by 3 percent. The introduction of DRGs also resulted in a 30 percent reduction in the use of antibiotics in inpatient care, the average number of tests, and the number of outpatient visits. The overall experience with DRG payments has been positive. Medical care expenditure for a given basis diagnosis decreased by an average of 8.3 percent, and the average length of stay dropped by 3 percent in participating institutions (Kwon 2003).

(continued)

implemented by most of the ECA countries in the sample (as has also been the case in many of the comparator countries, see box 6.3).

Governance

Governance is a broad concept that includes the overall capacity of the government to administer services and the mechanisms for monitoring and oversight of various institutions to ensure accountability. Various studies have tried to link governance variables with health sector performance measured by outputs and outcomes. Wagstaff and

BOX 6.3 (continued)

Ireland. Ireland was one of the first countries in Europe to introduce DRGs to pay for hospital services (in 1993). Hospitals work within a global budgeting framework that is adjusted according to their case mixes. A portion of the hospital budget is based on the case-mix adjustment. The additional funds gained as a result of this process may be used at the discretion of the hospital. For hospitals with over 5,000 discharges annually, 20 percent of the inpatient budget is determined on a case-mix basis and 80 percent is estimated on the basis of historical costs. Hospitals are classified according to their specialist and teaching status. It is planned that by 2007, about 50 percent of the hospitals budget will be determined on a case-mix basis. Since 1980, the number of inpatient hospital beds dropped by 21 percent, inpatient admissions increased about 6 percent, average length of stay decreased about one-third. Outpatient activity meanwhile increased by 40 percent in the same period. The number of day care beds increased from 284 in 1990 to 721 in 2000, and the number of discharges treated on a day basis increased from 124,769 in 1990 to 324,504 in 2000. (Wiley 2005).

Spain. Although each autonomous region of Spain can determine its precise approach, in general, hospitals are funded on a global budget basis, determined by historical costs with annual adjustments for such factors as inflation and changes in service delivery. Increasingly, an adjustment for activity is being integrated within the budgeting process. Since 1997–98, several regional systems have incorporated a case-mix adjustment. For example, 30 percent of the inpatient budget in Catalonia is estimated based on DRGs, whereas Valencia uses a combination of capitation and DRGs (Langenbrunner and Wiley 2002). Activities that are especially sophisticated (transplants, for instance), expensive (dialysis, for instance), or that are regarded as priority interventions because of the length of waiting lists (for example, major outpatient surgery) remain outside the case base system for budgeting and have their financing calculated separately. The cost of treatments in these categories is added to the financing of overall activity by cases, to give the total prospective budget for each hospital.

Source: Authors, based on Kwon (2003), Wiley (2005), and Langenbrunner and Wiley (2002).

Claeson (2004) use the Country Policy and Institutional Assessment (CPIA) score as a proxy for good governance and find that the elasticity of health outcomes to expenditure depends on a country's CPIA score. At the margin, spending has a larger impact on health outcomes in better-governed countries: for example, at a CPIA score of 4—one standard deviation above the mean—a 10 percent increase in the share of GDP devoted to public spending on health leads to a 7.2 percent decline in the maternal mortality rate, while at CPIA levels below 3, increased spending has no statistically significant impact on health. Similarly, Rajkumar and Swaroop (2002) find that public spending on health reduces both child and infant mortality rates in countries that have good governance, and it is more effective as the level of corruption goes down.

Weak governance in the health care system is evident in several ways in ECA countries. The first is the prevalence of informal payments. Informal payments generate an incentive for providers to discriminate among patients based on their ability to pay, which undermines the quality of and access to health care for those who cannot pay the expected bribe. The additional transactions and lack of transparency can also reduce the overall efficiency of delivery.

In addition, poor procurement and prescription practices for medical devices and pharmaceuticals are common in many ECA countries. This is a critical public finance issue because the diffusion of medical technologies and pharmaceutical expenditures can rapidly drive up health expenditures. With the shift from inpatient care to outpatient care and from treatment of communicable diseases to management of chronic diseases, the demand for pharmaceuticals is likely to continue to increase over the years. For example, total spending on pharmaceuticals across OECD countries has increased an average of 32 percent from 1998 to 2003, and its growth has outpaced that of total health expenditures over the same period in most OECD countries.[11] In the Slovak Republic, expenditure on pharmaceuticals increased dramatically from 1995 to 2002 and accounted for 32 percent of total health expenditures in 2002. The share of spending on drugs in Poland went from 13.7 percent in 1999 to 19.6 percent in 2003. This high pharmaceutical expenditure is the result of changes in both prices and volumes, variables that are affected by both supply forces (such as the type of drugs available, extent of competition and transparency, and quality of regulation) and demand forces (the aging of populations, asymmetry of information on drug prices and availability, and lack of consumer knowledge about what constitutes state of the art treatment). A variety of solutions have been implemented to contain the growth rate of spending on pharmaceuticals, and at least three types of measures are related to improved governance: (a) more transparent pharmaceutical procurement systems; (b) the right incentives for providers to prescribe medical diagnosis and prescriptions; and (c) a transparent prescription dispensing system.

The Slovak Republic implemented a successful reform in its pharmaceutical policy that addressed the issues mentioned above. Among other measures, the country (a) introduced a flat prescription fee to limit unnecessary demand; (b) fixed the ratio of price to reimbursement in cases of price reduction after categorization;[12] (c) mandated insurance companies to reimburse patients on the basis of the lowest price in every therapeutic category (as determined on the basis of daily dose requirement and published in a widely circulated handbook, with pharmacies being required to explain the substitutability and availability of drugs and the different copayments associated with them to patients); (d) opened competition among pharmaceutical providers (conducted online so that all bidders have complete information about the bids of their competitors); (e) changed the staffing of the Categorizing Committee, which sets copayments for procedures and drugs, to favor economists over doctors; and (f) increased the frequency of drug categorization from once a year to four times a year (Chawla 2005).

The final area where governance in health could be improved is the management and accountability of health provision. Inadequate stewardship and monitoring is observed at various levels. Health insurance funds may not monitor hospital behavior or control costs. Hospitals may not be directly accountable for maintaining a balanced budget. Quality in delivery is often overlooked. In addition, health care facilities in ECA are often managed by medical doctors, who have less experience in management, including financing, accounting, and operations. Arrears in the health sector have continued to grow in most ECA countries, while international focus countries have implemented successful reforms to improve transparency. Box 6.4 describes the reforms of CENABAS in Chile and the separation between the prescribing and the dispensing of drugs in Korea.

Access to Health Care

One of the central objectives of a well-functioning health system is to guarantee access to at least a basic package of benefits to the entire population. This has proven to be a difficult objective to achieve in many ECA countries. In Albania, for example, only 33 percent of individuals who reported being sick sought care.[13] In Georgia, 43 percent of those who reported being sick sought care in 2001, and in Armenia only 29.5 percent. Some of the comparator countries have achieved universal coverage through a variety of means, but it has taken a long time to reach that goal.

BOX 6.4

Chile and Korea: Improving Governance

Chile: Reform of CENABAS

Over 1995 to 1998, the Chilean Central Supply Facility (CENABAS) changed from a budget-supported government supply facility to a self-financing purchasing intermediary between Health Service Areas (HSAs) and private suppliers. During the reform, CENABAS developed a computerized auction-style bidding process to enhance competition among bidders to lower purchasing prices. CENABAS also established advisory services for HSAs and hospitals to improve their capacity for purchasing, stockpiling, and financial management. In addition, CENABAS developed an information and communication network with all HSAs and major hospitals. As a result, CENABAS was able to streamline its warehouse by 50 percent, its transportation costs by 11 percent, its stock margins by 10 percent, and its staff costs by 12 percent. Response time has fallen by half, and transparency and accountability have improved due to the computerized bidding process. Challenges remain for CENABAS to define the scope of the items to be purchased and the scope of primary care facilities to be covered.

Korea: The Separation Reform

Until July 2000, the physician's role of prescribing and the pharmacist's role of dispensing drugs were not separated in Korea. Doctors could dispense drugs at clinics, and pharmacies could sell some specialty drugs to patients without a doctor's prescription. Doctors and pharmacies competed with each other for the profit margin on drugs. Prescribing drugs was one of the important sources of doctors' income, and doctors had incentives to overprescribe drugs. To reduce overuse of pharmaceuticals and increase accountability for prescriptions, Korea implemented a reform starting in 1999 to separate the physician's role of prescribing and the pharmacist's role of dispensing drugs. The reform has triggered several physicians' strikes as their incomes have fallen; these have been settled through incremental increases of medical fees as compensation for the income loss. The overall outcome of separation has been positive because it has promoted the professional specialization of physicians and pharmacists, reduced inappropriate prescriptions, and created the potential for better-informed consumers.

Sources: World Bank 2000; OECD 2003.

In contrast, the entire population in Korea is now covered for the risk of medical illness, either through the National Health Insurance, a SHI scheme financed by mandatory contributions, or throughout the Medical Aid Program (MAP), a social assistance program for the poor financed though general taxation. The benefit is identical in both programs, and all patients except some MAP beneficiaries have to make substantial payments toward their treatment (table 6.5).[14]

Thailand is also illustrative. Expansion was also pursued over time, starting in 1975. Before introduction of universal health insurance coverage, four separate schemes covered different groups of the population.[15] The government elected in 2001 initiated health-financing reform and implementation of universal health care coverage. The universal coverage scheme (UCS) replaced the public welfare scheme and the voluntary health card, and incorporated all the uninsured under the same umbrella. The UCS is financed entirely through general tax revenue. The Civil Servant Medical Scheme and social security schemes are as before. Three systems remain: compulsory health insurance for formal employees, civil servants' insurance, and universal insurance covering the rest of the population. An analysis of the impact of the program on poverty and incidence of catastrophic payments for health showed that the UCS program has had a significant positive impact and has benefited the poorer quintiles more than the rest.[16]

Extending coverage universally did not eliminate out-of-pocket payments in countries such as Korea and Thailand, and in some cases additional coverage was achieved at the expense of limiting the benefit package substantially. The universal insurance system in Thailand still charges a notional copayment of $0.70 per visit to limit unnecessary demand, while in Korea a limited benefit scheme excludes certain high-cost services or imposes high copayments. The excluded services and treatments include patient transport, glasses and contact lenses, care not considered essential to daily living (for example, plastic surgery), and other high-cost services that are expected to be covered subject to future affordability, such as magnetic resonance imaging and ultrasonic diagnosis. There is no cap to copayments but some compensation is given for high cost cases.

TABLE 6.5

Copayments for Services Covered by National Health Insurance in the Republic of Korea

Health service and facility	Copayment
Inpatient	20 percent of total treatment cost
Outpatient	
General hospital	Per-visit consultation fee + 55 percent of treatment cost
Hospital	Per-visit consultation fee + 40 percent of treatment cost
Clinic	30 percent of treatment cost

Source: OECD 2003.

As coverage increased in Thailand, so did spending. The increase in coverage spanned the 1980s and 1990s, and during that time total health spending as a percentage of GDP increased from 3.7 (1980) to 5.2 (1990). The public share of spending also increased from 26.5 percent in 1980 to 40.3 percent in 1990 (OECD 1999). During the last decade, spending as a percentage of GDP remained relatively stable.

Overcapacity in Health Service Delivery

The current oversupply of hospital infrastructure in most ECA countries is a legacy of the Soviet period. The disproportionate number of hospital beds has become a drain on public resources in the health sector and is symptomatic of structural problems in health care provision. Large capacity combined with long length of hospital stays and low occupancy rates generates large fixed costs for the system. The overcapacity also perpetuates a model that treats many cases on an inpatient basis, when modern technology would allow for outpatient treatment at a lower cost.

Reforms involving closure of public hospitals or reduction of hospital beds would free up significant resources, but they are highly unpopular. There has been a trend toward reducing hospital beds in many ECA countries (figure 6.8 and 6.9), as well as in most of Western Europe. However, the average number of hospital beds in ECA is still much higher than that in the international focus group, as shown in table 6.6. ECA focus countries have 54 hospital beds per 10,000 population while the international focus group has 38. Ukraine has the highest hospital bed density, 87 per 10,000 population, followed by the Slovak Republic with 70 hospital beds per 10,000 population.

Georgia has made significant progress in downsizing the hospital sector. During the 1970s and 1980s, many hospitals and polyclinics were built in Georgia, mainly for military reasons because of the country's strategic location. By 1990, Georgia had 384 hospitals, approximately 1,400 polyclinics and ambulatories, and 53,039 hospital beds. Although health care had a strong inpatient focus, occupancy rates were at most 50 percent, and in many hospitals as low as 10 percent. The government of Georgia embarked on a series of reforms to decrease the number of hospitals to a more manageable number, as well as to change the ownership structure and financing arrangements. The first stage of reform in the hospital sector changed ownership structure and made each hospital responsible

FIGURE 6.8

Hospitals per 100,000 population, 1990 and 2004 (or latest year available)

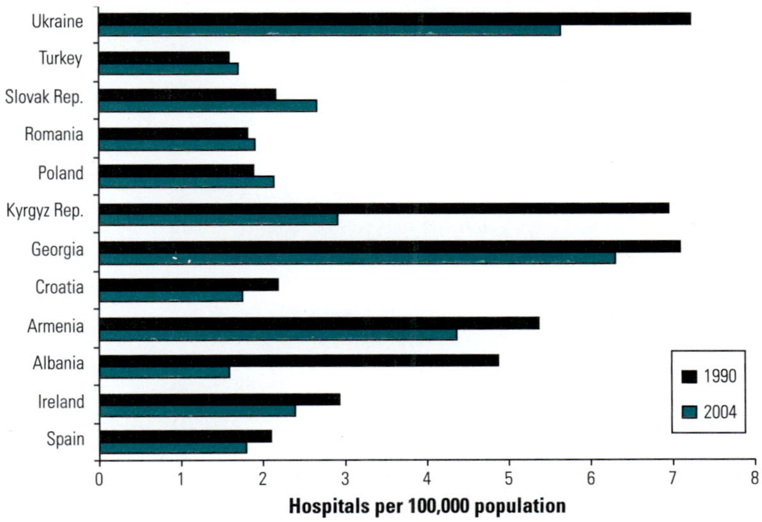

Sources: European Health for All database, WHO Regional Office for Europe, 2006.

FIGURE 6.9

Acute Hospital Beds Per 100,000 Population, 1990 and 2004 (or latest available year)

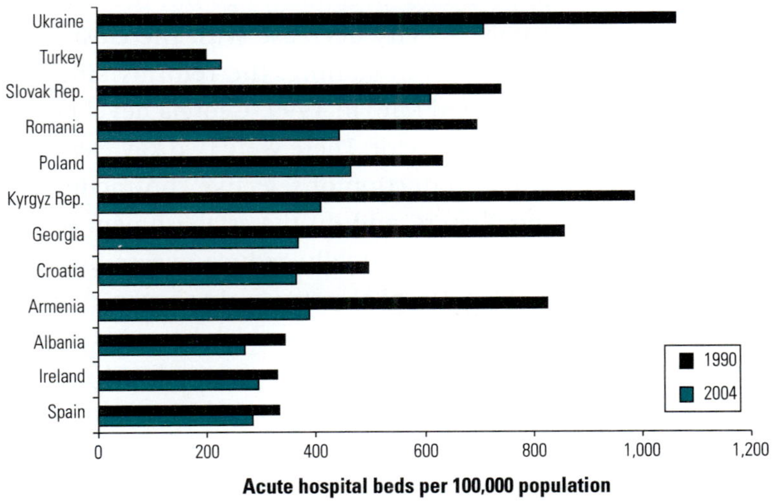

Sources: European Health for All database, WHO Regional Office for Europe, 2006.

TABLE 6.6
Health Care Resources, 2004 or Latest Year Available

Country	Physicians (per 1,000 population)	Nurses (per 1,000 population)	Hospital beds (per 10,000 population)
Albania	1.31	3.62	30
Armenia	3.59	4.35	44
Croatia	2.44	5.05	55
Georgia	4.09	3.47	—
Kyrgyz Republic	2.51	6.14	53
Poland	2.47	4.90	55
Romania	1.90	3.89	66
Slovak Republic	3.18	6.77	70
Turkey	1.35	1.70	26
Ukraine	2.95	7.62	87
Average (ECA)	*2.58*	*4.75*	*54*
Chile	1.09	0.63	25
Ireland	2.79	15.20	35
Korea, Republic of	1.57	1.75	71
Spain	3.30	7.68	37
Thailand	0.37	2.82	22
Uganda	0.08	0.61	—
Vietnam	0.53	0.56	23
Average (comparator countries)	*1.39*	*4.18*	*38*

Source: WHO database and OECD 2005.
Note: — = Not available.

for generating running costs through contracts with public purchasers and fee-for-service charges. It was envisaged that this process would force unprofitable hospitals to go out of business. Although there was some capacity decrease with the closure of some hospitals and reductions in staffing, the reforms failed to reduce capacity at the expected rate. In 1999, Georgia developed a plan to rationalize the hospital sector. There were two key elements of these reforms: (a) the introduction of selective contracting for hospital services with purchasers, and (b) the establishment of the Hospital Restructuring Fund to formally reduce excess hospital capacity, led by a master plan. Hospital restructuring began in 2000, guided by the master plan, which identified which hospitals should remain open and which should be closed or privatized.[17] The number of hospitals in Georgia has decreased by 109 since the early 1990s, but to reach the target for hospital closure according to the master plan, another 174 hospitals would need to be closed or consolidated during the next two stages of restructuring to be completed by 2010 (World Bank 2004c).

Adjusting to Aging Populations

Financing and delivering health care for the elderly population is a growing concern in health care systems all over the world. However, the exact impact of aging on health spending is still subject to debate. Some researchers find that aging populations exert pressure on health spending, while others maintain that people are becoming healthier as they age, at least in high-income settings, ameliorating the effect on health spending. Gottret and Schieber (2006) project the change in total health spending over time in various regions as a result of changes both in the number of people and in the age-gender composition of the population. Total health spending in ECA is expected to rise 14 percent from 2005 to 2025, with 1 percentage point due to increases in the population and 13 percentage points due to changes in the age-gender structure. Given that the gender structure is quite stable, the change would largely be due to age structure changes, especially increases in the older population. This is a low figure compared to other regions; for example, in Latin American, population changes are expected to lead to an increase of 47 percent in health spending. An upcoming World Bank report estimates the impact of aging in each ECA country and concludes that it is likely to increase spending in most but not all countries (EBRD 2007). If the current levels of benefits are maintained, public spending on health is expected to increase only modestly in Poland and Romania by 2050 (compared to 2005 levels) and to actually fall in Armenia.

The aging population and a rising number of elderly are likely to change the epidemiological profile of the populations, increasing the burden of noncommunicable diseases, and put new pressures on the provision and use of long-term care services for the elderly. However, public expenditures on formal and informal long-term care will depend on policies governing eligibility and benefits. The key to containing expenditures will lie in designing less expensive delivery arrangements. Increasing preventive health care should reduce the burden in the long run because a significant portion of chronic disease conditions could be prevented through the promotion of healthy lifestyles, screening, and primary and secondary preventive care. There seems to be no advantage in SHI or general tax–funded models when it comes to long-term elderly care. Different mechanisms are used to mobilize resources for the provision of long-term care services: special long-term care insurance (as in Germany), general taxes (as in Austria), a combination of insurance and general taxes (as in Japan), and special programs (as in the Netherlands).

The Sustainability of SHI and its Relation to Labor Markets

One of the most debated issues in the discussion on funding mechanisms for health care is the distortionary effect of payroll contributions paid to finance SHI systems. The revenue for SHI comes primarily from contributions from gross wages, levied on employers and employees, which increases labor costs for employers and reduces net income for employees. The sustainability of SHI is largely related to the payroll tax rate and the number of contributors. The payroll tax rate in ECA countries devoted to health is on average relatively high.

The debate over the effect of payroll taxes on competitiveness and unemployment has a long history and is reviewed in depth in chapter 9. Most observers agree that payroll taxes are likely to increase the level of informality in the economy (Wagstaff 2006), particularly in developing countries, and thus incorporating a sufficient number of workers into social risk-pooling schemes may be difficult. Baeza and Packard (2006) identify several factors that prevent informal or self-employed workers from joining SHI systems in Latin American countries; some of these factors are also valid for ECA countries. In some cases there is no legal mechanism for informal or self-employed workers to participate in SHI schemes because Bismarckian SHI applies only to salaried workers. And the perception of a large gap between contributions and benefits—particularly where health services are weak—reduces the desire of workers to enter the formal sector to gain access to risk-pooling.

Given those barriers, how can contributory risk-pooling be extended to the informal and self-employed sectors? Baeza and Packard suggest four options: (a) facilitate (through regulation) participation of self-employed and informal workers in contributory health insurance (which is extremely hard to achieve given that their income is unobservable and participation is purely voluntary); (b) improve enforcement of mandatory participation; (c) increase means-testing for access to publicly subsidized health services; and (d) reduce the contribution-benefits gap.

Spain, with a long tradition of a Bismarckian SHI system, has moved to a Beveridge model of financing. The General Health Act of 1986 changed the Spanish health care system dramatically. Before the act, multiple health care networks coexisted, with a significant proportion of health care financed through the social security system managed by the Ministry of Labor. From the late 1980s on, Spain gradually shifted from a payroll tax–financed social security scheme to a national health service financed by general taxation. In 1989, three years after the act, the funding sources for health care were drastically modified, with 70 percent financed from general taxation and 30 percent from payroll tax contribution. In the mid-1990s, it was agreed that all health financing would come from general taxation, and the payroll tax should be phased out progressively by 2000. In 1999, one year ahead of schedule, the entire health care budget in Spain came from general taxation. Regions in Spain receive health care funding from the central government on a per capita basis, adjusted by other factors. Regions have varying degrees of independence for management of resources. Coverage is almost universal and guarantees a fairly comprehensive package of benefits to all Spanish citizens, regardless of labor status or personal wealth (Baeza and Packard 2006).

Conclusions

This chapter has reviewed patterns of health spending, health-financing systems, and their relation to health outcomes in the ECA focus and international comparator countries. While higher GDP per capita and thus higher absolute levels of health spending are correlated with better health outcomes, no specific relationship emerges between financing method and either health spending or health outcomes. On average, ECA and comparator countries spend a similar percentage of GDP on health (approximately 6.1 percent), although there is significant variation between countries within each group. Among ECA focus countries, the group of countries with Bismarckian (SHI) models have a larger percentage of health spending coming from public sources, whereas in comparator countries the public sector spends more in tax-financed than in SHI systems.

The goal of achieving a well-functioning health care system that can provide a basic package of services to the entire population in a financially sustainable manner has not been achieved to date in many of the countries in the sample. Neither the level of public spending nor the financing model seem to dominate when it comes to fulfilling this goal or to achieving better health outcomes. Countries with both general tax funding and SHI schemes have put in place delivery mechanisms that work efficiently and reach a large share of the population. The keys under either type of system are to provide appropriate incentives to patients, insurers, and providers through payment mechanisms; to target the provision of basic care to vulnerable groups; to introduce good procurement practices; to strengthen accountability at all levels; and to emphasize monitoring and quality assurance. Public health policies, including promotion of healthier lifestyles, food safety, and improved sanitation, are also likely to be cost effective and sustainable ways to promote better health outcomes. Of course, broader public policies—beyond health—also affect health outcomes, including better education and policies to promote economic growth and good governance overall.

The mode of health financing may have impacts beyond health, however, given the differences in tax incidence between general revenue financing (whether through direct or indirect taxes) and financing through labor taxes. These issues of tax policy are

Notes

The authors are grateful for the research assistance provided by Qing Wu, Elena Rydralova, and Shweta Jain.

1. Individual health risk has no impact on the level of contributions.
2. Croatia, Poland, Romania, and the Slovak Republic.
3. Several studies have been implemented using micro data to look at the determinants of health spending. These studies find that in addition to income, prices of health care seem to matter, but there is no consensus on how important an effect price generates. The estimated price elasticity of health care spending tends to be small but is consistent with significant reductions in spending, particularly when the price paid by households is originally near zero (Docteur and Oxley 2003).
4. The impoverishing effect of out-of-pocket spending has been documented in both ECA and comparator countries. Wagstaff, van Doorslaer, and Watanabe (2002) analyzed the impact of household spending on health on poverty using data from the Vietnam Living Standards Survey for 1993 and 1998. In 1993, 38 percent of households in the sample registered out-of-pocket payments for health in excess of 5 percent, and 34 percent spent more than 15 percent of their nonfood consumption on out-of-pocket payments. Out-of-pocket payments were found to increase the poverty headcount ratio by 4.4 percentage points in 1993 and 3.4 percentage points in 1998. A similar analysis for Chile (Bitran et al. 2004) showed that approximately 90 percent of households in the poorest consumption quintile spent more than 15 percent of income on out-of-pocket health spending. Those in the private health insurance system were more likely to fall into poverty because of out-of-pocket payments because of the limitations of the private system in covering catastrophic shocks. In Albania it was estimated—using Living Standards Measurement Survey 2002 data—that about 26 percent of people reported health care payments greater than 10 percent of total incomes, and about 9 percent reported health spending above 25 percent of their income. The percentage of individuals below the poverty line increased from 25 to 34, and extreme poverty doubled from 5 to 10 percent, when health out-of-pocket spending was taken into account (World Bank 2006e).
5. "Amenable conditions" derives from the concept of deaths from various causes (such as pregnancy and childbirth, tuberculosis, diabetes mellitus,

pneumonia, and appendicitis) that should not occur in the presence of timely and effective health care.

6. Several approaches have been developed to better quantify the contribution of health care systems to population health. Immunization rates and standardized death rates from certain causes, such as cancer of the cervix, diabetes mellitus, cardiovascular disease, and tuberculosis, provide evidence of coverage of preventive care and the extent by which better systems could reduce unnecessary deaths from preventable diseases. A different approach is to look at tracer conditions, that is, select a particular health condition, the treatment of which captures some of the complexities involved in health care systems. Nolte, Bain, and McKee (2006) propose to look at diabetes at young age as a condition to measure the performance of health systems, arguing that the effective treatment of the disease requires the coordination of different actors. Diabetes is well defined, easy to diagnose, prevalent worldwide, and growing as a condition that affects a larger share of the population. Treating diabetes successfully involves good screening for the disease, reducing the risk of complications, access to essential medicines like insulin, good monitoring, and adequate prevention. The variable used to measure performance is the ratio of the standardized death rate from diabetes for ages 0–39 to age-standardized incidence for the 0–14 year-old group as an indicator of overall survival from the disease and therefore an indication of quality of treatment and care. The study contained few countries from the sample in this report, finding significant variation in performance. For example, Romania has a ratio of 0.13 and Poland 0.08, while the lowest ratio in the sample included in this study for which available data exist is Spain, with 0.02. The large variation across countries suggests differences in the ability of health systems to provide adequate care for people with diabetes.
7. Other studies on the relationship between public spending and outcomes tend to confirm these results (Berger and Messer 2002; Wagstaff and van Doorslaer 2001; Bidani and Ravallion 1997.
8. Also see discussion in chapter 9 on the relationship of these results to the overall quality of governance.
9. The output efficiency scores are not reported in this chapter because less variation in output efficiency scores is observed among ECA focus countries and international comparator countries.
10. For a complete description of the advantages and disadvantages of different payment mechanisms, see Langenbrunner and Wiley (2002).
11. Outpatient drugs only (OECD 2005b).
12. If the pharmaceutical company decreases the price of a drug after the positive list is published, the ratio between the reimbursement paid by the health insurance company and the copayment paid by the patient remains the same.
13. According to the 2004 household survey.
14. The successful implementation of universal coverage is largely the result of an incremental introduction of progressive innovations. In 1977, only 8.8 percent of the population in Korea was covered by formal social security insurance. In that year, two programs were established: MAP for the population with income below a certain level and a medical insurance

program that provides coverage for employees and their immediate family members working in enterprises of 500 or more people. Two years later, the coverage was expanded to enterprises with 300 or more employees and civil servants and teachers in private schools, and in 1981 coverage was extended to enterprises with 100 or more people. By 1988, the government expanded medical insurance coverage in rural areas to almost 7.5 million more people. In 1989, the government extended medical insurance to the uncovered population, mainly self-employed urban workers. So by 1989, 12 years after beginning the first reform, Korea successfully achieved universal health insurance. For more details see OECD (2003).

15. These were (a) the Civil Servant Medical Benefit Scheme covering government employees and dependents, noncontributory, financed fully by general tax revenue; (b) the public welfare scheme covering low-income households, the elderly, and children under 12, financed fully by general tax revenue (under two separate programs, the medical welfare scheme, and the Type B Fee exemption scheme); (c) the social security scheme and workers compensation fund covering private employees, financed by contributions equally from government, employer, and employee; and (d) voluntary Health Card Scheme covering the borderline poor who are not eligible for the public welfare scheme, with about 50 percent subsidized by the general tax and fixed fees that households contribute each year.
16. For example, the total number of households facing catastrophic expenditure in 2000 was fairly evenly distributed across the five quintiles, 15 percent in the first quintile, 25 percent in the second, and almost equally at 20 percent in the third, fourth, and fifth. After UCS implementation, the percent distribution in the first and second quintiles fell significantly, while it increased in the fourth and fifth. Overall poverty from out-of-pocket spending on health decreased, from 4.4 percent in pre-UCS 2000 to 1.8 percent in 2004. See Limwattananon, Tangcharoensathian, and Prakongsai (2005).
17. The master plan was completed in 1998. With more than 50 hospitals, Tbilisi was selected as the first priority for restructuring. Phase I of the plan has been completed. For the most part, this has involved the consolidation of some facilities in Tblisi, Kutaisi, Poti, and several other cities in Georgia. These mergers have meant that in the initial stages, several facilities have been combined to form one legal entity, so that on paper at least the number of facilities has decreased. Eventually some of the excess property within these consolidated groups was sold off.

CHAPTER 7

Pensions

Anita Schwarz
with contributions from Ufuk Guven

Public pension systems represent a large share of public spending throughout the Europe and Central Asia (ECA) region. As noted in chapter 2, relative to international comparator countries the levels of pension spending are significantly higher in ECA (figure 7.1). Much of the explanation for the difference lies in demographics and historical evolution—countries with older populations tend to spend more. However, within the ECA region some countries with younger populations, such as Turkey, spend more than some countries with much older populations, such as Armenia and Georgia, suggesting that pension policy also plays a role in determining the level of pension spending. ECA countries tend to have more costly systems with more generous benefits than non-ECA high-growth comparators. Given the finding in chapter 3 that high levels of public transfers are associated with lower economic growth, ECA countries need to look at their competitors in the world economy and decide whether the policies they are following will allow them to achieve the levels of long-run growth they desire for their populations.

FIGURE 7.1

Pension Spending in ECA and Comparator Countries, 2004 or Latest Available Year

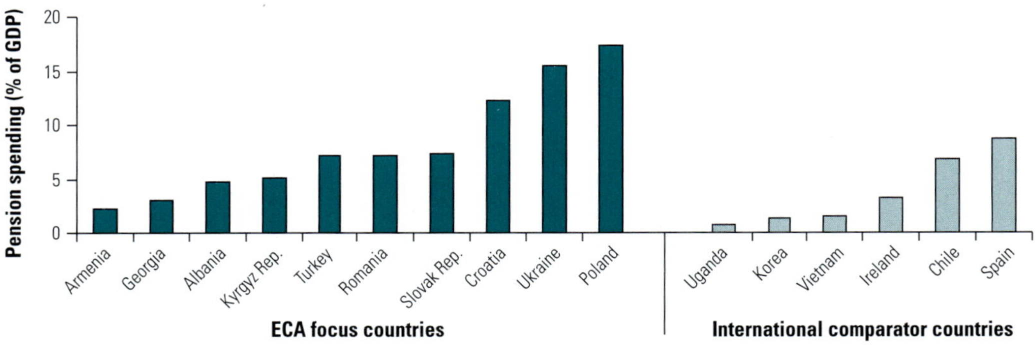

Source: World Bank Social Protection database.

Characteristics of ECA's Pension Systems

The ECA region is old relative to the international comparators (figure 7.2). More than 10 percent of the population in two-thirds of the ECA focus countries is over age 65. By contrast, only two of the seven non-ECA comparators have populations with 10 percent or more of the people over age 65.

Furthermore, pension systems in ECA are longstanding and therefore "mature." When a pension system financed on a pay-as-you-go basis first begins, it only collects revenue. Individuals make contributions, but almost no one has enough contributions in the first years to receive a pension. A few contributors may suffer disability soon after the pension system starts, but this tends to have a small effect. Thus, "immature" systems have few expenditures and generally run surpluses. As the systems mature, contributors begin to reach retirement age, increasing expenditures of the pension system. Finally, when all old-age retirees have spent their entire working lives as contributing members of the pension system—a process that may take 50 to 60 years—the system is judged to be mature. Expenditures are much higher in mature systems, and whether these systems remain in financial balance or run deficits depends on the relative generosity of the benefit parameters relative to the contribution parameters. Most ECA countries have fully mature pension systems that have been in existence for at least 50 years (figure 7.3). In the comparator coun-

FIGURE 7.2

Old-Age Populations in ECA and Comparator Countries, 2004 or Latest Available Year

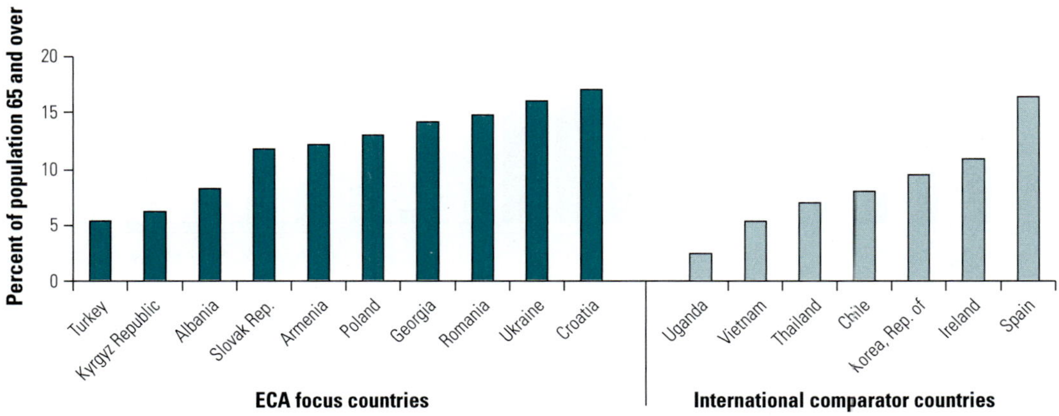

Source: UN Population Statistics.

tries, by contrast, pension systems are often much younger, with the exception of Chile, Ireland, and Spain. In the youngest of these systems, Thailand, the pension system has been functioning only since 1999. A few disabled and survivors are currently collecting pensions, but no contributors have paid into the system long enough to collect an old-age pension.

Based on age and system maturity, pension systems in Spain and Ireland are reasonably comparable to those in many ECA countries. However, a third feature of ECA countries makes them different from even these older countries with well-established pension systems, and that is the mismatch between pension coverage and contributor coverage. Countries around the world have different coverage rates in their pension systems, whether old-age coverage (the percentage of the elderly population receiving pensions) or contributor coverage (the percentage of the working-age population or labor force contributing to the pension system). Countries usually have either low coverage for both contributors and pensioners or high coverage for both, although there are a few exceptions. Most of the Organisation for Economic Co-operation and Development (OECD) countries have high coverage for both, while middle-income countries tend to have moderate coverage, and low-income countries low coverage. ECA countries are unique in that labor force participation and contributor coverage had historically been close to 100 percent for both men and

FIGURE 7.3
Maturity of Pension Systems

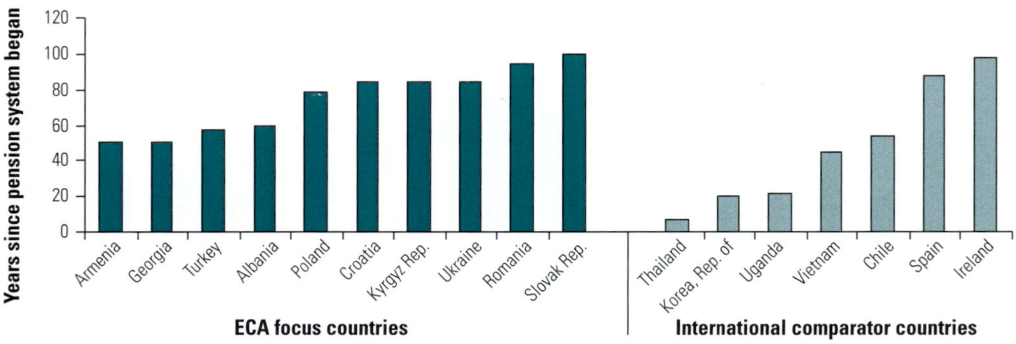

Source: Author's calculations.

women. As a result, most of the elderly are eligible for pensions and are receiving them. However, the situation is very different for today's workers. Labor force participation has dropped, particularly among women given the loss of state-provided childcare and other benefits, and unemployment rates are high. Even among those working, the informal sector attracts a substantial portion of the labor force, particularly in the lower-income countries. As a result, ECA countries are faced with unusually high pension expenditures arising from the high share of beneficiaries among the elderly, but such spending is not supported by high contributions given the declining revenue base.

Figure 7.4 shows the percentage of elderly receiving pensions compared with the percentage of working-age population making contributions in ECA and comparator countries. The elderly are defined as those 65 and older, while the working-age population is defined as those between the ages of 15 and 64, inclusive.[1] If countries from around the world were presented in this figure, most would lie relatively close to the 45-degree line, whether high-income countries with high coverage for both elderly and working age or low-income countries with low coverage for both elderly and working age. Where the pension system is immature or where coverage is growing, which is the case in many emerging market economies, such as the Republic of Korea and Thailand, the countries lie above the 45-degree line. ECA countries all lie below the 45-degree line and many substantially below, suggesting that pension expenditures in these countries are higher than pension revenues, even more so than suggested by pure demographics. Among the international comparators, only Vietnam,

FIGURE 7.4
Coverage Rates for Elderly and Working-Age Populations

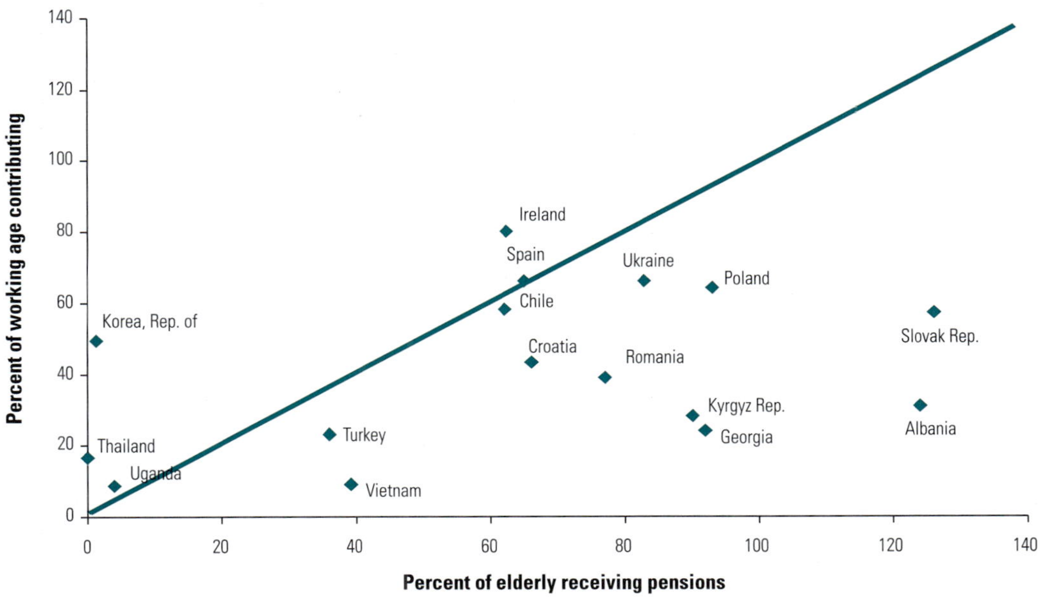

Source: World Bank Social Protection database.

which shares some of the transition history of the ECA countries, lies significantly below the 45-degree line. Chile also lies below, but not significantly so. Turkey, which does not share the transition history of the other ECA countries, also lies below the 45-degree line, largely because of its abnormally low retirement age, which currently stands at 45 for women and 47 for men. The low retirement age reduces the number of working-age individuals who are active contributors to the pension system.

Fiscal Implications

The immediate implications of this imbalance between contributors and pensioners in ECA are fiscal, with high levels of expenditures in the pension system but moderately low revenues to finance such expenditures. The initial reaction of many ECA countries to this fiscal imbalance has been to raise contribution rates even further to counteract the declining revenue. However, the original contribution rates were already high, having been set at a time when employers were not subject to market constraints and contributed whatever the state required. As discussed in chapter 9, these high payroll tax rates have been one among several factors encouraging the rapid growth of informal labor markets, further decreasing revenues to the pension system. Several countries have reduced payroll taxes recently in an effort to stem the growth of the informal sector and potentially raise revenues. Nevertheless, contribution rates are still high relative to the comparator countries, as shown in figure 7.5. Among the comparators, only Spain has contribution rates of similar magnitude to the ECA region, and half the ECA sample has rates above Spain's. Furthermore, lowering payroll tax rates is not necessarily the answer to the fiscal problem, at least in the short run. Experience to date in ECA and elsewhere suggests that formal sector employment may increase somewhat from lowering payroll taxes, but the increased employment is insufficient to actually raise revenues, resulting in an even larger shortfall between expenditures and revenues.

In the longer term, the fiscal issue could disappear if it were caused solely by an imbalance in coverage. As pensioners whose rights are based on the old system and their complete work histories leave the system and are replaced by today's workers with their incomplete

FIGURE 7.5

Pension System Contribution Rates in ECA and Comparator Countries

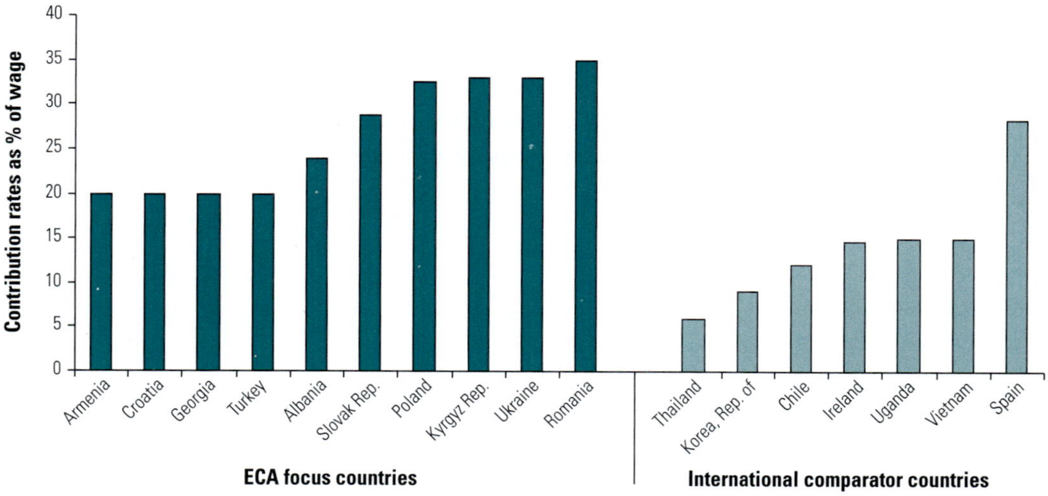

Source: Social security programs from throughout the world.

work histories, the number of pensioners will generally fall. The expenditures needed to support this fewer number of pensioners will thus be more consistent with the revenue being generated from workers. However, this adjustment will take place in the context of an aging population, which naturally tends to increase the number of pensioners relative to the number of contributors. Furthermore, the pension parameters themselves are still generous in these countries, suggesting that there might not be fiscal balance even if the countries were in a demographic steady state.

The long-term projections that are now available do not lead to the conclusion that the problem is only short term and will disappear as smaller numbers of today's contributors begin to retire. Detailed long-term projections of the pension system are available for half of the ECA focus countries: Albania, Georgia, Romania, the Slovak Republic, and Turkey. Some of these countries have put in place policy parameters that constrain the future growth of pension levels so that financial shortfalls are closed. However, social problems may well arise as a result. First, if individuals see extremely low rates of return from their pension contributions, they will have even less incentive to contribute, potentially increasing the rate of informalization. Second, at some point pensions may no longer fulfill their initial objective of providing poverty relief for the elderly, and political pressure to provide better pensions may force increases in pension levels beyond what is envisaged in today's legislation. If pension levels were to rise substantially, the pension systems would begin to face the same fiscal pressures as the countries that have not constrained their systems.

Georgia, for example, is one of the countries that has restricted pension levels. The pension benefit is virtually flat for most pensioners, aside from a few special categories. The benefit level is also extremely low, having been raised to 17.5 percent of the average wage in 2005 from an even lower level and having remained fixed since then in nominal terms. Even if the pension is indexed to inflation, benefits will fall and the pension system will run surpluses in future years (figure 7.6 and 7.7). The International Labour Organization (ILO) standard is that pension systems pay benefits equivalent to 40 percent of wages after 30 years of service. Already, the 17.5 percent being paid is well below that standard and is expected to fall farther given current parameters in the pension system. Should the government attempt to raise the pension level to ILO standards, expenditures would balloon, putting the pension system into significant deficit.

Albania is similar in many ways to Georgia. Pension benefits are not as low as in Georgia and there continues to be some differentia-

FIGURE 7.6
Georgia: Future Pension Benefit Levels

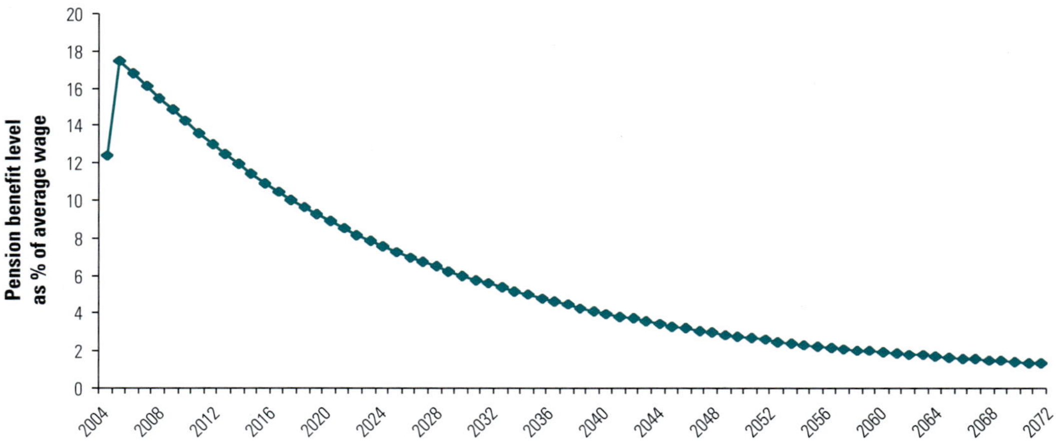

Source: Author's calculations derived from the World Bank's pension reform option simulation toolkit PROST model.

FIGURE 7.7
Future Financial Balance in Georgia's Pension System

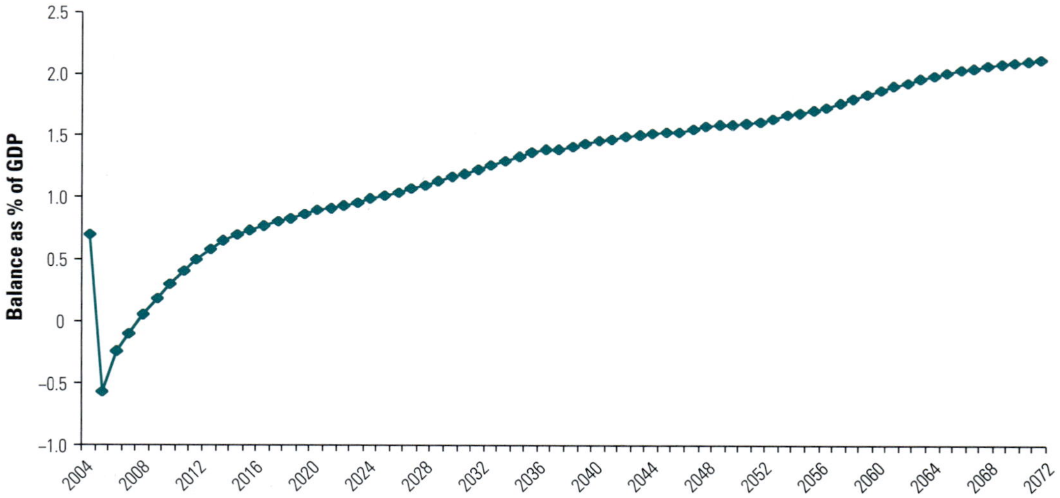

Source: Author's calculations derived from the World Bank's PROST model.

tion in pension levels, although 57 percent and 70 percent of male and female urban pensioners, respectively, and 100 percent of rural pensioners are receiving the minimum pension. However, as in Georgia, current parameters in the pension system result in a surplus in the long run and a considerable reduction in benefits. The Albanian system is driven by a maximum pension that is implicitly indexed only to inflation. As real wages grow, pension benefits will become increasingly constrained by the maximum pension that remains constant in real terms, resulting in declining pension levels relative to wages. Benefit levels are shown separately in figure 7.8 for urban and rural pensioners relative to their respective wages. The sharp initial upturn in rural pensions arises from a policy decision to equalize the urban and rural minimum pensions by 2012. Subsequently, both pension levels decline. Contributions are collected on current wages, and as benefits remain fixed in real terms while wages grow, the system will begin to run a surplus (figure 7.9). The surplus will be larger than in Georgia because the contribution rate is higher and Albania's younger population results in labor force growth throughout the period, in contrast to Georgia's declining labor force. In Albania, as in Georgia, the issue is whether these extremely low future pension levels will be socially sustainable.

Turkey is more typical than Georgia or Albania, in that it is expected to continue to run a deficit in the long run. However, it is clearly atypical for the ECA region, in that large numbers of elderly in Turkey are currently not eligible to receive pensions because they did not contribute to the system. The main problem in Turkey stems from the removal of a minimum retirement age in 1991, which left a 15-year contributory period as the primary eligibility condition, enabling people as young as 35 to retire. A 1999 law tried to fix the problem, but the government was unwilling to impose a higher retirement age immediately for those close to retirement. It chose instead to apply an extremely slow phasing in of normal minimum retirement ages, starting at 38 for women and 43 for men for the first cohorts to retire after the 1999 law. Eventually the ages were to be raised to 58 and 60, but these ages only apply to new entrants after 1999. Under the parameters in the 1999 law, the pension fund balance in Turkey would remain in deficit for the foreseeable future (figure 7.10). Deficits would stop growing in the medium term as the increasing retirement age counteracts the impact of an aging population. However, once the final retirement age has been reached, the deficits would quickly accelerate and continue to worsen throughout the period. Average pension benefit levels would remain fairly constant throughout the period and therefore are not shown separately. Legislation adopted by

FIGURE 7.8
Albania: Future Pension Benefit Levels in the Urban and Rural Sectors

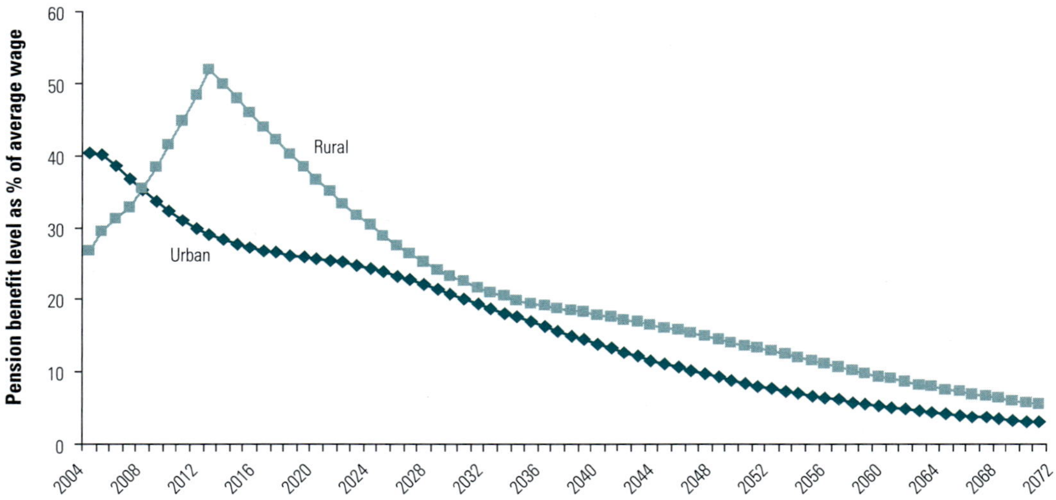

Source: Author's calculations derived from the World Bank's PROST model.

FIGURE 7.9
Future Financial Balance in Albania's Pension System

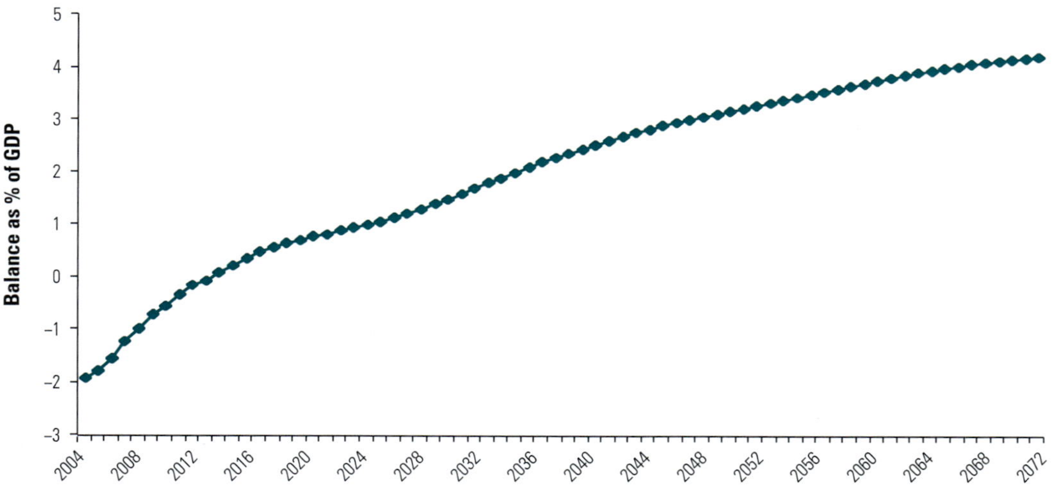

Source: Author's calculations derived from the World Bank's PROST model.

the Turkish Parliament in 2006 raised the retirement age still further to 65, but the law was declared unconstitutional in December 2006. Because it is unclear how the situation will be resolved, the simulations shown in figure 7.10 do not incorporate the new parameters.[2]

The Slovak Republic is also a more typical ECA country. It reformed its public pension system in 2004. Individuals receive points for each year of contribution, with the number of yearly points tied to the individual's salary (as compared with the average wage). Upon retirement, these points are monetized and converted into a pension. In 2005, the government introduced a privately managed defined-contribution pillar. Current contributors were given an 18-month window to choose whether they wanted to split their contribution, with a portion going to the funded pillar and the remainder to the public system, or to remain with the public system alone. New entrants to the labor force were automatically enrolled in the mixed system beginning in 2005.

Figure 7.11 shows the financial balance of the Slovak public system alone and with the addition of the funded system. The introduction of the funded option worsens the financial condition of the public

FIGURE 7.10

Future Financial Balance in Turkey's Pension System

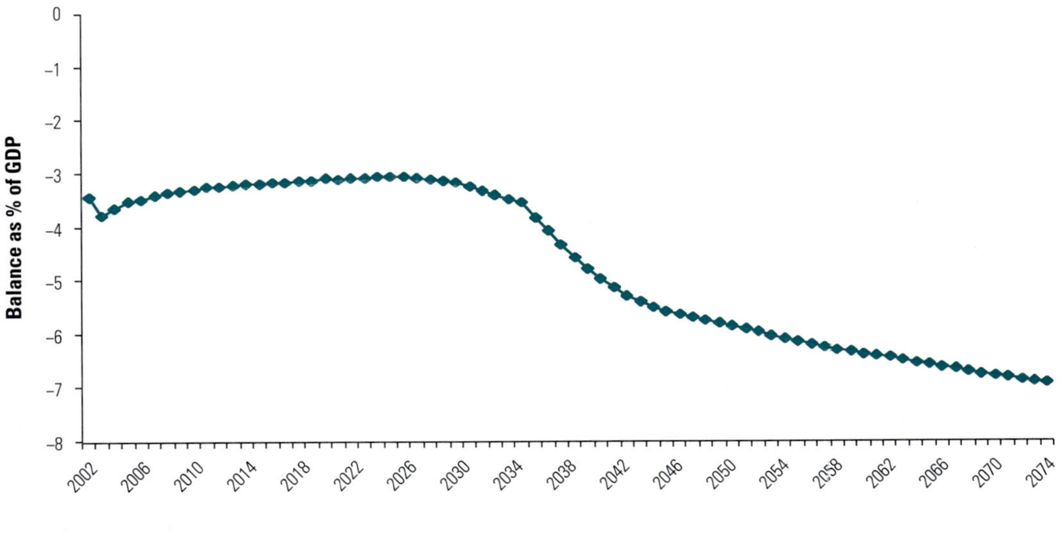

Source: Author's calculations derived from the World Bank's PROST model.

FIGURE 7.11
Future Financial Balance in the Slovak Republic's Pension System

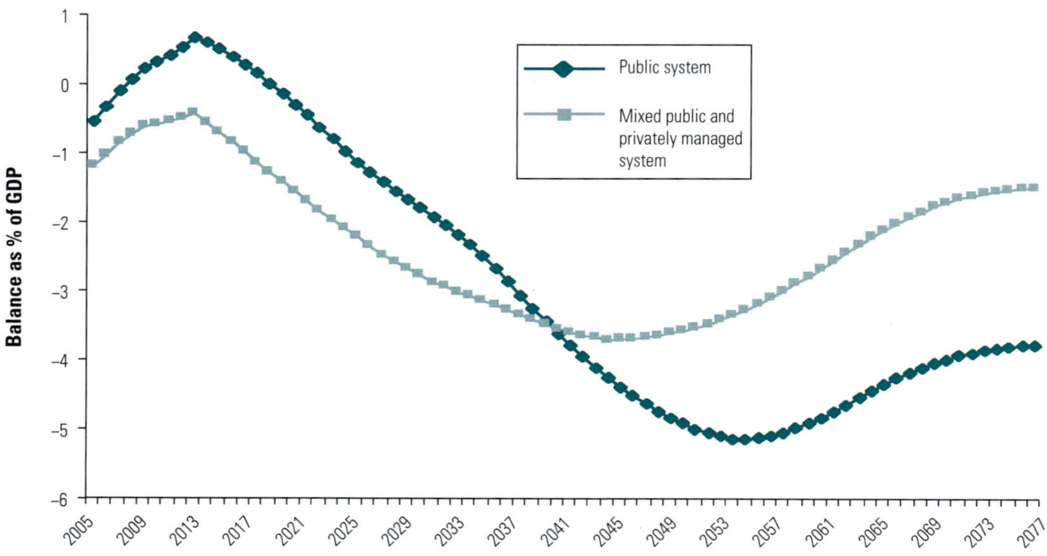

Source: Author's calculations derived from the World Bank's PROST model.

pension system in the short run, because contributors who choose to join the funded system contribute less revenue to the public system. Because the elderly had rights in the old system, the public system's expenditures do not change in the short and medium run but fall in the long run as these people leave the system altogether. Those who belong to the mixed system receive smaller public pensions in the longer run, lowering the expenditures of the public system and improving its balance. The initial improvement in the financial balance comes from parametric reforms of the public system introduced in 2004, including an increase in the retirement age.[3] The improvement over time reflects a new equilibrium between contributors and beneficiaries coming both from increased demographic stability and increased balance between coverage of contributors and beneficiaries. Average pension levels are expected to remain fairly constant through the simulation period for the mixed system and thus are not shown separately.

The final country, Romania, represents a mixture of the Georgian and Albanian systems and that of the Slovak Republic. The Slovak system maintains deficits in perpetuity, but pension levels do not decline over time. In Romania, the pension system approaches equilibrium but benefits do decline, although not as sharply as in Georgia or Albania (figures 7.12 and 7.13). The Romanians have also moved to a point system, but in their case the value of the point is left to the discretion of the policy maker. The average benefit given to a new retiree must lie between 30 and 50 percent of average wage after completion of the required length of service, which moves over time to 35 years for men and 30 years for women. The indexation of the pension postretirement is also discretionary, depending on the finances of the system. Baseline 2 shows the financial balance and the benefit ratios if the postretirement pension is indexed to inflation. Baseline 1, which shows a worse financial balance but higher benefit level, uses an indexation value some 50 percent higher than inflation, which has been typical of increases in recent years. In both cases, benefits fall below the ILO's 40 percent standard and fiscal balances improve in the very long run, as demographics stabilize and the coverage rates among contributors and beneficiaries become aligned.

In sum, while the long-run rebalancing between contributors and beneficiaries is expected to improve the fiscal balances of pension systems in ECA, it will not be sufficient to eliminate deficits while maintaining reasonable benefit levels in the future. Those countries that eliminate deficits are likely to do so at the cost of very low pensions, while those that maintain benefits are likely to remain in deficit.

FIGURE 7.12
Future Financial Balance in Romania's Pension System

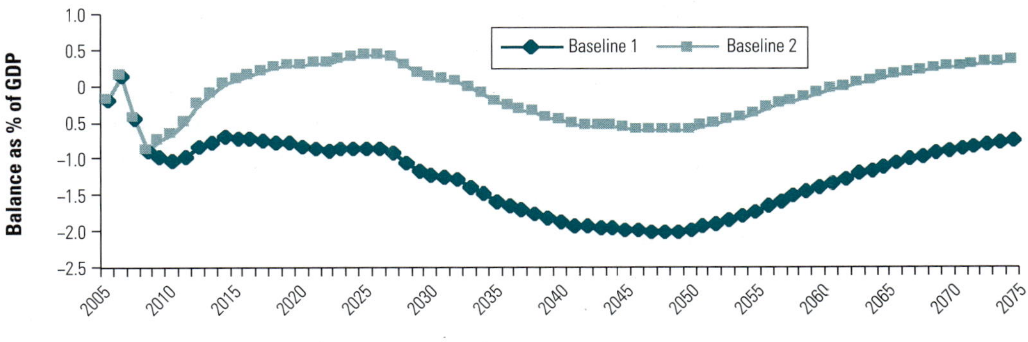

Source: Author's calculations derived from the World Bank's PROST model.

FIGURE 7.13
Romania: Future Pension Benefit Levels

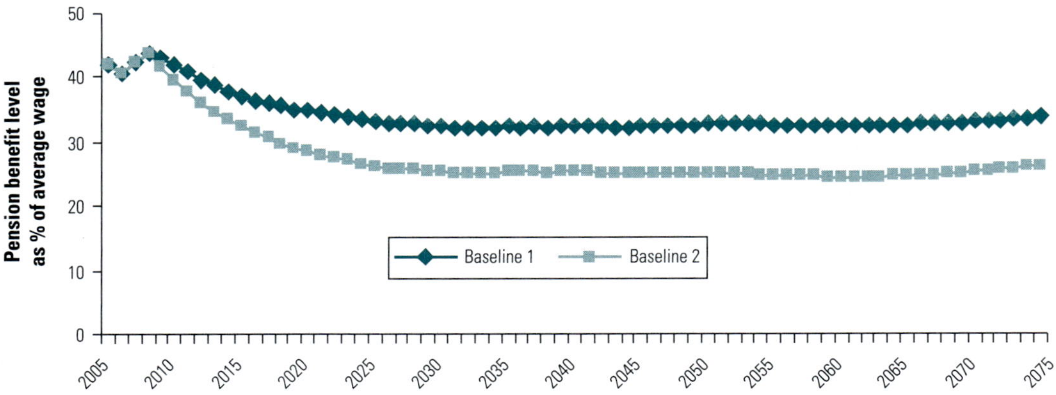

Source: Author's calculations derived from the World Bank's PROST model.

Social and Poverty Implications

While the fiscal problems associated with pension systems are very real, it is important to recognize that ECA's pension systems have had a positive impact on poverty reduction. Pensions are not necessarily well-targeted in the ECA region, but their coverage is widespread, and in some countries the benefit levels have been high enough to support multiple people on one benefit (World Bank 2005d). In other countries, however, the benefit is insufficient to keep most elderly households out of poverty. In Armenia, for example, the average pension is only 65 percent of the extreme poverty line. But even in Armenia, some 6–12 percent of the one-third of the population living in extended families where an elderly person would be poor without the pension, and an additional 5–14 percent of the population would be extremely poor without the pension (World Bank 2003a). Of eight countries reviewed for this study,[4] the pension played a significant role in reducing poverty in all but Croatia.

The situation is quite different in most of the developing world, where the elderly are less often the poorest members of society (Kakwani and Subbarao 2005). There tend to be fewer elderly in developing countries, and the really poor often do not survive until old age.

FIGURE 7.14
Future Drop in Elderly Receiving Pensions in Albania

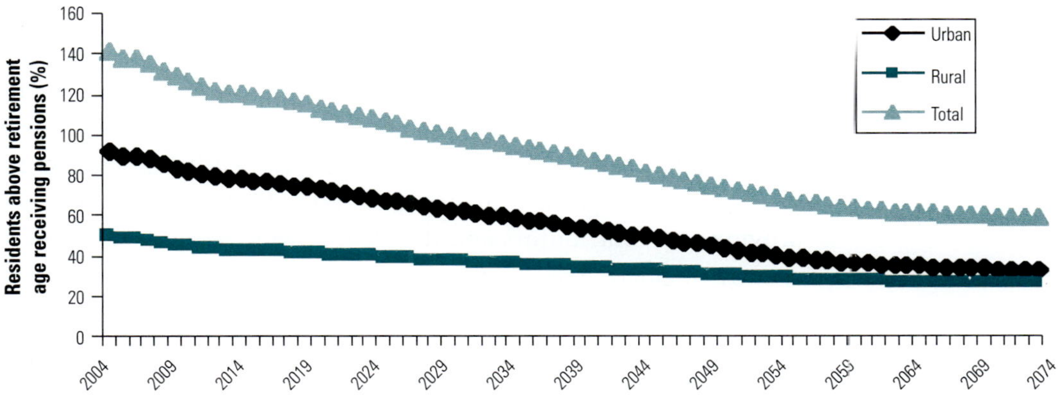

Source: Author's calculations derived from the World Bank's PROST model.

With much lower coverage, those who are covered by pensions tend to be the higher-income people within their cohort, often those with public sector or other formal sector employment. Furthermore, most developing countries have a high rate of cohabitation, with the elderly often residing in households with younger family members. Income sharing occurs in both directions, and there is little difference in poverty rates between the elderly and the younger generations. In contrast, in much of the developed world the elderly live as couples or alone (Whitehouse 2002). Without pensions, most of these elderly would be poor. Coverage is also relatively high despite lower women's labor force participation rates in some countries, because women often qualify for widow's pensions even when they have not been employed themselves.

ECA countries tend to fall in a middle ground. They have the high pension coverage of OECD countries, but cohabitation across generations is increasingly common as a means of income sharing. It is likely, however, that far fewer members of today's labor force in ECA will have pension rights when they retire. As a result, while the pension system reduces poverty today, it is less likely to play that role in the future. Figure 7.14 shows the potential future drop in elderly beneficiaries in Albania as a percentage of the elderly population. While the drop in Albania is particularly steep, all the ECA countries are likely to experience a fairly substantial fall in the percentage of elderly eligible to collect pensions in the future.

This drop in coverage has two implications for the future. First, because today's contributors tend to have higher incomes than noncontributors, transfers to cover pension system deficits in the future are likely to become more and more regressive, as future expenditures are focused on those lucky enough to have maintained high-paying formal sector jobs while the revenues are drawn from a broader population. To avoid this regressivity, pension systems must become increasingly self-financing, supported primarily by revenues provided by contributors and their employers. Second, as the percentage of elderly receiving pension benefits falls, governments may need to provide additional social assistance to the uncovered elderly to make sure they do not fall significantly below the poverty line. Thus, projections of fiscal improvements in the pension system may be misleading, offset by additional social assistance expenditures needed to alleviate old-age poverty of the uncovered elderly.

Options for Reform

What scope exists for further parametric reform in today's pension systems? Parameters in ECA focus countries and non-ECA high-growth comparators may look similar on average; thus it may not be readily apparent that ECA countries have scope for further reform. However, many of the comparator countries are on quite different points in the evolution of their pension systems. Young countries with rapidly expanding labor forces or with very new pension systems can afford to provide generous benefits because their pension expenditures are quite small. It is only when these countries face fiscal constraints that they must tighten their pension parameters.

Retirement Age

A critical parameter is the retirement age, which is still relatively low in ECA countries. Retirement ages already legislated for future retirees are shown in figure 7.15. However, it should be noted that the ages shown for the ECA countries are not the ages in force today. In all cases, the ages shown are the eventual retirement ages when all current laws become fully effective. Current retirement ages are considerably lower. Furthermore, countries often allow early retirement to certain older workers, and most ECA countries make generous use of such provisions. So not only are legal retirement ages, which are

FIGURE 7.15
Retirement Ages in ECA and Comparator Countries

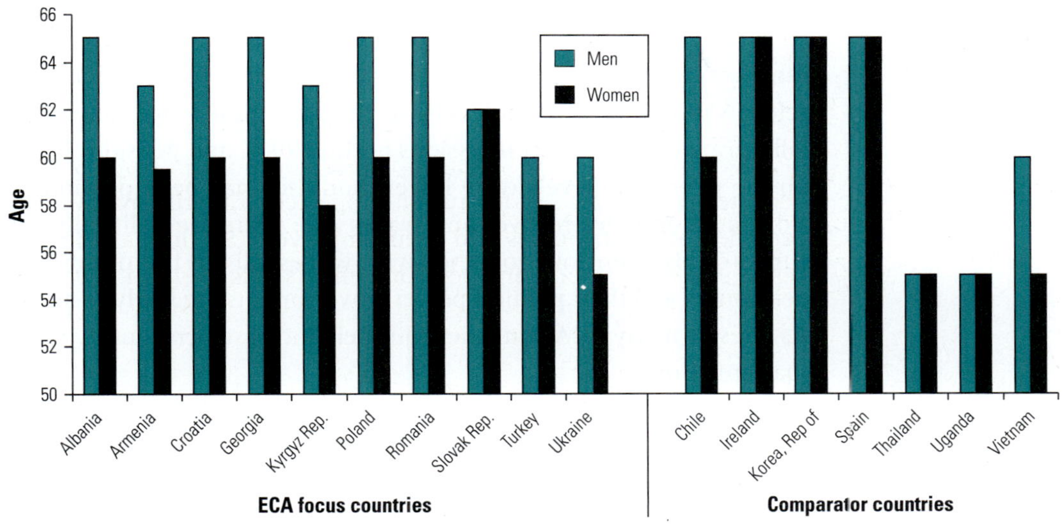

Source: World Bank Social Protection database.

lower in ECA countries than in comparator countries with older populations, lower than what is shown, but effective retirement ages are also often substantially lower than the legal retirement age.

Two trends stand out in figure 7.15. First, with the exception of the Slovak Republic, none of the ECA sample countries have equalized retirement ages for men and women. By contrast, five of the seven international comparators apply the same ages for men and women. There is little justification for maintaining an age differential between men and women. Women live longer than men—much longer in ECA,[5] and maintaining a lower retirement age for women results in an almost doubling of the period during which benefits are received for women relative to men. Second, while the younger comparator countries tend to have lower retirement ages, the older comparator countries have moved the retirement age to 65 for both men and women. Among ECA countries, the retirement age is only slowly moving to 65 for men, and no country among the sample has yet adopted 65 as the retirement age for women. Retirement age is a powerful parameter within the pension system, and this analysis suggests that there is still room for a further tightening of the official retirement age and for reducing the practice of freely allowing early retirement.

Indexation

Indexation is another parameter that can help to reduce pension costs. However, the issue is highly politicized given wage trends during transition. Before 1991, pensions were provided in a non-market-constrained economy and were generally relatively high. Since then most countries faced with high pension spending have undertaken reforms to reduce pension levels. At the same time wages tended to fall during the transition recessions in the 1990s, and pensions based on the new wage levels were lower than they had been previously. Now, as economies recover and wages rise, there are political pressures to raise pensions together with wages. Given the number of pensioners and their political power, governments are likely to agree. As a result many ECA countries routinely increase pensions by more than inflation.

Table 7.1 shows the indexation schemes in the ECA focus countries and the comparator countries. Of the 10 ECA countries, just three have legislation that links pension increases to inflation only, and only Poland actually follows price indexation (and has done so just since 2005). The majority of the rest have routinely awarded higher increases than inflation would justify, some by law and some on an ad hoc basis. Indexation in Armenia and Georgia is ad hoc and is routinely below the inflation rate, which explains their low levels of pension expenditures. Ukraine had legislated indexation to consist of 20 percent of wage growth and 80 percent inflation unless the inflation rate is higher than wage growth (in which case it became 100 percent inflation). However, before the last election, the previous government dramatically increased the level of the minimum pension, raising expenditures almost 50 percent. The government was subsequently forced to underindex pensions to reduce costs. Among the international comparators, three countries index to inflation and a fourth increases pensions on an ad hoc basis meant to be in line with inflation. Only Ireland raises pensions along with average wages. Vietnam indexes pensions to growth in the minimum wage, which may or may not be linked to economywide average wage growth.

Benefits

Comparisons of benefit levels are difficult because of the different ways of computing benefits, but table 7.2 tries to provide some cross-country comparison. The accrual rate, which is the benefit paid per year of service (if applicable), covers a wide spectrum in both the ECA focus countries and the comparator countries. The situation is further

TABLE 7.1

Pension Indexation Post-Retirement in ECA Sample and International Comparator Countries

Country	Inflation (%)	Wage (%)	Other
Albania	100	n.a.	Set to inflation by law, but in practice always higher
Armenia	n.a.	n.a.	Ad hoc basis
Croatia	50	50	
Georgia	n.a.	n.a.	Ad hoc basis
Kyrgyz Republic	n.a.	n.a.	Ad hoc basis
Poland	100	n.a.	
Romania	n.a.	n.a.	Ad hoc, but usually higher than inflation
Slovak Republic	50	50	
Turkey	100	n.a.	Set to inflation by law for main schemes, but in practice always higher
Ukraine	80	20	Slightly below inflation following the 2005 minimum pension increase
International Comparators			
Chile	100	n.a.	
Ireland	n.a.	100	
Korea, Republic of	100	n.a.	
Spain	100	n.a.	
Thailand	n.a.	n.a.	Ad hoc, but meant to accommodate inflation
Uganda	n.a.	n.a.	Paid as lump sum
Vietnam	n.a.	100	Grows with minimum wage

Source: World Bank Social Protection Database.
Note: n.a. = Not applicable.

complicated by the wide variety in benefit calculation schemes. In the traditional defined-benefit scheme, the accrual rate is the central feature. Individuals receive, for example, 2 percent of their average pensionable wage for every year they have contributed, subject to some minimum and maximum. There are still complications because different countries use different averaging periods—such as lifetime, three years, five years, or best three out of last ten—to calculate the pensionable wage. Furthermore, wages are rarely averaged at their nominal values to calculate the pensionable wage; they are typically revalued in line with inflation or average earnings growth to create a reasonable pensionable wage for the retiree.

At least four other types of benefit determination exist in this group of countries. Some countries—Armenia, Georgia, and Albania—make a flat payment irrespective of an individual's earnings, and in some cases irrespective of the years of contribution. This can be in lieu of or in addition to a pension linked to earnings or years of contribution. Because these flat payments are typically indexed on an ad hoc basis, they are difficult to convert to a comparable accrual rate. Among the comparators, Ireland calculates the pension as a flat payment based on years of service, and Korea has a component that is flat.

TABLE 7.2
Benefits Provided in ECA Pension Schemes and in Comparator Schemes

Country	Accrual rate	Details of formula calculation
ECA sample countries		
Albania	2%	Albania provides a basic pension equal to the minimum pension of about 38 percent of average wage for 35 years of service plus 1 percent of lifetime average wage per year of service, but the benefit is highly constrained by lim its on the maximum pension
Armenia	n.a.	Base pension of 3,000 drams plus 140 drams per year of contribution multiplied by a coefficient (roughly $US 6 for the pension and 0.25 per year of contribution
Croatia	0.825%	Covers only the public pension, which is calculated on a point system; there is a mandatory private part as well.
Georgia	n.a.	Flat rate of 28 lari per month (roughly $15)
Kyrgyz Republic	n.a.	Basic flat rate of 222.6 soms, but not less than 12 percent of average wage after 25/20 (25 for men, 20 for women) years of service plus 1 percent for each year before 1998 and notional account thereafter; minimum pension is 100 percent of minimum wage (roughly $5)
Poland	0.67%[a]	Notional account system, but with mandatory funded system
Romania	1.4% for men; 1.67% for women	Point system
Slovak Republic	1.19%	Point system but also has a mandatory funded pillar
Turkey	3.5% for first 10 years; 2% for next 15 years; 1.5% thereafter	n.a.
Ukraine	1%	n.a.
International comparator countries		
Chile	n.a.	Privately managed funded system
Ireland	n.a. years of contributions	Flat benefit designed to be approximately 34 percent of average wage after 35
Korea, Republic of	1.5%	Pensionable base is average of own lifetime earnings and average earnings of all insured for past three years
Spain	3%	n.a.
Thailand	1%	n.a.
Uganda	n.a.	Provident fund paying lump sum
Vietnam	3% for first 15 years; 2% for men and 3% for women for each additional year	n.a.

Source: World Bank Social Protection Database.
Note: n.a. = Not applicable. Accrual rate is the benefit earned per year of contribution as a percentage of previous wages.
a. Estimated by Whitehouse (2006).

A second type of benefit calculation uses the point system, where individuals get points for each year of contribution proportional to their contributory wage relative to average wage. These points are then converted to pensions at retirement. If the point value is indexed to average wage growth, as in the Slovak Republic, these systems are almost identical to the conventional defined-benefit system, with the value of the point as a percentage of average wage serving as an accrual rate. However, in other countries, such as Croatia, the value of the point is indexed to a mix of inflation and wage growth, suggesting that the point as a percentage of average wages will generally decline over time. In such systems there is no unique accrual rate. In other point systems, as in Romania, the value of the point is determined on an ad hoc basis within certain bounds, again yielding no unique accrual rate.

The third type of pension calculation is the notional account calculation, as used in Poland and the Kyrgyz Republic. In this case, an individual's contributions accumulate in an account on which an interest rate is paid, the rate tied to some indicator in the economy such as wage growth. On retirement, the accumulated account balance is converted into an annuity taking into account life expectancy at the age of retirement. Because the variable to which the notional interest rate is tied varies and life expectancy is expected to grow over time, again the accrual rate will not be unique.

Finally, the last form of benefit calculation is to allow the contributions to accumulate in an investment account that pays interest according to the investments of the fund. Pensions are determined at retirement from the account balance and current life expectancy. Poland, Croatia, and the Slovak Republic incorporate this type of system within their overall pension structure, and Chile and Uganda rely on it completely. But again, accrual rates are difficult to determine because they depend on the underlying changes in interest rates and life expectancies.

Given these complexities, it is difficult to determine whether benefit levels are higher or lower in ECA countries than in comparator countries on the basis of table 7.2. Benefit rates above 1.5 percent per year are generally not financially sustainable in the long run, which suggests that benefits in Turkey are probably too high. Albania also looks suspect, although its stringent maximum limits have resulted in much lower pensions than would appear to be the case on the basis of the formula alone.

Funded Pillars

Several ECA countries have moved to reduce their public pension liabilities not by parametric adjustments alone, but by also moving to privately managed defined-contribution systems. Croatia, Poland, and the Slovak Republic are among the countries that have introduced such funded pillars. In each of these cases, a portion of the total contribution is diverted to the privately managed funded accounts in return for a reduction in the public pension that individuals will receive upon retirement. Introducing such a system involves giving up current contribution revenue, resulting in a higher deficit in the short run, but it results in reduced public liabilities in the future.

Is this a strategy the rest of the ECA region should follow? For this strategy to work, individuals need to feel that their savings are safe, which requires that governments provide significant regulation and supervision of private pension funds. Investment strategies generally need to allow for foreign investment of some of the money. And the transition from one pension system to another must be fiscally affordable. Many of the early transformers have used privatization revenues to help offset the costs of the transition. Unless these preconditions exist in the remaining ECA countries, the policy is unlikely to provide adequate returns and may result in demands for further government intervention.

Contribution Rates and Coverage

Accompanying the move to flat income tax rates (see chapter 8), many policy makers in ECA countries have looked at the high payroll contribution rates and suggested that lower rates might result in higher revenue. Still others look at the enormous growth of informality in these countries and seek to lower contribution rates to stem the tide toward informality of labor markets. Many ECA countries have already lowered their pension contribution rates or are planning to do so soon in hopes of increasing coverage and compliance.

While formal sector employment may increase somewhat as a result of lower payroll taxes, international evidence suggests that the increase will be insufficient to counteract the reduced revenue from the lower tax rate, much less actually increase revenue, as discussed further in chapter 9. After reviewing a variety of international evidence, Hamermesh (1993) concludes that employment should be expected to increase about 0.3 percent for each percentage point of decrease in the payroll tax rate.[6] Because this magnitude is insufficient to keep revenue neutral, most countries cutting payroll taxes will experience an immediate reduction in revenue, threatening the surpluses in Albania and Georgia and exacerbating deficits in the others. In addition, there is a fundamental difference between pension contributions and other types of tax revenue. Each contribution in a pension system comes with a liability for future benefits. Assuming that the pension systems were actuarially balanced before, cutting the contribution rates without changing benefits puts them actuarially in deficit. Increasing the number of contributors in a scheme that is actuarially unbalanced will raise long-run deficits, making such a strategy a loser both in the short and long runs. Because most of the countries do not have actuarially balanced systems to begin with, raising the number of contributors only exacerbates the existing long-run deficit. While the increased formalization of workers may have other benefits, this potential negative fiscal consequence needs to be considered when enacting policies to increase formalization.

Internationally, contributor coverage seems to be related to income per capita, with higher income per capita leading to higher contributor coverage, as shown in figure 7.16. Some types of economic activity are more amenable to being included in the formal pensionable sector than others. The typical types of activities heavily engaged in by low-income countries, such as agriculture and very small scale business, are ones where compliance is difficult to enforce in every country. In addition, higher-income countries tend to have better institutional and administrative capacity to enforce compliance. But even in higher-income countries coverage rates are falling, not rising. As the economic structure changes in favor of smaller, more dynamic companies, and as job switching becomes more common in lieu of lifetime employment with a single large employer, workers and their

FIGURE 7.16

Pension Contributor Coverage in ECA Focus Countries Compared with International Averages

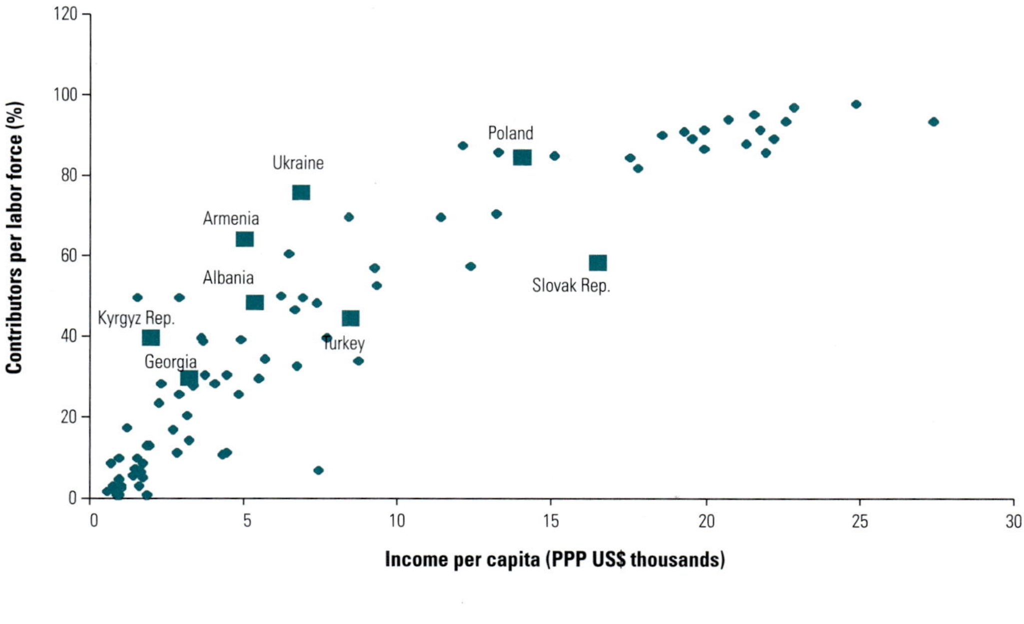

Source: Palacios and Pallarés-Miralles 2002.

Note: Data for ECA focus countries are from 2003 and 2004; for other countries, 1998.

employers are finding ways to avoid paying payroll taxes in even the richest countries. Thus, even the highest-income countries may have reached a plateau on coverage.

Figure 7.16 shows the results from a regression analysis of data from 87 countries (Palacios and Pallarés-Miralles 2002). What is clear from this analysis is that many of the ECA countries are still outliers even today. Albania, Armenia, Georgia, the Kyrgyz Republic, Poland, and Ukraine and all lie well above the internationally derived coverage graph, suggesting that these countries have higher coverage relative to other countries at their income levels. The likelihood of any of these countries increasing coverage further through either policy or administrative measures is low. Decreasing contribution rates would unambiguously reduce revenue. While this could potentially spur employment, it would put additional strain on pension financing. However, both the Slovak Republic and Turkey have greater potential to raise coverage. Croatia and Romania are not labeled on the figure because both countries lie essentially on the regression curve.

The move toward lower contribution rates without commensurate reductions in benefits is troubling on a number of other grounds. As the pension schemes earn less revenue, government resources earned from other sources are used to cover the resulting deficit as a supplemental source of finance. Because pensions are generally designed to be linked to contributions, which are themselves linked to wages, higher-income people generally receive higher pensions. As a result, tax revenue, which is often more broadly based than payroll taxes, is used to support pensions for a subset of the population that typically earns higher incomes than the overall population, and in such a way that the highest-income individuals get the highest benefit.

In the ECA context, the distinction between covered and uncovered segments among the retiree population is not yet that large, but it will grow in the next 25 years. However, in most countries greater benefits already go to higher-income individuals. Even in countries like Georgia, where benefits are almost equal, the categories receiving higher benefits and special privileges are all higher-income individuals. From an equity point of view, subsidizing pension systems from general revenues is an extremely regressive use of public finance. While this may be acceptable in the short run during a transition period in an ongoing reform, in many of the cases where contribution rates have been reduced, the imbalance is permanent and not likely to improve substantially over time.

The political economy of the social insurance system also becomes altered when the government starts making substantial contributions. When the system is just employer and employee financed, individuals who have not made contributions are not given pensions because they have not earned the right to a pension. However, when the system is half financed from government revenue it becomes difficult to deny pensions to those who contributed to general revenue but did not make explicit pension contributions. The government financing component makes pensions more a social policy than an acquired right that one has to pay contributions to earn, making it difficult for governments to deny similar benefits for the individuals who are among the poorest of the elderly.

In sum, governments need to consider a broad range of trade-offs in deciding whether to lower payroll taxes as a means of increasing employment and formalization. To the extent that formalization does increase, there may be significant fiscal costs, and to the extent that increasing pension deficits must be funded by general revenues, there may be serious equity and political economy issues. If pension benefits are linked to earnings, rather than being replaced, as in Georgia, by minimum social assistance payments across the board, it is critical that contribution rates be sufficient to keep them self-financing.

Two Strategies for Reform

Given the variance of income and institutional capacity within the ECA region, we would propose two separate reform strategies, one more appropriate for lower-income countries and the other for middle- and higher-income countries. In addition, it may be worth separating the design of the pension system for future retirees from the issue of how to finance the cost of today's large retiree population, although avoiding an abrupt change in policy suggests that there needs to be a transition between the two.

Lower-Income Settings

For the lower-income countries, the likelihood of raising coverage enough that most elderly of the future will receive pensions from a contributory pension system is small. Given that the bulk of the elderly will either receive no pensions or only small pensions because of incomplete contribution years, these countries need to consider other options for providing assistance to the elderly. The most likely options are a universal pension given to all individuals above a certain age, or a means-tested pension given to all individuals above a certain age and below a certain income level. Either option would be financed from general revenue but would not cause the equity problems found with government financing of contributory pensions, because the pensions would be available to all and the benefit would either be the same for all or would fall as income goes up.

One advantage of delinking the pension from contributions is that governments are then free to set the level of the pension based on what is financially feasible rather than on the basis of what is owed to a pensioner. While a universal pension is more expensive and less targeted, it is easier to administer, resulting in lower administration costs. If the pension is low enough, the affluent often do not bother to register, improving the targeting somewhat. And it is possible to tax the pension when income passes a certain threshold, again improving the overall targeting of the pension. However, a means-tested pension may be a better choice in countries where means-testing mechanisms are already established. The means-testing can be as rudimentary as checking whether the individual qualifies for some other type of pension if one exists. However, when other systems exist, the means-tested pension may reduce the incentives to make contributions to the contributory systems. Keeping the level of the social pension low or raising the threshold age at which the means-tested pension becomes available may limit the disincentives arising from instituting such a pension.

Depending on existing arrangements, the universal or means-tested pension can be complemented by a self-financing pension for either a subset of the population on a mandatory basis, such as the public sector or formal sector workers, or for the whole population on a voluntary basis. Middle- and higher-income individuals will want some mechanism to smooth their lifetime consumption and provide a living standard closer to what they were accustomed to during their working lives. Because such mechanisms may not automatically exist in an economy, the government may need to nurture their development or even provide them. Ideally, the pension should be provided on a defined-contribution basis by private providers. Such a system delivers the best return for the contribution in the context of an aging population and limits government liabilities toward a subgroup of individuals who either self-select themselves or are chosen as the ones to be covered under the system by the government. In either case, the individuals tend to be higher income and should not produce liabilities for the government. However, for such a system to succeed, financial markets and institutions must exist and function well at a rudimentary level at least, and the government needs to provide responsible supervision and regulation of the system. If the mechanism is provided on a voluntary basis, financial markets can be allowed to develop as the pension system itself grows. If the mechanism is provided on a mandatory basis, the financial market must already be at a certain level to make the mandatory pension contribution secure and worthwhile (Rocha and Rudolph 2007). However, aside from greater public responsibility when a system is mandatory, the distinction between mandatory and voluntary systems becomes blurred in an environment where enforcement and compliance are limited.

If the appropriate financial market conditions do not exist, the country could consider a small, self-financed, publicly managed pay-as-you-go system that is actuarially balanced in the long run for those who are able and willing to contribute. The important point is that this system must be self-financed and not rely on government subsidies, either in the short run or in the long run. Because it is not being provided to the entire population, it should not cause the government to incur net liabilities.

How does a country move from the current system of payroll-financed contributions to a universal pension financed out of general revenue? In Georgia, little transition is required. Georgia currently has a universal pension for all practical purposes. All elderly individuals with five years of work history receive a flat amount per month, with the exception of a few special categories. Almost all individuals can provide sufficient evidence of five years of work history because labor force participation was mandatory during socialism. Almost anything constitutes sufficient evidence because authorities do not have their own records with which to check work history. In Georgia, the authorities would merely have to declare the current pension to be universally available and would have to determine whether the current 20 percent social tax on wages is the least distortionary mechanism to finance this pension. Armenia is in a similar situation, as is Albania, to a lesser extent, as well as several other lower-income ECA countries. In Albania, well over half of current beneficiaries receive the minimum pension. For those who receive more already or expect to receive more based on past contributions, the government would incur transition costs in paying for the higher pensions these workers and pensioners have already accrued on the basis of contributions, while the contribution revenue disappears. However, there are ways of making these costs more manageable, such as by removing wage taxes only for those below a certain age or by raising both legal and effective retirement ages and making other adjustments to the benefits provided.

Middle-Income Settings

For middle-income countries, a contributory pension of some type would be beneficial. Pension systems serve two objectives: (a) to alleviate poverty among the elderly and (b) to allow pensioners to achieve similar levels of consumption during their retirement as they achieved during their working years. For the first objective, the social or universal pension is an appropriate tool, but because its focus is poverty alleviation it is unlikely to provide enough income to replace the previous income of middle- or high-income individuals. Because no society wants deprivation among the elderly, the primary focus has to be on the first objective in cases where resources and institutional capacity are limited. However, countries with more resources and more institutional capacity can also make some headway toward achieving the second objective.

Middle-income countries can look to the contributory pension system as the main foundation of their old-age support, expecting at least half or more of the labor force to actively contribute to the pension system. However, this contributory system would need to be complemented by some form of social assistance for those elderly who either do not contribute or for whatever reason cannot contribute. Because more than half of the elderly would have a contributory pension income during their old age, this social assistance should ideally be means-tested so that it focuses only on those who do not have contributory income. There are examples worldwide of higher-income countries that have chosen to provide all elderly with some basic pension, Canada being notable among these. This social pension can be provided to only those who have no contributory pensions or can include those who have contributory pensions, but at such low levels that they should receive some supplement from the state. In these cases, the social pension serves as an alternative to a minimum pension in the contributory system.

On the contributory side, the pension can take a number of forms. It can be a purely defined-contribution pension, where individuals and their employers put their contributions in individually owned retirement savings accounts that invest in a variety of financial market instruments that generate interest earnings for the workers. Upon retirement, these accounts are typically converted into annuities or other forms of periodic payment generating a stream of income for the elderly. The government in this case has the responsibility for supervising and regulating these retirement savings accounts, but does not face additional liabilities. There may be a small liability if the government provides a minimum pension guarantee to individuals, the size of which depends on the amount of the minimum pension and the conditions under which it becomes available. Chile, for example, has moved its pension system to a defined-contribution system. The other extreme is Ireland, which has a public contributory system but only provides individuals with a flat payment depending on years of service but not related to previous income level or the amount of individual contributions. In between are countries like Spain, which provide a public pension related to both the level of contributions and the years of service.

In looking at future contributory systems, countries need to be careful to design a structure that is self-financing in both the short run and long run. There is obviously a relationship between the level of benefit to be financed and the payroll contribution rate that will finance this benefit in a sustainable way. Despite the historically high benefit rates in the ECA region, countries now have to consider more modest benefit rates for at least three distinct reasons. First, the high labor taxes required to finance a high level of benefits clearly distort the labor market, both discouraging business investment and reducing formal employment. Tying contributions to benefits, so that these labor taxes are regarded as deferred income rather than distortionary taxes, is an improvement but has not reduced distortions as much as had been hoped (see chapter 9).

Second, individuals have different preferred time paths for their consumption. Some prefer to save early in life and consume later in life. Others with higher discount rates prefer to consume when young and to live more sparely in old age. Individuals will be happiest when they are allowed to live as they wish. Governments, however, are interested in preventing old-age poverty and are generally not willing to allow old-age deprivation even if that were the individual's choice. In addition, individuals can be myopic and not make the correct choices early in life. While these are arguments for government mandates for pension contributions, these are not arguments for a high level of mandatory benefits or for the high payroll taxes required to finance high benefits. Governments need to think of modest mandatory contributory systems, not the generous systems of the past.

Finally, pensioners typically need far less income than working-age people. The household size for a pensioner is typically smaller, reducing the number of people requiring support. Furthermore, nutrition requirements fall with age, the elderly rarely pay payroll taxes and often pay less in other taxes as well, and the elderly can engage in less costly activities than working-age individuals whose time is more constrained. The one expense category that increases markedly for the elderly is health care, including pharmaceuticals.

Each country needs to evaluate the appropriate requirements of a pensioner, taking into account its own health care system and what the pensioner needs to spend out of his or her pension to accommodate health needs. While historical pension systems in ECA provided 60–100 percent of gross wages earned while working, mandatory pension systems should typically provide only about 40 percent of the average wage at a cost of about 15–20 percent of the wage as contribution. Individuals can be encouraged to save beyond this level through other systems.

In what form should this pension be provided? In an ideal world, individuals should save money as mandated by government and then finance a pension from these resources when they cannot work. Such a system eliminates liabilities for governments, eliminates arbitrary intergenerational transfers, and results in the least distortionary incentives for individuals. However, when public pension systems were first being designed in Europe and elsewhere, sufficiently secure financial institutions did not exist to intermediate between generations. Thus, governments became the intermediary, taking contributions from one generation and using them to pay benefits to the older generation, with the promise that the next generation's contributions would be used to pay benefits to the current contributing generation. When these systems first began, there were few elderly and many workers, and it was possible to pay generous benefits for the few elderly with minimal contributions from each of many workers. The systems then became politicized, and additional and more generous benefits were added in response to political pressures. Demographic changes also began to equalize the sizes of the beneficiary populations with the contributing populations, forcing rises in contribution rates, while changes in benefits or benefit eligibility was strongly resisted, resulting in fiscal problems for most European and other OECD pension systems today.

ECA countries should not replicate the historical path of the more developed countries, but rather find an approach that suits where they are today and that is appropriate given their demographic and institutional situations. While the domestic financial markets of many ECA countries are not much different from what Western Europe faced when it made the choice of publicly provided pension systems, the demographics are much less favorable, with many ECA countries having rapidly aging societies. Given these demographic conditions, pay-as-you-go public pension systems, where contributing generations pay for the benefits of the elderly, will be quite expensive as the contributing populations shrink relative to the beneficiary populations. These systems are also difficult to dismantle, suggesting that even younger countries want to be careful in instituting such systems. However, international financial institutions do exist that can handle savings from individuals, although exchange rate issues may limit the extent to which countries may wish to have their pension savings invested abroad. Furthermore, savings systems do impose financial market risk on individuals who may have limited capacity to absorb such risk. For these reasons, countries like Poland and the Slovak Republic have chosen to adopt a mixed design, where part of the pension continues to be provided through the public system (which might ultimately offer lower rates of return but may be less variable), and the remainder is invested by the individual in private pension funds (which are expected to offer higher rates of return). While the ideal weighting of the two parts of the pension system depends on many factors (including preferences for public versus private provision), and the design of the public part can take many forms (from Poland's notional accounts to the Slovak Republic's point system to Turkey's conventional defined-benefit system), most middle-income ECA countries would be best served if their modest contributory pension systems included elements of both a savings system and a pure publicly provided system. As noted above, these need to be complemented with mechanisms to provide for those who are unable to contribute for whatever reason. Given the modest scale of the benefits, they also need to be complemented with opportunities for individuals to save more and accumulate more generous pensions if desired.

The system just described would be an ideal system if the policy maker were starting from no pension system. But all ECA region countries already have pension systems, and these initial conditions will strongly determine how quickly or even if such a system can be adopted. Two primary obstacles arise in moving to a mixed contributory system. First, when individuals contribute to their own savings accounts, that portion of their contributions can no longer be used to finance benefits for the current elderly, requiring additional government financing to cover these benefits. Depending on the number of elderly, the level of their benefits, and the extent of contributions diverted to individual accounts, these costs can be formidable. Second, domestic financial markets may not provide sufficient and secure assets in which these savings can be invested. While countries such as Poland, the Slovak Republic, Croatia, and Romania—which are members of the European Union—face fewer problems with investing abroad, countries like Kazakhstan (which has also adopted the individual savings account approach) may face greater difficulties. Exchange rate risks and domestic opposition to foreign investment of scarce domestic capital may limit foreign investment options while domestic options are scarce.

Regardless of whether a funded pillar is feasible, public pay-as-you-go systems can be reformed by raising retirement ages, reducing early retirement, only linking increases in pensions to inflation, adjusting benefits where needed, and improving administration and governance. At the same time, countries should try to deepen their domestic financial markets, which will improve economic performance and welfare regardless of the pension system. When transition costs to a funded pillar are not formidable and when domestic financial systems are deep enough, the country can consider adopting a funded system if it so desires.

Conclusions

This chapter has reviewed the fiscal implications of pension systems in ECA and suggested paths for reform to balance fiscal needs with social protection and poverty reduction among the elderly. ECA faces a unique combination not present in other high-growth comparators: (a) a historical legacy of high pension coverage and generous pension benefits; (b) a rapid decline in recent years in labor force participation and thus in the number of pension contributors; and (c) a rapidly aging population. This combination of factors creates strong fiscal pressures, and none of the systems surveyed will achieve fiscal balance in either the near term or the long term under current projections while providing reasonable benefits to contributors. It will be necessary to still further alter parameters—raising retirement ages, lowering benefit levels, and limiting indexation—if countries are to reduce fiscal pressures and free up public resources for growth-enhancing expenditure.

The chapter proposes separate strategies for low-income and middle-income countries. As a basic system, low-income countries should opt for a simple low-rate benefit available to all elderly people (or targeted to the poor) and financed out of general government revenues (as is being adopted, for example, in Georgia). This can be supplemented by contributory systems for subsets of workers, but the latter should be wholly self-financing to avoid regressive fiscal transfers. Middle-income countries have the administrative capacity and financial systems to support contributory systems for a broader set of workers and can draw from various models that have been successful elsewhere. Again, parameters should ideally be set to ensure self-financing, which would require a reduction in benefits in most ECA countries.

Reforms will inevitably meet political resistance, and strong leadership over the long term will be required. However, the importance of these reforms must not be underestimated—they are essential for sustained economic growth.

Notes

1. For the ECA countries, in most cases age-specific data on pensioners and contributors was compared with age-specific population data. However, the data correspond to specific years for which data were available rather than the same year for all countries. For the international comparators, data on pensioners and contributors were not age-specific; all pensioners were attributed to an elderly population and all contributors were attributed to working-age population. Had the same methodology been applied to ECA countries, they would have appeared even farther to the right than shown in figure 7.4, given the prevalence of early retirement in ECA countries. While the data shown are not strictly comparable, it does serve to illustrate a fundamental difference between ECA and non-ECA countries.
2. The 2006 law included a further increase in the retirement age to 65 for men and women, phased in between 2036 and 2048, and also changed other pension parameters.
3. The package of Slovak reforms included a slightly higher contribution rate, rising from 28.00 percent to 28.75 percent; a lower accrual rate of 1.19 percent per year, down from 2.00 percent for the first 25 years and 1.00 percent subsequently for a maximum of 67 percent; inclusion of lifetime wages in computation of pensions rather than highest 5 of last 10 years' salary; lower indexation, 50 percent to inflation and 50 percent to nominal wage growth, compared to the previous 100 percent to nominal wage growth; higher retirement ages of 62 for both men and women phased in from the previous 60 for men and 53–57 for women depending on the number of children they had; and a tying of contributions to benefits with the point system, making the ceiling on contributions the same as the ceiling on pensionable wage.
4. Albania, Armenia, Croatia, Georgia, the Kyrgyz Republic, Poland, Turkey, and Ukraine.
5. While men's life expectancies in ECA countries tend to be significantly lower than those for men in Western Europe, the differential for women's life expectancies with Western European countries is much lower, resulting in an even larger difference between men's and women's life expectancies in ECA countries.
6. Hamermesh (1993) provides a comprehensive survey of empirical studies of labor demand over a variety of countries and calculates this consensus estimate.

PART 3

Selected Issues in Taxation

CHAPTER 8

Flat Income Tax Reforms

Pablo Saavedra
with contributions from
Anton Marcincin and Juraj Valachy

A number of countries in Europe and Central Asia (ECA) have implemented so-called flat income tax reforms since the mid-1990s, with Estonia taking the lead in 1994.[1] These reforms vary significantly from country to country, and none of them represent a literal flat tax on all sources of income. Some countries have implemented a flat rate only on the personal income tax (PIT), others have complemented that with rate and exemption changes on the corporate income tax (CIT) but at a different rate level, and yet others have implemented a flat (or proportional) rate at the same level for the PIT and the CIT. The publicity stemming from this reform has led to similar proposals and debate in other ECA countries, including Poland, Slovenia, the Czech Republic, and Hungary. This chapter explores the experience of ECA countries in undertaking flat tax reforms and the effects of such reforms in three areas: (a) revenue collection, (b) tax structure, and (c) tax compliance.

The Flat Income Tax

A flat income tax can be defined as one that levies a flat rate (that is, a proportional rate) on all sources of income of individuals and businesses, but avoids double taxation. For the PIT, this reform provides an alternative to the more common progressive schedule of rates, whereby higher income brackets are taxed at higher rates and a variety of exemptions and deductibles are available to reduce the tax liability. In the case of the CIT, a flat tax reform focuses on curtailing the loopholes and exemptions that this tax tends to build up over time and establish a single proportional rate for all kinds of businesses.[2] This reform typically affects many aspects of an economy, including revenue collection, tax compliance, administrative costs, economic efficiency, investment behavior and productivity, labor supply, and income distribution.

Proponents commonly put forward several arguments in favor of flat rate income tax reform, claiming that it

- reduces the complexity of the tax system and thus administrative costs;
- creates incentives—through lower and simpler rates and clearer rules—for accurate reporting of income and consequently higher compliance by taxpayers;
- lowers marginal tax burdens, creating incentives for investment and saving;
- reduces inefficiencies in the economy by avoiding double taxation and reducing tax-induced distortions in investment behavior (see box 8.1); and
- promotes labor force participation, including for individuals in higher income brackets that may also have higher skills.

For every argument there is a counterargument, however. Some claim that allowances and tax credits compromise the simplicity of such reforms and complicate their administration, offsetting the positive effect of flat rates. It is also clear that investment and savings behavior may depend on economic drivers that go well beyond this limited reform. Furthermore, the effects of taxes on labor markets are difficult to pin down, particularly given high rates of evasion and poor data quality. In addition, detractors point particularly to the negative effects that flat tax reforms are likely to have on equity, although this argument is also often contested (see boxes 8.1 and 8.3).

Flat Income Taxes in ECA

The transition agenda during the early 1990s focused primarily on macroeconomic stability and core structural reforms such as privatization. Detailed issues of tax design tended to be off the radar screen, but they began to gain attention in the mid-1990s when the Baltic

BOX 8.1

Efficiency and Equity Considerations of Flat Tax Reforms

Both economic efficiency and income distributional effects are core concerns for policy makers. Moreover, equity and efficiency arguments may imply trade-offs in tax design. With regard to efficiency, income taxes are considered critically important in affecting individuals' or firms' decisions on investment, saving, and labor. The less a tax affects economic behavior, the better it is for efficiency. In theory, a flat rate across all types of income should have less of an effect on the investment and saving decisions of economic agents than a tax with highly differentiated rates on various types of income. A flat rate is also thought to minimize the practice of tax arbitrage—the shifting of tax liability from a higher-taxed to a lower-taxed category of income. It can be designed to avoid the double taxation of income, for example, once at the corporate level and a second time when dividends are received by shareholders, which not only raises the overall tax burden but can also distort investment financing options of firms. With regard to labor supply and its quality, low tax rates and less progressive tax structures may tend to increase the participation of highly skilled individuals, particularly if labor supply is highly elastic. However, proportional rates may negatively affect labor participation by low-income groups if mechanisms are not in place to exempt these individuals at least partially from the tax.

Flat taxes are often criticized, however, on equity grounds. Taxpayers with the same level of income (no matter the source) may bear the same tax burden (horizontal equity), but richer taxpayers—who have greater "ability to pay"—do not bear a heavier burden in proportional terms than poorer ones (vertical equity). However, the vertical equity of a flat tax system can be enhanced through the use of tax-free allowances, which remove the poorest from the tax net. Moreover, it can also be argued that vertical equity is enhanced by closing loopholes and removing exemptions, particularly because higher-income taxpayers (typically comprising more sophisticated taxpayers that perform tax planning) typically take more advantage of the loopholes in the system (and may thus pay less tax than lower-income taxpayers, even in progressive tax systems). Moreover, equity needs to be analyzed from a broader fiscal perspective because the public expenditures financed through the tax system can be highly progressive, making the public budget an instrument of redistribution overall.

Source: Author.

countries—led by Estonia in 1994 and soon followed by Lithuania (1994) and Latvia (1995)— implemented flat rates on income taxes. Attention waned once again during the Russian and Asian crises of the late 1990s, but the reform captured worldwide attention with the Russian Federation's implementation of a flat rate on personal income in 2001. Other ECA countries followed, most prominently the Slovak Republic and Ukraine in 2004 and Georgia and Romania in 2005. The flat tax reform has gained increasing attention among scholars and policy makers around the world, as countries in Eastern Europe and the Caucasus have moved to implement different variants of this reform (figure 8.1).

None of the variants in ECA is a "flat tax" in its most theoretical shape, however. The reforms in ECA countries have focused on flat (or proportional) rates for the PIT and a flat rate on the CIT, although some countries (such as Ukraine and Russia) have not aligned their PIT and CIT rates at the same level, and some have focused only on the former and not the latter. Moreover, the reforms have often introduced tax-free allowances or special deductions for certain categories of individuals.

The flat tax rates applied to the PIT and CIT vary significantly across countries that have undertaken these reforms. The lowest rate for the PIT is 12 percent in Georgia, followed closely by Ukraine with 13 percent.[3] On the other end are the Baltic countries: Lithuania introduced a rate of 33 percent, Latvia a rate of 25 percent, and Estonia a rate of 26 percent. Russia has the highest CIT rate, with a combined rate up to 35 percent.[4] Other countries with high CIT rate are Ukraine and,

FIGURE 8.1
Flat Tax Reforms in ECA

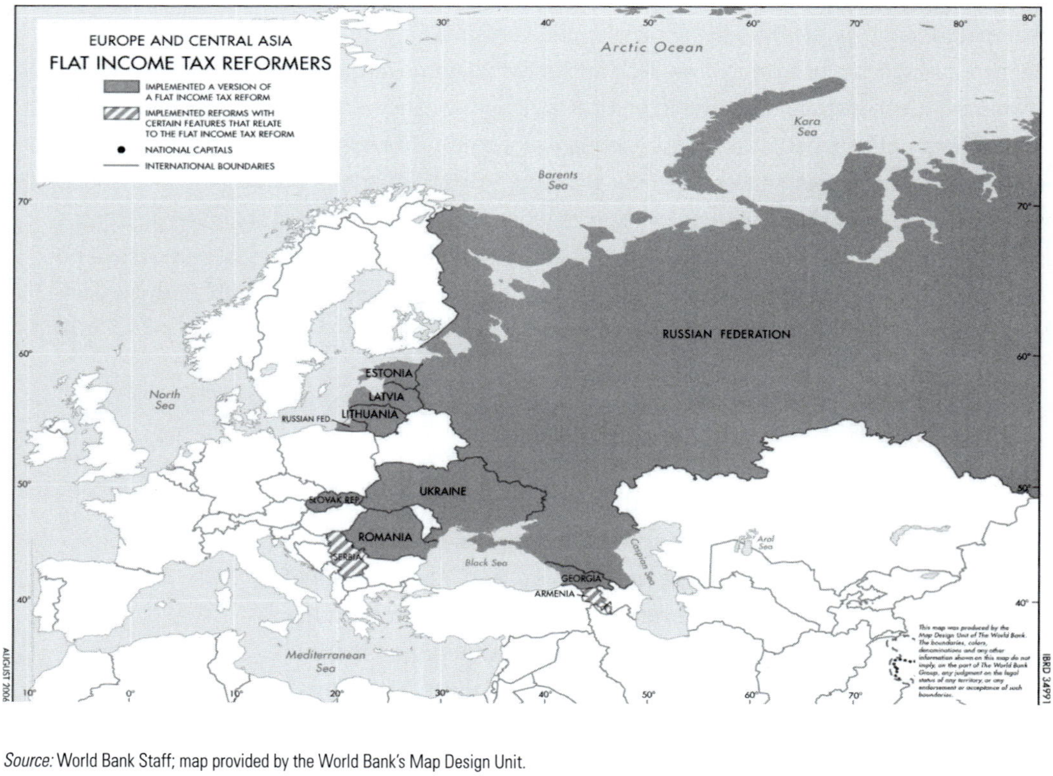

Source: World Bank Staff; map provided by the World Bank's Map Design Unit.

again, the Baltic countries (see table 8.1). Four out of the nine countries that implemented variations of this reform—Estonia, Romania, Serbia and Montenegro, and the Slovak Republic—have a flat rate at the same level for the PIT and the CIT. The other five— Georgia, Latvia, Lithuania, Russia, and Ukraine—have different rates for these two taxes.[5]

The large differences in rates from country to country may reflect in part the timing of the reform. The Baltic countries implemented this reform in a time of tight fiscal constraints in the mid-1990s, and the danger of having an unmanageable drop in revenues pushed the governments toward higher rates. The other countries, particularly the latecomers that implemented the reforms from 2004 onward, enjoyed more buoyant growth rates in their economies and better fiscal balances at the time of implementation.

Differences in rates selected during reforms also reflect the prereform rate schedules, revenues collected from each bracket, and overall effective tax rates. Comparing the rates selected by each country with its own former progressive rate schedule is helpful in understanding the intended goals of policy makers. In addition, looking at the former rate schedules helps to visualize the potential gains in simplicity that arise from a flat rate, particularly with the PIT (see table

TABLE 8.1

Personal Income and Corporate Income Tax Rates, by Country

Country	Personal income tax rate	Year of personal income tax reform	Current corporate income tax rate (%)	Future rate change plans
Estonia	23	1994	23 (26)	Government plans to reduce personal and corporate income tax rates to 20% by 2009. The corporate rate was recently reduced from 26% to the current 23%.
Lithuania	27	1994	15	The personal income tax rate was reduced from 33% to 27% in 2006, and a further reduction to 24% is expected for 2008.
Latvia	25	1995	15	The corporate rate was lowered from 19% to the current 15% in 2003.
Russian Federation	13	2001	30 (35)	The post-reform rate was not strictly a single rate tax. Some types of income were taxed through both personal income taxes and a unified social tax.
Serbia	14	2003	14	There are discussions about further decreasing this rate.
Ukraine	15	2004	25	Ukraine increased the personal rate from 13% to 15% in 2007. There are plan to reduce the corporate rate gradually starting in 2009.
Slovak Republic	19	2004	19	n.a.
Georgia	12	2005	20	n.a.
Romania	16	2005	16	n.a.

Sources: World Bank country reports; IMF staff reports.
Note: n.a. = Not applicable.

8.2), as discussed further below. However, in selecting rates, policy makers have tended to overlook existing payroll taxes, which share a significant portion of their base with the PIT. This disjointed rate policy and the problems it may generate are discussed further below (see also chapter 9).

A key feature of flat rate income tax reforms in ECA countries is the existence of allowances and deductibles, which is a departure from the pure form of a flat income tax. The simplest way to set an allowance is to establish a threshold below which income is free of tax regardless of any characteristics of the taxpayer. However, as with rates, allowances and deductibles vary significantly across countries in ECA that have implemented the reform.

The level of allowances increased in most countries with the move to flat tax structures, but to different degrees. In the Slovak Republic, for example, the level of allowances almost doubled in real terms, and new tax credits were introduced to enhance progressivity (see table 8.3 and box 8.2). Ukraine also increased the level of allowances significantly but narrowed their focus. Previously the allowance was granted independent of any individual characteristics,[6] but after the reform it could only be claimed for the education expenses of

TABLE 8.2

Rates and Rates Schedule Before and After Reform

Country	Flat personal income tax rate for the year after the reform	Schedule of rates (by income bracket) before the reform, or top rate
Georgia	12	Up to GEL 200 =12%
		GEL 201 to 350= GEL 24 + 15% of the amount in excess of GEL 200
		GEL 351 to 600 = GEL 46.5 + 17% of the amount in excess of GEL 350
		Over GEL 600 = GEL 89 + 20% of the amount in excess of GEL 600
		The presumptive tax varies from GEL 10 to GEL 150 monthly based on the type of activity and the size of the population where the enterprise is located.
Russian Federation	13	Below 3,168 rubles: 0%
		3,168 to 50,000: 12%
		50,000 to 150,000: 20%
		Above 150,000: 30%
Slovak Republic	19	Income range, rate on the rate + fixed amount
		Sk 0–Sk 90,000: 10% + Sk 0
		Sk 90–Sk 180,000: 20% + Sk 9,000
		Sk 180,000–Sk 396,000: 28% + Sk 27,000
		Sk 396,000–Sk 564,000: 35% + Sk 87,480
		Sk 564,000 and more: 38% + Sk 146,280
Estonia	26	Top personal income tax rate in 1993: 33%
Latvia	25	Regressive schedule starting at 25%
Ukraine	13	Top tax rate 40% (see Section D) [[AU: Section D of what?]]
Romania	16	Progressive tax from 18% to top rate of 40%

Sources: World Bank various country reports; Ivanova, Keen, and Klemm (2005) for Russia; IMF staff reports; World Bank World Tax Database.
Note: 1.78 Georgian GEL = US$ 1; 27.20 Russian rubles = US$ 1; 129.69 Slovak Sk = US$1; all average exchange rates for 2006.

TABLE 8.3

Personal Income Tax Allowances and Credits Before and After Reform in the Slovak Republic, 2003 and 2004

Allowances and credits	2003 (before reform)	2004 (after reform)
Allowances		
Taxpayer	Sk 38,760 (Sk 48,000 if handicapped)	Sk 80,832
Spouse	Sk 12,000 if had no income	Sk 80,832 minus spouse's income
Old age pensioners	Sk 0 (Sk 8,400 if partially disabled; Sk 16,800 if disabled)	Sk 0
Dependent child	Sk 16,800 (Sk 22,800 if handicapped)	Sk 0
Tax credits		
Dependent child	Sk 0	Sk 4,800 only if parent's annual gross income exceeds 6 times minimum wage (minimum wage is Sk 36,480)

Source: Ministry of Finance, Slovak Republic.
Note: 29.69 Sk = US$1.(average exchange rate for 2006).

dependent children (although this has become more complicated since the reform with added allowances. Overall, countries that have set higher proportional rates for the PIT have also tended to be more generous with allowances. At the other extreme, Georgia eliminated allowances completely, which went hand in hand with a very low flat rate of 12 percent.

Revenue Effects of Flat Tax Reforms

Although the behavior of tax revenues varied across countries after the implementation of reforms, on average the reforms do not appear in and of themselves to have had a significant impact on revenues, whether positive or negative (see annex 8A, which presents a cross-country empirical analysis of this reform). This is line with findings for other countries where the reform itself seems to have had little to do with revenue mobilization performance (see box 8.3 on the evaluation of Russia's flat tax reform performed by Ivanova at al. [2005]). In addition to other variables in the country's economy, a variety of design variables affect revenue outcomes, including the rates and allowances established. Figure 8.2 shows how collections in personal and corporate income taxes evolved in the first two years after reforms in selected countries.

Changes in revenue collection reflect in part the goals pursued by policy makers with the reforms. In most cases, policy makers did not want revenues to decline dramatically, and thus rates and allowances were selected in some countries to have a neutral revenue effect and in others to allow a manageable drop in collections as a way to

BOX 8.2

The Distributional Impact of Tax and Social Benefit Reforms in the Slovak Republic

Since 2002, the Slovak Republic has implemented an extensive package of social and structural reforms driven by an increased emphasis on employment and competitiveness. Before the reforms, the Slovak Republic had an effective but fiscally unsustainable safety net, with a high tax wedge that created barriers to job creation and discouraged individuals with low earning potential from actively seeking employment. To address these problems, the government simultaneously reformed its tax and transfer systems in 2004, introducing a flat PIT at 19 percent (reduced from previous rates of 10–38 percent) and reducing its average transfers by 16 percent. The reduction of the PIT rate was accompanied by a substantial increase in deductions and tax credits to reduce the tax burden for households with lower incomes and higher numbers of dependent children.

A recent World Bank report examined the distributional and poverty impacts of the combined tax and social transfer reforms. The study found that the combined effect of the reforms of the tax and benefits regime was to increase the disposable income of the majority of households that were entitled to benefits. The only households that suffered a decline in disposable income were those with three or more children in which all of the adults were unemployed and thus entitled to a higher schedule of benefits before the reform, and even then the maximum potential loss was limited

The fact that the combined overall effect on poverty was positive despite a 16 percent reduction in transfers means that the effect of the PIT reform itself was highly positive. Indeed, without the benefit reduction the tax reform would have reduced poverty by as much as 17 percent. The Slovak tax system became more progressive after 2004, and the poorest households benefited most from the tax reform. This shows that it is possible to increase the progressivity of the tax system by introducing a flat tax rate with a simultaneous change in the structure of deductible items and tax credits.

Source: World Bank 2005c.

reduce overall and marginal tax burdens. In 1994 Lithuania introduced a proportional rate of 33 percent—the highest marginal PIT rate in the country's rate schedule before the reform—and revenues actually went up as a result (Keen, Kim, and Varsano 2006). Russia also set its flat rate to avoid significant revenue losses in the short term. Close to 90 percent of Russian taxpayers had been in tax brackets with rates below the flat rate established by the reform in 2001, and about 60 percent of PIT collections had come from the 12 percent rate bracket.[7]

BOX 8.3

Russia's Flat Tax Reform

In 2001, Russia unified its progressive marginal rates for the PIT, from the previous 12, 20, and 30 percent rates to a single rate of 13 percent. In the following year, revenue from the PIT increased by 46 percent (about 26 percent in real terms) and by one-fifth relative to GDP. This successful revenue performance attracted much attention and triggered emulation of the reform in Eastern Europe. In 2005, Ivanova, Keen and Klemm used individual and household-level panel data from the Russian Longitudinal Monitoring Survey to examine the impact of Russia's tax reform on tax revenue and compliance.

This study drew several important lessons applicable to other countries considering adopting similar reforms. The authors found that the reform itself did not drive the growth of PIT revenues. In fact, PIT payments, as well as the combination of PIT and social insurance payments, fell for all groups except those initially paying at low tax rates and basically unaffected by the reform. Rather, they found that lower tax rates increased compliance and improved the reporting of income. Compliance for the individuals who benefited most from the reform (higher-income taxpayers) increased by 18 percentage points (from 52 percent to 70 percent), while it remained unchanged for the individuals who were unaffected by the rate change (lower-income individuals whose taxes before the reform were levied at rates below the flat rate established by the reform).

This study concludes that Russia's tax reform did not "pay for itself" because tax payments by most income groups actually fell. The authors attribute the postreform increase in PIT revenue to improved compliance and conclude that, although the improvement in compliance could be credited to the flat tax reform, it might also reflect the impact of strengthened tax administration undertaken about the same time. Other developments unrelated to the tax reform, including real wage growth, strong energy prices, and wider structural reforms, also played a role.

Source: Ivanova, Keen, Klemm 2005.

One of the Slovak Republic's goals with its reform was to reduce the overall tax burden and the high marginal income tax rates, but in a fiscally prudent way. In the first year of implementation, PIT revenues dropped by 0.8 percent of GDP (table 8.4). However, the overall number of returns increased, including for the self-employed, leading to a small increase in PIT revenues in 2005.

CIT collections before the reform stood at 2.5 percent of GDP. CIT collections dropped to 2.3 percent of GDP in 2004, the first year of the reform, but soared to above the prereform level in 2005. This turnaround occurred despite a reduction in the CIT rate from 25 to 19 percent, a reduction in the tax on capital gains from 36.3 to 19.0

FIGURE 8.2

Changes in PIT and CIT Revenue Collection in Selected Countries

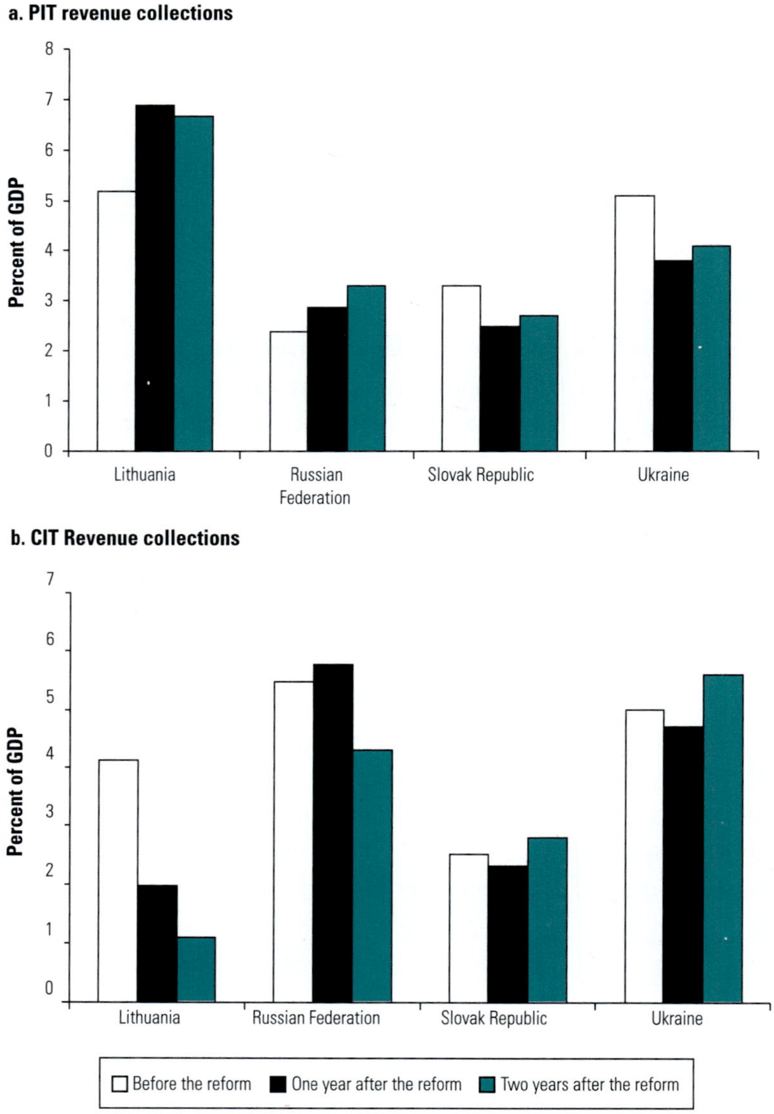

Source: World Bank; Bank staff calculations.

percent, and the elimination of the tax on dividends (formerly taxed at 15 percent). A key reason for the revenue increase was the expansion in the tax base resulting from the elimination of exemptions. The Slovak Republic went further than most other countries in closing tax loopholes (box 8.4) as it reduced tax rates.

TABLE 8.4
Tax Collections in the Slovak Republic, 1993–2005

Indicator	1993–99	2000	2001	2002	2003	2004	2005
Total personal income tax revenues (Sk million)	.---	31,839	34,623	37,115	39,594	33,379	39,805
% of GDP	3.7	3.4	3.4	3.3	3.3	2.5	2.7
% of general government	16.4	16.9	19.2	18.0	18.2	14.6	14.6
Total corporate income tax revenues (Sk million)	26,351	21,728	29,760	30,639	31,265	41,463	
% of GDP	4.6	2.8	2.1	2.7	2.5	2.3	2.8

Source: Act on Income Tax No. 595/2003 and 366/1999.
Note: 29.69 Sk = US$1.(average exchange rate for 2006).

Ukraine also wanted to reduce high marginal tax rates, acknowledging that revenues might fall in the short term. Fiscal authorities expected that PIT revenues would drop by about 0.5 percent of GDP during the first year of the reform (2004) but would fully recover in 2005. PIT revenues actually fell by 1.3 percent of GDP in the first year, significantly more than anticipated. Revenues recovered in 2005 to 4.1 percent of GDP, but remained below the prereform level by 1 percentage point of GDP (see figure 8.3). CIT revenues remained at almost the same level during the first year and grew further in 2005, despite the rate reduction from 30 to 25 percent in 2004. As in the Slovak Republic, the drop in the CIT rate was offset by closed loopholes. Overall tax revenues dropped from 30.6 to 29.2 percent of GDP and then surged to 35 percent of GDP in 2005. This surge was driven by buoyant collections of the value added tax (VAT) (which explains 66 percent of the surge), the recovery of PIT and CIT, and increases on labor taxes (primarily resulting from real wage growth).

Changes in Tax Structure

In both Ukraine and the Slovak Republic, the flat tax reforms led to a shift toward greater reliance on indirect taxes. However, the reasons were different in the two countries. In Ukraine, the balance between direct and indirect taxes changed only slightly in the first year of reform, because the drop in PIT and CIT collections was partly compensated for by a small increase in payroll taxes. The change in the tax structure was more prominent in 2005 because of increasing revenues from the VAT. In the Slovak Republic, a marked shift from direct to indirect taxation occurred in the first year of the reform and

BOX 8.4

PIT and CIT Loopholes Closed in the Slovak Tax Reform

The following special treatments, applying to both the PIT and the CIT base, were abolished:

- Income of taxpayers in farming, forestry, and water management
- Income from yields on government bonds and securities denominated in foreign currency, and from yields from mortgage debentures
- International grants
- Operational revenues of small-scale power plants and environmentally friendly equipment

In the CIT, several tax exemptions and concessions were abolished:

- Tax exemptions of income from business activities of colleges, high schools, primary schools, and educational establishments
- Tax concessions on selected research and development activities
- Tax concessions for creating jobs for partially disabled persons (Sk 10,000 for each) and for severely disabled persons (Sk 24,000) when the enterprise was not subject to a reduced CIT rate

In the PIT, the following exemptions were abolished:

- Supplementary pension insurance paid by the employer
- Several allowances (total allowances reduced from six to three)
- 10 percent tax rate on use of the Social Fund
- Revenues from sale of securities (previously exempt if three years between purchase and sale, or if annual revenues did not exceed Sk 50,000)
- Income of members of military missions working abroad and paid in foreign currency
- Income paid by health care institutions to blood and biological materials donors
- Earned interest on deposits in construction saving societies, and on state aid

Source: Ministry of Finance, Slovak Republic.

Note: Average exchange rate in 2006 was US$1 = 29.69 Sk.

accelerated further in 2005 (see figure 8.4). The overall tax burden went down, but the burden of direct taxes proportionally more. Such a shift in tax structure was an explicit policy goal, and the Slovaks increased the rates of indirect taxes—the VAT and excises taxes—to protect against revenue declines from the move to a flat income tax. Cross-country regression results also confirm that the reform brings a change in tax structure through a shift away from direct taxes toward indirect taxes (annex 8A)

FIGURE 8.3
Tax Collections in Ukraine, 2000–05

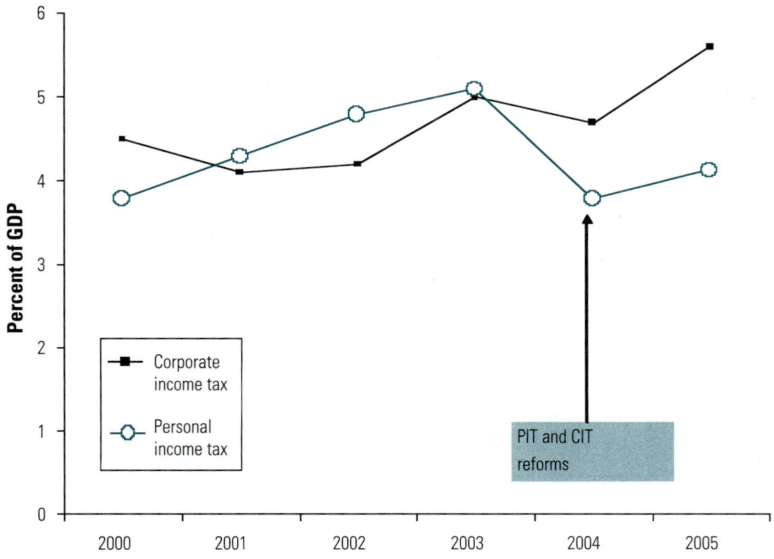

Sources: Ministry of Finance, Ukraine; Bank staff calculations.

Simplicity and Compliance

Improved simplicity and compliance are two main selling points of flat rate income taxes. Results from cross-country analysis suggest that compliance seems to be affected positively by the reform when CIT and PIT have the same flat rate (annex 8A). The extent to which flat rates simplify the system depends in part on other features of the reform, including changes in deductibles and allowances. In the Slovak Republic, both the definition of the tax base and the tax rate structure were simplified significantly for individuals and legal entities, and the increased simplicity was acknowledged as very positive by both local taxpayers and foreign investors. The fact that the number of self-employed tax returns increased by 14.6 percent in the first year of the reform is further evidence of increased simplicity and compliance (table 8.5).

Ukraine had a progressive tax rate structure before the reform (see table 8.6). The brackets were adjusted for inflation once a year in each annual budget law on an ad hoc basis, and even the rates applied to each bracket were subject to change. This produced an unstable environment for taxpayers. Greater simplicity and certainty were two

FIGURE 8.4
Changes in Tax Structures in Ukraine and the Slovak Republic

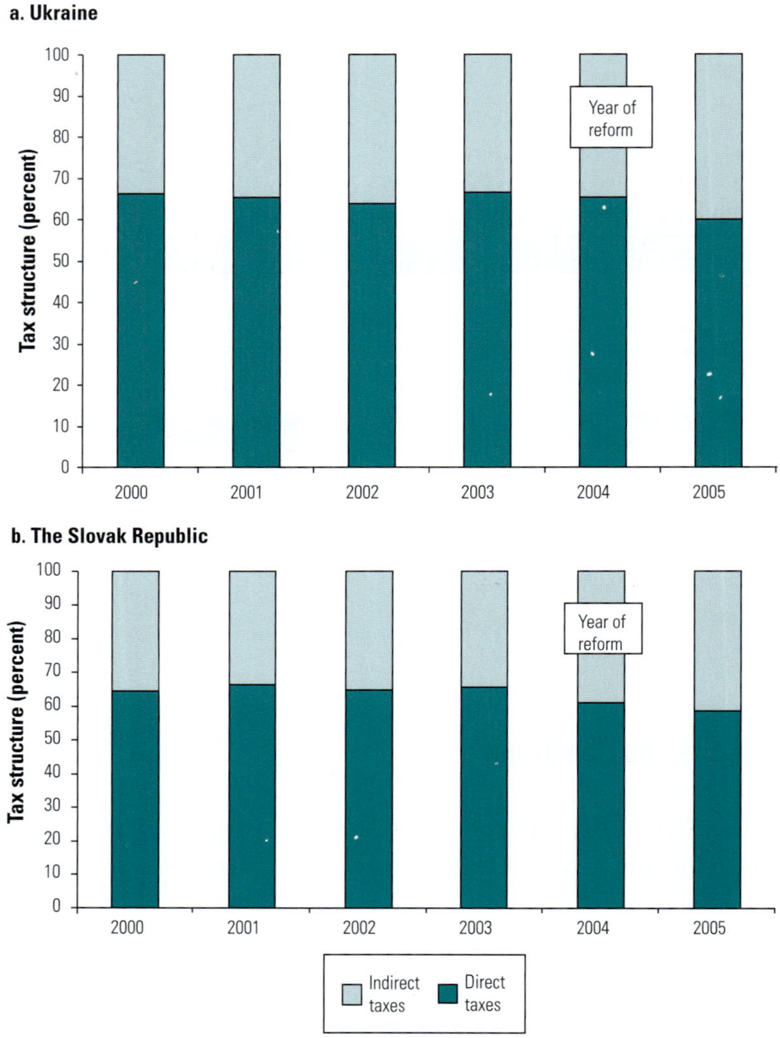

Sources: Ministry of Finance, Ukraine; Ministry of Finance, the Slovak Republic; Bank staff calculations.

of the successes of the reform in Ukraine. Despite some added complexity in the verification process for claimed allowances,[8] the reform brought about lower PIT compliance costs for taxpayers and their employers. Before the reform, an individual had to fill out an independent declaration in every workplace and for every additional source of independent income, and the taxpayer had to add up all income on a separate form and send all of the forms together to the

TABLE 8.5

Increase in Number of Personal Income Tax Returns after Reform in the Slovak Republic

	2000	2001	2002	2003	2004
Number of tax returns, self-employed	375,235	383,788	375,399	389,453	446,206
Year-over-year change, percent	--	2.3	-2.2	3.7	14.6

Sources: Ministry of Finance of Slovak Republic, Tax Office of Slokak Republic, Bank Staff calculations.

TABLE 8.6

Ukraine Personal Income Tax Rates and Income Brackets Before and After Reform, 2003 and 2004

Tax rate before reform (2003)		Tax rate after reform (2004)
		19 percent
Income range	*Tax rate + fixed amount*	
Sk 0–Sk 90,000	10 percent + Sk 0	
Sk 90–Sk 180,000	20 percent + Sk 9,000	
Sk 180,000–Sk 396,000	28 percent + Sk 27,000	
Sk 396,000–Sk 564,000	35 percent + Sk 87,480	
Sk 564,000 and more	38 percent + Sk 146,280	

Note: 29.69 Sk = US$1.(average exchange rate for 2006).

State Tax Service to determine tax liability. The rate assigned to each taxpayer had to be updated annually in all of the taxpayer's workplaces for the calculation of tax withholding. Following the reform, only one form is needed to determine tax liability, and income taxes can be withheld at source at the single rate. The benefits of increased simplicity can hardly be overstated, particularly given Ukraine's very poor international ranking on compliance costs (World Bank 2006c).

A quick analysis shows that growth in PIT and CIT collections in the Slovak Republic in 2005 (the second year of the reform) was driven by factors beyond growth in wages and GDP, respectively. Figure 8.5 shows changes in nominal PIT collections with respect to changes in nominal wages in the economy and changes in nominal CIT collections with respect to nominal GDP growth (at factor prices). These elasticities[9] are calculated for the year before the reform, 2004 (the first year of the reform), and 2005. Elasticity (ε_t) greater than one indicates that PIT (or CIT) revenues grew faster than the tax base in period t, while elasticity ε_t less than one indicates the opposite. Elasticities above one signal, even if rudimentarily, some improvement in compliance in the absence of policy changes (that is, changes in tax base or rate, or both). Because policy changes did occur with the reform in 2004, the elasticities for 2004 do not reveal much about compliance. However, the elasticities for 2005 (the second year of the reform) are good indicators because no sig-

FIGURE 8.5

Slovak PIT and CIT Revenue Elasticities, 2002–05

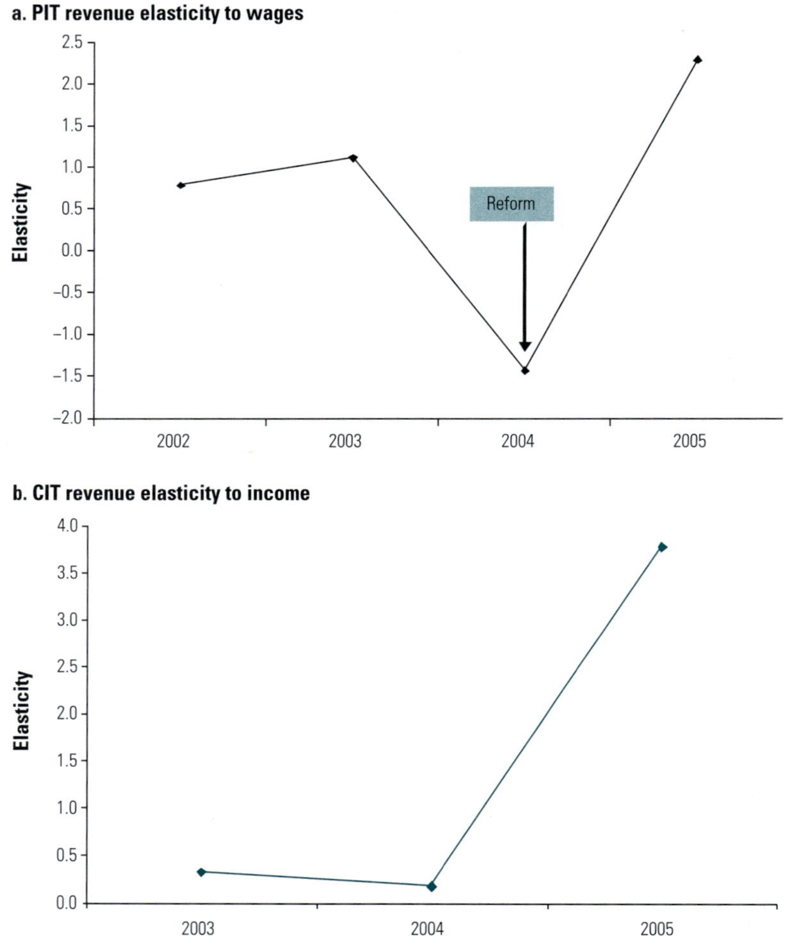

Sources: Ministry of Finance, the Slovak Republic; Bank staff calculations.

Note: PIT revenue elasticity to wages is calculated as $\varepsilon_t = (\%\Delta PITcollection)/(\%\Delta TaxBase[(wages)])$.

Note: CIT revenue elasticity to income is calculated as $\varepsilon_t = (\%\Delta CITcollection)/(\%\Delta TaxBase[(GDP_{fp})])$.

nificant change in rate or base took place that year. In fact, the elasticities for both PIT and CIT for 2005 are well above one, signaling that collection increases in that year were driven by factors beyond wage growth in the economy (for the PIT) and GDP growth (for the CIT)—most likely higher compliance.

Improvements in compliance are not as evident in Ukraine. The PIT reform was undertaken partly with the hope of providing an adequate incentive for taxpayers and their employers to report income accurately and thus to improve compliance and revenues for the government. Even though the government anticipated a drop in collections in 2004, it expected to reach prereform collection levels in 2005 and continue to expand revenues over the medium term. However, two years after the reform, PIT revenues were close to prereform levels. Figure 8.6 shows changes in nominal PIT collections in Ukraine with respect to changes in nominal wages in the economy. Lower rates in 2004 led to falling PIT collections, which explains the downward line in 2004. Collections recovered in 2005 and 2006 (projected), but the elasticities for these two latter years were still below one, suggesting that wage growth was driving the revenue increases rather than improvements in compliance.[10]

Several factors have inhibited improvements in compliance in the PIT in both the Slovak Republic and Ukraine. First, the high consolidated rates of payroll taxes (see chapter 9)[11] discourage PIT reporting because both taxes share almost the same base (in both the Slovak Republic and Ukraine). The link between payroll taxes (contributions) and pension benefits is weak, almost nonexistent in Ukraine, which also diminishes the incentives to report income accurately. Employers and employees may enter into collusion to set the "take-home pay" for the employee, which is composed of a registered

FIGURE 8.6

Ukraine PIT Revenue Elasticity with Respect to Wages, 2000–06

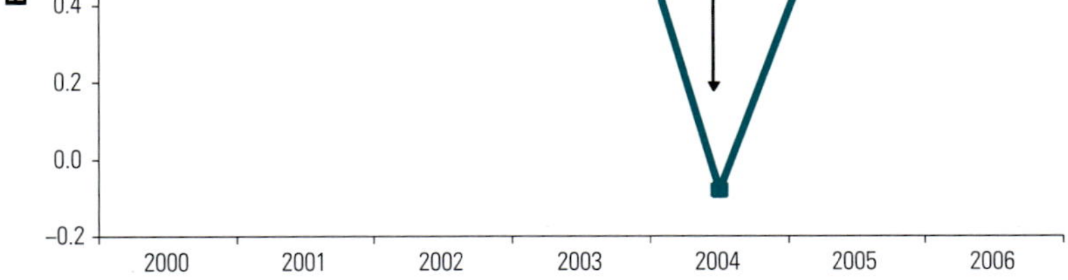

Sources: Ministry of Finance, Ukraine; Bank staff calculations. Data for 2006 are Bank staff estimates based on January–September performance.

Note: PIT revenue elasticity to wages is calculated as $\varepsilon_T = (\%\Delta PITcollection)/(\%\Delta TaxBase[(wages)]$.

amount that appears in the books to establish tax liability and a portion that is paid in cash and is not registered in the books. This practice is particularly common in countries in the Commonwealth of Independent States, and the key driver in these agreements is the high rate of payroll taxes (see chapter 9). Moreover, tax liability under the Simplified Tax System[12] in place in Ukraine is considerably lower than the rate for the PIT (and CIT) or for payroll taxes. Thus, taxpayers have been migrating to this system through evasion and avoidance schemes, thereby undermining the bases of all major taxes, including the PIT and the CIT.

The CIT in Ukraine, however, has shown good performance that can be attributed to improved compliance. Figure 8.7 shows elasticities of CIT collections with respect to GDP (at factor prices) in the prereform and postreform periods. After the drop in elasticity in 2004 (a consequence of the rate change), the elasticity in the second year (2005) rises to a level well above that before the reform. The behavior of these elasticities indicates that collections are driven by factors other than growth in the tax—presumably improvements in compliance. However, this result may also be influenced by the continued growth in foreign direct investment that began before the reform.

Tax administrations do not appear to have contributed to better compliance after the reform in either Ukraine or the Slovak Republic. In Ukraine, the revenue authorities (both the State Tax Administration [STA] and the four social insurance funds) have followed a slow

FIGURE 8.7

Ukraine CIT Revenue Elasticity with Respect to GDP, 2002–05

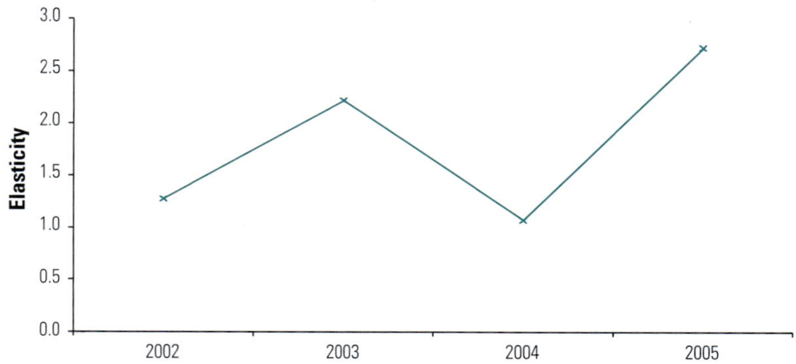

Sources: Ministry of Finance, Ukraine; Bank staff calculations.

Note: CIT revenue elasticity to income is calculated as $\varepsilon_t = (\%\Delta CITcollection)/(\%\Delta TaxBase[(GDP_{fp})]$.

pace in their modernization. Despite increases in revenues over two years since reform, the STA continues to impose high compliance costs and is weak in core areas such as taxpayer registration, compliance monitoring, and audit. Additionally, the collection of PIT and payroll taxes by the STA and the four different social insurance funds, respectively, is poorly coordinated. The Slovak STA also imposes high compliance costs on taxpayers according to international comparisons. The recent World Bank Doing Business Survey (World Bank 2006c) ranks both Ukraine and the Slovak Republic near the bottom on thus issue—lower than any other EU-8 country except Hungary). A proposal to consolidate and strengthen tax administration was put forward with the tax reform, but political resistance was strong and consolidation never took place.

A positive aspect of the Slovak Republic's reform was the communication campaign. This campaign was geared to counter political opposition and address public concerns, and it may have helped encourage compliance as well. From an early stage, the government team in charge of the reform involved a variety of stakeholders, including private sector representatives, nongovernmental organizations, and academics, in discussions to create a consensus on the objectives and, later, on specific features of the reform. The government was very transparent and allowed several think tanks to participate in the process of estimating the fiscal impact of the reform and to present their results in jointly organized seminars and conferences. Journalists and the general public had ready access to relevant information, including through a specially designed Web site. Communication through the mass media was constant and helped to create support in the general population and the business community.

Conclusions

Flat tax reforms have been widespread in ECA and in general appear to have had positive effects on simplicity and compliance. They have not as a rule led to either revenue collapse or revenue surges. Rather, the revenue impacts have generally depended on the goals of the reform and design features of the tax, such as the tax rates selected. If collections dropped more than expected during the first year of the reform, they typically improved thereafter, reflecting either growth in tax bases or improved compliance (or both). Several countries with a high tax burden on the economy aimed the reform at reducing the burden of direct taxes (as well as the overall tax burden), and in such cases manageable reductions in real collections may even have had positive implications for competitiveness and growth in the economy. A shift away from direct toward indirect taxes was noticeable in most cases analyzed. In some countries, such as the Slovak Republic, this was a conscious policy decision and is likely to have a positive influence on economic growth (as discussed in chapter 3).

The experiences with flat income tax reforms in ECA point to several lessons. First, the key objectives of the reform should be clearly articulated before turning to specific design issues. In the rush to implement the apparently successful reforms of other countries, governments may overlook their core objectives. There are different objectives for this type of reform, such as improving compliance, broadening the tax base, bringing simplicity to the system, mobilizing higher or lower revenue, reducing the tax burden in the country, and shifting the tax burden from direct to indirect taxation; some of these objectives run counter to each other. Clear objectives should drive design features, such as rates, allowances, tax credits, and the like, as well as other parallel reforms needed.

Second, if revenue neutrality is one of the goals of the reform, tax policy in other areas may need to be adjusted as a safeguard against some drop in revenues in the PIT and CIT. If, in parallel, another goal is to shift the burden away from direct taxes and toward indirect taxes, tax policy and administration for the VAT and excises should be strengthened before or in tandem with a flat income tax reform.

Third, a comprehensive curtailment of income tax loopholes and ad hoc exemptions is essential to expand tax bases and prevent undue revenue loss with flat income tax reforms. Countries that closed loopholes and reduced exemptions had greater success with simplification, compliance, and revenue collection.

Fourth, success in expanding the PIT tax base and improving PIT compliance depends in part on complementary reforms in social insurance and contributions. Payroll taxes have almost the same base as the PIT in most countries in ECA, and high marginal rates of payroll taxes (social insurance contributions) can be a major obstacle to improved PIT compliance after the reform.

Fifth, modernization of tax administration is a key complementary institutional reform. Simultaneous reforms in tax administration will complement policy changes in helping in achieve the goals of the reform (whatever they may be) with fewer fiscal risks.

Sixth, allowances are critical to the achievement of equity goals. Allowances have proven to be an important safety net for lower-income taxpayers and have enhanced the equity of flat tax reforms. It is important to evaluate trade-offs carefully and set allowances at appropriate thresholds. Allowances should be kept simple, however, to avoid administrative complexity.

Seventh, the timing of the reform is critical. Governments have been able to avoid unmanageable revenue losses by implementing tax reforms during times of strong growth and sound fiscal frameworks.

Finally, communicating the reform, its goals, and its characteristics, and obtaining consensus from all stakeholders is important for success. Informing the public is critical for PIT and CIT reforms and can help to reduce political obstacles. For the CIT, a highly publicized campaign on the benefits of transparency and the need to close loopholes can help counter industry lobbyists who may argue against elimination of exemptions for certain industries.

Annex 8A Cross-Country Analysis of Flat Tax Reform

Data and Variables

Type of variables	Specific variable	Source
Dependent	Revenue collection (PIT, CIT) as % of GDP	Study database and IMF GFS
	Revenue structure: direct taxes/total tax revenue; and indirect taxes/total tax revenue	Study database and IMF GFS
	Tax compliance proxy	BEEPS
Institutional	Tax administration quality	BEEPS and CPIA
	Corruption (several measures including corruption in tax administration)	BEEPS, CPIA
	Other business climate variables	BEEPS
Economic and business cycle (other controls)	Per capita GDP, and change in per capita GDP	WDI, LDB
	Per capita GDP growth	WDI, LDB
	Foreign direct investment	WDI, LDB
	Inflation	LDB
	Real wage growth	EBRD, ILO

Note: BEEPS = Business Environment and Enterprise Performance Survey; CPIA = Country Policy and Institutional Assessment; EBRD = European Bank for Reconstruction and Development; GFS = Government Finance Statistics; ILO = International Labour Organization; LDB = Live Database; WDI = World Development Indicators.

Methodology

To analyze the effects of this reform on compliance, revenue mobilization, and tax structure, this study used first differencing methods and the method of difference-in-difference estimations (D-in-D) with extensions (a brief description is presented below). This latter method helps in evaluating a policy reform implemented by a group of countries in a sample that also includes countries without the reform. This panel contains a treatment group of countries (that is, countries that have implemented a flat rate income tax reform) and a control group of countries that have not implemented the reform inside and outside ECA; this latter group is the counterfactual group of countries.[13]

Assume a model:

$$Y_{it} = \beta o + \alpha_i + \gamma_t + \beta R_{it} + \varepsilon_{it} \qquad \text{(Eq 8A.1)}$$

where Y_{it} is a policy outcome indicator (that is, tax revenues, tax compliance, tax structure); βo is a common intercept term; α_i is a country-specific intercept term (fixed effect); γ_t is a time-specific intercept term; $\beta 1$ is the impact of a policy on Y_{it} where $R_{it} = 1$ if the policy is in place, $R_{it} = 0$ otherwise.

The objective is to compare outcomes over time between the treatment and control groups to obtain an estimate of the impact of the policy (on average). In the basic model, the treatment group is observed at two periods: postpolicy: $Y_{it} = \beta o + \alpha_i + \gamma_t + \beta 1$; and prepolicy: $Y_{it} = \beta o + \alpha_i$. The difference between the pre- and postpolicy changes can be measured as

$$\Delta^T = (\beta o + \alpha_i + \gamma_t + \beta 1) - (\beta o + \alpha_i) = \gamma_t + \beta 1 \qquad \text{(Eq 8A.2)}$$

Similarly, for the control group, postpolicy: $Y_{it} = \beta o + \alpha_i + \gamma_t$; prepolicy: $Y_{it} = \beta o + \alpha_i$. The difference between the pre- and postpolicy changes for the control group can be measured as

$$\Delta^C = (\beta o + \alpha_i + \gamma_t) - (\beta o + \alpha_i) = \gamma_t \qquad \text{(Eq 8A.3)}$$

The true impact of the policy is determined by taking the *difference in difference* between the control and the treatment groups. Therefore, the impact of the policy can be calculated by

$$\Delta = \Delta^T - \Delta^C = (\gamma_t + \beta 1) - \gamma_t = \beta 1 \qquad \text{(Eq 8A.4)}$$

Consistent estimates of $\beta 1$ in Eq 8A.4 can be obtained with the first difference estimator[14] of Eq 8A.5:

$$\Delta Y_{it} = \gamma_t + \beta 1 \Delta R_{it} + \Delta \varepsilon_{it} \qquad \text{(Eq 8A.5)}$$

The D-in-D model can be extended to include other variables of interest besides the treatment R_{it}. A more general model includes a vector of regressors X_{it} and the equation to be estimated becomes

$$\Delta Y_{it} = \gamma_t + \beta 1 \Delta R_{it} + \Delta X_{it}'\xi + \Delta \varepsilon_{it} \qquad \text{(Eq 8A.6)}$$

Eq 8A.6 can also be used to estimate β1 if data is available for more than two time periods (by adding a dummy variable for each time period to account for secular changes that are not being modeled), or in the event that some countries start with treatment at different time periods (Wooldridge 2002). In such cases, β1 cannot be written as in Eq 8A.4 but its interpretation is similar: it is the change in the average value of *Y* due to the reform (*R*), all else being equal. The model used to estimate treatment effects with various time periods and differences across countries in the treatment implementation is given in Eq 8A.7:

$$\Delta Y_{it} = \gamma_0 + \sum_{t=3}^{T} \gamma_t d_t + \beta 1 \Delta R_{it} + \Delta X_{it}'\xi + \Delta\varepsilon_{it} \qquad \text{(Eq 8A.7)}$$

Cross-Country Regression Results

Cross-country regressions do not point to either a decrease or increase in PIT revenues as a result of a move to a flat income tax.[15] For countries that implemented flat rate PIT reforms in ECA, regardless of the type of reform and rate of the CIT (that is, the first treatment group in table 8A.1), the results are not statistically significant in any specification. The only variable that is significant at a 10 percent confidence level is real wage increases. In the countries that implemented the reform with PIT and CIT at the same rate (second treatment group in table 8A.1), there are some indications that PIT revenues tend to fall after the reform. However, these results are not robust in all specifications.

The results for changes in CIT revenues are also unclear (table 8A.2). Results were inconclusive in various different model specifications. Empirically, CIT revenues do not seem to be significantly affected by the reform. This is in line with what was observed in the country case studies, where revenue losses from reduced rates were compensated for by base expansion, particularly the closure of loopholes and exemptions. These regressions only evaluate data until 2004, so additional observations in the future may change these results.

Regression results confirm that the reform brings a change in tax structure through a shift away from direct taxes toward indirect taxes (table 8A.3). The result is highly significant in all specifications regardless of the type of flat tax reform, that is, both for reforms with a flat rate on PIT but with a different rate on the CIT and for reforms that aligned PIT and CIT rates at the same level.

The results are even stronger for the countries that aligned the flat rate at the same level for both CIT and PIT. These results are quite robust under different specifications (and robustness tests) and even

TABLE 8A.1
Effect of the Reform on Personal Income Tax Revenues

Dependent variable: PIT revenues % of GDP	Model specification (1)	Model specification (2)	Model specification (3)	Model specification (4)	Model specification (5)
Reform treatment PIT reform (regardless type of reform in CIT)	0.075 [0.453]	0.067 [0.452]	0.074 [0.458]		
Treatment if reform has same rates for PIT and CIT (FLAT)				-0.194 [0.324]	-0.676 [0.105]***
CPIA revenues efficiency		-0.025 [0.091]	-0.183 [0.164]	-0.179 [0.162]	-0.039 [0.167]
Inflation CPI					0 [0.000]*
Real wage index	0.014 [0.008]*	0.014 [0.008]	0.014 [0.009]*	0.015 [0.009]*	0.009 [0.009]
GDP growth	-0.005 [0.008]	-0.004 [0.008]	-0.003 [0.008]	-0.003 [0.008]	-0.004 [0.008]
PC GDP	0 [0.000]	0 [0.000]	0 [0.000]	0 [0.000]	0 [0.000]
Constant	0.13 [0.334]	0.126 [0.335]	0.124 [0.336]	0.136 [0.351]	0.329 [0.365]
Observations	213	213	213	213	195
R-squared	0.07	0.06	0.07	0.07	0.08

Source: Bank Staff estimations.
Note: CIT = Corporate income tax; CPI = Consumer Price Index; CPIA = Country Policy and Institutional Assessment; PIT = personal income tax.
* Significant at 10 percent level. *** Significant at 1 percent level. Robust standard errors in brackets.

TABLE 8A.2
Effect of the Reform on Corporate Income Tax Revenues

Dependent variable: CIT revenues % of GDP	Model specification (1)	Model specification (2)	Model specification (3)	Model specification (4)
Treatment if reform has same rates for PIT and CIT (FLAT)	-0.232 [0.197]	-0.226 [0.184]		
Treatment if CIT reform			-0.069 [0.139]	-0.078 [0.144]
CPIA revenue efficiency		-0.006 [0.106]		-0.005 [0.106]
CPIA overall	0.035 [0.189]			
GDP growth	-0.037 [0.015]	-0.035 [0.023]	-0.035 [0.023]	-0.035 [0.023]
PC GDP	0.002 [0.001]***	0.002 [0.001]***	0.002 [0.001]***	0.002 [0.001]***
Inflation CPI	0 [0.001]			
Constant	0.393 [0.477]	0.397 [0.766]	0.399 [0.764]	0.397 [0.766]
Observations	220	229	230	229
R-squared	0.18	0.18	0.17	0.17

Source: Bank Staff estimations.
Note: CIT = Corporate income tax; CPI = Consumer Price Index; CPIA = Country Policy and Institutional Assessment; PC = per capita GDP; PIT = personal income tax.
* Significant at 10 percent level. *** Significant at 1 percent level. Robust standard errors in brackets.

TABLE 8A.3

Effect of the Reform on Revenue Structure, Using Ratio of Direct Taxes to Total Tax Revenues

Dependent variable: TAX STRUCTURE 1—ratio of direct taxes/total tax revenues	Model specification (1)	Model specification (2)	Model specification (3)	Model specification (4)	Model specification (5)	Model specification (6)
Treatment if reform has same rates for PIT and CIT (FLAT)	-3.637 [0.439]***	-3.604 [0.505]***	-3.672 [0.582]***			
Treatment PIT reform				-3.111 [1.067]***	-3.14 [1.097]***	
Treatment CIT reform						-2.525 [1.403]*
CPIA fiscal		-0.133 [0.549]		-0.125 [0.546]		-0.129 [0.546]
Real wage index	0.003 [0.036]	0.003 [0.036]	0.002 [0.037]	0.01 [0.036]	0.01 [0.036]	0.006 [0.036]
Inflation CPI	0.001 [0.000]**	0.001 [0.000]**	0.001 [0.000]**	0.001 [0.000]**	0.001 [0.000]**	0.001 [0.000]**
GDP growth	-0.084 [0.081]	-0.08 [0.084]	-0.083 [0.082]	-0.079 [0.083]	-0.083 [0.082]	-0.084 [0.083]
PC GDP	0.003 [0.002]	0.003 [0.002]	0.003 [0.002]	0.002 [0.002]	0.002 [0.002]	0.003 [0.002]
Constant	0.221 [1.072]	0.21 [1.081]	0.217 [1.075]	0.883 [1.215]	0.894 [1.210]	0.234 [1.085]
Observations	199	198	198	198	198	198
R-Squared	0.05	0.05	0.05	0.06	0.06	0.06

Source: Bank Staff estimations.

Note: CIT = Corporate income tax; CPI = Consumer Price Index; CPIA = Country Policy and Institutional Assessment; PC = per capita GDP; PIT = personal income tax.

* Significant at 10 percent level. *** Significant at 1 percent level. Robust standard errors in brackets.

when using different ratios to evaluate changes in tax structure. Table 8A.4 shows a modified dependent variable, that is, the ratio of indirect taxes to total tax revenues. The signs on the coefficients change clearly to the opposite direction, accounting for the new relationship that the modified dependent variable imposes.

Compliance seems to be affected positively by the reform when CIT and PIT have the same flat rate. The set of regressions in table 8A.5 shows as a dependent variable a proxy variable for compliance gathered from the BEEPS (see note a to table 8A.5). The results show that a flat rate at the same level for both PIT and CIT has a statistically significant positive effect on the compliance proxy. These results are robust in most specifications.

Tax administration seems to be a key factor for improving compliance because the regression results indicate that more burdensome tax administrations may deter compliance, even in the presence of this reform.

TABLE 8A.4

Effect of the Reform on Revenue Structure, Using Ratio of Indirect Taxes to Total Tax Revenues

Dependent variable: TAX STRUCTURE 2—ratio of indirect taxes/total tax revenues	Model specification (1)	Model specification (2)	Model specification (3)	Model specification (4)	Model specification (5)	Model specification (6)
Treatment if reform has same rates for PIT and CIT (FLAT)	4.71 [1.142]***	4.684 [1.295]***	4.715 [1.294]***			
Treatment PIT reform				2.597 [0.959]***	2.588 [0.983]***	
Treatment CIT reform						1.944 [1.302]
CPIA fiscal		0.317 [0.672]				
D.realwageindex2005	0.037 [0.048]	0.038 [0.049]	0.037 [0.048]	0.029 [0.047]	0.029 [0.047]	0.033 [0.047]
D.inflationcpi	0 [0.000]	0 [0.000]	0 [0.000]	0 [0.000]	0 [0.000]	-0.001 [0.000]
D.gdpgrowthannual	0.042 [0.083]	0.032 [0.084]	0.039 [0.082]	0.042 [0.082]	0.039 [0.082]	0.045 [0.083]
D.gdppercapconstant2000us	-0.003 [0.002]	-0.003 [0.002]	-0.003 [0.002]	-0.002 [0.002]	-0.003 [0.002]	-0.003 [0.002]
Constant	0.158 [0.982]	0.188 [0.997]	0.17 [0.996]	-0.409 [1.099]	-0.396 [1.118]	0.132 [0.984]
Observations	199	198	198	199	198	199
R-Squared	0.06	0.06	0.06	0.06	0.06	0.06

Source: Bank Staff estimations.

Note: CIT = Corporate income tax; CPI = Consumer Price Index; CPIA = Country Policy and Institutional Assessment; PC = per capita GDP; PIT = personal income tax.
* Significant at 10 percent level. *** Significant at 1 percent level. Robust standard errors in brackets.

Notes

1. Hong Kong (China) pioneered this reform over 50 years ago. A few other countries outside the ECA region, such as Bolivia (in the early 1990s), also implemented a flat rate on the personal income tax.
2. Hall and Rabushka (1983, 1985), most prominently, proposed the idea of a flat tax for the United States as a combination of a tax on wages and a tax on the cash flow of business, both at the same rate.
3. Ukraine raised the PIT rate from 13 percent to 15 percent in 2007, a measure announced in advance in 2004.
4. The rate of 30 percent (which includes federal and regional portions) can be increased by municipal "piggybacking" taxes that may raise the overall rate up to 35 percent.
5. The Slovak Republic also established its value added tax (VAT) rate at 19 percent.
6. The allowance granted to taxpayers before the reform was very simple. The first 17 Ukrainian hryvnias (5.05 Hrv = US$1) of monthly income was free of tax and all income after that threshold was taxed under the rate schedule established. The threshold amount was established every year in the annual budget document.

TABLE 8A.5

Effect of the Reform on Compliance

Dependent variable: BEEPS question Q43a—proxy for compliance[a]	Model specification (1)	Model specification (2)	Model specification (3)	Model specification (4)	Model specification (5)	Model specification (6)	Model specification (7)
Treatment if reform has same rates for PIT and CIT (FLAT)	5.128 [1.582]***	5.101 [2.467]**	2.140 [3.363]*	2.956 [2.574]			
Treatment CIT reform					1.425 [2.389]**	-0.076 [3.403]	
Treatment PIT reform							-0.076 [3.403]
CPIA accountability Pub Sect-Corr	5.533 [5.696]			4.326 [5.270]		4.268 [5.415]	4.268 [5.415]
BEEPS Q54h—Tax rates as major obstacle, 1=no obstacle 4 = major obstacle				-0.405 [3.718]		-1.225 [3.456]	-1.225 [3.456]
BEEPS Q54i—Tax administration as major obstacle, 1=no obstacle 4 = major obstacle			-5.231 [3.504]*	-7.657 [2.499]**	-4.754 [4.113]	-7.543 [3.638]*	-7.543 [3.638]*
BEEPS Q54q—Corruption as major obstacle, 1 = no obstacle 4 = major obstacle					-5.22 [4.988]		
PCGDP	0.024 [0.010]			0.021 [0.009]**	0.013 [0.007]*	0.022 [0.009]**	0.022 [0.009]**
Observations	26	27	27	26	27	26	26
R-Squared	0.56	0.44	0.42	0.67	0.52	0.66	0.66

Source: Bank Staff estimations.

Note: CIT = Corporate income tax; CPI = Consumer Price Index; CPIA = Country Policy and Institutional Assessment; PC = per capita GDP; PIT = personal income tax. * Significant at 10 percent level. *** Significant at 1 percent level. Robust standard errors in brackets.

a. The BEEPS question is as follows: "Recognizing the difficulties that many firms face in fully complying with taxes and regulations, what percentage of total annual sales do you estimate the typical firm in your area of business reports for tax purposes?"

7. Author's calculations based on a sample of 2,414 individuals in the Russian Longitudinal Monitoring Survey of the Carolina Population Center at the University of North Carolina, as described in Ivanova, Keen, and Klemm (2005).
8. The new allowance system in Ukraine did create some administrative difficulties. The new allowance works differently from its predecessor in several ways. First, the new allowance is only for deductions based on education expenses. Second, the allowance may be from zero up to the threshold established. The threshold amount is obtained by multiplying the "subsistence minimum" times 1.4. The subsistence minimum is a notional amount set by the government each year in the annual budget; this amount is above the minimum wage in Ukraine (the "minimum subsistence" level was Hrv 386.7 (5.05 Hrv = US$1) in 2004). Because the allowance is only for education expenses, the tax administration must verify that the supporting documents (school and university

receipts) are generated by state-accredited educational institutions and for the corresponding fiscal period. Officials in the Ministry of Finance and the State Tax Administration have stated that because this process is by and large manual, its administration has added complication.

9. The elasticity of the PIT is calculated as follows:

$$\varepsilon_t = (\%\Delta PITcollection) / (\%\Delta TaxBase\left[(wages)\right])$$

The elasticity of the CIT is calculated as follows:

$$\varepsilon_t = (\%\Delta CITcollection) / (\%\Delta TaxBase\left[(GDP_{fp}\right])$$

10. A similar result was found for Russia (Ivanova, Keen, and Klemm 2005). Reported wage growth has been much faster than—in some years double—GDP growth in Ukraine. It is possible that part of this rapid wage growth is really a "de-shadowing" of the economy, that is, a signal of more accurate reporting of income that had previously been concealed, and thus of improved compliance. A counterargument, however, is that wage growth in the public sector has been growing rapidly (in some years outpacing private sector wage growth), and public sector wages are rarely concealed.
11. In Ukraine, currently, the rate may reach 42 percent of wage income. The employer contribution rate alone is close to 37 percent, which covers contributions to the four social insurance funds.
12. The Simplified Tax System was established by Presidential decree in 1998 as a temporary measure to foster small business. However, its design, with high thresholds for eligibility (up to US$200,000 in annual turnover for legal entities and US$100,000 for individuals), no limitation on types of activity, and considerably lower tax liability than in the regular system, has created a number of problems for the tax system. It creates incentives for taxpayers to migrate out of the regular tax system, leading to vertical and horizontal inequities among taxpayers. It also generates economically inefficient choices for taxpayers, and it undermines the bases and the collection efficiency of major taxes (payroll taxes, the PIT, the VAT and, more marginally, the CIT).
13. The sample of countries includes all ECA countries in addition to several non-ECA developing and developed countries (called international comparators in this report).
14. For a detailed explanation concerning estimation of the first difference model, see Cameron and Trivedi (2005).
15. The cross-country analysis is based on time-series panel data that include 38 ECA and non-ECA countries (called international comparators in this report). The methodologies used are first-differencing and extensions and difference-in-difference estimatio

CHAPTER 9

Taxation of Labor

Jan Rutkowski
with contributions from Mateusz Walewski

Economic growth results from both a higher quantity of factors of production—labor and capital—and higher productivity in the use of those factors of production. Because labor is an important economic input, higher employment rates will lead to higher GDP, other things being equal. Yet employment has declined markedly in countries of the Europe and Central Asia (ECA) region since the start of transition. The share of the working-age population employed in most ECA countries is now well below the European Union's (EU's) average and in most cases below the Lisbon target of 70 percent (World Bank 2005a). Unemployment rates are high, in many cases well over 10 percent of the labor force.

These poor employment outcomes in ECA—including low labor force participation, high unemployment, and substantial informal employment—are often blamed on high taxes on labor. These taxes discourage both labor demand (by raising labor costs to employers) and labor supply (by lowering the real consumption wage of workers). They create a "tax wedge" between labor cost to the employer and the worker's take-home pay (see box 9.1) and thereby reduce both employment and economic growth.[1] Is this conventional wisdom justified? Are labor taxes in ECA higher than in countries with comparable income levels? If so, why? Do they have a discernible impact on employment outcomes and, if so, how can their negative impact be limited?

This chapter addresses these questions.[2] It finds that the tax wedge on labor in ECA is indeed relatively high from an international perspective, mainly because of expensive social security systems.[3] It confirms that high labor taxes have a negative impact on employment. Those ECA countries where the tax wedge on labor is high tend to have worse employment outcomes than those where it is low, and regression analysis confirms the significant relationship between tax rates and employment.[4] Finally, the study recommends two main ways to limit the negative impact of the tax wedge on employment. The first is to lower social security contributions, which account for the bulk of the tax wedge, by rationalizing the social security system (for example, limiting early retirement options and the abuse of disability and sickness benefits) and perhaps by switching the financing of some social benefits away from labor contributions to general taxation. The second is to use tax reductions targeted at low-skilled workers and youth, the two groups whose employment is most negatively affected by high labor taxes. However, expectations should be realistic. Reductions in social security contribution rates that are feasible from a fiscal perspective are likely to bring about a rather modest employment effect.

Labor Taxes in ECA

Labor taxes are high in ECA countries, accounting for about 40 percent of total labor cost on average.[5] If a worker receives the equivalent of US$100 in net wage, the employer incurs a labor cost on average of US$167. There is significant variation among countries, however (figure 9.1), with the tax wedge being highest in Hungary (45.8 percent) and lowest in Georgia (26.7 percent). Among country groups (figure 9.2), the tax wedge ranges from 33 percent in low-income CIS to close to 43 percent in the EU-11[6] and Turkey. It increases with income levels, indicating that the generosity of the social security system tends to increase more sharply than the tax base in ECA.

In virtually all ECA countries the tax wedge on labor is higher than in countries at similar income levels in other regions of the world (figure 9.2). The average tax wedge for EU-11 is somewhat lower than that for EU-15,[7] but there is an enormous gap in GDP per capita between these two groups of countries. The high relative labor tax burden is clearest if one compares ECA and non-ECA focus countries selected for this study (table 9.1). In the middle-income ECA coun-

BOX 9.1

Taxes on Labor: Concepts and Definitions

Labor taxes include personal income tax, social security contributions paid by employees, and payroll taxes —that is, social security contributions and other taxes paid by the employer. Consumption taxes are not considered a component of labor taxes in this chapter.

Social security contributions finance social security benefits such as old-age pensions, disability pensions, survivors' pensions, sickness benefits, and unemployment benefits. Strictly speaking, they should not be regarded as taxes if employees value the benefits they finance and would demand a compensating wage increase if the benefits were abolished. Thus, the term labor taxes should be regarded as short for "labor taxes and contributions."

Total labor cost is a sum of gross wage earnings of employees and payroll taxes paid by the employer.

Net take-home pay (net wage) is the difference between gross earnings and personal income tax and social security contributions paid by the employee.

Tax wedge is the difference between total labor cost to the employer and the net take-home pay of the employee, expressed as a percentage of the total labor cost.

Annex 9A presents details on the components of the tax wedge in ECA countries.

Source: Author.

tries, represented by Poland, Romania, and the Slovak Republic, social security contributions account for 45 to 49 percent of the gross wage—far higher than in Chile and the Republic of Korea, where they account for 13 and 16 percent, respectively. This substantial gap reflects the fact that middle-income ECA countries have developed expensive social security systems that resemble those in high-income Western Europe. However, even a comparison with Spain, another non-ECA comparator country, points to a marked disproportion between the high social security contribution rates in the middle-income ECA countries and their levels of income. Spain's GNI per capita is about three times as high as in Poland and the Slovak Republic and seven times as high as in Romania. Still, social security contributions in Spain account for 37 percent of the gross wage, some 10 percentage points lower than in the middle-income ECA countries.

A similar picture emerges when one looks at low-income ECA countries. In Albania, Armenia, and the Kyrgyz Republic, social secu-

FIGURE 9.1
Tax Wedge on Labor, 2006

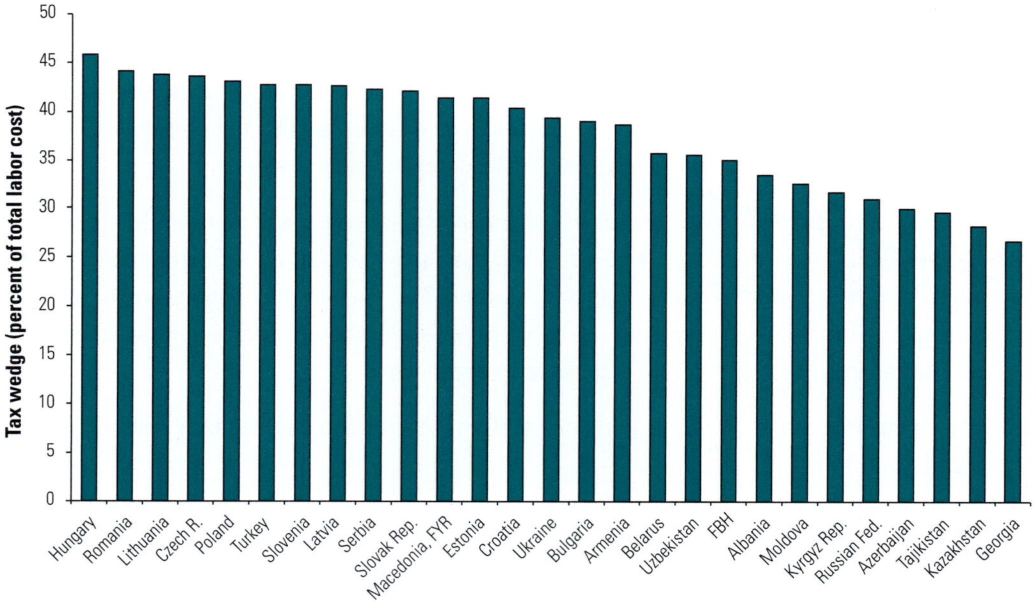

Source: World Bank.

FIGURE 9.2
Tax Wedge on Labor: ECA and Selected Comparator Countries, 2006

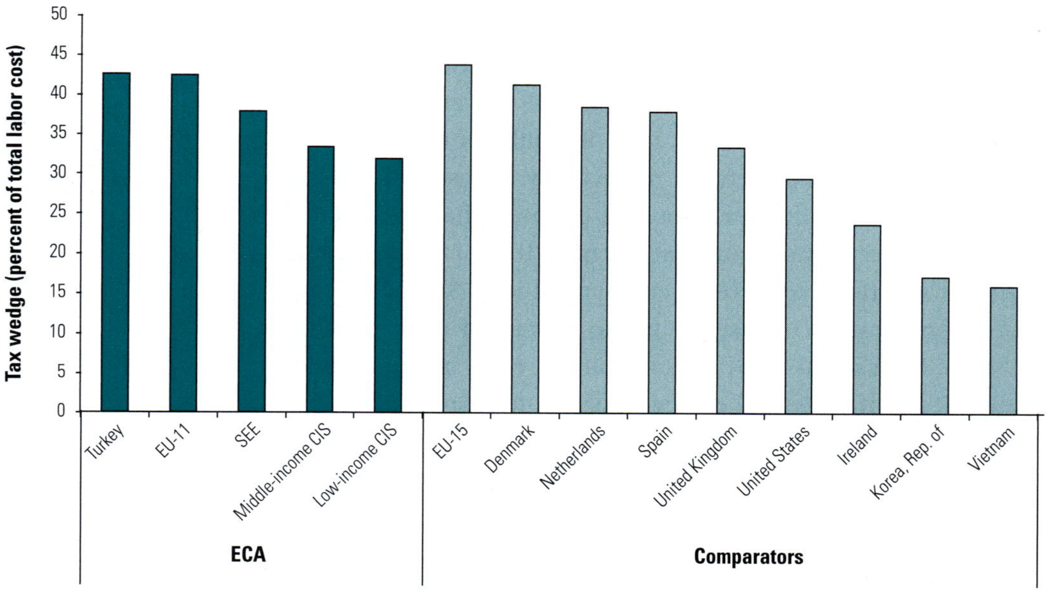

Source: World Bank, Eurostat, and OECD data; Bank staff calculations.

FIGURE 9.3

Tax Wedge and GDP per Capita, 2006 or Latest Available Year

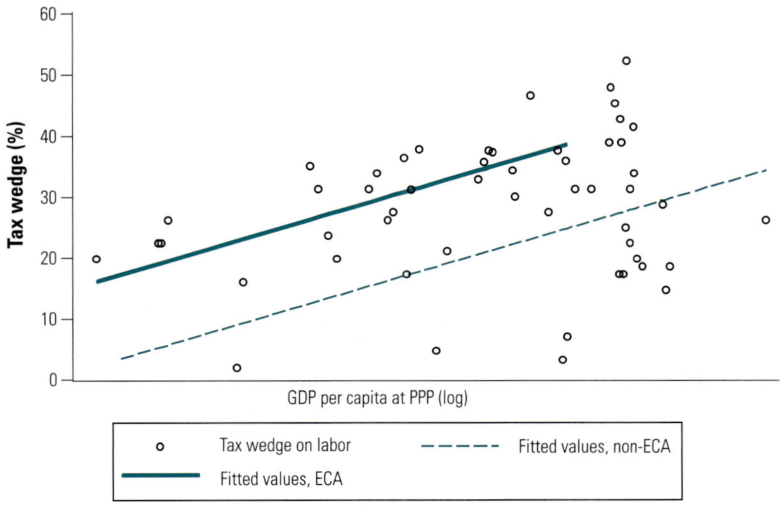

Source: World Bank for ECA; Eurostat, OECD, and World Bank for comparator countries; Bank staff calculations.

Note: PPP = Purchasing power parity.

rity contributions account for 29 to 37 percent of the gross wage. In contrast, in Thailand and Uganda they account for 11 percent and 15 percent, respectively.[8] Social security contributions in low-income ECA countries are two to three times as high (as a percentage of gross wages) as in comparator low-income countries.

More systematic confirmation that labor taxes are disproportionately high in ECA comes from regression analysis. In a simple regression of the tax wedge on log GDP per capita (at purchasing power parity), the ECA dummy variable, which represents ECA specificity, is highly significant (figure 9.3), and the mean difference in the labor tax rate is estimated at 10.9 percentage points. If one uses the typical range of estimates of employment-to-tax wedge elasticities obtained for Organisation for Economic Co-operation and Development (OECD) countries (Nickell 2003), this would correspond to a 1 to 3 percent lower rate of employment.

Several reasons could hypothetically explain a high level of labor taxes, including (a) high social security contributions to finance generous social benefits (pensions, health care, unemployment); (b) high

TABLE 9.1

Labor Taxes and Employment Outcomes in Focus Countries, 2005 or Latest Available Year

Country	Tax wedge[a]	Social security contributions rate[b]: Employer's part (%)	Social security contributions rate[b]: Employee's part (%)	Personal income tax rate[c] (%)	Labor force participation rate (%)	Employment/ population ratio[d]	Unemployment rate (%)	Memorandum: Shadow economy (% of value added)	Memorandum: GNI per capita (US$ at PPP)
ECA countries									
Albania	33.4	30.4	11.5	1.6	65.7	48.8	14.4	35.3	2,120
Armenia	38.5	22.0	15.0	10.0	61.0	52.3	9.4	49.1	1,060
Croatia	40.3	17.2	20.0	10.0	64.4	56.5	13.8	35.4	6,820
Georgia	26.7	20.0		12.0	65.0	65.1	12.6	68.0	1,060
Kyrgyz Rep.	31.6	21.0	8.0	9.2	68.8	60.9	9.9	41.2	400
Poland	43.1	20.4	25.4	6.1	63.5	54.8	19.0	28.9	6,100
Romania	44.1	32.5	17.0	8.9	62.2	65.4	8.0	37.4	2,960
Slovak Rep.	42.0	35.6	13.4	7.9	69.5	60.4	18.1	20.2	6,480
Turkey	42.7	21.5	15.0	15.4	54.7	47.6	10.3	34.3	3,750
Ukraine	39.2	38.0	3.5	12.5	67.7	59.7	8.6	54.7	1,270
Comparator countries									
Chile	30.0	0.0	12.6	—	58.7	57.4	8.0	20.9	5,220
Ireland	23.8	10.8	5.0	10.6	70.4	57.1	4.4	15.3	34,310
Korea, Rep of	17.3	9.0	7.1	2.7	65.7	64.0	3.7	28.8	14,000
Spain	38.0	30.6	6.3	12.7	69.7	62.0	11.4	22.0	21,530
Thailand	14.3	5.6	5.0	—	77.7	72.2	1.5	54.1	2,490
Uganda	13.6	10.0	5.0	—	84.5	—	3.2	45.4	250
Vietnam	16.1	12.0	6.0	0.0	80.1	—	2.1	17.9	540

Sources: EUROSTAT, ILO Laborsta, Social Security Programs Throughout the World at http://www.socialsecurity.gov/policy/docs/progdesc/ssptw/; UNICEF TransMONEE; World Bank WDI databases.

Note: — = not available.

a. The sum of social security contributions and personal income tax (effective) as percentage of total labor cost.

b. Social security contributions as percentage of gross wage.

c. Effective rate for an average worker.

d. Population of working age.

reliance on labor taxes (particularly personal income taxes) to finance overall public spending; or (c) a narrow tax base (resulting from relatively low levels of formal employment), which requires high taxes even if benefits or overall spending are more modest. Of these, high labor taxes in ECA primarily reflect the first—high levels of public spending, particularly on social security.[9] As shown in figure 9.4a, a close relationship exists between the tax wedge on labor and social expenditures as a share of GDP across a sample of OECD countries. The tax wedge on labor in ECA OECD member countries (Czech Republic, Hungary, Poland, and the Slovak Republic as well as Turkey) is even higher than the one predicted based on the level of social expenditures alone and, indeed, ECA's high tax wedge is associated with high spending overall in ECA countries (figure 9.4b). Given that the share of labor taxes in total tax revenues in EU-8 coun-

FIGURE 9.4

High Labor Taxes Driven by High Government Spending, Especially Social Expenditures

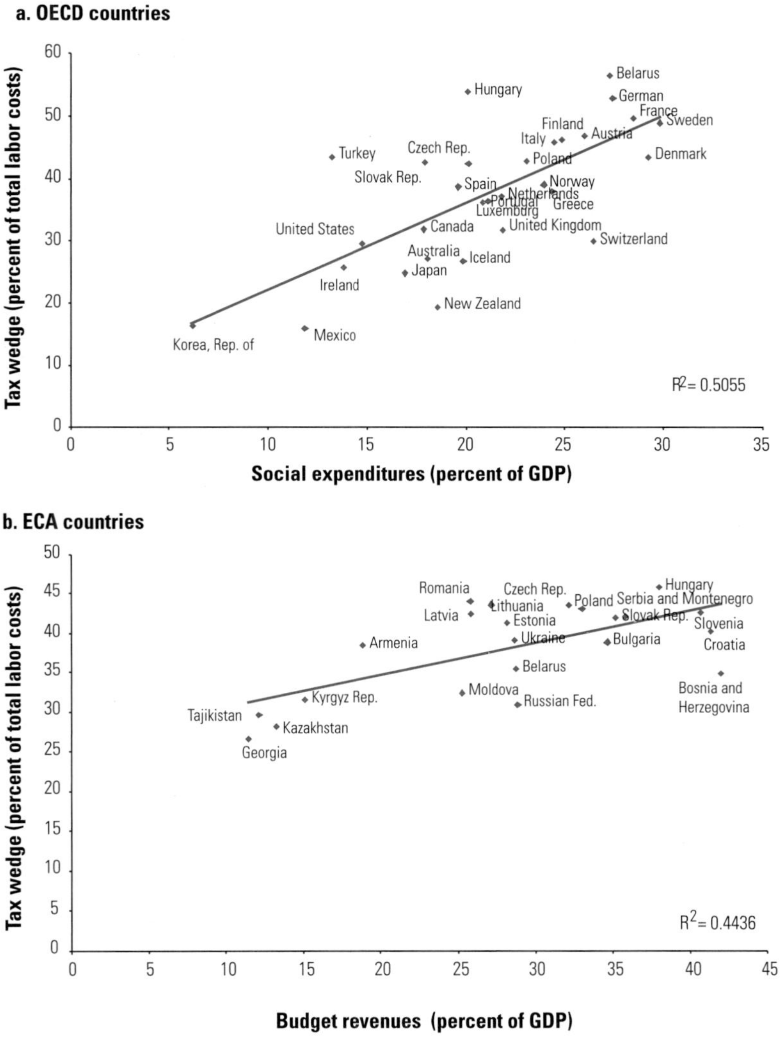

Sources: OECD data on social expenditures, www.oecd.org; Bank staff calculations

tries is not significantly higher than in the OECD overall or in the EU-15 (figure 9.5), it is likely that the high tax wedge in ECA countries is also due in part to the narrowness of the tax base (and its flip side, the significant size of the informal economy).

Social security contributions are the dominant component of labor taxes in ECA. Social security contributions (paid by both the employer

FIGURE 9.5

Reliance on Labor Taxation in EU-8, EU-15, and OECD

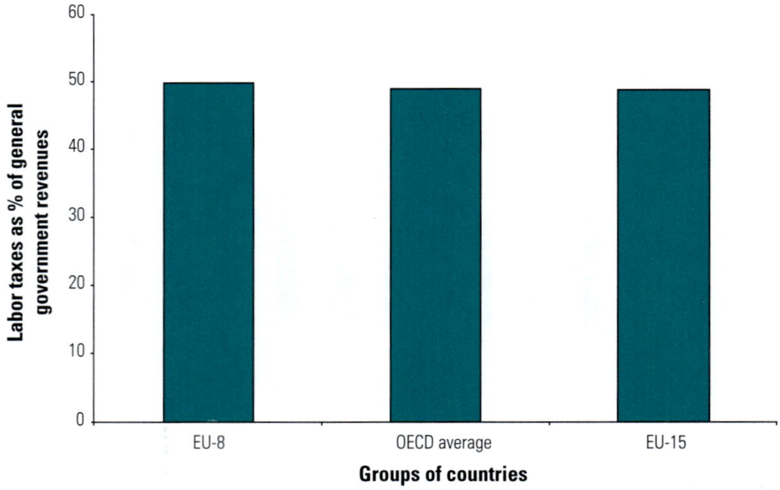

Sources: Eurostat database on Government Finance Statistics at http://epp.eurostat.ec.europa.eu for EU-8 and EU-15 countries; data are for 2004. OECD Web site for OECD countries; data are for 2005.Bank staff calculations.

Note: General government comprises central, state, and local governments, and social security funds.

and the employee) account for 77 percent of the tax wedge (figure 9.6) on average, on par with Spain and the Netherlands and significantly higher than in Ireland, the United Kingdom, and Denmark. Indeed, high personal income tax rates do not appear to be a factor behind the high tax wedge in ECA because in most ECA countries the effective personal income tax (PIT) rates are relatively low (figure 9.7).[10] In EU-11 countries, the average effective PIT rate is about 13 percent, which is 4 percentage points lower than the EU-15 average (figure 9.8). Still, the EU-11 average is higher than the PIT rate in some of the EU-15 countries, such as Ireland and the Netherlands. And the PIT rate in Korea, at about 3 percent of income, is significantly lower than in virtually all ECA countries.

Social security contributions are paid largely by the employer in ECA. Employers pay 60–70 percent of social security contributions in EU-11, Southeastern Europe (SEE) and Turkey, and 80–90 percent in low- and middle-income CIS (figure 9.9). Accordingly, employees pay only a minor part.[11] Among the comparator countries there is no clear pattern as to which party is responsible for paying social security contributions. In Ireland, Spain, and Vietnam, as in ECA, the employer pays the bulk of social security contributions. In the United

FIGURE 9.6

Share of Social Security Contributions in the Tax Wedge in ECA, 2006 or Latest Available Year

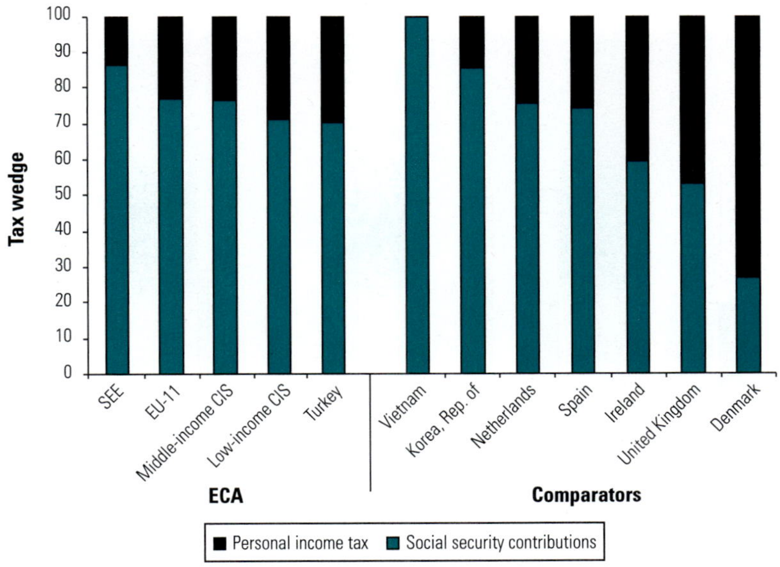

Sources: Eurostat, OECD, World Bank; Bank staff calculations.

FIGURE 9.7

Effective Personal Income Tax Rates, ECA Countries, 2006 or Latest Available Year

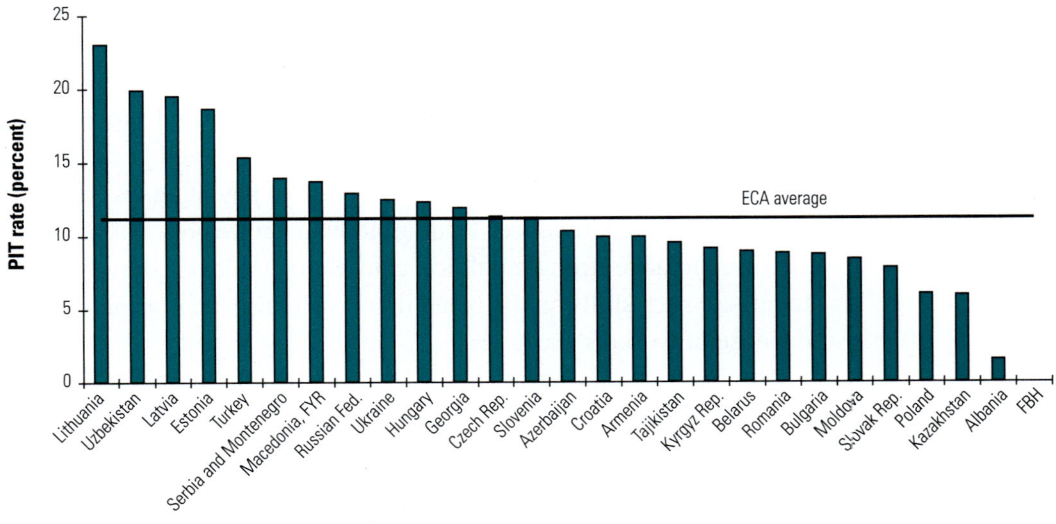

Source: World Bank.

FIGURE 9.8

Effective Personal Income Tax Rate, ECA and Comparators, 2006 or Latest Available Year

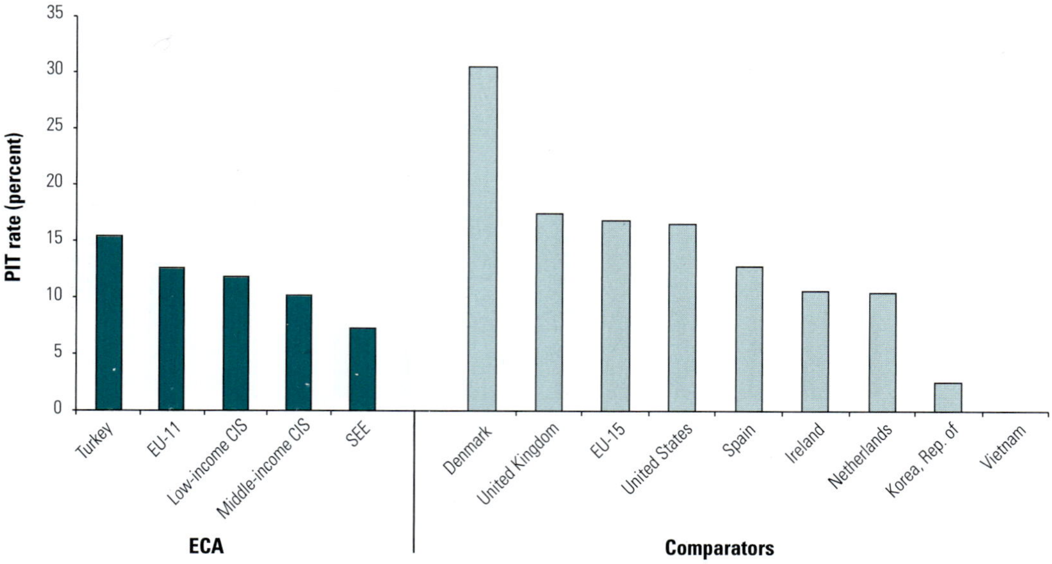

Sources: Eurostat; OECD; World Bank; Bank staff calculations.

Kingdom and Korea, the responsibility is divided approximately equally between both parties. And in the Netherlands and Denmark, the bulk of social security contributions are paid by employees.

This bias toward taxing the employer rather than the employee reflects historical legacy and political economy considerations. Under communism, state-owned enterprises paid social security contributions on behalf of their workers. The state paid for and provided all social security. This pattern has been largely preserved because it is politically difficult to shift the responsibility for paying taxes from the employer to the employee. Trade unions in the region, which often continue to have stronger political clout than employers, have tended to oppose such shifts on the belief that it will raise firms' profits at the expense of workers' earnings.

This bias toward taxation of the employer results in extremely high rates of payroll tax (that is, social security contributions paid by the employer), as shown in figure 9.10. On average, employers in ECA must add 27 percent to gross wages as social security payments. The variation across the region is substantial. Payroll taxes are particularly high in middle-income CIS and in EU-11, where they approach 30

FIGURE 9.9

Employers' and Employees' Shares in Social Security Contributions in ECA, 2006 or Latest Available Year

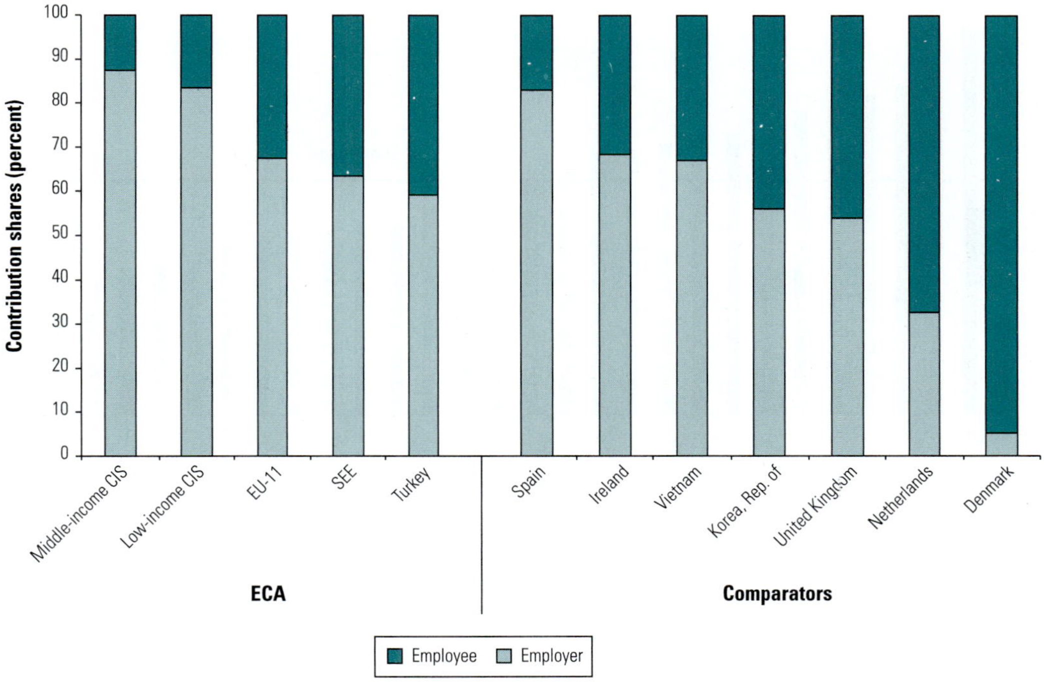

Sources: Eurostat, OECD, World Bank; Bank staff calculations.

percent. They are somewhat lower—less than 25 percent—in low-income CIS and in Turkey (figure 9.11). In Slovenia and Bosnia and Herzegovina the payroll tax rate is only about 15 percent, while in the former Yugoslav Republic of Macedonia it is as high as 45 percent (figure 9.10).[12] Among the comparator countries, only Spain's payroll tax rate is comparable to that in EU-11 and middle-income CIS, while in countries as diverse as Vietnam, Korea, the Netherlands, and Ireland it is around 10 percent (figure 9.11). Thus, the payroll tax rates in ECA are some two to three times higher than in other countries.

The three most important programs financed out of social security contributions in ECA are pension insurance, health insurance, and unemployment insurance. On average, pension contributions account for some 70 percent of all social security contributions (paid by both employers and employees), health care contributions account for slightly above 20 percent, and unemployment insurance accounts for about 7 percent (figure 9.12). Of course, the structure of social

FIGURE 9.10

Social Security Contributions Paid by Employer

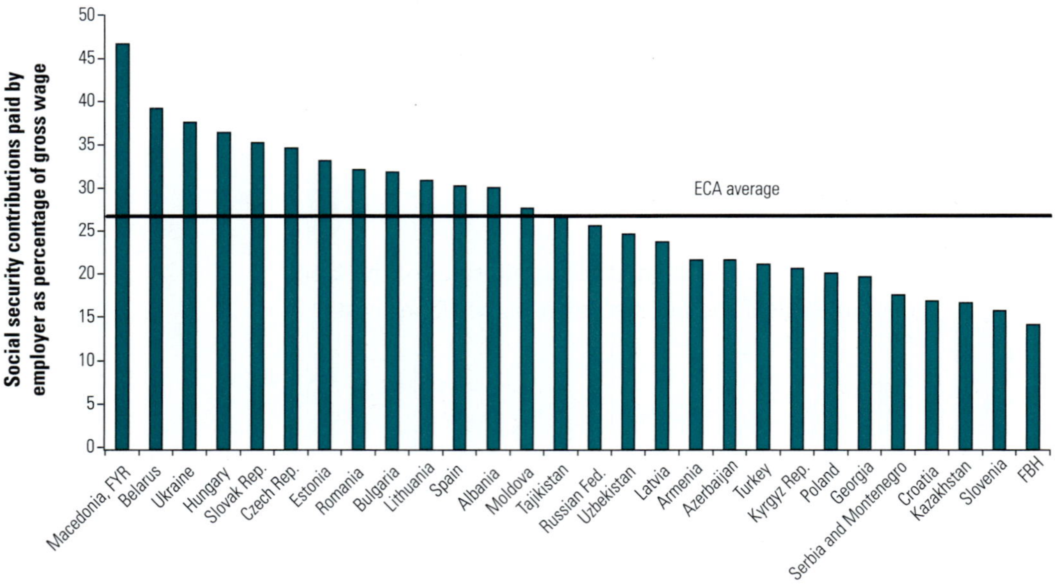

Source: World Bank.

FIGURE 9.11

Social Security Contributions Paid by Employers, ECA and Selected Comparators, 2006 or Latest Available Year

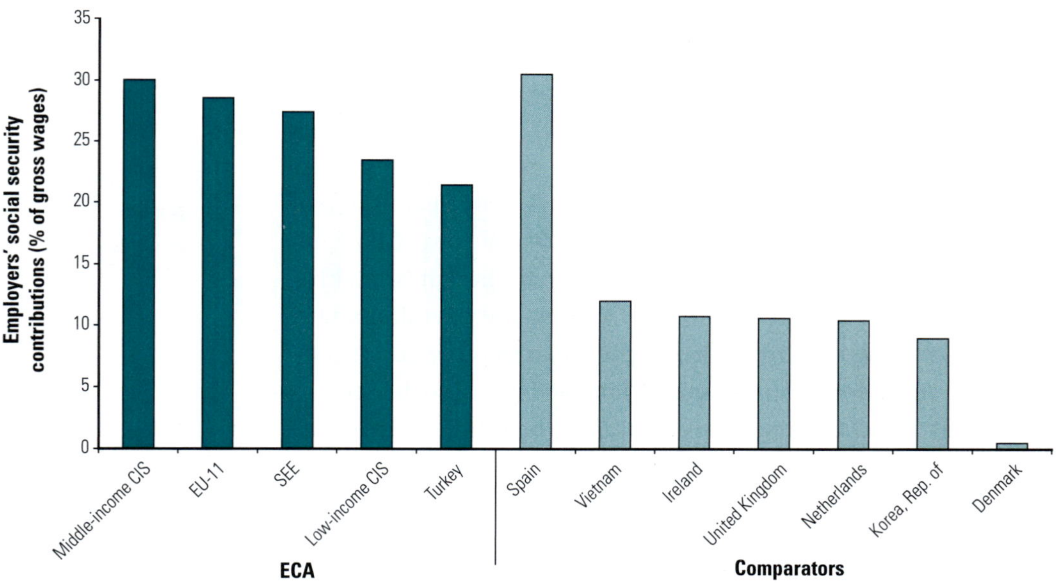

Sources: Eurostat, OECD, World Bank; Bank staff calculations.

security contributions varies substantially across countries because of demographic and systemic differences. One important factor affecting the structure of contributions is whether health care is insurance based (and thus financed out of contributions) or universal (and thus financed out of general taxation), as discussed in chapter 6.xiii

Labor Taxation, Employment, and Economic Growth: Theory and Evidence

Labor taxes affect both the demand and the supply sides of the labor market. Labor demand falls if the tax results in higher labor costs[14]—because the tax is levied on employers and they are unable to pass the increase onto workers, or because the tax is levied on workers and they are able to pass the tax on to employers and protect their real consumption wage. Labor supply falls if the tax results in a lower real consumption wage—because the tax is levied on workers and they are unable to offset it with commensurately higher wages, or it is

FIGURE 9.12
Structure of Social Security Contributions, 2006

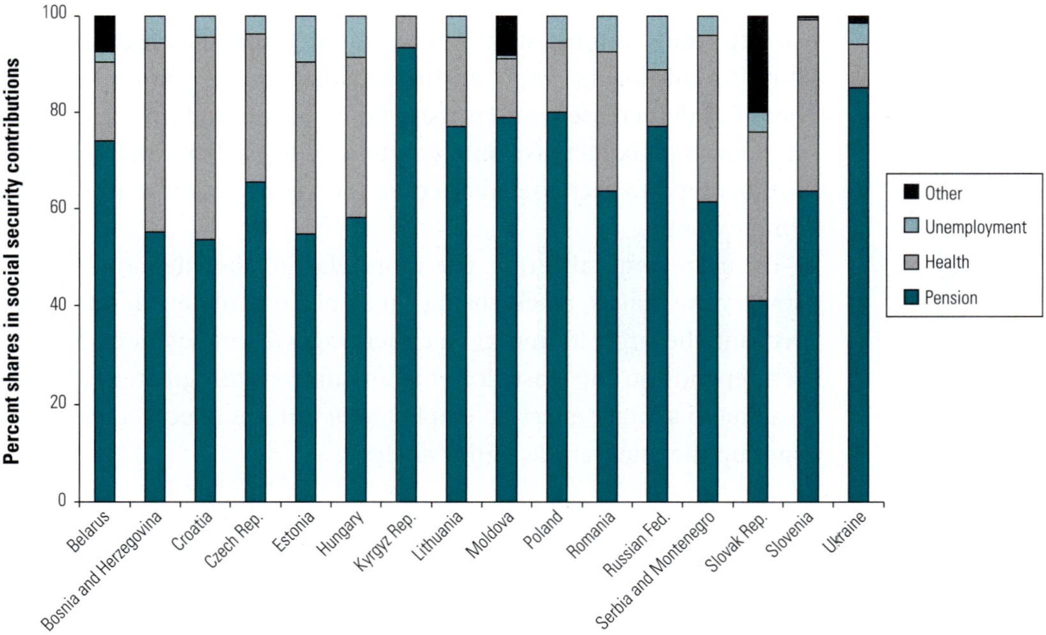

Source: World Bank.

levied on employers and they are able to shift it to workers through lower wages. The effect of the combination of the fall in labor demand and in labor supply is lower employment.

What Determines the Impact of Labor Taxes on Employment?

The employment and wage effects of labor taxes depend on two important factors: labor market conditions and labor market institutions. If job opportunities are scarce and unemployment is high, as in most ECA countries, employers' bargaining power tends to be strong, while employees' bargaining power tends to be weak. Under such conditions workers bear the burden of taxation in the form of lower wages. Even if the tax is levied on employers, they are able to shift it backward onto wages, without an increase in labor costs. The resulting fall in wages discourages labor supply and may lead to a fall in labor force participation. In contrast, when the labor market is buoyant and employers find it difficult to fill job vacancies, the bargaining power of workers is strong. Under such a scenario, employers tend to bear the burden of taxation. Even if the tax is levied on workers, they are able to pass it onto employers by claiming an offsetting pay rise. The resulting increase in the labor cost inhibits labor demand and may also cause a fall in employment.

Labor market institutions matter because they influence the relative bargaining power of employers and workers. For example, strong trade unions, strict employment protection legislation, a binding minimum wage, and the availability of unemployment benefits all increase workers' bargaining power and thus their ability to pass a tax increase onto employers. These labor market institutions tend to increase labor costs, protecting wages at the cost of employment.

In more general terms, the more elastic labor demand[15] is the smaller the impact, all else being equal, of a payroll tax on total labor cost and the larger its impact on either wages or employment. The latter depends on the elasticity of labor supply, with greater elasticity leading to a larger effect on employment but less effect on wages. To sum up the implications of this analysis,

- An increase in the tax wedge can give rise to *unemployment* as a *temporary* disequilibrium phenomenon (until wages adjust to lower demand). In contrast, it will cause a *permanent* fall in *employment* for as long as the negative labor demand shift caused by the tax increase is not offset by a commensurate positive demand shift (reflecting, for example, higher labor productivity and thus a fall in unit labor cost).

- Given that labor demand and labor supply tend to be inelastic in the short run, the employment impact of an increase in the tax wedge is likely to be limited. Most of the impact is likely to be on wage rates, and whether employers or workers will bear the brunt of wage shifts depends on the relative elasticity of labor demand and labor supply (see below). But the negative employment effect of an increase in labor tax will be larger in the longer run as firms find ways to substitute capital for (more expensive) labor.
- An increase in labor taxes will have the strongest effect on employment of worker groups for whom labor demand is most elastic. These include low-skilled workers, youth, older workers, and women. The negative employment effect will be amplified if the elasticity of labor supply of those groups is high.
- The negative employment effect of payroll taxes will be stronger if labor market regulations (such as minimum wage or unemployment benefits) or strong trade unions limit the downward wage adjustment and the tax cannot be absorbed by a commensurate fall in wages.
- In addition, an increase in labor taxes also raises the costs of formal employment relative to informal (that is, untaxed) employment, and as such may contribute to a fall in formal and an increase in informal employment. This may have important fiscal implications because larger informal employment means lower tax revenues. It may also affect economic growth because informal firms may remain suboptimally small and continue to lack access to infrastructure, credit markets, and legal institutions (de Soto 1989; Loayza, Oviedo, and Serven 2005).

What Is the Evidence?

The evidence provided by empirical studies carried out to date[16] supports the view that the size of the tax wedge has a significant effect on labor costs and employment, but evidence that labor market flexibility reduces tax wedge effects is not as strong. Nickell's review of existing studies on OECD countries concludes that "tax rates are a significant factor in explaining differences in the amount of market work undertaken by the working age population in different countries... a 10 percentage point rise in the tax wedge reduces labor input by somewhere between one and three percent of the population of working age" (Nickell 2003: 8). This is a significant although relatively small effect. For example, the difference in the tax wedge would explain around one-quarter of the overall difference in the employment rate between the United States and the big three countries of continental Europe—France, Germany, and Italy.

A recent comprehensive study by Bassanini and Duval (2006) using pooled cross-section/time series data for OECD countries over the period 1982–2003 found that a 10 percentage point reduction in the tax wedge would be associated with a drop in the unemployment rate of 2.8 percentage points. The unemployment effects of high tax wedges are found to be largest in those countries where binding minimum wage floors prevent tax shifting to workers.

The literature blames higher labor taxes not only for an increase in European unemployment but also for a slowdown in economic growth. This strong message emerges from an influential article by Daveri and Tabellini, who argue that "if wages are set by strong and decentralized trade unions, an increase in labor taxes is shifted onto higher real wages. This has two effects: First, it reduces labor demand, and thus creates unemployment. Secondly, as firms substitute capital for labor, the marginal product of capital falls; over long periods of time this in turn diminishes the incentive to invest and growth" (Daveri and Tabellini 2000: 48). According to their estimates, the observed rise of 14 percentage points in labor taxes between 1965 and 1995 in the EU could account for a rise in EU unemployment of roughly 4 percentage points, a reduction of the investment share of output of about 3 percentage points, and a growth slowdown of about 0.4 percentage points a year.[17]

The literature for ECA countries is limited. However, a recent World Bank study on Turkey (Betcherman and Pagés 2007) concludes that labor tax cuts would not have a major impact on formal employment. An across-the-board reduction of 5 percentage points in pension contributions paid by employers would bring about a 0.8 percent increase in employment overall and would reduce the unemployment rate by about 0.2–0.3 percentage points. The effect would be stronger—an increase in employment of almost 1.5 percent—if the reduction in pension contributions were targeted at workers younger than 30 years old, who have less bargaining power to capture most of the tax reduction in higher wages. Some studies hint that there may be an asymmetric reaction to changes in labor tax rates, with an increase in the tax wedge leading to employment reduction but a decrease leading more to wage growth because wages may be more rigid downward than upward (World Bank 2005b). In Chile, for example, payroll taxes were reduced dramatically, around 25 percentage points, from 1979 to 1986, but the reduction was fully trans-

BOX 9.2

Chile: Social Security Reform and the Incidence of Payroll Taxation

In 1981, Chile began to phase out its "traditional" state-run pay-as-you-go social security system financed by employees and their employers in favor of mandatory individual private accounts. Beginning in 1983, wage earners and salaried employees entering the work force were no longer covered by the old system and were instead required to pay a proportion of their earnings to a private pension fund of their choice. Workers under the old system were given the choice of joining the new system or remaining in the old one. However, if they stayed in the old system they would be responsible for paying the full share of the payroll tax (with no employer contributions).

As part of the transition to the new system, employers were required to increase workers' wages and salaries by about 18 percent at the time the new system went into effect. The employers' burden in paying these higher wages and salaries was ameliorated by the elimination of the employer share of the payroll tax, and workers under the old system did not see any reduction in their pay when they picked up the employers' former share of the payroll tax. The new employee contribution rate, 12.6 percent, was much lower than the combined employer-employee payroll tax it replaced.

However, this sharp reduction in the payroll tax burden on Chilean firms had no effect on employment. The elimination of the employer social security contributions did not lower labor costs but was fully offset by higher wages. As put by Gruber who analyzed a large sample of manufacturing firms in Chile over the 1979–1986 period "the shift in financing of social insurance in Chile in the early 1980s did not have important consequences for labor market efficiency. The reduced costs of payroll taxation to firms appear to have been fully passed on to workers in the form of higher wages, with little effect on employment levels" (Gruber 1995: 26–27).

Source: http://www.natlaw.com/pubs/spchlb1.htm; Gruber 1995.

lated into higher wages with no employment effect (box 9.2). In contrast, a 10 percent increase in payroll taxes in Colombia in the late 1980s and early 1990s resulted in a 1.4–2.3 percent decrease in net wages and a 4–5 percent reduction in employment (Kugler and Kugler 2003).[18]

Finally, there is evidence that higher labor taxes are associated with larger shadow economies for countries at similar levels of per capita income. Regressions on a rich country sample (14 countries) in the mid-1990s indicated that a unit standard deviation tax difference of 12.8 percentage points is associated with, among other things, a rise in the shadow economy of 3.8 percent of GDP, which corresponds to a 24 percent increase in the size of the shadow economy evaluated at the mean (Davis and Henrekson 2004).

Many factors besides tax rates, including cultural factors, corruption, and enforcement capacity, clearly also affect the level of informality. Economic development has historically involved a gradual shift from informal into formal employment as well as an increase in the size of government coupled with increasing tax rates. Thus, many high-income OECD countries combine high tax rates with a relatively low incidence of undeclared work (OECD 2004). In a sample of 69 developing and developed countries, higher tax rates are associated with lower—not higher—unofficial activity as a percentage of GDP (Friedman et al. 2000). Furthermore, administrative capacity and governance also matter. A comparison of tax rates and the extent of tax evasion between the Czech Republic and the Slovak Republic, for example, led to the conclusion that "the most important determinant of tax evasion ... is not a divergence between tax rates, but rather the difference in opportunities for tax evasion in each country" (Hanousek and Palda 2003).

Empirical analysis undertaken for this study confirms that higher labor taxes have a negative impact on total employment. As seen in figure 9.13, the average labor force participation rate in ECA countries where the tax wedge is highest (top quartile) is almost 5 per-

FIGURE 9.13
Labor Force Participation Rate by Quartiles of Tax Wedge, ECA, 2004

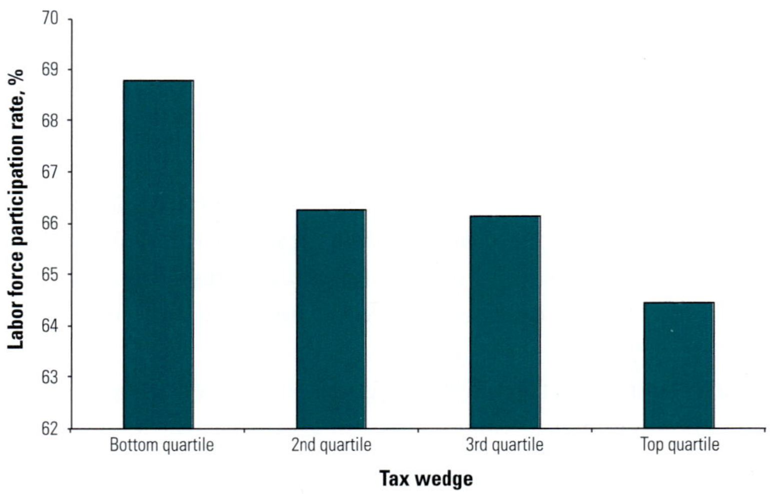

Source: World Bank.

centage points lower than in those countries where the tax wedge is the lowest (bottom quartile).[19] Holding other relevant variables constant, a higher tax wedge is clearly associated with lower labor force participation rates and lower employment-to-population ratios (annex 9B table 9B.2 A). Specifically, a 1 percentage point increase in the tax wedge is estimated to result in a 0.3–0.6 percentage point drop in both the labor force participation rate and the employment-to-population ratio in ECA.[20] If the tax wedge were reduced by 5 percentage points (roughly one standard deviation), say from 44 percent (as in Romania) to 39 percent (as in Bulgaria), this would be expected to result in a 2.3 percentage point increase in the labor force participation rate.[21] This result is in line with those obtained for the OECD countries using better data and more advanced econometric techniques (Nickell 2003). Box 9.3 discusses measurement issues associated with identifying the relationship between the tax wedge and employment in transition economies.

Furthermore, the analysis provides evidence that labor market flexibility may mitigate the negative employment effect of labor taxes. As indicated earlier, the tax wedge is expected to have a stronger negative impact on employment in more rigid labor markets, where wages are slow to adjust to downward shifts in labor demand because of, for example, strict employment protection or a high minimum wage. The results suggest that high firing costs may aggravate the effect of the tax wedge on the labor force participation rate, while a high minimum wage may amplify the negative impact of the tax wedge on the employment-to-population ratio in ECA. However, these results should be subject to further verification using better data and more advanced techniques, especially because a more thorough analysis for a larger sample of OECD countries failed to produce strong evidence in favor of the hypothesis that flexibility reduces tax wedge effects (Nickell 2003).

Additional evidence on a detrimental effect of the tax wedge on employment comes from a pooled cross-section time-series regression for the eight new EU member states (annex 9B, table 9B.1).[22] The results suggest that an increase in the tax wedge has slowed down employment growth from what it otherwise might be given prevailing GDP growth. The effect is significant and its magnitude quite large: a 1 percentage point increase in the tax wedge led to a 0.5 percentage point decrease in the employment growth rate. Several caveats are in order, however. First, this result may be somewhat biased because other potentially important determinants of employment growth were not included in the regression equation (such as labor saving technological progress and other sources of

BOX 9.3

Tax Wedge and Employment Measurement Problems

Correct identification of the relationship between the tax wedge and employment outcomes assumes that the latter are properly measured. However, constructing an accurate employment measure is difficult, especially in the context of transition. The first issue involves data. Ideally, a measure of formal employment would be used because this is the type of employment that is affected by taxes on labor. However, available data as a rule refer to total (formal and informal) employment because employment data published by the International Labour Organization (the only source of consistent labor market information) come from Labor Force Surveys, which by design measure total employment. To the extent that the tax wedge affects the distribution of employment between the formal and informal sectors rather than total employment, using the total employment measure as a dependent variable will bias the results toward insignificance.

The transitional nature of labor markets in ECA also complicates the analysis. Apparently favorable employment outcomes in some CIS countries, such as Moldova or Ukraine, may instead be a symptom of delayed enterprise restructuring. While open unemployment may be low, hidden unemployment is large because labor is underutilized in unprofitable enterprises. More open unemployment will emerge once enterprise restructuring accelerates. However, high open unemployment in some EU-8 countries, such as Poland or the Slovak Republic, may be a sign of intensive enterprise restructuring and associated gains in labor productivity. Eventually firms will translate these gains in productivity into investment and employment growth; the first signs of this process are already noticeable. Because labor markets are in transition, regressions using outcomes to date as a dependent variable may produce biased results.

Source: Author.

productivity gains). Second, the analysis covers a period of intensive enterprise restructuring and shedding of redundant labor, and it is uncertain to what extent the results would carry over to a more steady-state situation.[23] Finally, it is uncertain to what extent the results are valid for the whole ECA region given its heterogeneity. Results obtained for the developed, mostly urban, and formal economies of EU-8 countries may not hold for the significantly less developed, largely rural, and informal economies of low-income CIS countries.

Past studies have shown that the employment of less skilled workers appears to be more sensitive to changes in the tax wedge than that of more skilled workers. Góra et al. (2006), using panel regressions for a sample of 27 OECD countries (including EU-8 countries) for two years (1997 and 2003), found that the tax wedge has a statistically significant and strong negative effect on the employment rate of unskilled prime-age male workers, but no effect on that of skilled workers. Data were not sufficient to test this hypothesis ECA-wide.[24]

Finally, the regression analysis does not support the notion that payroll taxes paid by the employer are more detrimental to employment than taxes paid by the employee. In both cases the effect on labor force participation is negative (with regression coefficients around -0.2), although not always statistically significant. The impact and true incidence of the tax does not appear to depend on who is formally liable to pay it, which is in line with theoretical expectations.[25]

Policy Options

How can countries limit the negative impact of labor taxes on employment? Focus should be placed on reducing social security contributions because they represent the dominant part of the tax wedge. There are three main ways to lower social security contributions:

- *Improve the efficiency of the social security system by tightening eligibility, limiting system abuse, strengthening revenue collection, and curbing informality.* In most ECA countries there is substantial room to improve the efficiency of the social security systems by limiting leakages. Areas where significant economies are possible include early retirement programs, disability pensions, and sickness benefits.[26] There is less room to reform unemployment benefit programs (World Bank 2005a).[27] According to some estimates, if there were no early retirement schemes in Poland, social security contributions could be reduced by one-third (Góra 2006), and if expenditures on disability pensions were reduced to the average OECD level, the rate of social security contributions could be reduced by an additional percentage point
- *Limit the insurance-based portion of the social protection system by moving more to tax-financed universal benefits.* The principal way of doing so is to move some benefits from the insurance system to the universal system and, accordingly, to fund them with general revenues rather than payroll taxes. Examples include family and maternity benefits, health care (as discussed in chapter 6), flat rate

social pensions (as discussed in chapter 7), flat rate unemployment benefits, and services to the unemployed.

- *Reduce social security contributions, particularly for workers for whom the elasticity of labor demand is relatively high and the pass-through effect (whereby lower contributions are captured through higher wages) is limited.* Payroll tax reductions (or hiring subsidies) targeted at low-skilled workers and youth, who are most hit by unemployment, might improve their employment chances by lowering their cost to employers. Such targeted reductions (or subsidies) may also be efficient in terms of how much fiscal "cost" is required to achieve a desired increase in employment. Because both the elasticity of labor demand (Hamermesh 1993) and the elasticity of labor supply (Davis and Henrekson 2004) are higher for less skilled than for more skilled workers, a change in the after-tax wage will elicit a stronger demand or supply response (depending on whether the employer or the employee benefits from the tax rate reduction). Evidence suggests that low-skilled workers are less likely to capture the tax cut through higher wages (Betcherman and Pagés 2007), implying that the primary impact is likely to be through greater labor demand.

Targeted tax reductions have been implemented in a number of countries, including Belgium, France, and the Netherlands. France introduced payroll tax subsidies in 1993 and the system is still in place in a modified form. The program provides payroll tax exemptions for low-wage workers according to a sliding scale up to a threshold of 1.33 times the minimum wage, when the subsidy is stopped. The maximum exemption is 18.2 percentage points in employer's payroll tax for minimum wage workers. Crépon and Desplatz (2002) estimated that each reduction in labor cost of 1 percentage point led to a rise in employment of 1.6 percent in manufacturing and 1.8 percent in nonmanufacturing, and the unskilled labor content increased substantially. These changes in employment were due to two effects: substitution between factors of production—as less skilled labor was substituted for more skilled labor and capital—and expanded profitability and output (because reduced labor costs enabled firms to lower prices and thus boost demand). More generally, evaluations of different payroll tax reduction programs show that they can have a significant positive effect on the employment of unskilled workers, but often at a high fiscal cost (see OECD, 2004, table 3.2, p. 124 for examples of reductions in social insurance contributions for low-paid jobs).

Such programs also have weaknesses, however. First, they generate significant deadweight losses when subsidies are received by firms that would hire additional workers anyway without the subsidy (OECD 2003b).[28] Moreover, targeted employment subsidies tend to help targeted groups find jobs largely at the expense of other groups of workers. Such substitution effects significantly limit the impact of targeted subsidy programs on overall employment (OECD 2003b). In addition, these programs can create low-pay "traps" as payroll tax reductions for low-paid jobs make the tax system more progressive and it becomes more expensive for companies to award wage increases at the bottom of the wage ladder (OECD 2003b). Indeed, the programs may carry a stigma or additional administrative restrictions that lead to a low take-up rate among employers.[29] Finally, tax cuts targeted at low-paid workers may entail implementation difficulties because they encourage underreporting of wages so as to benefit from the tax credit. This underreporting may increase the fiscal cost of the subsidies still further.

Despite these disadvantages, a narrowly targeted scheme may prove to be an efficient way of improving employment chances of disadvantaged worker groups in some ECA settings. High unemployment and high labor demand and supply elasticities among the youth and the low-skilled makes these two groups obvious targets. Thus, one option is to target a reduction in social security contributions to low-paid workers, for example, those earning up to 1.3 times the minimum wage (possibly using a sliding scale). Another option is to target it to workers below a certain age limit, such as 25 years old. However, the programs need to be carefully designed and provide for both ex ante assessment of associated fiscal costs and ex post evaluation of their effects on employment among the target groups.

Many ECA countries have adopted the options outlined above. For example, in Poland in the early 2000s, the family benefit was moved out of the social insurance system and began to be financed out of general taxation rather than social insurance contributions. Similarly, Bulgaria began to finance active labor market policies from the general budget rather than the contribution-financed Employment Fund. Further examples of social security reforms for ECA focus countries are contained in box 9.4.

In closing, it is important to point out that changes in the structure of taxation, if not accompanied by a reduction in the overall tax burden, can be expected to bring about only modest improvement in employment outcomes. As the OECD *Jobs Study* (1994: 275) remarks, "Changes in the mix of taxes by which government raises revenues can be expected, at most, to have a limited effect on unemployment".[30] A similar view is presented in the recent survey of evidence on labor taxes and unemployment by Daveri (2002) who writes, "we should not expect much employment gain from reductions in labor taxation when the overall tax burden stays unchanged. In other words ... the structure of taxation does not appear to matter very much" (p. 14).[31] This takes us back full circle to chapters 2 and 3, which discuss the impact of the overall size of government on economic growth. To achieve and sustain long-term growth, the basic message of this chapter—and of this study overall—is that governments need to strive for a reasonable role for government, reflected in a modest tax take and structures of public spending in general, and social benefits in particular, that are compatible with that level of taxation.

BOX 9.4

Reduction of the Tax Wedge in ECA

In recent years many ECA countries have undertaken reforms of their social security systems with an explicit aim of reducing the tax wedge on labor and improving labor market incentives. Examples of reforms in selected ECA focus countries are presented below.

Albania. In 2006, Albania reduced social security contributions by 9 percentage points, including a 6 percentage point reduction in pension contributions (to 23.5 percent) and a 3 percentage point reduction in unemployment insurance (to 2 percent). If the impact of these reforms—an increase in formal employment—proves positive, the government also plans to reduce health insurance contributions (currently at 3.4 percent). The cut in contributions was coupled with a substantial rise in pensions (20 percent for rural and 5 percent for urban pensions). The government is prepared to cover any emerging deficit, which will mean a partial switch from a contribution-financed to a general revenue–financed system.

Armenia. A major problem of the social security system in Armenia, as in many low-income countries, is ineffective revenue collection due to poor administrative capacity. To address this problem the administration of social security contributions was moved from the social security system to general tax administration, whose tax collection capacity is better developed. The effect of this administrative change was significant: in 2005, when the reform was implemented, social security payments increased by 34 percent (compared with nominal GDP growth of 18 percent). This example demonstrates that the efficiency of the social security system can be greatly enhanced by improvements in administration, in particular more effective collection of contributions.

(continued)

BOX 9.4 (continued)

Croatia. Croatia has gradually reduced the tax wedge on labor from an extremely high to a more moderate level through a substantial reduction in both social security contributions and PIT rates. In 1994 the tax wedge accounted for almost 53 percent of total labor costs—much above the already high ECA average. At the same time labor force participation was low and unemployment high. To improve both labor demand and labor supply, the government initiated a gradual reduction in labor taxes. Over time the wedge was reduced to about 40 percent, still high but much lower than 10 years earlier. Social security contributions paid by the employer were reduced by 5.8 percentage points over 10 years (from 23 percent of gross wage in 1994 to 17.2 percent in 2004), whereas those paid by the employee were reduced by 4.4 percentage points (from 24.4 percent in 1994 to 20 percent in 2004). Simultaneously, the effective PIT rate (for a worker at the average wage) was cut by 7.8 percentage points (from 17.8 percent in 1994 to 10 percent in 2004). In 2004 the pension contribution accounted for 20 percent of worker gross wage and was paid only by the employee, whereas in 1994 it had accounted for 27 percent of gross wage and was split evenly between the employer and the employee. The benefit replacement rate for pensions fell from 75 percent in 1990 to 46 percent in 2005 through stricter eligibility conditions (extended retirement age, increased decrement for early retirement, extension of the calculation period), and health insurance for pensioners was moved from payroll to general taxation. Moreover, the reduction in the contribution rates was financed by the widening of the contribution base and by improving compliance (Anusic, O'Keefe, and Madzarevic-Sujster 2003). A further 2.5 percentage point reduction in social security contributions was achieved by moving the child benefit out of the social insurance system and switching to general tax financing. There has been no reduction in the health insurance contribution rate (15 percent of gross wage), although currently it is paid only by the employer, whereas in 1994 it was split evenly between both parties. Similarly, unemployment insurance (1.7 percent) was not reduced, but it is currently paid only by the employer, with the total rate unchanged. Overall, Croatia has maintained a roughly even split between the employer and employee share in social security contributions, in contrast to most ECA countries where social security contributions are still largely paid by the employer.

Georgia. In 2004, Georgia simplified and consolidated its social security system and introduced a unified 20 percent social security contribution paid only by the employer. The reform entailed a 3 percentage point reduction in the total social security contribution rate (including the elimination of 1 percent unemployment insurance contribution paid by the employee) and the replacement of a range of different contributions (pension, health, unemployment) by a single one. The reduction in the social security contribution rate was coupled with measures to improve the efficiency of the system. Nonetheless, the social security system requires budgetary transfers to cover the gap between expenditures and revenues. In addition to lower tax rates, a substantial liberalization of the labor code, which went into effect in 2006, enticed many firms to move from the informal to the formal sector. As a result social security revenues have increased.

(continued)

BOX 9.4 (continued)

Kyrgyz Republic. In 2005, the Kyrgyz Republic moved away from contribution financing to general tax financing of unemployment and other social security benefits (but not pensions). The Employment Fund and the Social Insurance Fund were eliminated, and the responsibility for paying the relevant benefits was taken over by the government budget. This allowed the government to lower the rate of social security contributions paid by the employer from 25 to 23 percent. The rate paid by the employee remained unchanged at 8 percent.

Romania. Recently initiated reforms of the social security system in Romania consist of two elements: reducing payroll tax rates (social security contribution paid by employers) and switching to financing of some benefits by general taxation rather than by payroll taxes. Given that reductions refer only to contributions paid by the employer, an additional effect of the reform will be a somewhat more balanced distribution of contributions between the employer and the employee. Specifically, the payroll tax rate in 2007 is expected to be 3.25 percentage points lower than in 2005. This reduction consists of a 2.25 percentage point cut in pension contributions, a 0.25 percentage point cut in health insurance, and a 0.75 percentage point cut in unemployment insurance. As a result, the employer social security contribution rate will be lowered to 28.5 percent, whereas that of the employee will remain at 17 percent of the gross wage.

Source: World Bank.

Annex 9A Labor Taxes in ECA, 2006

TABLE 9A.1

Labor Taxes in ECA, 2006

	Tax wedge[a]	Social security contributions		Personal income tax[b]
		Employer's part	Employee's part	
Albania	33.4	30.4	11.5	1.6
Armenia	38.5	22.0	15.0	10.0
Azerbaijan	29.8	22.0	4.0	10.4
Belarus	35.5	39.6	1.0	9.0
Bosnia and Herzegovina (FBH)	34.9	14.5	25.5	0
Bulgaria	39.0	32.2	10.5	8.8
Croatia	40.3	17.2	20.0	10.0
Czech Republic	43.6	35.0	12.5	11.4
Estonia	41.4	33.5	3.0	18.7
Georgia	26.7	20.0	0	12.0
Hungary	45.8	36.8	13.5	12.4
Kazakhstan	28.2	17.0	10.0	6.0
Kyrgyz Republic	31.6	21.0	8.0	9.2
Latvia	42.5	24.1	9.0	19.6
Lithuania	43.7	31.2	3.0	23.1
Macedonia, FYR	41.4	47.1	0	13.8
Moldova	32.4	28.0	5.0	8.5
Poland	43.1	20.4	25.4	6.1
Romania	44.1	32.5	17.0	8.9
Russian Federation	31.0	26.0	0	13.0
Serbia and Montenegro (Serbia)	42.2	17.9	17.9	14.0
Slovak Republic	42.0	35.6	13.4	7.9
Slovenia	42.6	16.1	22.1	11.3
Tajikistan	29.6	27.0	1.0	9.6
Turkey	42.7	21.5	15.0	15.4
Ukraine	39.2	38.0	3.5	12.5
Uzbekistan	38.0	25.0	2.5	20.0

Source: World Bank and Eurostat for EU-8 countries. Bank staff calculations.

Note: FBH = Federation of Bosnia and Herzegovina, which is one of two entities that constitute Bosnia and Herzegovina. The other entity, Republika Srpska, is not covered in this table b/c data are not available.

a. The tax wedge is calculated as a sum of social security contributions paid by the employer and the employee and the personal income tax expressed as a percentage of total labor cost. Total labor cost is gross wage plus employers' social security contributions. Gross wage is net wage plus employee's social security contributions and the personal income tax.

b. Data refer to effective rates on average wage.[[AU: What is this note supposed to be attached to?]] [note b) added to "personal income tax" in last column]

TABLE 9A.2

Panel Regression Results (Fixed Effects): Tax Wedge on Labor Slows Down Employment Growth in EU-8 Countries, 1996–2003

Variable	Coefficient	Standard error	t-Statistic	Prob.
GDP growth rate	0.425504	0.154645	2.751481	0.0076
Tax wedge	-0.531383	0.290770	-1.827498	0.0719
Fixed effects				
R-squared	0.238370	Mean dependent variable		-0.002334
Adjusted R-squared	0.109037	S.D. dependent variable		0.026545
S.E. of regression	0.025056	Sum squared resid		0.033275
F-statistic	16.58761	Durbin-Watson stat		1.886317

Source: Góra et al. 2006.
Note: The sample covers EU-8 countries during the period 1996–2003 resulting in 63 total panel observations.

Annex 9B Results of Regression Analysis

Regression analysis allows one to determine a separate impact of an independent, or "focus," variable (here the tax wedge) on the dependent variable (here different measures of employment outcomes), controlling for the effects of other independent or "conditioning" variables. For this exercise two sets of independent variables were chosen based on economic theory and earlier studies on the employment effects of labor taxes (Nickell [2003] contains a summary). The first set concerns economic structure and growth, including GDP growth, GDP per capita, share of agriculture, size of shadow economy, and quality of governance as measured by a corruption index. The second concerns labor market institutions, including employment rigidity, firing costs, and the minimum wage. One key question is whether the relationship between employment outcomes and the tax wedge is robust or fragile to alterations in the independent variables (Levine and Renelt 1991). We found that the relationship is reasonably robust in that it remains with the theoretically predicted sign and is statistically significant in most specifications. Moreover, the coefficient on the dependent variable—the tax wedge—changes within reasonable limits across specifications.

As a rule, a theoretical variable (for example, labor market flexibility) can be measured in many different ways and can be proxied by an array of indicators. In such cases we experimented with different available indicators (employment rigidity index, firing costs index, severance pay from the Doing Business database, for instance) and chose the one that performed best in the regression analysis (was of the theoretically predicted sign and most significant). Specification 1 uses the full set of available control variables, while specification 2

TABLE 9B.1

Regression Results: All Else Equal, High Tax Wedge IS Associated with Worse Employment Outcomes in ECA Countries

A. Dependent variable: labor force participation rate

	Specification			
Explanatory variables	(1)	(2)	(3)	(4)
Tax wedge on labor	-0.573 *	-0.563 **	-0.325	-0.274
	0.075	0.017	0.554	0.267
Economic structure and growth				
GDP per capita	0.001	0.001 **	0.001 **	0.001 **
	0.331	0.044	0.036	0.027
Agriculture (share in value added)	-0.041	-0.042	-0.088	-0.090
	0.776	0.754	0.602	0.561
Informal economy (share in value added)	-0.001			
	0.998			
Corruption index	0.108			
	0.949			
GDP growth rate	0.195	0.183	0.235	0.203
	0.804	0.699	0.645	0.655
Labor market flexibility				
Firing cost (weeks of wages)	-0.064	-0.063	0.584	0.585
	0.257	0.211	0.134	0.109
Minimum wage (% of average wage)	0.009		-0.033	
	0.907		0.948	
Interactions: tax wedge and labor market flexibility				
Firing cost x tax wedge			-0.016 *	-0.016 *
			0.082	0.063
Minimum wage x tax wedge			0.001	
			0.924	
Constant	85.317	85.518	75.521	74.447
	0.000	0.000	0.000	0.000
Observations	27	27	27	27
F-statistics	2.67	3.92	9.08	12.2
R-squared	0.353	0.352	0.425	0.424

Source: Bank staff calculations.

Note: Regressions with robust standard errors. P-values below coefficients. * Significant at 10 percent level. ** Significant at 5 percent level. *** Significant at 1 percent level.

omits variables without the correct sign or significance. Specifications 3 and 4 add interaction terms between the tax wedge and labor market variables assumed to mediate the impact of the tax wedge on employment.

Our analysis has a number of limitations, including small sample size and unavailability of data for some potentially important variables, such as union bargaining power (union density, bargaining coverage) and the bargaining structure (centralized versus decentralized bargaining). The use of cross-section data means that we did not control for unobservable country specific characteristics (so-called fixed effects) that may be behind differences in employment outcomes. Many variables, in particular the more qualitative ones such as the quality of governance or the extent of employment protection, are susceptible to considerable measurement error. Finally, some results, particularly regarding informality, may be affected by reverse causality (endogeneity). A high tax wedge encourages informality, but informality may in turn drive the tax wedge.

To conclude, we found a robust association between the tax wedge and labor force participation rates across ECA countries. Because of data limitations these results should be viewed as tentative and subject to further verification.

Notes

1. An increase in labor taxes can also affect economic growth through a more indirect channel. To the extent an increase in the tax wedge gives rise to higher labor costs (for example, in the presence of strong unions) firms are induced to substitute capital for labor. This leads to a fall in the marginal product of capital, which over long periods diminishes the incentive to invest and to grow (Daveri and Tabellini 2000).
2. This study on labor taxation is the first one that covers the entire ECA region. Most existing empirical work is limited to OECD countries (Daveri and Tabellini 2000; Nickell 2003; OECD 1995). Studies on labor taxation in ECA are few and are limited to eight new EU member states (EU-8) (World Bank 2005b; Vork et al. 2007). A few studies focus on selected ECA countries: Dolenc and Vodopivec (2005) examine the effects of the tax wedge in Slovenia, Gora et al. (2006) in Poland, and Betcherman and Pagés (2007) in Turkey.
3. Information on various components of labor taxes and contributions is not available on a regular basis for most ECA countries. Data on employment outcomes are also incomplete and not always comparable, as is information on labor market institutions, which condition the impact of the tax wedge on employment outcomes. These data deficiencies limit the scope of the analysis and the conclusions that can be drawn from it.

Accordingly, the findings presented in this chapter should be treated as tentative and subject to further, more thorough tests.

4. The evidence on the correlation between the tax wedge and employment outcomes in ECA provided in the chapter should be regarded as tentative because of the transitional nature of labor markets in ECA (employment outcomes may not be in equilibrium), the short period of observation, and data limitations (for example, lack of information on potentially important control variables reflecting the heterogeneity of ECA's economic structures).
5. The median in ECA is 39.2 percent (Ukraine), and the unweighted arithmetic mean is 37.8 percent. The tax wedge was estimated based on nominal rates of social security contributions. These rates may differ from actual ones if wages are underreported. Informality in wage payments is widespread in some ECA countries, which means that the nominal tax rates overestimate the actual tax rates on wages. However, the underreporting of wages is caused exactly by the high nominal tax rates. Hence, the nominal rates are important for understanding the behavior of firms and workers and thus labor market dynamics.
6. The EU-11 comprise new EU member states, known as EU-10 (Bulgaria, Czech Republic, Estonia, Hungary, Latvia, Lithuania, Poland, Romania, the Slovak Republic, and Slovenia) and Croatia, which is an EU accession country.
7. The median tax wedge in ECA is higher than the tax wedge in some EU-15 countries such as the Netherlands, a developed welfare state. The EU-15 comprises Austria, Belgium, Denmark, Finland, France, Germany, Greece, Ireland, Italy, Luxembourg, the Netherlands, Portugal, Spain, Sweden, and the United Kingdom.
8. In Thailand, social security contributions are also paid by the government on behalf of employees (2.5 percent of gross wages).
9. High social security spending in ECA countries results mainly from wide coverage and often lax eligibility criteria, rather than from a high level of benefits. Old-age pensions (the main social security item) are a good example. High pension spending largely reflects the high coverage rate and the low actual (and nominal) retirement age, and not necessarily high pension benefits (see chapter 7).
10. The Baltic states (Estonia, Latvia, and Lithuania) and Uzbekistan are notable exceptions, with the PIT rate close to or above the EU-15 average.
11. Here we are looking at what party (the employer or the employee) is formally responsible for paying the tax. But, as will be explained later, the actual incidence of taxation does not depend on which party (the employer or the employee) the tax is levied on, but on the elasticity of labor demand and labor supply, which in turn determine the ability of each party to shift the tax to the other party.
12. This example shows that vastly different models evolved from the one model prevailing in the former Yugoslavia.
13. In some cases, peculiarities of tax administration obscure the picture. For example, in Poland health insurance is financed out of an earmarked part of PIT. The tax is collected by the Social Insurance Fund along with other social security contributions and then subtracted from PIT liabilities.

14. This assumes that labor productivity and product prices are unchanged. The latter assumption means that employers are not able to shift the tax increase forward in the form of higher product prices.
15. The elasticity of demand for labor (or supply of labor) refers to the percentage change in demand (or supply) given a percentage change in the real wage.
16. See de Haan, Sturm, and Volkerink (2003) and World Bank (2005b) for a more in-depth literature survey.
17. A cautionary note is in order, however. Although recent research with aggregate data has strengthened the case for an empirical link between labor taxes and unemployment, whether the pattern of detected partial correlation is to be interpreted in a causal sense remains highly controversial (Daveri 2002). Thus some skepticism remains. "… we still don't know whether labor taxes have statistically significant and economically important effects on labor costs and employment" (Daveri 2002: 15).
18. A further question is whether the division of social security contributions between the employer and the employee matter. Empirical evidence on the impact of tax structure is very limited and there is no definite answer to this question. According to conventional wisdom, taxes levied on the employer should have a stronger effect on employment than taxes levied on the employee. Garcia and Sala (2006) found, in contrast, that in continental Europe heavier taxation of the employee relative to that of the employer leads to higher unemployment, although this result does not appear to hold for Anglo-Saxon or Nordic countries . The result for continental Europe is consistent with the model where trade unions have significant power in wage setting and wage bargaining takes place mainly at the sector level (that is, is neither decentralized as in Anglo-Saxon countries nor centralized as in Nordic countries), and workers (unions) do not accept lower wages in return for benefits received as a result of higher taxes. Under such conditions, higher social security contributions paid by employees translate into wage increases, thereby pushing unemployment upward. Further research is necessary to see how, if at all, the tax structure affects employment under different institutional settings. But the result obtained by Garcia and Sala demonstrates that the conventional wisdom is not necessarily correct.
19. Simple correlation analysis also suggests a negative relationship between the tax wedge on labor and employment outcomes. The tax wedge correlates negatively with the total employment-to-working-age-population ratio ($r = -0.11$) and with the labor force participation rate ($r = -0.30$) and positively with the unemployment rate ($r = 0.17$) Data on employment-to-population ratio were calculated using the ILO's Laborsta database, and data on labor force participation and unemployment rates come from the World Bank World Development Indicators.
20. This is in line with the result obtained by Vork et al. (2007) for the eight ECA new EU member states using panel data regression for 1996–2004.
21. Reducing the tax wedge by one standard deviation (5 percentage points) is a massive undertaking given broader fiscal constraints. For example, it would require cutting the employee social security contribution rate by as much as 7 percentage points. But such a reduction is achievable, as exemplified by labor tax cuts and attendant social security reforms in

some ECA countries (see box 9.). Currently, Poland plans to reduce the employee social security contribution rate by 7 percentage points.

22. The Czech Republic, Estonia, Hungary, Latvia, Lithuania, Poland, the Slovak Republic, and Slovenia.
23. In this context it is noteworthy that no statistically significant effect of the tax wedge on employment growth was found using an identical regression equation for a sample of OECD countries (excluding EU-8) during the same period (Gora et al. 2006). This may indicate that the observed relationship, if not spurious, is specific to a period of intensive enterprise restructuring associated with the economic transition.
24. Regressions conducted for this study found a negative but insignificant correlation between the tax wedge and the female employment rate (-0.33), although the small sample size limited the analysis. Data limitations also prevented an examination of the impact of the tax wedge on youth employment.
25. The standard result is that for a short period after the tax is imposed (one to five years), employers may bear over 50 percent of the employer tax burden. But over the longer term labor will bear at least two-thirds of the overall employer and employee payroll taxes (Dahlby 1993).
26. Plans to limit early retirement may be difficult to implement due to political economy reasons. However, a clear vision and determination on the part of the government, and tripartite dialogue can facilitate the process. For example, the Polish government is now discussing ambitious plans to curb early retirement with trade unions and employers' representatives.
27. In most ECA countries fewer than 20–30 percent of the registered unemployed qualify for benefits. In most CIS countries the registered unemployed are only a fraction of the all (ILO) unemployed, which is explained by low benefits of registration.
28. For instance, according to employer surveys in the Netherlands, between 20 and 60 percent of new recruits would have been hired without the financial support.
29. Close monitoring of employers' behavior is necessary to curb abuse.
30. However, Daveri and Tabellini (2000) claim that the distortionary effects of labor taxes are much bigger than those of capital and consumption taxes. Accordingly, they recommend reducing labor taxes with a compensating increase in consumption taxes.
31. This represents a reversal of the author's earlier view. In Daveri and Tabellini (2000) the authors were confident of the validity of the prescription of reducing labor taxes with a compensating increase in consumption taxes.

References and Other Resources

Adam, C, and D. L. Bevan. 2005. "Fiscal Deficits and Growth in Developing Countries." *Journal of Public Economics* 89 (4): 571–97.

Afonso, António, Christiane Nickel, and Philipp C. Rother. 2006. "Fiscal Consolidations in the Central and Eastern European Countries." *Review of World Economics* 127 (2): 402–21.

Afonso, A., L. Schuknecht., and V. Tanzi. 2006. "Public Sector Efficiency: Evidence for New EU Member States and Emerging Markets." ECB Working Paper No. 581, European Central Bank, Frankfurt.

Alesina, Alberto, and Silvia Ardagna. 1998. "Tales of Fiscal Adjustment." *Economic Policy* 13 (27): 487–546.

Alesina, Alberto, and Roberto Perotti. 1995. "Fiscal Expansions and Fiscal Adjustments in OECD Countries." NBER Working Paper No. 5214, National Bureau of Economic Research, Cambridge, MA.

———. 1997. "Fiscal Adjustment in OECD Countries: Composition and Macroeconomic Effects." IMF Staff Papers 44 (2): 210–48.

Amos, Paul. 2005. "Reform, Commercialization and Private Sector Participation in Railways in Eastern Europe and Central Asia." Transport Papers Series No. 4, World Bank, Washington, DC.

Anderson, B., and B. Silver. 1986. "Infant Mortality in the Soviet Union: Regional Differences and Measurement Issues." *Population and Development Review* 12 (4): 705–38.

Anusic, Zoran, Philip O'Keefe, and Sanja Madzarevic-Sujster. 2003. "Pension Reform in Croatia." Social Protection Discussion Paper No. 0304, World Bank, Washington, DC.

Appleton, S., and J. Mackinnon. 1996. "Enhancing Human Capacities in Africa." In *Agenda for Africa's Economic Renewal,* ed. B. Ndulu and Nicolas van de Walle, 109–49. Washington, DC: Transaction Publishers.

Arellano, M., and S. Bond. 1991. "Some Tests of Specification for Panel Data: Monte Carlo Evidence and an Application to Employment Equations." *Review of Economic Studies* 58 (2): 277–97.

Aschauer, D. 1989. "Is Government Spending Productive?" *Journal of Monetary Economics* 23: 177–200.

Åslund, Anders, and Nazgul Jenish. 2005. "The Eurasian Growth Paradox." Peterson Institute for International Economics, Washington, DC.

Audric, S., P. Givord, and C. Prost. 2000. "Estimation de l'impact sur l'emploi non qualifie des mesures de baisse de charges." Revue Economique 51 (3): 513–22.

Baeza, C., and T. Packard. 2006. "Beyond Survival: Protecting Households from Health Shocks in Latin America." Washington, DC: World Bank, and Palo Alto, CA: Stanford University Press.

Baldacci, Emanuele, Benedict Clements, Sanjeev Gupta, and Qiang Cui. 2004. "Social Spending, Human Capital, and Growth in Developing Countries: Implications for Achieving the MDGs." Working Paper WP/04/217, IMF, Washington, DC.

Baldacci, Emanuele, Maria Teresa Guin-Siu, and Luiz de Mello. 2003. "More on the Effectiveness of Public Spending on Health Care and Education: A Covariance Structure Model." *Journal of International Development* 15 (6): 709–25.

Ball, Laurence, Douglas Elmendorf, and N. Gregory Mankiw. 1995. "The Deficit Gamble." Harvard Institute of Economic Research Working Paper No. 1710, Harvard University, Cambridge, MA.

Barro, R. 1990. "Government Spending in a Simple Model of Endogenous Growth." *Journal of Political Economy* 98 (5): S103–25.

———. 1991. "Economic Growth in a Cross Section of Countries." *Quarterly Journal of Economics* 106 (2): 407–43.

———. 1997. *Determinants of Economic Growth: A Cross-Country Empirical Study.* Cambridge, MA: MIT Press.

Barro, Robert J., and Jong-Wha Lee. 1993. "International Comparisons of Educational Attainment." *Journal of Monetary Economics* 32 (3): 363–94.

———. 2001. "International Data On Educational Attainment: Updates and Implications." *Oxford Economic Papers* 53 (3): 541–63.

Barro, R., and X. Sala-i-Martin. 1992. "Convergence." *Journal of Political Economy* 100 (2): 223–51.

———. 1995. *Economic Growth.* New York: McGraw-Hill.

Barrow, Lisa, and Cecilia Elena Rouse. 2005. "Causality, Causality, Causality: The View of Education Inputs and Outputs from Economics." Working Paper No. 2005-15, Federal Reserve Bank of Chicago.

Bassanini, Andrea, and Romain Duval. 2006. "Employment Patterns in OECD Countries: Reassessing the Role of Policies and Institutions." Economics Department Working Paper No. 486, OECD, Paris.

Beck, Thorsten, and Luc A. Laeven. 2005. "Institution Building and Growth in Transition Economies." Policy Research Working Paper No. 3657, World Bank, Washington, DC.

Benhabib, J., and M. Speigel. 1994. "The Role of Human Capital in Economic Development: Evidence from Aggregate Cross-Country Data." *Journal of Monetary Economics* 34 (2): 143–73.

———. 2005. "Human Capital and Technology Diffusion." In *Handbook of Economic Growth,* ed. Philippe Aghion and Steven N. Durlauf. Amsterdam: North Holland.

Berger, Louis. 2002. "Transport Infrastructure Regional Study (TIRS) in the Balkans." Final Report for Agence Française de Developpement and European Conference of Ministers of Transport, Paris.

Berger, M. C., and J. Messer. 2002. "Public Financing of Health Expenditures, Insurance, and Health Outcomes." *Applied Economics* 34 (17): 2105–13.

Berryman, Sue E. 2000. *Hidden Challenges to Education Systems in Transition Economies.* Washington, DC: World Bank.

Betcherman, Gordon, Karina Oliva, and Amit Dar. 2004. "Impacts of Active Labor Market Programs: New Evidence from Evaluations with Particular Attention to Developing and Transition Countries." Social Protection Discussion Paper No. 0402, World Bank, Washington, DC.

Betcherman, Gordon, and Carmen Pagés. 2007. "Estimating the Impacts of Labor Taxes on Employment and the Balances of the Social Insurance Funds in Turkey." Draft Synthesis Report, World Bank, Washington, DC.

Bidani, B., and M. Ravallion. 1997. "Decomposing Social Indicators Using Distributional Data." *Journal of Econometrics* 77 (1): 125–39.

Bils, Mark, and Peter J. Klenow. 2000. "Does Schooling Cause Growth" American Economic Review 90 (5):1160–83.

Bird, R., J. Martinez-Vazquez, and B. Torgler. 2004. "Societal Institutions and Tax Effort in Developing Countries." Working Paper 04-06, International Studies Program, Andrew Young School of Policy Studies, Georgia State University.

Bitran, R. U. Giedion, and R Muñoz, 2004. "Fondos de riesgo, ahorro y prevención: estudio regional de políticas para la protección de los más pobres de los efectos de los choques de salud: Estudio de caso de Chile. Background paper for the regional study "Beyond Survival: Protecting Households from the Impoverishing Effects of Health Shocks." Santiago, Chile.

Bleaney, M. F., N. Gemmell, and R. Kneller. 2001. "Testing the Endogenous Growth Model: Public Expenditure, Taxation and Growth over the Long-Run." *Canadian Journal of Economics* 34 (1): 36–57.

Bloom, D., D. Canning, and Jaypee Sevilla. 2001. "The Effects of Health on Economic Growth: Theory and Evidence." NBER Working Paper No. 8587, National Bureau of Economic Research, Cambridge, MA.

Briceño-Garmendia, Cecilia, Antonio Estache, and Nemat Shafik. 2004. "Infrastructure Services in Developing Countries: Access, Quality, Costs and Policy Reform." Policy Research Working Paper No. 3468, World Bank, Washington, DC.

Bruns, Barbara, Alain Mingat, and Ramahatra Rakatomalala. 2003. *Achieving Universal Primary Education by 2015: A Chance for Every Child.* Washington, DC: World Bank.

Bunker, J. P., H. S. Frazer, and F. Mosteller. 1995. "The Role of Medical Care in Determining Health: Creating an Inventory on Benefits." In *Society and*

Health, ed. B. J. Amick, S. Levine, A. R. Tarlov, and D. Chapman Walsh. New York: Oxford University Press.

Burnside, Craig, and David Dollar. 2000. "Aid, Policies, and Growth." *American Economic Review* 90 (4): 847–68.

———. 2004. "Aid, Policies, and Growth: Revisiting the Evidence." Policy Research Working Paper No. 3251, World Bank, Washington, DC.

Burtless, Gary. 1996. *Does Money Matter? The Effect of School Resources on Student Achievement and Adult Success.* Washington, DC: Brookings Institution Press.

Calderon, Cesar. 2006. "Infrastructure and Productivity Growth in the ECA Region: A Macroeconomic Approach." Unpublished, World Bank, Washington, DC.

Calderon, Cesar, and Luis Serven. 2004. "The Effects of Infrastructure Development on Growth and Income Distribution." Central Bank of Chile Working Paper No. 270, Santiago.

Cameron, Colin, and Pravin Trevedi. 2005. *Microeconometrics: Methods and Applications.* New York: Cambridge University Press.

Campos, Nauro F., and Fabrizio Coricelli. 2002. "Growth in Transition: What We Know, What We Don't, and What We Should." *Journal of Economic Literature* 40 (3): 793–836.

Canning, David, and Esra Bennathan. 2000. "The Social Rate of Return on Infrastructure Investment." Policy Research Working Paper No. 2390, World Bank, Washington, DC.

Canning, Mary, Martin Godfrey, and Dorota Holzer-Zelazewska. 2006. "Financing Higher Education." In *Current Issues in Fiscal Reform in Central Europe and the Baltic States 2005,* ed. Thomas Laursen. Washington, DC: World Bank.

Card, David, and Alan B. Krueger. 1996. "The Economic Return to School Quality." In *Assessing Educational Practices: The Contribution of Economics,* ed. William E. Becker and William J. Baumol. Cambridge, MA: The MIT Press.

Cashin, P. 1995. "Government Spending, Taxes, and Economic Growth." IMF Staff Papers 42 (2): 237–69.

Chawla, Mukesh. 2005. "Managing Health Expenditures in New EU Member States: Options for Reforms." PowerPoint presentation, World Bank, Washington, DC.

Chen, Sheng-Tung, and Chien-Chiang Lee. 2005. "Government Size and Economic Growth in Taiwan: A Threshold Regression Approach." *Journal of Policy Modeling* 27 (9): 1051–66.

Chu, K. 1995. Unproductive Public Expenditures: A Pragmatic Approach to Policy Analysis. IMF pamphlet series no. 48. Washington, DC: IMF.

Chu, Ke-young, and Gerd Schwartz. 1994. "Output Decline and Government Expenditures in European Transition Economies." IMF Working Paper No. 94/68, IMF, Washington, DC.

Coleman, J. S., and E. Q. Campbell, with C. F. Hobson, J. McPartland, A. M. Mood, F. D. Weinfield, and R. L. York. 1966. *Equality of Educational Opportunity.* Washington, DC: US Office of Education.

Coricelli, Fabrizio. 1997. "Fiscal Policy: A Long-Term View." In *Fiscal Policy in Transition: Forum Report of the Economic Policy Initiative No. 3.* 39–52. London: Center for Economic Policy Research.

COWI. 2003. "The Regional Balkans Infrastructure Study (REBIS)." Denmark.

Crépon, Bruno, and Rozenn Desplatz. 2002. "Evaluation of the Effects of Payroll Tax Subsidies for Low Wage Workers." Unpublished, CREST and Direction de la Prévision.

Crouch, Luis, and Tazeen Fasih. 2004. "Patterns in Educational Development: Implications for Further Efficiency Analysis." Unpublished, World Bank, Washington, DC.

Currie, Janet, and Enrico Moretti. 2003. "Mother's Education and the Intergenerational Transmission of Human Capital: Evidence from College Openings." *Quarterly Journal of Economics* 118 (4): 1495–532.

Dahlby, Bev. 1993. "Payroll Taxes." In *Business Taxation in Ontario,* ed. Allan Maslove. Toronto: University of Toronto Press.

Daveri, Francesco. 2002. "Labor Taxes and Unemployment: A Survey of the Aggregate Evidence." CeRP Working Paper 18/02, Center for Research on Pensions and Welfare Policies, Moncalieri, Italy.

———. 2003. "Labor Taxes and Unemployment: A Survey of the Aggregate Evidence." In *Pension Policy in an Integrating Europe,* ed. E. Fornero and O. Castellino. Cheltenham: Edward Elgar.

Daveri, F., and G. Tabellini. 2000. "Unemployment and Taxes: Do Taxes Affect the Rate of Unemployment?" *Economic Policy* 15 (30): 47–104.

David, A., B. Hall, and A. Toole. 2000. "Is Public R&D a Complement or Substitute for Private R&D? A Review of the Econometric Evidence." *Research Policy* 29 (4–5): 497–529.

Davies, Sara, and Martin Hallet. 2002. "Interactions between National and Regional Development." Hamburgisches Welt-Wirtschaftgs-Archiv Discussion Paper No. 207, European Commission, Brussels.

Davis, Steven J., and Magnus Henrekson. 2004. "Tax Effects on Work Activity, Industry Mix and Shadow Economy Size: Evidence from Rich-Country Comparisons." NBER Working Paper No. 10509, National Bureau of Economic Research, Cambridge, MA.

Davoodi, H., and D. Grigorian. 2006. "Tax Potential and Tax Effort: Factors Behind the Stubbornly Low Tax Collection in Armenia." Paper presented at "Armenia: Public Sector Governance and Economic Efficiency" conference, World Bank, Washington, DC, January 14–15.

Dee, Thomas S. 2004. "Are There Civic Returns to Education?" *Journal of Public Economics* 88 (9-10): 1697–720.

De Haan, J., J.-E. Sturm, and B. Volkerink. 2003. "How to Measure the Tax Burden on Labour at the Macro-Level." CESifo Working Paper No. 963, CESifo Group, Munich.

De la Fuente, A. 1997. "Fiscal Policy and Growth in the OECD." CEPR Discussion Paper No. 1755, Centre for Economic Policy Research, London.

———. 2002. "Convergence across Countries and Regions: Theory and Empirics." CEPR Discussion Paper No. 2465, Centre for Economic Policy Research, London.

De la Fuente, A., and R. Doménech. 2000. "Human Capital in Growth Regressions: How Much Difference Does Data Quality Make?" OECD Economics Department Working Paper No. 262, Paris.

Delannoy, Francoise. 2000. "Education Reforms in Chile, 1980–98: A Lesson in Pragmatism." Country Studies, Education Reform and Management Publication Series, vol. 1, no. 1, World Bank, Washington, DC.

de Melo, Martha, Cevdet Denizer, and Alan Gelb. 1996. "Patterns of Transition from Plan to Market." *The World Bank Economic Review* 10 (3): 397–424.

de Soto, Hernando. 1989. *The Invisible Revolution in the Third World.* New York: Harper Row.

Devarajan, Shanta, M. Holmes, C. Humphreys, A. Moon, and V. Swaroop. 2001. "Guidelines for the World Bank's Work on Public Expenditure Analysis and Support (including PERs)." Unpublished, World Bank, Washington, DC.

Devarajan, S., V. Swaroop, and H. Zou. 1996. "The Composition of Public Expenditure and Economic Growth." *Journal of Monetary Economics* 37 (2–3): 313–44.

Diamond, A. M. 1999. "Does Federal Funding 'Crowd In' Private Funding of Science?" *Contemporary Economic Policy* 17 (4): 423–31.

Di Gropello, Emanuela, ed. 2006. *Meeting the Challenges of Secondary Education in Latin America and East Asia: Improving Efficiency and Resource Mobilization.* Washington, DC: World Bank.

Dillinger, William. 2006. "Intergovernmental Fiscal Relations." In *Current Issues in Fiscal Reform in Central Europe and the Baltic States 2005,* ed. Thomas Laursen. Washington, DC: World Bank.

Docteur, E., and H. Oxley. 2003. "Health Care Systems: Lessons from the Reform Experience." Economics Department Working Paper No. 374, OECD, Paris.

Dolenc, Primoz, and Milan Vodopivec. 2005. "Tax Wedge on Labor: Slovenia vs. EU and OECD Countries." Managing the Process of Globalization in New and Upcoming EU Members, Proceedings of the 6th International Conference of the Faculty of Management, Koper Congress Centre, Bernardin, Slovenia, November 24–26.

Duret, E. 1999. Dépenses publiques et mortalité infantile: les effets de la décentralisation. Revue d'Economie du Dévelopment 4: 39–68.

Easterly, William, and Sergio Rebelo. 1993. "Fiscal Policy and Economic Growth: An Empirical Investigation." *Journal of Monetary Economics* 32 (3): 417–58.

Easterly, W., C. A. Rodriguez, and K. Schmidt-Hebbel. 1994. *Public Sector Deficits and Macroeconomic Performance.* Oxford and New York: Oxford University Press for the World Bank.

Ebinger, J. 2006. "Measuring Financial Performance in Infrastructure: An Application to Europe and Central Asia." Policy Research Working Paper 3992, World Bank, Washington, DC.

EBRD (European Bank for Reconstruction and Development). 2004. *Transition Report 2004: Infrastructure in Transition.* London.

———. 2007. "Life in Transition: A Survey of People's Experiences and Attitudes." EBRD, London.

EBRD-World Bank. 2005. "Business Environment and Enterprise Performance Survey." World Bank, Washington, DC.

Elmendorf, Douglas W., and N. Gregory Mankiw. "Government Debt." NBER Working Paper No. W6470, National Bureau of Economic Research, Cambridge, MA.

Elton, M. Nagy. 2002. "The Determinants of Tax Effort in Arab Countries." Working Paper Series No. 0207, Arab Planning Institute, Kuwait.

Engen, E. M., and J. Skinner. 1996. "Taxation and Economic Growth." NBER Working Paper No. 5826, National Bureau of Economic Research, Cambridge, MA.

Estache, Antonio. 2006. "Infrastructure: A Survey of Recent and Upcoming Issues." PREM and INF Vice Presidencies, World Bank, Washington, DC.

European Commission. 2005. *Key Data on Education in Europe 2005.* Luxembourg: Office for Official Publications of the European Communities.

European Observatory on Health Care Systems. 2002. "Health Care Systems in Transition: Armenia." Copenhagen, Denmark, WHO Regional Office for Europe.

———. 2005. "Health Care Systems in Transition: Ukraine." WHO Regional Office for Europe, Copenhagen, Denmark.

Fernandez, Enric, and Paolo Mauro. 2000. "The Role of Human Capital in Economic Growth: The Case of Spain." International Monetary Fund Working Paper WP/00/8, IMF, Washington, DC.

Fidrmuc, Jan. 2001. "Forecasting Growth in Transition Economies: A Reassessment." Unpublished, Center for European Integration Studies (ZEI), University of Bonn.

Figueras, J., R. B. Saltman, R. Busse, and H. R. F. Dubois. 2004. "Patterns and Performance in Social Health Insurance Systems in Western Europe." In *Social Health Insurance Systems in Western Europe,* ed. R. B. Saltman, R. Busse, and J. Figueras. European Observatory on Health Systems and Policies. Berkshire, UK: Open University Press.

Filer, Randall K., and Daniel Münich. 2000. "Responses of Private and Public Schools to Voucher Funding: The Czech and Hungarian Experience." William Davidson Institute Working Paper No. 360, Ann Arbor, MI.

Filmer, D., J. Hammer, and L. Pritchett. 2000. "Weak Links in the Chain: A Diagnosis of Health Policy in Poor Countries." *World Bank Research Observer* 15 (2): 199–224.

Filmer, D., and L. Pritchett. 1999. "The Impact of Public Spending on Health: Does Money Matter?" *Social Science and Medicine* 49 (10): 1309–23.

Fischer, Stanley. 1993. "The Role of Macroeconomic Factors in Growth." *Journal of Monetary Economics* 32 (3): 485–512.

Fischer, Stanley, and Ratna Sahay. 2000. "The Transition Economies After Ten Years." NBER Working Paper No. 7664, National Bureau of Economic Research, Cambridge, MA.

Fischer, Stanley, Ratna Sahay, and Carlos Vegh. 1996. "Stabilization and Growth in Transition Economies: The Early Experience." *Journal of Economic Perspectives* 10 (2): 45–66.

Fiszbein, Ariel, ed. 2001. "Decentralizing Education in Transition Societies." In *Decentralization, Local Governments, and Education Reform in Post-Communist Poland,* ed. T. Levitas and J. Herczynski. Open Society Institute, Yerevan, Armenia.

Flug, K., A. Spilimbergo, and E. Wachtenheim. 1998. "Investment in Education: Do Economic Volatility and Credit Constraints Matter?" *Journal of Development Economics* 55 (2): 465–81.

Fölster, S., and M. Henrekson. 2001. "Growth Effects of Government Expenditure and Taxation in Rich Countries." *European Economic Review* 45 (8): 1501–20.

Friedman, Eric, Simon Johnson, Daniel Kaufmann, and Pablo Zoido-Lobaton. 2000. "Dodging the Grabbing Hand: The Determinants of Unofficial Activity in 69 Countries." *Journal of Public Economics* 76 (3): 459–93.

Gallagher, M. 1993. "A Public Choice Theory of Budgets: Implications for Education in Less Developed Countries." *Comparative Education Review* 37 (2): 90–106.

Garcia, Jose Ramon, and Hector Sala. 2006. "The Tax System Incidence on Unemployment: A Country-Specific Analysis for the OECD Economies." IZA Discussion Paper No. 2226, Bonn.

Gerdtham, U.-G., and B. Jonsson. 1991. "Price and Quantity in International Comparisons of Health Care Expenditures." *Applied Economics* 23 (9): 1519–28.

Glewwe, Paul, and Harry Anthony Patrinos. 1999. "The Role of the Private Sector in Education in Vietnam: Evidence from the Vietnam Living Standards Survey." *World Development* 27 (5): 887–902.

Global Water Intelligence. 2005. *Water Market Europe: Opportunities in EU Accession, the Framework Directive, and the CIS.* Oxford UK: Media Analytics Limited.

Godoy, Sergio, and Joseph E. Stiglitz. 2006. "Growth, Initial Conditions, Law and Speed of Privatization in Transition Countries: 11 Years Later." NBER Working Paper No. 11992, National Bureau of Economic Research, Cambridge, MA.

Góra, Marek. 2006. Idà wybory, b´dà prezenty dla wszystkich, Rzeczpospolita, 24 lipca.

Góra, M., A. Radziwill, A. Sowa, and M. Walewski. 2006. "Tax Wedge and Skills: Case of Poland in International Perspective." CASE Report Series No. 64, Center for Social and Economic Research, Warsaw.

Gottret, P., and G. Schieber. 2006. *Health Financing Revisited: A Practioner's Guide.* Washington, DC: World Bank.

Grier, K., and G. Tullock. 1989. "An Empirical Analysis of Cross-National Economic Growth 1950–1980." *Journal of Monetary Economics* 24 (1): 259–76.

Grossman, Philip J. 1990. "Government and Growth: Cross-Sectional Evidence." *Public Choice* 65 (3): 217–27.

Gruber, Jonathan. 1995. "The Incidence of Payroll Taxation: Evidence from Chile." NBER Working Paper No. 5053, National Bureau of Economic Research, Cambridge, MA.

———. 2000. "Health Insurance and the Labor Market." In *Handbook of Health Economics,* edition 1, volume 1, ed. A. J. Culyer and J. P. Newhouse, 645–706. Amsterdam: Elsevier.

Guellec, D., and B. van Pottelsberghe. 1999. "Does Government Support Stimulate Private R&D?" *OECD Economic Studies* 29 (1997/II): 95–122.

Guichard, S., M. Kennedy, E. Wurzel, and C. André. 2007. "What Affects Fiscal Consolidation? Some Evidence from OECD Countries." Conference Paper, OECD, Paris.

Gupta, Sanjeev, Hamid R. Davoodi, and Erwin R. Tiongson. 2002. "Corruption and the Provision of Health Care and Education Services." In *Governance, Corruption, & Economic Performance,* ed. George T. Abed and Sanjeev Gupta. Washington, DC: International Monetary Fund.

Gupta, Sanjeev, L. Leruth, L. de Melo, and S. Chakravarti. 2003. "Transition Economies: How Appropriate is the Size and Scope of Government?" IMF Working Paper 01/55, IMF, Washington, DC.

Gupta, Sanjeev, Marijn Verhoeven, and Erwin R. Tiongson. 2002. "The Effectiveness of Government Spending on Education and Health Care in Developing and Transition Economies." *European Journal of Political Economy* 18 (4): 717–37.

Guryan, Jonathan. 2003. "Does Money Matter? Estimates from Education Finance Reform in Massachusetts." University of Chicago Graduate School of Business, Chicago, IL.

Gwilliam, Kenneth, and Zmarak Shalizi. 1999. "Road Funds, User Charges and Taxes." *The World Bank Research Observer* 14 (2): 159–85.

Gyimah-Bremponga, K., and M. Wilson. 2004. "Health, Human Capital and Economic Growth in Sub-Saharan African and OECD Countries." *Quarterly Review of Economics and Finance* 44 (2): 296–320.

Hall, Robert E., and Alvin Rabushka. 1983. *Low Tax, Simple Tax, Flat Tax.* New York: McGraw-Hill.

———. 1985. *The Flat Tax.* First edition. Stanford, CA: Hoover Institution Press.

Hallak, Jacques, and Muriel Poisson. 2005. "Ethics and Corruption in Education: An Overview." *Journal of Education for International Development* 1(1).

Hamermesh, Daniel S. 1993. *Labor Demand.* Princeton, NJ: Princeton University Press.

Hanousek, J., and F. Palda. 2003. "Why People Evade Taxes in the Czech and Slovak Republics: A Tale of Twins." In *The Informal Economy in the EU Accession Countries: Size, Scope, Trends and Challenges in the Process of EU Enlargement,* ed. B. Belev, 139–74. Sofia: Center for the Study of Democracy.

Hansen, B. 1999 "Threshold Effects in Non-Dynamic Panels: Estimation, Testing and Inference." *Journal of Econometrics* 93 (2): 345–68.

———. 2000. "Sample Splitting and Threshold Estimation." *Econometrica* 68 (3): 575–603.

Hanushek, E. A. 1986. "The Economics of Schooling: Production and Efficiency in Public Schools." *Journal of Economic Literature* 24 (3): 1141–77.

———. 1989. "The Impact of Differential Expenditures on School Performance." *Educational Researcher* 18 (4): 45–65.

———. 1996. "Measuring Investment in Education." *Journal of Economic Perspectives* 10 (4): 9–30.

———. 1997. "Assessing the Effects of School Resources on Student Performance: An Update." *Educational Evaluation and Policy Analysis* 19 (2): 141–64.

Hanushek, Eric A., and Dennis D. Kimko. 2000. "Schooling, Labor-Force Quality, and the Growth of Nations." *The American Economic Review* 90 (5): 1184–208.

Hanushek, Eric A., and Ludger Wössmann. 2007. "The Role of Education Quality in Economic Growth." Policy Research Working Paper No. 4122, World Bank, Washington, DC.

Hauner, D., and M. S. Kumar. 2005. "Financial Globalization and Fiscal Performance in Emerging Markets." IMF Working Paper No. 05/212, IMF, Washington, DC.

Hauptmeier, S., M. Heipertz, and L. Schuknecht. 2006. "Expenditure Reform in Industrialized Countries: A Case Study Approach." European Central Bank Working Paper No. 634, Frankfurt am Main, Germany.

Havrylyshyn, Oleh. 2001. "Recovery and Growth in Transition: A Decade of Evidence." IMF Staff Papers 48 (Special Issue): 53–87.

Havrylyshyn, Oleh, Ivailo Izvorski, and Ron van Rooden. 1998. "Recovery and Growth in Transition Economies 1990–97: A Stylized Regression Analysis." IMF Working Paper No. 98/141, International Monetary Fund, Washington, DC.

Hedges, Larry V., and Rob Greenwald. 1996. "Have Times Changed? The Relation between School Resources and Student Performance." In *Does Money Matter? The Effect of School Resources on Student Achievement and Adult Success,* ed. Gary Burtless, Washington, DC: Brookings Institution Press.

Heggie, Ian G., and Piers Vickers. 1998. Commercial Management and Financing of Roads. Technical Paper No. 409. Washington, DC: World Bank.

Heitger, B. 2001. "The Scope of Government and Its Impact on Economic Growth in OECD Countries." Kiel Working Paper No. 1034, Kiel Institute for the World Economy, Germany.

Heller, Peter. 2005. "Understanding Fiscal Space." Policy Discussion Paper 05/4, International Monetary Fund, Washington, DC.

Herrera, Santiago, and Gaobo Pang. 2005. "Efficiency of Public Spending in Developing Countries: An Efficiency Frontier Approach." Policy Research Working Paper No. 3645, World Bank, Washington, DC.

Howitt, P. 2005. "Health, Human Capital and Economic Growth: A Schumpeterian Perspective." In *Health and Economic Growth: Findings and Policy Implications,* ed. G. Lopez-Casasnovas, B. Rivera, and L. Currais, 19–40. Cambridge, MA: MIT Press.

Hudson, J., and J. Teera. 2004. "Tax Performance: A Comparative Study." *Journal of Enternational Development* 16 (6): 785–802.

Humphreys, Martin, and Martha Lawrence. 2005. "Railway Reform in the Western Balkans." Europe and Central Asia Region Working Paper Series Vol. 1, No. 2, Infrastructure Department, World Bank, Washington, DC.

IEA (International Energy Agency). 2002. World Energy Outlook 2002. Paris: IEA.

———. 2004. World Energy Outlook 2004. Paris: IEA.

IMF (International Monetary Fund). 2002. "Government Finance Statistics Manual 2001 Companion Material: Classification of GFSM 1986 Data to GFSM 2001 Framework." IMF, Washington, DC.

———. 2004a. "The Government Finance Statistics Manual 2001 and its Relationship with the European System of Accounts 1995." IMF, Washington, DC.

———. 2004b. "Public Investment and Fiscal Policy." Fiscal Affairs Department and Policy Development and Review Department, International Monetary Fund, Washington, DC.

———. 2006. "Government Finance Statistics Yearkbook." IMF, Washington, DC.

———. 2007. *World Economic Outlook.* Washington, DC: IMF.

Ivanova, A., M. Keen, and A. Klemm. 2005. "The Russian Flat Tax Reform." IMF Working Paper No. 05/16, IMF, Washington, DC.

JP Morgan. 2006. "Emerging Markets Debt and Fiscal Indicators." JP Morgan, New York, October.

———. 2007. "Emerging Markets Debt and Fiscal Indicators." JP Morgan, New York, April.

Kakwani, Nanak, and Kalanidhi Subbarao. 2005. "Ageing and Poverty in Africa and the Role of Social Pensions." Social Protection Discussion Paper No. 0521, World Bank, Washington, DC.

Kamps, C. 2004. "New Estimates of Government Net Capital Stocks for 22 OECD Countries 1960–2001." IMF Working Paper 04/67, International Monetary Fund, Washington, DC.

Karosadnize, Tamuna, and Camrin Christensen. 2005. "Georgia: A New Beginning for Georgia's University Admissions." In *Stealing the Future: Corruption in the Classroom—Ten Real World Experiences,* ed. Bettina Meier and Michael Griffin, 36–43. Berlin: Transparency International.

Kaufmann, D., A. Kraay, and M. Mastruzzi. 2006. "Governance Matters V: Governance Indicators for 1996–2005." World Bank, Washington, DC.

Keen, M., Y. Kim, and R. Varsano. 2006. "The Flat Tax(es): Principles and Evidence." IMF Working Paper No. 06/218, IMF, Washington, DC.

Kihwan, Kim, and Danny M. Leipziger. 1997. "Korea: A Case of Government-Led Development." In *Lessons from East Asia,* ed. Danny M. Leipziger. Ann Arbor, MI: The University of Michigan Press.

Kneller, R., M. F. Bleaney, and N. Gemmell. 1999. "Fiscal Policy and Growth: Evidence from OECD Countries." *Journal of Public Economics* 74 (2): 171–90.

Kugler, A., and M. Kugler. 2003. "The Labor Market Effects of Payroll Taxes in a Middle-Income Country: Evidence from Colombia." IZA Discussion Paper No. 852, Bonn.

Kutzin, J. 2001. "A Descriptive Framework for Country-Level Analysis of Health Care Financing Arrangements." *Health Policy* 56 (3): 171–204.

Kwon, Soonman. 2003. "Payment System Reform for Health Care Providers in Korea." *Health Policy and Planning* 18 (1): 84–9.

Landau, D. 1986. "Government and Economic Growth in the Less Developed Countries: An Empirical Study for 1960–80." *Economic Development and Cultural Change* 35 (1): 35–75.

Langenbrunner, J. C., and M. Wiley. 2002. "Hospital Payment Mechanisms: Theory and Practice in Transition Countries." In *Hospitals in a Changing Europe,* ed. M. McKee and J. Healy, 150–176. Buckingham, UK: Open University Press.

Leamer, E. E. 1985. "Sensitivity Analyses Would Help." *American Economic Review* 75 (3): 308–13.

Lee, Y., and R. H. Gordon. 2005. "Tax Structure and Economic Growth." *Journal of Public Economics* 89 (5–6): 1027–43.

Levacic, Rosalind, and Peter Downes. 2004. *Formula Funding of Schools, Decentralization and Corruption: A Comparative Analysis.* Paris: International Institute for Educational Planning, UNESCO.

Levine, Ross, and David Renelt. 1991. "A Sensitivity Analysis of Cross-Country Growth Regressions." Working Paper Series No. 609, World Bank, Washington, DC.

———. 1992. "A Sensitivity Analysis of Cross-Country Growth Regressions." *American Economic Review* 82 (4): 942–63.

Levitas, Tony, and Jan Herczynski. 2002. "Decentralization, Local Governments and Education Reform in Post-Communist Poland." In *Balancing National and Local Responsibilities: Education Management and Finance in Four Central European Countries,* ed. Kenneth Davey, 113–90. Budapest: Local Government and Public Service Reform Initiative, Open Society Institute.

Limwattananon, S., V. Tangcharoensathian, and P. Prakongsai. 2005. "Equity in Financing Healthcare: Impact of Universal Access to Healthcare in Thailand." Working Paper No. 16, Equitap Project, Thailand.

Loayza, Norman V., Ana Maria Oviedo, and Luis Serven. 2005. "The Impact of Regulation on Growth and Informality: Cross-Country Evidence." Policy Research Working Paper N. 3623, World Bank, Washington, DC.

Lochner, Lance, and Enrico Moretti. 2004. "The Effect of Education on Crime: Evidence from Prison Inmates, Arrests, and Self-Reports." *American Economic Review* 94 (1):155–89.

Lucas, Robert E. 1988. "On the Mechanics of Economic Development." *Journal of Monetary Economics* 22 (July): 3–42.

Mankiw, N. Gregory, David Romer, and David Weil. 1992. "A Contribution to the Empirics of Economic Growth." *Quarterly Journal of Economics* 107 (2): 407–37.

McKee, M. 2003. "Reducing Hospital Beds: What are the Lessons to be Learned?" Policy Brief No. 6, Copenhagen, Denmark, WHO regional office for Europe.

McKeown, T. 1976. *The Role of Medicine: Dream, Mirage or Nemesis?* Princeton: Princeton University Press.

Merlevede, Bruno. 2003. "Reform Reversals and Output Growth in Transition Economies." *Economics of Transition* 11 (4): 649–69.

Middleton, J., A. Ziderman, and A. Van Adams. 1993. *Skills for Productivity: Vocational Education and Training in Developing Countries.* New York: Oxford University Press for the World Bank.

Mincer, Jacob. 1970. "The Distribution of Labor Incomes: A Survey with Special Reference to the Human Capital Approach." *Journal of Economic Literature* 8 (1): 1–26.

———. 1974. *Schooling Experience and Earnings.* New York: Proquest Info and Learning.

Mingat, A., and Jee-Peng Tan. 1992. "Education in Asia: A Comparative Study of Cost and Financing." A World Bank Regional and Sectoral Study, World Bank, Washington, DC.

———. 1998. "The Mechanics of Progress in Education: Evidence from Cross-Country Data." Policy Research Working Paper No. 2015, World Bank, Washington, DC.

Mizala, Alejandra, Pilar Romaguera, and Dario Farren. 2002. "The Technical Efficiency of Schools in Chile." *Applied Economics* 34 (12): 1533–52.

Nickell, S. 2003. "Employment and Taxes." CESifo Working Paper No.1109, CESifo Group, Munich.

Nolte, E., C. Bain, and M. McKee. 2006. "Diabetes as a Tracer Condition in International Benchmarking of Health." *Diabetes Care* 29 (5): 1007–11.

Noss, A. 1991. "Education and Adjustment: A Review of the Literature." Policy Research and External Affairs Working Paper WPS 701, World Bank, Washington, DC.

Nourzad, F., and M. Vrieze. 1995. "Public Capital Formation and Productivity Growth: Some International Evidence." *Journal of Productivity Analysis* 6 (4): 283–95.

OECD (Organisation for Economic Co-operation and Development). 1991. "Reviews of National Policies for Education: Ireland." OECD, Paris.

———. 1994. *The OECD Jobs Study: Evidence and Explanations.* Paris: OECD.

———. 1995. "Taxation, Employment and Unemployment." The OECD Jobs Study, OECD, Paris.

———. 1998. "Reviews of National Policies for Education: Korea." OECD, Paris.

———. 1999. *OECD Health Data 1999.* Paris: OECD.

———. 2000. "OECD Economic Outlook 68: Links between Policy and Growth: Cross-Country Evidence." OECD, Paris.

———. 2003a. *Employment Outlook: Towards More and Better Jobs.* Paris: OECD.

———. 2003b. "OECD Reviews of Health Care Systems: Korea." OECD, Paris.

———. 2004. *Employment Outlook.* Paris: OECD.

———. 2005a. "Financing Water Supply and Sanitation in EECCA." Conference of EECCA Ministers of Economy/Finance, Environment and Water and their Partners from the OECD. Yerevan, Armenia, November 17–18.

———. 2005b. *OECD Health Data 2005.* Paris: OECD.

———. 2006a. *Education at a Glance: OECD Indicators 2006.* Paris: OECD.

———. 2006b. *OECD Factbook 2006: Economic, Environmental, and Social Statistics.* Paris: OECD.

Padovano, F., and E. Galli. 2001. "Tax Rates and Economic Growth in the OECD Countries (1950–1990)." *Economic Inquiry* 39 (1): 44–57.

———. 2002. "Comparing the Growth Effects of Marginal vs. Average Tax Rates and Progressivity." *European Journal of Political Economy* 18 (30): 529–44.

Palacios, R., and M. Pallarés-Miralles. 2002. "International Patterns of Pension Provision." Social Protection Discussion Paper No. 0009, World Bank, Washington, DC.

Parry, Taryn Rounds. 1997. "Decentralization and Privatization: Education Policy in Chile." *Journal of Public Policy* 17 (1):107–33.

Piancastelli, M. 2001. "Measuring the Tax Effort of Developed and Developing Countries: Cross-Country Panel Data Analysis, 1989–95." Discussion Paper, Instituto de Pesquisa Econõmica Aplicada, Rio de Janeiro.

Poot, Jacques. 2000. "A Synthesis of Empirical Research on the Impact of Government on Long-Run Growth." *Growth and Change* 31 (4): 516–46.

Preker, A., M. Jakab, and M. Schneider. 2002. "Health Financing Reforms in Central and Eastern Europe and the Former Soviet Union." In *Funding Health Care: Options for Europe,* ed E. Mossialos, A. Dixon, J. Figueras, and J. Kutzin. Berkshire, UK: Open University Press.

Pritchett, Lant. 2001. "Where Has All the Education Gone?" *World Bank Economic Review* 15 (3): 367–91.

———. 2006. "Does Learning to Add Up Add Up? The Returns to Schooling in Aggregate Data." In *Handbook of the Economics of Education,* ed. Eric A. Hanushek and Finis Welch. Amsterdam: North Holland.

Psacharopoulos, George, and Harry A. Patrinos. 2004. "Returns to Investment in Education: A Further Update." *Education Economics* 12 (2): 111–34.

Purfield, Catriona. 2003. "Fiscal Adjustment in Transition: Evidence from the 1990s." *Emerging Markets Finance and Trade* 39 (1): 43–62.

Pushak, Taras, Erwin R. Tiongson, and Aristomene Varoudakis. 2007. "Public Finance, Governance, and Growth in Transition Economies: Empirical Evidence 1992–2004." Background paper for Fiscal Policy and Economic Growth. World Bank, Washington, DC.

Rajkumar, A., and V. Swaroop. 2002. "Public Spending and Outcomes: Does Governance Matter?" Policy Research Working Paper No. 2840, World Bank, Washington, DC.

Rudolph, Heinz, and Roberto Rocha. 2007. "Enabling Conditions for Second Pillars." Unpublished, World Bank, Washington, DC.

Ross, K., and R. Levacic, eds. 1999. *Needs-Based Resource Allocation in Education via Formula Funding of Schools.* Paris: IIEP-UNESCO.

Sachs, Jeffrey D. 1996. "The Transition at Mid-Decade." *American Economic Review* 86 (2): 128–33.

Sala-i-Martin, Xavier, Gernot Doppelhofer, and Ronald I. Miller. 2004. "Determinants of Long-Term Growth: A Bayesian Averaging of Classical Estimates (BACE) Approach." *American Economic Review* 94 (4): 813–35.

Saltman, R. B. 2004. "Social Health Insurance in Perspective: The Challenges of Sustaining Stability." In *Social Health Insurance Systems in Western Europe,* ed. R. B. Saltman, R. Busse, and J. Figueras. European Observatory on Health Systems and Policies. Berkshire, UK: Open University Press.

Sanchez-Robles, B. 1998. "Infrastructure Investment and Growth: Some Empirical Evidence." *Contemporary Economic Policy* 16 (1): 98–108.

Sargsyan, Gvorg, Ani Balabanyan, and Denzel Hankinson. 2006. *From Crisis to Stability in the Armenian Power Sector: Lessons Learned from Armenia's Energy Reform Experience.* Washington, DC: World Bank.

Schaffer, M. E., and G. Turley. 2001. "Effective versus Statutory Taxation: Measuring Effective Tax Administration in Transition Economies." EBRD Working Paper N. 62, EBRD, London.

Schneider, F. 2004. "The Size of the Shadow Economies of 145 Countries All over the World: First Results over the Period 1999 to 2003." IZA Discussion Paper No. 1431, Institute for the Study of Labor, Bonn.

———. 2005. "Shadow Economies of 145 Countries All over the World: What Do We Really Know?" *European Journal of Political Economy* 21 (3): 598–642.

Schneider, F., and B. Torgler. 2006. "What Shapes Attitudes towards Paying Taxes? Evidence from Multicultural European Countries." IZA Discussion Paper 2117, Institute for the Study of Labor, Bonn.

Schultz, T. P. 2005. "Productive Benefits of Health: Evidence from Low-Income Countries." IZA Discussion Paper No. 1482, Institute for the Study of Labor, Bonn, Germany.

Selowsky, Marcelo, and Ricardo Martin. 1997. "Policy Performance and Output Growth in the Transition Economies." *American Economic Review* 87 (2): 349–53.

Serven, L. 2006. "Infrastructure: Macroeconomic Issues." Unpublished Powerpoint presentation, World Bank, Washington, DC.

Sianesi, Barbara, and John Van Reenen. 2002. "The Returns to Education: A Review of the Empirical Macro-Economic Literature." CEE Discussion

Paper No. 0006, Centre for the Economics of Education, London School of Economics.

Skarbinski, J., H. Walker, L. Baker, A. Kobaladze, Z. Kirtava, and T. Raffin. 2002. "The Burden of Out-of-Pocket Payment for Health Care in Tbilisi, Republic of Georgia." *JAMA* 287 (8): 1043–9.

Stotsky, J. G., and A. WoldeMariam. 1997. "Tax Effort in Sub-Saharan Africa." Working Paper No. 97/107, IMF, Washington, DC.

Summers, L. 1989. "Some Simple Economics of Mandated Benefits." *American Economic Review* 79 (2): 177–83.

Tanzi, V. 1981. "A Statistical Evaluation of Taxation in Sub-Saharan Africa." IMF Occasional Paper No. 8, IMF, Washington, DC.

Tanzi, V., and K. Chu, eds. 1998. *Income Distribution and High-Quality Growth.* Cambridge, MA: MIT Press.

Theil, H. 1970. "On the Estimation of Relationships Involving Qualitative Variables." *American Journal of Sociology* 76 (1): 103–54.

TransMONEE database. 2006. UNICEF Innocenti Research Centre, Florence.

Tsang, Mun. 1997. "The Cost of Vocational Training." *International Journal of Manpower* 18 (1/2): 63–89.

Vandenbussche, Jerome, Philippe Aghion, and Costas Meghir. 2006. "Growth, Distance to Frontier and Composition of Human Capital." *Journal of Economic Growth* 11 (2): 9–127.

Van Zon, A., and J. Muysken. 2001. "Health and Endogenous Growth." *Journal of Health Economics* 20 (2): 169–85.

Vork, Andreas, Reelika Leetmaa, Alari Paulus, and Sten Anspal. 2007. "Tax-Benefit Systems in the New Member States and Their Impact on Labour Supply and Employment." Praxis Working Paper No. 26, Tallinn, Estonia.

Wagstaff, Adam. 2006. "Social Health Insurance Reexamined." Policy Research Working Paper No. WPS4111, World Bank, Washington, DC.

Wagstaff, A., and M. Claeson. 2004. *The Millennium Development Goals for Health: Rising to the Challenges.* Washington, DC: World Bank.

Wagstaff, A., and E. Van Doorslaer. 2001. "Paying for Health Care: Quantifying Fairness, Catastrophe, and Impoverishment, with Applications to Vietnam, 1993–98." Policy Research Working Paper No. 2715, World Bank, Washington, DC.

Wagstaff, A., E. van Doorslaer, and N. Watanabe. 2002. "On Decomposing the Causes of Health Sector Inequalities with an Application to Malnutrition Inequalities in Vietnam." *Journal of Econometrics* 112 (1): 207–23.

Walewski, Mateusz. 2006. "Labor Market Effects of Labor Taxes in ECA." Unpublished background paper prepared for the ECA Public Finance and Economic Growth Study, Warsaw.

Whitehouse, Edward. 2006. *Pensions Panorama: Retirement Income Systems in 53 Countries.* Washington, DC: World Bank.

Whitehouse, W. 2000. "How Poor Are the Old? A Survey of Evidence from 44 Countries." Social Protection Discussion Paper No. 0017, World Bank, Washington, DC.

Widmalm, F. 2001. "Tax Structure and Growth: Are Some Taxes Better Than Others?" *Public Choice* 107 (3–4): 199–219.

Wiley, M. M. 2005. "The Irish Health System: Developments in Strategy, Structure, Funding, and Delivery Since 1980." *Health Economics* 14 (S1): S169–86.

Willoughby, Christopher. 2006. "Public/Private Balance in Transport Infrastructure and Services: A Global Overview." Unpublished background paper for Independent Evaluation Group Evaluation of World Bank Assistance to the Transport Sector, 1995–2005, World Bank, Washington, DC.

Wooldridge, Jeffrey M. 2002. *Econometric Analysis of Cross Section and Panel Data.* Cambridge, MA: MIT Press.

World Bank. 1989. *Educational Development in Thailand: The Role of World Bank Lending.* A World Bank Operations Evaluation Study, Operations Evaluation Department. Washington, DC: World Bank.

———. 1993. *The East Asian Miracle: Economic Growth and Public Policy.* New York: Oxford University Press.

———. 2000. "Implementation Completion Report on Republic of Chile Health Sector Reform Project." Report No. 19806, World Bank, Washington, DC.

———. 2002. *Transition: The First Ten Years.* Washington, DC: World Bank.

———. 2003a. "Armenia: Poverty Assessment." Report No. 27192-AM, World Bank, Washington, DC.

———. 2003b. "Pro-Poor Health Financing Schemes in Thailand: A Review of Country Experience." Working Paper No. 31009, World Bank, Washington, DC.

———. 2003c. "Turkey: Road Improvement and Traffic Safety Project." Implementation Completion Report, Europe and Central Asia Region, World Bank, Washington, DC.

———. 2004a. "Competing in the Global Economy: An Investment Climate Assessment for Uganda." World Bank and Uganda Manufacturers Association Consultancy and Information Services, Washington, DC.

———. 2004b. *A Framework for the Development of the Transport Sector in South East Europe. Europe and Central Asia Region.* Washington, DC.

———. 2004c. "Georgia: Review of the Health Sector." Report Number 29413-GE, World Bank, Washington, DC.

———. 2004d. "Georgia: Secondary and Local Roads Project." Project Appraisal Document. Cr. 3938-GE, World Bank, Washington, DC.

———. 2004e. "Kyrgyz Republic Public Expenditures Review: Fiscal Policies for Growth and Poverty Reduction." Economic Report No. 28123, World Bank, Washington, DC.

———. 2004f. "Millennium Development Goals for Health in Europe and Central Asia: Relevance and Policy Implications." Working Paper No. 33, World Bank, Washington, DC.

———. 2004g. *World Development Report 2004: Making Services Work for Poor People.* Washington, DC: World Bank.

———. 2005a. *Enhancing Job Opportunities: Eastern Europe and the Former Soviet Union.* Washington, DC: World Bank.

———. 2005b. "EU-8 Quarterly Economic Report, Special Topic: Labor Taxes and Employment in the EU-8." World Bank, Warsaw.

———. 2005c. "The Quest for Equitable Growth in the Slovak Republic: A World Bank Living Standards Assessment." Report No. 32433-SK, PREM unit, ECA region, World Bank, Washington, DC.

———. 2005d. "Ukraine: Poverty and Inequality in a Growing Economy." Report No. 34631-UA, World Bank, Washington, DC.

———. 2006a. "Albania: A Public Expenditure and Institutional Review." Volumes I and II. Report No. 36453-AL. Poverty Reduction and Economic Management Unit, Europe and Central Asia Region, World Bank, Washington, DC.

———. 2006b. "Dimensions of Urban Poverty in the Europe and Central Asia Region." Policy Research Working Paper No. 3998, Infrastructure Department, Europe and Central Asia Region, World Bank, Washington, DC.

———. 2006c. *Doing Business in 2006.* Washington, DC: World Bank.

———. 2006d. *Infrastructure in the Europe and Central Asia Region: Approaches to Sustainable Services.* Report No. 36227-ECA, Infrastructure Department. Washington, DC: World Bank,.

———. 2006e. "Albania Health Sector Note." Report No. 32612-AL, World Bank, Washington, DC.

———. 2006f. "Measuring Financial Performance in Infrastructure." Report No. 36058-ECA, Infrastructure Department, Europe and Central Asia Region, World Bank, Washington, DC.

———. 2006g. *People and Power: Electricity Sector Reforms and the Poor in Europe and Central Asia.* Washington, DC: World Bank.

———. 2006h. "Selected Issues in Fiscal Reform in Central Europe and the Baltic Countries 2005." World Bank, Warsaw.

———. 2006i. "Turkey: Country Economic Memorandum: Promoting Sustained Growth and Convergence with the European Union." Volumes I and II. Report No. 33549-TR, Poverty Reduction and Economic Management Unit, Europe and Central Asia Region, World Bank, Washington, DC.

———. 2006j. "Turkey: Public Expenditure Review." Report No. 36764-TR, Poverty Reduction and Economic Management Unit, Europe and Central Asia Region, Washington, DC.

———. 2006k. World Development Indicators database.

———. 2007. "The Third Transition: Exploring the Impact of Changing Demographic Structures in Eastern Europe and the Former Soviet Union." ECA Region, World Bank, Washington, DC.